SELECTED ISSUES IN
EQUITY
COMPENSATION
19TH EDITION
2023

Michael J. Album, Barbara Baksa, Colin Diamond, William Dunn, Steven D. Einhorn, Jennifer George, Sorrell Johnson, Thomas LaWer, Joshua McGinn, Eric Orsic, Henrik Patel, Joseph Phelps, Carlisle F. Toppin, Marlene Zobayan, and Jacobin Zorin

See **www.nceo.org/CEP** for our CEP Exam Prep Course
and other resources for CEPI exam candidates

The National Center for Employee Ownership
www.nceo.org

Selected Issues in Equity Compensation, 19th ed.

Editing and book design by Scott Rodrick

Copyright © 2023 by The National Center for Employee Ownership. All rights reserved. No part of this book may be reproduced or transmitted in any form or by any means, electronic or mechanical, including photocopying, recording, or by any information storage and retrieval system, without prior written permission from the publisher.

The National Center for Employee Ownership
Phone (510) 208-1300
www.nceo.org

Originally published as *Stock Options: Beyond the Basics* in September 1999. Second edition August 2000. Third edition January 2003.

New edition, titled *Selected Issues in Stock Options*, January 2004.

Second edition of *Selected Issues*, titled *Selected Issues in Equity Compensation*, February 2005. Third edition January 2006.
Fourth edition January 2007. Fifth edition February 2008. Sixth edition February 2009. Seventh edition February 2010. Eighth edition February 2011. Ninth edition February 2012. Tenth edition February 2013. Eleventh edition February 2014. Twelfth edition March 2015. Thirteenth edition February 2016. Fourteenth edition February 2017. Fifteenth edition March 2019. Sixteenth edition January 2020. Seventeenth edition January 2021. Eighteenth edition January 2022. Nineteenth edition January 2023.

ISBN: 978-1-954990-21-0

Contents

Chapter 2: Federal Securities Law Considerations for Equity Compensation Plans   47

Eric Orsic

Chapter 3: State Securities Law Considerations for Equity Compensation Plans   127

Joseph Phelps

Chapter 4: Preparing for an Initial Public Offering   149

Jacobin Zorin

Chapter 5: Executive and Equity Compensation Considerations After an IPO   175

Jacobin Zorin

Chapter 6: Equity Considerations in Merger and Acquisition Transactions   241

Sorrell Johnson

Chapter 7: Handling Death Under an Equity Compensation Plan   267

Michael J. Album and Steven D. Einhorn

Chapter 8: Evergreen Provisions for Equity Compensation Plans   289

Thomas LaWer

Chapter 9: Repricing Underwater Stock Options   299

Colin Diamond and Henrik Patel

Chapter 10: Equity Awards in Divorce   327

William Dunn and Jennifer George

Chapter 11: Designing and Implementing an Employee Stock Purchase Plan   337

Barbara Baksa

Chapter 12: The Role of the Transfer Agent   391

Joshua McGinn

Chapter 13: Annual Meetings   403

Joshua McGinn

Chapter 14: State Mobility Issues for Equity Compensation   419

Marlene Zobayan

Preface

More and more companies are realizing that their employees are their most important asset. To attract, retain, and reward employees, many companies use stock options and related plans, often in "broad-based" programs that include most or even all employees. Our standard introductory guide for company owners, managers, and advisors is *The Stock Options Book,* which covers a multitude of issues relating to stock options and stock purchase plans.

This book goes a step beyond *The Stock Options Book* with extensive information on crucial issues such as administration, securities laws, and divorce. It is not a comprehensive overview like *The Stock Options Book* but rather is more selective and detailed. It is not meant to be an introduction to the field or to be a guide to all advanced issues.

We hope you find this book useful and that it inspires you to become more involved with stock plans. To read about the other information resources that we at the National Center for Employee Ownership (NCEO) offer, including many other publications on stock plans, communicating to employees, and creating an ownership culture, visit our website at www.nceo.org or see the back of this book.

Changes in the 19th Edition (2023)

For the 19th edition, the glossary and chapters 1, 2, 4, 5, 11, 12, and 14 were updated.

CHAPTER

1

Administering an Employee Equity Plan

Carlisle F. Toppin

CONTENTS

Portions of this chapter were originally written by Mark A. Borges. Rachel Southorn assisted with drafting section 1.3 of the present chapter.

1

For many years, equity compensation has been a popular non-cash means for compensating employees. While companies generally grant equity to their senior management as an integral piece of the long-term incentive component of the executive compensation program, many companies also grant equity at various levels within the organization. Moreover, broad-based employee stock plans that grant restricted stock or stock options to all or substantially all employees, long used by smaller businesses, are now used by larger corporations as well.

A multitude of complex and, at times, confusing tax, accounting, corporate, and securities laws affect the adoption, implementation, operation, and administration of employee stock plans. These laws are supplemented by an array of other provisions, ranging from the detailed requirements of the national securities exchanges to the general common-law principles of contracts. While the terms and conditions of individual employee stock plans vary from company to company, the characteristics of all employee stock grants are heavily influenced by the various rules that govern their use.

Stock plan administrators, who manage the day-to-day operations of the plan, must ensure that all equity transactions are processed and settled timely and accurately. This requires a comprehensive knowledge of the various types of equity awards (broadly including stock options and restricted stock) and the actions to be taken at the various stages over the term of such awards (e.g., grants, exercises, vesting, forfeitures, and the issuance and disposition of the acquired shares). Stock plan administrators must work closely with their companies' internal legal, accounting, finance, tax, and payroll teams, as well as with external stockbrokers, transfer agents, and third-party administrators to provide accurate information related to equity transactions and ensure compliance with applicable laws, regulations, and other guidance.

These laws, regulations, and other guidance are well-documented elsewhere. Less understood are the administrative considerations that arise in operating the plans. This chapter discusses the more common administrative aspects of employee stock plans.

1.1   Establishing the Plan

When a company decides to implement an employee stock plan, management commissions the preparation of a formal plan document.

Typically, the plan's structure, as well as its specific terms and conditions, are determined in consultation with the company's legal counsel, accountants, and outside compensation or benefits specialists. Factors taken into consideration in designing the plan include the cost to the company and to the proposed participants, the projected dilution of shareholders' ownership interests, the potential liquidity alternatives for participants, the financial accounting results for the company, and the income tax and securities law consequences to participants and the company from the operation of the plan.

Most employee stock plans are "omnibus plans" that allow for the grant of multiple types of equity compensation awards, e.g., incentive stock options (ISOs), nonqualified stock options (NSOs), stock appreciation rights (SARs), restricted stock awards (RSAs), restricted stock units (RSUs), and performance-based grants. This variety permits flexibility in granting the appropriate form of equity to the intended recipients, while maintaining an effective limit on the total number of shares of stock available for issuance under the plan. Typically, the company's legal counsel prepares the plan documents. Once management is satisfied with the plan's design and structure, the plan is presented to the company's board of directors for consideration and adoption. Because under the corporate laws of most states, the board of directors must authorize any issuance of shares of the company's stock, generally board approval is required before the implementation of an employee stock plan.

Following adoption by the board of directors, the employee stock plan is then submitted to the company's shareholders for approval. Shareholder approval is required if the company's securities are listed on a national securities exchange (such as the New York or American stock exchanges or the Nasdaq Stock Market). In addition, shareholder approval may be a requirement under state corporate law or the company's charter documents. Even if shareholder approval is not required, there may be distinct advantages to obtaining shareholder approval of the plan. For example, the preferential tax treatment the Internal Revenue Code (the "Code") affords to ISOs is available only if the plan has been approved by the company's shareholders. In addition, compliance with certain provisions of the federal securities laws may be made easier if the plan has been approved by shareholders.

1.2   Developing Policies and Procedures

1.2.1   Policies

Many companies establish formal policies and procedures to facilitate the efficient administration of their employee stock plans. Policies broadly set forth the objectives of the equity compensation program and guide the day-to-day plan administration, while allowing for some flexibility in decision-making. Policies may be driven by business principles, competition, marketplace influences, guidelines developed by proxy advisors to institutional shareholders, and laws and regulations.

A comprehensive employee stock plan policy should address how grant recipients are determined, how the size of grants (number of shares) is determined, which type of equity award to grant, how the mix of such awards among levels and positions should be allocated, when and how often equity awards are to be granted, how the vesting criteria and schedule are to be determined, and which circumstances not specifically defined in the plan or grant agreement will affect the award.

1.2.2   Procedures

Procedures, on the other hand, narrowly detail the individual processes and rigidly provide step-by-step actions to be followed to implement policies and provisions of the employee stock plan. Examples of procedures include the company's internal grant approval process, transaction recordation, and tax collection. Moreover, the procedures should coordinate (1) internal communications between the stock plan administrator and the board of directors or its compensation committee, plus the human resources, payroll, legal, and finance departments; as well as (2) external communications with brokers (who facilitate transactions), transfer agents (who perform the recordkeeping of the share issuances), and any third-party administrators (who administer the employee stock plan if this function is outsourced).

1.2.3   Common Situations for Policies and Procedures

An effective employee stock plan should have policies and procedures that collaborate to broadly ensure timely, accurate and compliant operation of the plan and more narrowly address how awards are to be handled in specific situations.

1.2.3.1 Timing of Stock Option Grants

In view of the high degree of investor interest in the timing of stock option grants and to prevent manipulation, a formal grant policy, as well as specific procedures for processing grants, can be an effective means of minimizing the risk of option backdating resulting from either deliberate efforts to manipulate option grant dates or incomplete, inadequate, or inconsistent grant practices. Many companies establish a policy to disclose a fixed schedule for when options will be granted during the year. In some instances, this schedule is preannounced by the company. Other companies make it a policy to restrict the grant of stock options to predetermined time periods, such as during a specified period following the release of the company's quarterly or annual financial results.

1.2.3.2 Stock Ownership and Holding Guidelines

Consistent with the guidelines set forth by proxy advisors to institutional shareholders, a company should establish a stock ownership policy that requires senior executives to obtain a certain number of shares within a set timeframe and mandates them to maintain meaningful stock ownership during their tenure to align their interests with those of the shareholders. A minimum holding value of three times cash compensation is generally expected by proxy advisors. The policy should:

- Identify the employees subject to the ownership guidelines (e.g., position, title, level, or named executive officer status);
- define the level of ownership, which may be based on a factor of salary or cash compensation or the value or number of shares to be held, and state whether the minimum holding varies between positions or levels;
- set forth which shares are considered owned under the policy (e.g., unrestricted shares and time-based restricted stock, while excluding outstanding stock options);

• determine the value attributed to the shares, which may be defined as the value of the shares based on the current market value or a fixed value regardless of market movement; and

• establish the ramifications of falling below the policy's ownership requirements and set forth a grace period for individuals newly subject to the policy to achieve the required ownership level.

Of the proxy advisory firms, Institutional Shareholder Services (ISS) is one of the more vocal when it comes to stock ownership guidelines. Not all shares that may be disclosed in the proxy are included in ISS's equity ownership tables. Specifically, unexercised options (vested and unvested) and unearned performance-based awards are not included. However, unvested time-based restricted stock and RSUs and deferred awards that are no longer forfeitable are included.

1.2.3.3 Leaves of Absence

From time to time, employees will be permitted to take leaves of absence from their positions with the company. If the employee holds an equity grant, the plan administrator will face various questions concerning the status of the award during the leave of absence. For example, the employee stock plan or the grant agreement may address how vesting will be calculated during the leave of absence. In the absence of an express provision, the company may want to establish a policy regarding whether the employee will receive vesting credit during all or any portion of the leave. Under certain circumstances, companies toll the vesting period (that is, suspend vesting) during particular leaves of absence. In general, vesting is tolled on leaves of absence where other benefits also are tolled, such as an extended personal leave. In creating a policy regarding leaves of absence, the company will need to ensure that it is not tolling vesting on any employee who is on a protected leave status. With respect to stock options, the company may want to establish a policy regarding whether the employee will be permitted to exercise the stock option while on leave.

1.2.3.4 Insider Trading Policy

Insider trading policies and procedures are necessary for publicly held companies to ensure compliance with federal securities laws that prohibit the purchase or sale of securities by persons who are aware of material nonpublic information about the company. If the company's insider trading policy includes a specific period when certain employees will be prohibited from selling company stock, then it should impose a closed trading window on selling shares through any captive brokerage firm.

1.3 Selecting an Equity Compensation Platform

While it is possible for companies that award equity grants to only a very small number of employees to track those grants in a spreadsheet, companies will reach a point in their growth where leveraging an equity compensation platform is essential. In addition, there may be points when a company's current platform is no longer suitable. When selecting a platform, the company should go through the rigor of a request for proposal (RFP), which allows it to compare the advantages and challenges of multiple platforms and providers before finalizing a relationship.

Many equity compensation database providers combine a software solution with some level of services. The comprehensive offerings should be considered when selecting a platform. The needs of each company will vary depending on the size of the equity compensation program, the complexity of the grants awarded, and the corporate structure. When selecting an equity compensation platform, companies should not only consider their current needs but should also try to anticipate their future requirements.

Before initiating inquiries with a service provider, the company should create a list of known and anticipated needs and rate them in order of importance. Considerations should include, for example, the extent of automation needed to eliminate or minimize manual inputs, employer status (e.g., whether the company is publicly traded or privately held), demographics of the award recipients, grant types offered, share pool adjustments, accounting treatment, and securities filings.

1.3.1 Automation

Efficiency and accuracy are improved with automation. When selecting an equity compensation platform, consider the ability to integrate the equity compensation platform with the company's human resources and financial systems. If the equity compensation platform will exist as another stand-alone system, assess the ability to exchange data with the company's other systems and external providers (brokers, transfer agents, and third-party administrators) via import and export functions. In addition, assess the user interface for ease of use by the plan administrator and employees.

1.3.2   Employer Status

Whether the company is publicly traded or privately held will significantly influence what the company needs from an equity compensation platform. Public companies will need to comply with SEC requirements and manage the tax deduction limit under Code Section 162(m) for compensation payable to certain executive officers during their active employment and beyond. Private companies will need to manage their capitalization tables ("cap tables"), which provide an analysis of the company's ownership percentages among series of common and preferred stock, equity dilution, and the value of equity in each round of investment by founders, investors, and other owners.

1.3.3   Award Recipient Demographics

The demographics of award recipients are significant when selecting an equity compensation platform for many reasons, including:

- The award recipient's status as an employee (active or former) or nonemployee service provider determines the tax treatment of and withholding requirements associated with the award.
- Employees who earn more than $1 million in equity compensation and other supplemental wages in any given year become subject to higher flat rate U.S. federal income tax withholding.
- If the company and the award recipient are covered under Code Section 162(m), then corporate deductions for all compensation in excess of $1 million paid to such recipient in a given year may not be allowed.

Tax reporting and withholding obligations can become complex for companies with employees working in various jurisdictions, whether throughout the U.S. or globally. This is exacerbated by mobile employees who work in several jurisdictions, since the company will need to track their work locations during the period the award is earned for purposes of sourcing the income and allocating tax withholding among the jurisdictions. Where the awards have a provision to accelerate vesting for retirement-eligible employees, the company will need to determine the vesting dates for these employees for purposes of collecting certain payroll taxes and in some cases income taxes.

The company should assess the ability of the equity compensation platform to manage these and other situations.

1.3.4   Grant Type

The types of equity compensation awards granted under the employee stock plan will also affect the features the company will need from its equity compensation platform. With respect to ISOs, for example, the platform should automatically identify portions of the award that will be treated as NSOs to the extent the $100,000 first exercisable rule has been exceeded. The company may need to assess the equity platform's ability to manage employee elections to accelerate or defer restricted stock taxation and manage performance-based grants, which may have vesting events that cannot be standardized and may require manual inputs.

1.3.5   Share Pool Adjustment

The equity compensation platform should track the share reserve (or "share pool") in a manner that conforms to the plan's methodology. Specifically, determine whether the platform accommodates the stock plan's "fungible" share ratio, in which shares are counted against the plan's share pool differently based on the type of award being granted. Also, ensure the equity platform reverts shares to the pool following cancellations, forfeitures, and use to cover taxes.

1.3.6   Expense and Accounting

Before selecting a platform, the company should understand how the system will provide valuation, expense amortization, and tax accounting reporting for grants under the company's employee stock plan.

Most equity compensation platforms include the functionality to value stock options using the Black-Scholes model. If the company requires different valuation models, it will need to assess the platform's ability to perform this function.

Members of the company's finance and accounting functions should be part of the multidisciplinary team involved in selecting the equity compensation platform. The collaborative team should assess the platform's quarterly and annual financial reporting and tax accounting functionality.

The company should also consider whether any special circumstances may arise that will affect expense and tax accounting—for example, a modification, a repricing, or an acquisition. If the company has a history of such actions or anticipates that one may occur, it will be important to understand how the platform will manage the associated expense.

1.3.7   Securities Filings

In selecting an equity compensation platform, the company should understand the extent to which the platform can be used to manage securities filings. Many equity compensation platforms have functionality that allows for tracking and reporting for Section 16 insiders. The company should assess the extent to which the platform will assist with completing and filing Forms 3, 4, and 5. The platform should also provide reports for other securities filing requirements such as proxy and financial reporting. Multinational companies should assess the level of support the platform provides to aid in the securities and tax filings required by international jurisdictions.

1.4   Administering Events Common to All Equity Awards

Certain standard, routine processes are generally common among the various equity awards, regardless of award type—ISOs, NSOs, SARs, RSAs, or RSUs. The awards are granted and eventually vest or become forfeited; shares are issued and are subject to taxation (unless an exemption applies).

1.4.1 Granting Equity Awards

1.4.1.1 Plan Participation

Under an employee stock plan, both the selection of recipients and the timing of grants are typically reserved to the discretion of the board of directors or appropriate board committee that is to serve as the plan administrator. Companies use a wide variety of approaches and policies for determining which employees should receive grants. In some instances, only members of senior management are eligible to receive equity. Other companies grant equity compensation to all managers. Some companies even grant equity to all employees regardless of their job descriptions.

Some companies grant equity to newly hired employees, while others grant equity only to employees who have completed a specified term of service with the company or directly affected the achievement of corporate goals. Equity grants are frequently used as a form of merit bonus, in combination with or in lieu of a salary increase or in conjunction with a promotion. It is not uncommon for a company to make periodic (for example, annual) uniform stock grants to all employees. In general, the grants are consistent with the company's intentions behind establishing the equity plan—to recruit, retain, motivate, reward, and align the interests of shareholders and employees.

ISOs may only be granted to employees of a company, while other types of equity compensation such as NSOs, SARs, and restricted stock may be granted to employees, nonemployee directors, consultants, advisors, and other service providers to the company.

1.4.1.2 Number of Shares Granted

Under an employee stock plan, the number of shares of stock to be granted pursuant to an equity award is typically determined by the board of directors or appropriate board committee that has been designated as the plan administrator. Companies use a wide variety of approaches to determine grant sizes. Typically, a company establishes guidelines for determining the number of shares of stock to be subject to each grant. Often, these guidelines are set as a range of shares based on job classification or length of service. The number of shares of stock may be determined on an employee-by-employee basis (often based on individual performance), by job classification, or based on the company's overall performance over a specified period of time. The number of shares of stock also may be determined as a percentage of the employee's annual salary or based on a desired overall dollar value for the award. Typically, a company will establish an annual budget for the number of shares to be granted over the course of the year, with the allocation among employees determined on the basis of guidelines such as those described in the preceding sentences.

With performance-based equity awards becoming more common, a question may arise as to the number of shares of stock to be credited against the plan's share reserve for a performance-based grant. This issue is relevant where the award provides for variations in the number of shares earned (or available to exercise, in the case of options) based on the actual level of performance achieved. These awards provide for a target performance level and often set forth a threshold performance level below which no shares will be earned and a maximum performance level at which the number of shares that may be earned is capped. These are typically expressed as a percentage of the target (e.g., the maximum payout may be 150% of the payout at target). In this instance, even though the performance outcome will not be known at the time of grant, it is customary for the company to assume that the actual performance will be at the maximum performance level to ensure that an adequate number of shares has been reserved for the award and, perhaps more importantly, to guard against inadvertently exceeding the limit of the plan share reserve.

1.4.1.3 Internal Approval Process

Companies find it beneficial to establish internal approval procedures around their grants of equity compensation. The exact nature of these procedures varies from company to company, but in all cases they should address such matters as who will be recommended for equity compensation grants, the size of the recommended grants, and whether any special terms and conditions will be attached to them. These decisions are usually made by the human resources department and other benefits personnel, possibly with input from various management-level employees. For example, in the case of newly hired employees, the hiring manager may provide the first level of grant recommendation or approval. For merit grants, an employee's direct supervisor may provide the recommendation.

Next, all grants, regardless of origin, are incorporated into a formal proposal to be submitted to the company's board of directors or appropriate board committee for review and approval. If the board of directors has delegated responsibility for equity grants to a subcommittee of the board, such as the compensation committee or a special equity compensation committee or to an executive officer (or group of executive officers), the recommendations will be considered and approved. Alternatively, the committee may make its own recommendations, which are submitted to the full board for review and final approval. Grants generally become effective as of the date of board action (although the terms of the plan or the specific grant authorization may provide otherwise).

A company should document the entire internal approval process, including the grant date, the number of shares subject to the award, the exercise price if the grant is an option, and the identity of the intended recipient. The company also should consider documenting the identities of the persons who authorized the award and the related authorization date. This authorization should be reflected in the board or committee meeting minutes or in a written consent in lieu of a meeting. To the extent that the board of directors delegates responsibility for grants to an executive officer (or group of executive officers), there should be restrictions on the scope of this authority (for example, limits on the size of awards and permissible recipients). In addition, the board of directors should regularly audit the activities resulting from this delegated responsibility to ensure that this authority is not being misused. In the event that an employee is inadvertently left off the list of recommendations for a grant, the company should have a policy in place for how this situation will be handled. Depending upon the particular facts and circumstances, the remedy may involve simply adding the individual's name to the grant list or placing the individual on a subsequent list to be submitted for board or committee approval. This is particularly important for stock option grants, because the company will want to avoid the tax, legal, and investor relations problems that result from granting an option with an exercise price that is lower than the grant date fair market value.

To comply with Section 404 of the Sarbanes-Oxley Act of 2002, companies should ensure their internal control systems cover administration of their employee stock plans, from the initiation of grants through final approval by the company's board of directors or appropriate board committee. In establishing the internal approval process, it is imperative that the company segregate the required duties appropriately to ensure that the individuals who gather and formulate the information that is presented to the board of directors or board committee are not the same individuals who record the approved awards. The principal areas that should be incorporated in the control system include both grant procedures and the reporting of grants and awards within the company, particularly with respect to interdepartmental communications. Finally, these procedures should be routinely evaluated and tested to ensure they contain no material deficiencies.

In addition, care should be taken when administering an employee stock plan where the board of directors has delegated grant approval to a subcommittee to ensure that grants conform to the guidelines that have been established with respect to the subcommittee's scope of authority. Frequently, the charter of the subcommittee will state that the subcommittee may approve awards only to certain groups of employees within specified ranges of value. It is imperative that any audit of grant procedures verify that these guidelines have been followed precisely. If grants have been processed that did not follow the specified guidelines, then the grants are not valid.

1.4.1.4 Grant Agreement

Companies generally document equity compensation grants by preparing formal grant agreements (commonly referred to as "award agreements"). The grant agreement is a written or electronic document that specifies the terms and conditions of the grant. The grant agreement typically contains the following:

- name of the grant recipient
- effective date of the grant

- type of grant (e.g., ISO, NSO, SAR, RSA, RSU)
- number of shares of stock covered by the award
- exercise price if the grant is a stock option or SAR
- applicable dividend and voting rights if the grant is in the form of restricted stock
- vesting schedule and acceleration and forfeiture events
- expiration and termination provisions

In addition, if the grant is a stock option or SAR, the agreement usually sets out the procedures the optionee must follow to exercise it, the permissible forms of payment of the exercise price, and other related matters. If the grant is restricted stock, the agreement may set forth the procedures for making an 83(b) election to accelerate taxation on RSAs or for making an election to defer issuance of the shares for RSUs. Alternatively, the agreement may simply make reference to the provisions within the plan document that are not specific to any particular grant.

For private companies, the agreement may set forth the liquidation rights, including a right of first refusal clause that provides the company with the first chance to buy the shares at the same price and terms as another offer; a put option that gives the recipient the right to sell the shares to the company; a call option that gives the company the right to buy the shares back from the holder; a tag-along clause that requires the majority shareholder to allow the minor shareholders to join in on a sale of the company; or a drag-along clause that requires the minor shareholders to sell their shares in a sale of the company. If the grant is for "qualified stock" of an NSO or an RSU under a broad-based plan of a private company, the agreement sets forth the procedures for making a fairly new "83(i) election" to defer taxation of the shares for up to five years if the company allows these elections.

An equity grant represents a contract between the company and the recipient. For this reason, requiring recipients to formally acknowledge and accept the terms and conditions governing an award will help eliminate possible contract disputes during its term. Since the grant agreement sets out the obligations of the recipient in connection with the receipt of the grant and acquisition of the shares, most companies require that the recipient sign (or acknowledge receipt of) the grant agreement. When acceptance is required to effectuate an award, companies may put an expiration date on the acceptance. A company should set a time limit within which a recipient must sign and return the grant agreement (or acknowledge acceptance of the grant conditions). The company should address whether there is to be a penalty for failure to return an executed agreement (or make the required acknowledgement). In addition, the company should provide a formal method for a recipient to actively decline the grant. The plan administrator should ensure that records of grant acceptances and rejections are retained.

However, some companies do not require an affirmative acceptance of the award, taking the position that a grant agreement is legally binding with or without a signature—particularly in the case of stock options, which require action on the part of the employee to purchase the shares. Before taking such a position, it is important to discuss the consequences with the company's legal counsel.

1.4.1.5 Collateral Documents

In addition to the grant agreement, the company may provide several other documents to a grant holder. For purposes of compliance with applicable federal and state securities laws, it is customary for the company to provide each optionee with a copy of the employee stock plan or with a document (often referred to as the plan "prospectus") that summarizes the principal terms and conditions of the plan, describes the tax consequences of participation in the plan, and advises the grantee where to obtain additional information about the company and the plan.

When grants are made under an omnibus plan, which gives the company flexibility to grant various types of equity awards, other relevant documents may include: a stock option exercise notice, a Section 83(b) election form that can be used to notify the company that the grant holder has elected accelerated taxation of RSAs at grant, a deferral election form to defer taxation of RSUs, memoranda describing the company's exercise procedures, investment representation letters or statements (in the event the underlying shares have not been registered with the SEC), an escrow agreement and instructions for restricted stock and options that may be exercised for unvested shares of stock, a form of promissory note and security agreement for option exercises by a company loan, the appropriate forms for conducting a broker-assisted "same-day-sale" to settle stock awards, and guidance that answers the most frequently asked questions about equity grants and contains instructions on exercise procedures. If the company maintains an internal employee website, some or all of these documents or information may be posted there. Companies may also require that recipients acknowledge receipt of these documents.

1.4.1.6 Special Provision for Privately Held Companies

Securities Act Rule 701 provides an exemption from the registration requirements of Section 5 of the Securities Act of 1933 for privately held companies with employee stock plans that are used to offer and sell their own securities (including stock options) to their employees and other permitted recipients. Among the conditions that must be satisfied to rely on the Rule 701 exemption is an information delivery requirement. Specifically, a company relying on Rule 701 must deliver to each employee receiving a grant of stock a copy of the employee stock plan pursuant to which the award has been granted. In addition, if the aggregate sales price or amount of securities sold during any consecutive 12-month period exceeds $10 million (increased from $5 million in 2018), the company must provide certain additional written information to the employees and other recipients receiving grants of stock under the company's employee stock plan within a reasonable period of time before the date of sale. This information includes: (1) a summary of the material terms of the plan (or, if the plan is subject to the Employment Retirement Income Security Act of 1974 [ERISA], a copy of the summary plan description required by ERISA); (2) information about the risks associated with investment in the company's securities; and (3) financial statements required to be furnished by Part F/S of Form 1-A under Regulation A as of a date no more than 180 days before the date of the sale of the stock in reliance on the exemption. To maintain confidentiality of their financial condition, most privately held companies are reluctant to simply distribute their financial statements to their employees (as well as to nonemployees and prospective employees who may be receiving grants). Consequently, many of these companies will establish a controlled environment where this information can be accessed and reviewed, but not retained (for example, a binder containing the company's financial statements that employees may review, or a customized website to which the employees are granted access). It is important for privately held companies to establish a procedure to provide this information to their employees and other grant recipients for review before the grant of restricted stock or the exercise of vested stock options to ensure compliance with Rule 701.

1.4.2 Vesting

Generally, an award holder earns either his or her shares or the right to exercise his or her stock option over a specified period of time. The process of earning the shares or the right to exercise the option is commonly referred to as "vesting." The vesting period set forth in the grant agreement is commonly referred to as the "vesting schedule."

The shares underlying RSAs are released to the grant holder upon vesting, and RSUs are usually converted to shares upon vesting—although it is possible to defer this in some situations. Stock options typically become exercisable upon vesting. (Occasionally, a company permits an optionee to exercise his or her stock option immediately as of the date of grant, subject to a right of repurchase in favor of the company should the optionee leave the company before a specified date.)

1.4.2.1 Vesting Schedule

Vesting typically occurs either in one lump sum after a specified period of time (so-called "cliff vesting") or in cumulative increments (often called "graded vesting"). Generally, a vesting schedule provides that at the completion of designated intervals or periods of service, a predetermined percentage of the shares are earned under restricted stock or become available for purchase under a stock option. These interim dates are called "vesting dates." Typically, vesting is measured from the date a stock option is granted (the "vesting commencement date"). However, some companies set the vesting commencement date earlier than the grant date by measuring vesting from the date the optionee was hired or commenced providing services to the company or some other specified date.

A company adopts a vesting schedule that best suits the incentive, retention, or other objectives of its employee stock plan. Many companies provide grants with annual vesting schedules (that is, the option shares vest in equal annual installments over a period of several years—typically, three, four, or five years) or grants in which a portion cliff-vests after one year with monthly or quarterly vesting for the duration of the schedule. For administrative convenience, a company may time the vesting of restricted stock to occur on a regular cadence (e.g., the last day of a calendar quarter) for all grants.

It is also possible to structure equity grants to vest upon the achievement of a specified company performance goal, such as achievement of a specified earnings-per-share, revenue, or profitability target, or for stock options to become exercisable based on a performance goal. Like grants that are subject to service-based vesting requirements, performance-based grants may vest either in one lump sum after a specified performance goal has been satisfied or in cumulative increments after one or more performance goals are met.

1.4.2.2 Fractional Shares

From time to time, procedural questions may arise in connection with grants of equity compensation, such as how fractional shares of stock are to be allocated under the vesting schedule. Most companies do not wish to show fractional shares vesting on a vesting date and either drop or round the fractional amount. If the fraction is dropped, it is merely allocated to a later vesting period until the aggregate amount equals a whole share. If the fraction is rounded, it is usually rounded to the nearest whole share, and, if rounded down, the fractional amount is allocated to a later period until a whole share can be shown.

1.4.3 Withholding, Depositing and Reporting Employment Taxes

1.4.3.1 Tax Withholding

Once the amount subject to tax (taxable income) is determined, the company must reckon with its tax withholding obligation. Where the award recipient is a nonemployee (e.g., consultant, independent contractor, or nonemployee director), the company does not withhold taxes on the income recognized from the equity award. Where the award recipient is an employee of the company or was an employee when the shares were earned, arrangements must be made to satisfy any tax withholding obligations that arise in connection with a tax event. The timing of such an event may vary depending on the award type. Explanations of the taxes, collection, remittance, and reporting are discussed in this section, while the timing of the tax withholding obligations is discussed in section 1.5 of this chapter for stock options and section 1.6 for restricted stock.

The company's tax withholding obligation consists of several types of taxes: federal income tax, the Social Security insurance portion of the Federal Insurance Contributions Act (FICA), the Medicare insurance portion of FICA, state income tax (if applicable), and state disability or unemployment insurance (if applicable).

For federal income taxes purposes, the income an employee recognizes from equity awards is treated as supplemental wages (i.e., wages that are not regular wages such as a base salary or hourly wages). An employee's supplemental wages that do not exceed $1 million in a calendar year may be withheld in one of two ways. Either the compensation income resulting from the equity award may be aggregated with an employee's regular salary payment for the period and withholding computed on the total amount (the "aggregate method"), or the company may apply the "optional flat rate withholding method" and withhold at a flat percentage (currently 22%).[1] However, a mandatory flat rate (currently 37%) applies to supplemental wages in excess of $1 million that an employee receives during a calendar year. The withholding taxes collected by the company are only an estimate of the employee's ultimate tax liability. It may be necessary for the employee to make additional quarterly tax deposits, depending on the employee's personal tax situation (or to remit additional amounts owed when tax returns are filed).

FICA is made up of two separate taxes: (1) the old age, survivor, and disability insurance (or Social Security) tax, and (2) the hospital insurance (or Medicare) tax, both of which are imposed on the employee and the company. The current tax rate for Social Security is 6.2% for

---

1.   Tax and withholding rates, and the Social Security taxable wage base, are given with information available as of fall 2022 when this chapter was revised.

the employer and 6.2% for the employee (or 12.4% total). The current tax rate for Medicare tax is 1.45% for the employer and 1.45% for the employee (or 2.9% total). The Social Security component of FICA is collected up to an annual maximum $147,000 for 2022), while the Medicare component is collected against the employee's total income. There is an additional Medicare component to be withheld from employees who earn more than $200,000 in taxable wages ($250,000 for joint returns; $125,000 for married taxpayers filing a separate return). Currently, the rate for an employee's wages up to $200,000 is 1.45%, while the rate for wages in excess of $200,000 is 2.35%. The rate for employers remains constant at 1.45% on all taxable wages, since the additional Medicare tax component is imposed on only employees.

Many states follow the federal framework for income tax reporting and collection purposes and may require the withholding of state disability and unemployment taxes. Generally, state taxes are determined on the basis of the employee's state of residence. Some states and countries are enforcing laws that require individuals to pay local income tax on compensation for the period during which the individual worked in the state or country when that compensation was earned. Employers are required to report income and withhold taxes based on these local laws. Accordingly, the plan administrator should track the work locations of the award recipients during the vesting period as the award is earned, particularly with respect to mobile employees.

1.4.3.2 Methods of Collecting Tax Withholding

The company can collect the tax withholding by withholding from other wages payable to the employee at the same time, by requiring the employee to make a payment equal to the withholding amount in cash or by promissory note, by selling a sufficient number of shares through a broker to cover the taxes ("sell-to-cover"), or by retaining a sufficient number of shares ("withhold-to-cover").

Withholding from other wages payable to the employee at the same time may be appropriate for small amounts of supplemental wages attributable to equity awards, but may be insufficient to cover all of the withholding taxes due or may leave the employee with inadequate net pay where larger amounts are involved.

The employee may be required to remit the employee's portion of the withholding taxes due to the company. This payment method may involve a wire transfer or a check made payable to the company. The company should decide whether a bank or cashier's check is required for payment or whether a personal check is acceptable, and what the permissible time period is for remitting payment. Alternatively, the company may pay the taxes on the employee's behalf, subject to re-payment by the employee pursuant to the terms of a promissory note in favor of the company. However, companies that are subject to the reporting requirements of the Securities Exchange Act of 1934 (the "Exchange Act") are prohibited from extending credit or arranging for the extension of credit in the form of a personal loan to their directors and executive officers.

Sell-to-cover is one preferred method of tax payment. This involves selling shares on the market to generate adequate proceeds to cover the tax liability, with the remaining shares given to the employee. This method is available for broker-assisted transactions and marketable securities.

Withhold-to-cover is another preferred method of tax payment. Under this method, the company withholds a portion of the shares that are released. However, the company must pay the tax obligation from company funds, rather than using cash generated by the sale of stock in a sell-to-cover transaction. While a withhold-to-cover is administratively simpler, it may result in a significant cash outlay for the company, particularly if a large number of shares vest or are exercised on one day.

Officers and directors subject to Section 16 of the Exchange Act may, if certain requirements have been satisfied, elect to have shares withheld to pay withholding tax obligations without the transaction giving rise to a "sale" for purposes of the "short-swing profits" recovery provision of Section 16(b).

1.4.3.3 Depositing Employment Taxes

When making federal tax deposits, it is important to understand the "$100,000 next-day deposit rule." Under this rule, if during any deposit period, a company accumulates a tax liability of $100,000 or more, it must make a deposit by the next business day. For this purpose, when calculating a company's tax liability, the employees' withheld federal income tax, Social Security tax, and Medicare tax are to be included.

The timing of the employment tax withholding and deposit rules for stock awards is complicated by the Securities Exchange Commission (SEC) rule requiring brokers to settle securities transactions within two business days after their transaction date. This rule is commonly known as the "T+2" rule (short for "trading date plus two days"). In May 2020, the Internal Revenue Service (IRS) updated its Internal Revenue Manual, instructing its agents not to challenge the timeliness of employment tax deposits for NSOs, stock-settled SARs, or stock-settled RSUs that are made within one day of settlement, so long as the settlement complies with the T+2 rule.

Accordingly, the settlement date is used as the liability incurred date for purposes of determining the $100,000 next-day deposit obligation. The settlement date for NSOs and stock-settled SARs is the second business day after the exercise date. For stock-settled RSUs, the settlement date is the second business day after the payment initiation date. For example, if an employee exercised NSOs on Monday, the shares were delivered to the employee's brokerage account or sold to cover the exercise price and withholding taxes (settled) on Wednesday, and the employment tax withholding was deposited on Thursday, then the IRS will consider the deposit to be timely under the $100,000 next-day deposit rule.

Historically, a 2003 IRS administrative waiver of late deposit penalties applied only to the settlement of NSOs that complied with the then-existing "T+3" rule (when brokers had up to three business days to settle securities). The administrative waiver was expanded in 2020 to include NSOs, stock-settled SARs, and stock-settled RSUs, but it provided less time to deposit the employment taxes for consistency with the shorter T+2 settlement cycle in effect since September 5, 2017. In February 2022, the Securities Exchange Commission (SEC) proposed to further shorten the settlement cycle from two business days after the trade date ("T+2") to one business day after the trade date ("T+1"), effective March 31, 2024. The SEC is also exploring challenges that market participants may need to address to achieve a T+0 settlement cycle. As a corollary of a shorter settlement cycle, employers may be required to deposit employment taxes one day after (and potentially the same day as) the payment initiation date to satisfy the $100,000 next-day deposit rule.

1.4.3.4 Reporting

The company must furnish an employee (or former employee) who acquires shares from an equity award with a Form W-2 for the year of taxation reporting the compensation income recognized as wages and the taxes withheld. If the recipient is a nonemployee, the compensation income is not subject to withholding but must be reported on a Form 1099-NEC for the year of taxation. Before 2020, the tax reporting for nonemployee compensation was reported on a Form 1099-MISC.

1.4.3.5 Company Deduction

In general, a corporate tax deduction may be claimed when the award is taxable for income tax purposes to the employee, provided the company has reported the income on a Form W-2 for employees (or the appropriate Form 1099 for nonemployees). Notably, the timing of the deduction may differ between compensation attributable to RSAs and RSUs if the company does not report taxes on a calendar-year basis, as discussed further in section 1.6.7. The corporate deduction equals the amount of taxable income of the employee. However, shares issued to certain executive officers pursuant to the exercise or vesting of awards have additional tax considerations. In particular, Code Section 162(m) denies a corporate tax deduction for compensation in excess of $1 million paid to "covered employees" of a public company in a taxable year. In general, a company's "covered employee" group currently consists of the principal executive officer, the principal financial officer, the next five highest compensated officers, and any post-December 31, 2016, covered employee. For tax years beginning on or after January 1, 2027, the covered employee group will be expanded to include the next five highest compensated employees (in addition to the group of officers currently treated as covered employees).

1.4.3.6 Recharge Agreements

A "recharge agreement" is a formal agreement between a parent corporation and its foreign subsidiary pursuant to which the subsidiary reimburses the parent corporation for the cost of equity compensation. Companies enter into these types of agreements either to secure a corporate tax deduction at the subsidiary level for equity compensation awarded to its employees or to repatriate cash to the parent corporation. For U.S. tax purposes, a recharge payment is treated as a payment to the parent corporation in consideration for its stock, and the payment is not taxable to the parent corporation. Recharge agreements are a tax-efficient method of repatriating cash from the foreign subsidiary to the parent corporation. A recharge to a subsidiary in some countries can change the tax treatment of the equity compensation to the employee and may affect employer reporting and withholding responsibilities.

1.5   Administering Stock Options

1.5.1   Stock Options Overview

The fundamental difference between an ISO and an NSO is the tax treatment. Shares acquired from an NSO are taxed at exercise and again upon sale. The difference between the exercise price and the fair market value of the shares on the date of exercise (the "spread") is treated as wages, subject to ordinary income tax to the employee and deductible by the company. Any further appreciation or depreciation receives capital gains or capital loss treatment upon sale of the acquired shares. For ISOs, no tax is due until the employee sells the shares acquired on exercise. If the shares are held for the requisite statutory period, only long-term capital gains tax applies, and there is no corresponding deduction for the company. Alternatively, if the employee fails to hold the shares for the statutory period and engages in a disqualifying disposition, a mix of wages and capital gains applies. The company is entitled to a deduction to the extent wages are reported.

For employees to obtain the favorable tax treatment on ISOs, the plan administrator must assess compliance with the various tax rules and plan provisions: the exercise price cannot be less than the fair market value of the shares on the date of grant (or at least 110% of fair market value on the grant date for a more-than-10% shareholder), the recipient is an employee at the time of grant, the option has not expired at the time of exercise, exercise occurs while the individual is an employee or within three months after terminating employment (or 12 months for a termination by reason of a disability), and the employee has held the ISO shares for the greater of one year from the date of exercise and two years from the date of grant (the "statutory holding period") before disposing of them. There is a limit on how much of a grant is eligible for ISO treatment in that no more than $100,000 worth of shares may become exercisable in any calendar year (determined by the share price at grant). Shares over the limit are treated as NSOs.

1.5.2   Stock Option Term

When a stock option is granted, the grant agreement specifies the date the right to purchase the option shares will expire. This period within which the stock option must be exercised is referred to as the "option term." Typically, stock option terms range between five to ten years from the date the option is granted. In the case of an ISO, the maximum permitted option term is ten years from the grant date. If the optionee owns stock possessing more than 10% of the total combined voting power of all classes of the company's outstanding stock, the maximum permitted option term for an ISO is five years. When an optionee ceases to provide services to the company, the optionee may exercise the option within a predefined time period following such termination (the "post-termination exercise period"), but not later than the original expiration date of the option.

Once the stock option term has expired at the end of either the original option term or the post-termination exercise period, the employee may no longer purchase the option shares. While it is the obligation of the optionee to understand when he or she may exercise an option and when the option term will expire, many companies have implemented procedures to remind optionees of a looming expiration date to minimize, if not eliminate, the risk that an option will expire unexercised. (Such an occurrence can lead to significant personnel issues with the affected optionee, who will often view the company as having failed to notify the optionee of the potential forfeiture of what may be a significant economic benefit.) Companies handle this issue in a variety of ways. Some companies will remind optionees of upcoming option expirations. (Occasionally, these reminders will be accompanied by an acknowledgement of receipt.) In addition, some public companies will establish automatic exercise programs with their captive securities brokerage firms to automatically perform a sell-to-cover, same-day sale, or withhold-to-cover exercise before the expiration of any outstanding and unexercised in-the-money stock options to avoid an inadvertent failure to exercise.

1.5.3 Option Exercise Price

Typically, the exercise price of an employee stock option is equal to the fair market value of the granting company's stock on the grant date. Occasionally, a stock option plan permits the option exercise price to be less than fair market value (for example, 85% of the fair market value of the granting company's stock on the grant date). However, such provisions have become extremely rare, because an option with an exercise price below the fair market value of the underlying stock on the grant date may be considered to involve a deferral of compensation subject to Code Section 409A.

Most stock option plans stipulate how fair market value is to be determined. There are many methodologies employed to set fair market value for a public company, including (1) the closing price of the granting company's stock on the grant date, (2) the closing price of the granting company's stock on the date preceding the grant date, (3) the average of the high and low trading prices of the company's stock on the grant date, and (4) the average of the high and low trading prices of the company's stock on the date preceding the grant date. In the case of a privately held company, fair market value is frequently based on a formula prescribed by the company's board of directors or an external appraisal of the company's value.

1.5.4 Exercising Stock Options

1.5.4.1 Policies and Procedures

Consistent with the efficient administration of their equity compensation plans, many companies establish formal policies and procedures in connection with the exercise of their employee stock options. Formal guidelines for processing stock option exercises can serve as an effective means for ensuring that all company procedures are properly followed.

Formal plan policies are used to ensure that the intent of the plan is followed, even where adherence is complex. In addition, written procedures are used to comply with Section 404 of the Sarbanes-Oxley Act of 2002, which covers internal controls.

A comprehensive stock option plan policy should address:

- When the option may be exercised and the option shares purchased.

- The determination of the exercise date. Typically, the exercise date is the date that both the exercise notice and the payment (the option exercise price plus any associated withholding taxes) are received by the company.

- How applicable withholding taxes are to be calculated and collected. In most instances, this involves the calculation of fair market value for a cashless exercise.

- The different treatment for directors and officers subject to Section 16 of the Exchange Act and other trading restrictions. Section 16 regulates the trading of their own companies' securities by key corporate insiders, such as officers and directors, by requiring such insiders to publicly disclose their transactions in their companies' equity securities and to disgorge to their companies any "short-swing profits" realized from their trading activities in the companies' equity securities.[2] Other trading restrictions, such as Exchange Act Rule 10b-5 and Regulation BTR (Blackout Trading Restriction), may also limit the ability of officers and directors to exercise their stock options and sell the underlying option shares.

- Permissible exercise methods.

- Exercise limits.

A written procedure should address:

- the required documents for processing the exercise

- the tasks of the plan administrator

---

2. See section 2.3 of chapter 2 for more information on the "short-swing profits" recovery provision of Section 16(b)

- transfer agent communications
- broker communications (if applicable)
- interdepartmental communications

1.5.4.2 Exercisability

An optionee's right to exercise a stock option will be governed by the terms of the grant agreement. Where the stock option is exercisable only as the option vests, the optionee will be able to exercise the option only on or after the vesting date. Alternatively, where the stock option is exercisable before vesting, the optionee will be able to exercise the option at any time during its term. Generally, the date of exercise is considered to be the date on which the plan administrator or other designated representative of the company receives both an executed stock option exercise notice and payment of the total option exercise price for the number of option shares being purchased plus any associated withholding taxes.

1.5.4.3 Notice of Exercise

To purchase the shares of stock underlying a stock option, the optionee must follow the procedures established by the company for exercising the option. Typically, these procedures are set forth in the optionee's grant agreement or an accompanying document. At a minimum, these procedures require that the optionee provide written notice to the company stating his or her intention to exercise all or a portion of his or her vested options.

Most companies have established electronic exercise methods to alleviate many of the burdens to optionees and the company of processing exercises. Through these programs, optionees are able to exercise their stock options via a website or an automated telephonic system. Readily available from many securities brokerage firms, these systems eliminate most of the manual data entry that was historically associated with option exercises and can also reduce the number of optionee inquiries about exercise procedures.

Even so, many companies with electronic exercise procedures also allow optionees to exercise a stock option manually. To do so, the optionee completes and signs a stock option exercise notice identifying the stock option being exercised and indicating the number of option shares the optionee intends to purchase. The exercise notice may also indicate how the optionee intends to pay for the option shares. Most stock option plans regard online initiation of an exercise as notice of intent to exercise. For exercises conducted manually, companies require a written exercise notice as a prerequisite to a valid exercise to establish the exercise date and to document the optionee's intent to exercise.

The stock option exercise notice may also contain other information, such as (1) specific representations and statements by the optionee deemed necessary by the company to ensure compliance with all required federal and state securities laws, (2) information relevant to the form of payment that the optionee has selected to pay the total required option exercise price for the number of option shares being purchased, (3) specific statements pertaining to the tax withholding obligations of the optionee, if any, arising in connection with the exercise, and (4) specific statements regarding any restrictions and conditions imposed on the option shares.

Generally, if the stock option exercise notice is on paper, it should be submitted to the plan administrator or other designated representative of the company in person, or by registered or certified mail, return receipt requested, before the expiration date of the stock option, accompanied by full payment of the total required option exercise price for the number of option shares being purchased and any associated withholding taxes, plus any other required documents. Where the optionee is not a local employee, alternate procedures may be in place for the delivery of the stock option exercise notice and payment of the option exercise price and any associated withholding taxes.

Where the stock option is being exercised by means of a broker's "same-day-sale" exercise (see below), additional documents may have to be executed by the optionee in order to complete the transaction.

1.5.4.4 Methods of Payment

An employee stock option plan may provide for a variety of methods for exercising a stock option—that is, for paying the purchase price for the option shares. These payment methods include cash (usually in the form of a check), stock swaps, broker-assisted exercises (whether a "same-day sale" or a "sell-to-cover" exercise), and use of a promissory note. Some plans also permit the delivery of already owned shares of stock or the withholding of option shares from the stock option exercise to satisfy the withholding tax obligation arising from the exercise. Company policy should set out the methods available to the optionee and the relevant guidelines for each.

Cash Exercises. When conducting a cash exercise, at the time of exercise, the optionee is required to remit the total required option exercise price for the option shares being purchased plus any associated withholding taxes due to the company. Generally, payment is made in the form of a wire transfer or check made payable to the company. The company should decide whether a bank or cashiers' check is required for payment or whether a personal check is acceptable, whether separate checks are required for the total option exercise price and the taxes due, and the permissible time period for remitting payment.

Brokers' "Same-Day Sale" Exercises. A "same-day sale" exercise is a means by which an optionee can finance the exercise of a stock option by immediately selling through a securities brokerage firm all of the option shares underlying the stock option being exercised. The proceeds of the sale are remitted to the employee after deducting the total required option exercise price for the option shares being purchased plus any withholding taxes due to the company (which amounts are remitted directly to the company).

A company may make formal arrangements with one or more securities brokerage firms to facilitate "same-day sale" exercises. Not only do such arrangements simplify the administration of these programs, they also enable the transactions to be completed more expeditiously. In these arrangements, sometimes referred to as "captive broker" programs, the company keeps the securities brokerage firm or firms updated on outstanding stock options and vested shares, thereby enabling the optionee to contact the brokerage firm directly when he or she wants to exercise a stock option. To further simplify the administration of these transactions, some companies establish an "omnibus" account with one or more securities brokerage firms and transfer a block of shares to the account for the purpose of ensuring that sufficient shares are available to deliver upon the settlement of the sale.

Following the sale, the company is notified of the sale price so that the required withholding taxes, if any, can be calculated. This figure is then transmitted to the securities brokerage firm so that it can divide the sales proceeds between the company and the optionee.

Generally, within the settlement period (currently two business days from the trade date, or "T+2"), the securities brokerage firm will remit to the company the portion of the sales proceeds necessary to cover the total required option exercise price for the option shares being purchased and any associated withholding taxes due to the company. This amount is usually paid by check, by wire transfer, or through a deposit into the company's account at the securities brokerage firm.

Typically, the company does not instruct its transfer agent to deliver shares for the "same-day sale" to the securities brokerage firm until payment of the option exercise price has been made. Upon receipt of the shares, the transaction will be completed and the balance of the sale proceeds, less brokerage commissions, is remitted to the employee.

Where employees are not able to initiate a "same-day sale" transaction electronically, an optionee who wishes to execute such a transaction will first contact the plan administrator and indicate his or her decision to exercise a vested stock option. The optionee will complete the required forms for a standard stock option exercise (typically, a stock option exercise notice) and the additional forms necessary for a "same-day-sale" exercise (such as a set of irrevocable instructions to the company, a stock transfer power, a Form W-9, and, if a brokerage account needs to be established, a new account form or a margin agreement form).

Once the forms have been completed and the plan administrator has confirmed that the optionee does, in fact, have sufficient option shares to cover the proposed transaction, the exercise notice and the irrevocable instructions (which may be integrated into a single document) will be immediately transmitted to the securities brokerage firm. The securities brokerage firm will also be instructed as to how many option shares are to be sold (either just enough to cover the total required option exercise price for the transaction and any associated withholding taxes or some greater number, up to all, of the option shares).

For income tax purposes, it is important for a company to satisfy itself as to when the option exercise is deemed to occur in the context of a "same-day-sale" transaction—either the date that the stock option exercise notice is submitted or the date that payment of the total required option exercise price is received. To the extent that these are different dates, the amount of income realized from the exercise, if any, and the associated withholding taxes may vary. In addition, the determination may result in a difference between the exercise date and the sale date, thereby resulting in variations between the amount of gain reported by the company and by the securities brokerage firm. Companies employ various techniques to ensure that payment of the option exercise price is received or credited for the employee's benefit on the earliest possible date, such as providing in their stock option plans that delivery of the appropriate paperwork for a "same-day-sale" exercise will be an acceptable payment method or by arranging for immediate payment by, or receipt of a short-term "loan" from, a securities brokerage firm. The resolution of this matter for an individual company generally will be based upon the provisions of the company's stock option plan and the grant agreement, as well as by any applicable provisions of state corporate law.

Except as discussed below, officers and directors subject to Section 16 of the Exchange Act may participate in these "same-day-sale" exercise programs. As affiliates of the company, however, they are subject to certain restrictions not imposed on regular employees. For example, such "same-day-sale" exercise transactions may be restricted to the company's trading "window period." As affiliates, their sales of company stock also must be made in compliance with the conditions of Securities Act Rule 144, the resale exemption from the registration requirements of the Securities Act of 1933 that imposes certain conditions on any sale of securities by a company's officers and directors. In addition, in some circumstances, a "same-day sale exercise" may be viewed as involving either an extension of credit or an arrangement for the extension of credit in the form of a personal loan by the company, which is prohibited under Section 13(k) of the Exchange Act. This prohibition precludes the directors and executive officers of companies that are subject to the reporting requirements of the Exchange Act from engaging in certain types of "same-day-sale" exercises. Accordingly, a company should consult with its legal counsel before allowing directors and executive officers to engage in a "same-day-sale" exercise of a stock option to ensure its procedure does not violate Section 13(k).

For financial reporting purposes, the implementation of a broker's "same-day-sale" exercise program does not result in the recognition of a compensation expense, because the company receives the full option exercise price for the option shares purchased, the company actually issues the shares, and no payment related to the exercise originates with the company.

Brokers' "Sell-to-Cover" Exercises. Similar to a "same-day sale" exercise, a "sell-to-cover" exercise is a means by which an optionee can finance the exercise of a stock option by immediately selling through a securities brokerage firm that number of option shares from the stock option being exercised necessary to satisfy the payment of the total required option exercise price for the option shares being purchased plus any withholding taxes due to the company. The remainder of the shares acquired upon exercise are then retained by the optionee.

The process is similar to that of a "same-day sale" exercise, except that, rather than delivering cash proceeds to the optionee, the remaining (unsold) shares exercised are delivered to the optionee. Typically, these remaining shares would be held electronically in the optionee's brokerage account.

Stock Swaps. When an optionee elects to exercise a stock option by means of a stock swap, he or she is surrendering already owned shares of stock to pay the total required option exercise price for the option shares being purchased. Typically, the surrendered shares are valued at the fair market value of the company's stock on the date of exercise. An optionee will be permitted to engage in a stock swap exercise only if the stock option plan expressly authorizes the delivery of already owned shares of stock as a permissible payment method. The surrendered shares are either held by the company as treasury shares, returned to the plan share reserve for regrant (if permitted under the plan), or retired by the company (thereby reverting to the status of authorized but unissued shares).

Some employee stock option plans permit an optionee, in lieu of actually delivering shares to the company to exercise an option, to simply "attest" to owning sufficient shares to pay the total required option exercise price and, thereafter, receive from the company only the number of shares upon exercise that reflect the appreciation in the exercised option. In addition to the administrative benefits of this procedure, the attestation approach may provide additional recordkeeping and tracing advantages.

Officers and directors subject to Section 16 of the Exchange Act may, if certain requirements have been satisfied, engage in a stock swap without the transaction giving rise to either a "purchase" or "sale" for purposes of the "short-swing profits" recovery provision of Section 16(b).

For financial reporting purposes, generally the surrender of already owned shares of stock to pay the total required exercise price for the exercise of an employee stock option will not trigger the recognition of a compensation expense. In the rare case where the optionee has the ability to compel the company to repurchase his or her option shares, a stock swap could give rise to liability accounting treatment under ASC 718. Thus, if a stock option plan contains a "put" feature, the company should confirm the accounting consequences of a stock swap exercise before permitting such transactions.

Reload Stock Options. Some employee stock option plans provide for the grant of so-called "reload" stock options in connection with stock swap exercises. Essentially, a reload option feature provides that upon a stock swap exercise, the optionee will receive an automatic grant of a new stock option at the then-current fair market value of the company's stock for a number of shares of stock equal to the number of already owned shares surrendered to the company to complete the stock swap exercise.

Use of a Promissory Note. Some companies permit employees to deliver a promissory note to pay the total required option exercise price for the option shares being purchased. Generally, the promissory note will be a full recourse obligation secured by the option shares being purchased or other property acceptable to the company.

If the use of promissory notes is permitted, such arrangements must provide for the payment of at least the minimum amount of interest that is required under the Code. If the interest rate charged is less than the applicable federal rate, the IRS will treat a portion of the amount repaid as imputed interest, which may have significant income tax consequences to the employee and the company. The applicable federal rates are published by the IRS monthly.

In addition, if the stock option is intended to be an ISO, failure to provide for adequate interest for the promissory note may jeopardize the tax status of the option. Consequently, the promissory note must meet the interest requirements of Section 483 of the Code or interest will be imputed, thereby reducing the principal amount of the promissory note. To the extent that this occurs, the amount deemed paid for the option shares will be less than the fair market value of the company's stock on the date of grant. Because less than fair market value will be deemed paid for the shares, incentive stock option treatment will not be available, and the option may be considered to involve a deferral of compensation subject to Section 409A of the Code.

Under current accounting rules, a failure to provide for adequate interest in a promissory note may be viewed, under certain circumstances, as a reduction of the exercise price of the stock option and increase the compensation cost for financial reporting purposes. Thus, it will be necessary to confirm the accounting consequences of the use of a promissory note to exercise an option before permitting such transactions.

As previously noted, under Section 13(k) of the Exchange Act, companies that are subject to the reporting requirements of the Exchange Act are prohibited from extending credit or arranging for the extension of credit in the form of a personal loan to their directors and executive officers. Because this prohibition applies to the delivery of a promissory note to purchase company stock, directors and executive officers may not exercise a stock option through the delivery of a promissory note.

1.5.4.5 Exercise Restrictions

To control administrative costs, the company may adopt a formal policy establishing a minimum number of option shares that must be exercised at any one time. This may be especially important if the company's vesting schedule contemplates frequent vesting dates (such as monthly). For example, company policy may restrict the exercise of fewer than 100 option shares at a time unless the balance of the shares remaining in the award is less than the minimum exercise amount.

1.5.4.6 Exercise of Unvested Shares

As previously described, some companies permit optionees to exercise stock options before the date that the option shares vest. These unvested option shares will be subject to a right of repurchase in favor of the company in the event the optionee is an employee who terminates his or her employment (or a nonemployee who terminates his or her service) before the vesting date. This right of repurchase expires either all at once or as to incremental portions of the option shares over the vesting period. When an exercise for unvested option shares occurs, typically the shares are issued in the name of the optionee and then held in escrow until they vest. The option shares cannot be sold while they are held in escrow, nor can they be used as collateral for loans. Consequently, the optionee usually executes and delivers to the company a form of joint escrow agreement or escrow instructions when exercising a stock option for unvested shares.

The unvested share repurchase right held by the company will be exercisable only upon the termination of employment or service of the optionee and then only to the extent of any shares of stock previously acquired by the optionee that remain unvested on the date of termination. Typically, the grant agreement specifies the rights and obligations of the company and the optionee under this repurchase right.

If a company elects to exercise its unvested share repurchase right, the company must notify the optionee in writing within a specified period of time (usually two to three months following termination of employment) of its decision to repurchase some or all of the unvested shares. The decision to repurchase the unvested shares is typically made by the board of directors. Typically, the repurchase price is an amount equal to the original option price paid by the optionee for the option shares. Occasionally, the repurchase price is the lesser of the original option price paid by the optionee or the current fair market value of the shares. This payment is made in cash or by cancellation of any outstanding indebtedness of the optionee to the company. While, typically, the company holds the unvested shares pending vesting, if the option shares have been issued to the optionee, payment of the repurchase amount will not take place unless and until the certificate for the unvested shares is delivered to the company.

Since a right of repurchase on unvested option shares renders the shares nontransferable and is considered to be a "substantial risk of forfeiture," the optionee is normally not subject to taxation in connection with the purchase of the option shares until the shares vest. The optionee may elect to close the compensatory element of the purchase and accelerate the time at which gain will be realized (and at which taxes, if any, will be paid) to the date of exercise by making a so-called "Section 83(b) election."

1.5.4.7 Calculating the Income on Exercise

Upon the exercise of an NSO, an optionee will recognize ordinary income in an amount equal to the difference between the fair market value of the option shares on the exercise date and the option's exercise price (the option "spread"). In the case of a "same-day-sale" exercise, the fair market value of the option shares should be determined without regard to the optionee's actual sale price or any brokerage commissions paid on the transaction. Because the amount realized from the sale of the option shares may (and usually will) differ from the company's fair market value calculation, the optionee must account for this discrepancy. Note that this amount should not affect the optionee's recognized income (nor the company's income tax deduction). Instead, it should be treated as a capital gain or loss (depending upon whether the amount realized by the optionee is more or less than his or her adjusted basis in the option shares). In this situation, the amount realized by the optionee should equal the sale price net of any brokerage commission, while the optionee's adjusted basis in the option shares is the sum of the option's exercise price and the ordinary income recognized from the transaction. Some companies use the sale price as the fair market value amount for purposes of making the ordinary income calculation. This practice eliminates any discrepancy between the reported income and subsequent capital gain or loss.

The calculation for the exercise of an ISO is more complex. At the outset, a "same-day sale" or "sell-to-cover" will involve a disqualifying disposition because the ISO holding periods will not have been satisfied. The general rule applicable to NSOs is modified in the case of an

ISO. Section 422(c)(2) of the Code provides that if the amount realized from the sale is less than the fair market value of the option shares on the exercise date and the transaction would result in a realized loss by the optionee, the amount of ordinary income is limited to the difference between the amount realized and the optionee's basis in the option shares. In this case, any brokerage commissions incurred in the transaction would not be deducted in determining the amount realized by the optionee. If the ISO is exercised and held, either as a full cash exercise or the held portion of shares in a "sell-to-cover," the company must track the final disposition of shares to be able to determine the calculation of gain. Notably, some practitioners regard the ability to exercise an ISO by same-day sale or sell-to-cover as disqualifying the entire ISO (rather than a disqualifying disposition with respect to a portion of the shares sold to fund the exercise price and employment taxes). For this reason, many employers do not allow ISOs to be exercised under the same-day or sell-to-cover method.

1.5.4.8 Confirmation of Exercise

After processing the exercise, generally the plan administrator confirms the transaction by sending a written notice to the optionee. This notice should automatically be generated in the case of an exercise by electronic means. A copy of this notification should be retained by the plan administrator, a copy submitted to the accounting department with payment received for the option exercise price, and, if withholding of income and employment taxes are required, a copy of the notification also should be provided to the payroll department.

1.5.4.9 Section 6039 Reporting

Section 6039 of the Code requires a company to file an information return with the IRS and provide a written information statement to an employee whenever the company has transferred shares of stock to the employee in connection with the employee's exercise of an ISO. The information return to be filed with the IRS and the information statement to be provided to the employee must be on Form 3921 and contain the following information:

- name, address, and employer identification number (EIN) of the company transferring stock upon the exercise of the option

- name, address, and EIN of the company whose stock was transferred upon the exercise of the option (if different from the company identified in the first item in this list)

- name, address, and identifying number of the person to whom the stock was transferred upon exercise of the option

- date the option was granted

- date the option was exercised

- exercise price per share

- per-share fair market value of the stock at the time of exercise

- number of shares of stock transferred upon exercise of the option

IRS Form 3921 may be reported via a manual filing if the company has fewer than 250 reportable transactions in a calendar year. If the company has 250 or more reportable transactions in a calendar year, then the company must report the transactions electronically. For purposes of this form, each option exercise or stock transfer is a separate transaction, and therefore multiple transactions by a single optionee will trigger multiple filings. The forms are due to the IRS by February 28 of the year following the year of the transaction if manual forms are filed or March 31 if filing electronically. A penalty may be imposed for each statement not timely furnished or containing incomplete or incorrect information (an intentional failure to report is subject to a greater penalty).

1.6   Administering Restricted Stock

1.6.1   Restricted Stock Overview

RSAs and RSUs are economically the same, since both deliver the full value of the award when issued at no cost to the recipient, rather than the appreciation as in the case of a stock option. However, the mechanics of issuing shares differ between the two, and their timing of taxation may vary as well. The shares underlying an RSA are issued at the time of grant and are held in an escrow account until the restrictions lapse. At the company's discretion, the employee may be entitled to voting and dividend rights immediately. RSUs, on the other hand, represent a commitment from the company to issue stock after the vesting restrictions have lapsed. Normally, the tax event for the two award types is at vesting. However, the tax event for an RSA may be accelerated to the grant date by an 83(b) election or for an RSU deferred to a future date or event.

1.6.2   Granting of Restricted Stock

The plan administrator must process the grant of RSAs and RSUs and administer any elections associated with these awards. Processing the grant entails ensuring that the appropriate parties approved the award, the grant has been properly recorded and adjustments to the share pool made, and the employee has been notified of the grant and accepts the award (as required under many plans). The plan administrator must also manage any elections made under the awards that affect their tax treatment.

1.6.2.1   83(b) Election for RSAs

An employee may elect to have an RSA taxed at grant by making a Code Section 83(b) election within 30 days after the grant. Accordingly, income and FICA taxes become due at this point based on the fair market value of the awards at grant. The employee makes an 83(b) election by completing a statement that includes the following information: the employee's name, address, and taxpayer identification number; grant date and calendar year of the 83(b) election; description of the stock awarded and number of shares subject to the 83(b) election; the nature of the restriction or restrictions which the property is subject, such as a vesting schedule; the fair market value of the stock on the grant date; the amount (if any) paid for the shares; and a statement to the effect that copies of the 83(b) election have been furnished to the employer. The employee must also sign and date the 83(b) election form. The completed and signed statement must be mailed to the IRS within 30 days of the grant date to the IRS service center in which the employee files his or her tax returns. A copy must be submitted to the employer as well. Since 2016, the employee is no longer required to attach a copy of the 83(b) election to his or her federal income tax return.

In response to pandemic concerns with securing handwritten signatures, the IRS allows taxpayers to use electronic or digital signatures when signing certain forms that currently require a handwritten signature. The temporary deviation from the handwritten signature requirement applies to 83(b) elections that must be signed and postmarked during the period August 28, 2020, through October 31, 2023.

1.6.2.2 Deferral Election for RSUs

While an 83(b) election is not available with respect to RSUs, an employee with an RSU may elect to defer the issuance of the shares and the related income tax to a future date by making a timely deferral election under Code Section 409A. If permitted under the employee stock plan and award agreement, the deferral election generally may be made within 30 days after the grant date if vesting occurs more than one year after the deferral election is made. If the deferral election is made after the 30-day window but more than one year before the vesting date, the release of the shares must be deferred for at least five years from the original vesting date. For RSUs with a performance-based vesting schedule of at least 12 months, such deferral election may be made up to six months before the end of the performance period, provided other Section 409A conditions have been satisfied.

1.6.3 Dividends and Dividend Equivalents

When RSAs are granted, the shares are issued and are considered issued and outstanding stock of the company. Likewise, the employees holding these unvested awards are considered shareholders of the company. The company, in its discretion, may deny or provide the employee with dividend rights on the restricted shares. If dividends are paid on the unvested shares, the plan or award agreement may provide for the dividends to be paid at the same time as they are paid to other shareholders, although the restricted shares are unvested. Dividends paid on unvested restricted shares are treated as wages, not as dividend income, and thus are subject to tax withholding, reported on the employee's W-2, and deductible by the company. The plan administrator should have adequate controls to implement this treatment, whether automated through software, or through manual processes.

Alternatively, the dividends payable during the vesting period may be accumulated and paid to the grant holder when the restrictions lapse or may be forfeited if the underlying award is forfeited.

For RSUs, which represent a promise by the company to issue shares at a future date, the employee does not acquire shares at grant and is not a shareholder. As such, there are no dividend rights before issuance of the shares. However, the company may choose to pay dividend equivalents equal to the cash dividends paid to actual shareholders. Dividend equivalents may similarly be paid currently during the vesting period or accumulated and deferred. Such payments will be treated as wages.

1.6.4   Vesting of Restricted Shares

For RSAs, nontransferable shares are issued at grant and the restrictions lapse upon vesting. For RSUs, the company's commitment to issue shares materializes upon vesting. Assuming there are no Section 83(b) elections on the RSAs and no deferrals for the RSUs, the lapse of restrictions prompts a taxable event, and the applicable payroll taxes become due for employees. The plan administrator must coordinate the vesting and release of shares between the internal departments (human resources and payroll) and the external service providers (broker, transfer agent, and any third-party administrator) to collect the tax on the awards. Given the scheduled vesting date of the award, the plan administrator can generally plan ahead to source the award to the applicable jurisdictions for mobile employees and prepare for the tax withholding.

1.6.5   Release of Shares

The shares issued on the date of grant for an RSA are unvested and nontransferable, which entails additional considerations. Whether the company issues stock certificates electronically or in paper form, the certificates will need to include all appropriate restrictive legends. If the company is publicly traded, it may choose to issue the shares into a restricted account in the holder's name at the corporate transfer agent, with applicable restrictive legends noted.

With respect to RSUs, the issuance of shares generally occurs shortly after the vest date. However, the issuance may be deferred in either of two ways: (1) by an election to defer the release beyond the scheduled vesting date or (2) by accelerating the vesting date while maintaining the same release date. For example, many plans include provisions in which an employee's RSUs are no longer subject to a substantial risk of forfeiture once the employee becomes eligible to retire, but the shares will be released to that employee at the same time they are released to other participants, as originally scheduled. In the case of either a deferral election or an accelerated vesting, the shares become subject to FICA tax at vesting, but the income tax obligation is delayed until the distribution of the shares. The plan administrator must implement the appropriate tax treatment. If FICA taxes were not collected in the year of vesting and the three-year period for correction has lapsed, then FICA taxes must be collected along with the income tax withholding immediately following the release of the shares. Doing so, however, may result in higher FICA taxes if, at the time of vesting, the fair market value of the shares was less and the employee had exceeded the limit for Social Security taxes such that only Medicare taxes would have been payable on the shares at that time, and the employee has no other wages in the year the shares are issued.

1.6.6 Collection of Taxes on Restricted Stock

As previously discussed, the most common methods of collecting tax are sell-to-cover and withhold-to-cover. When shares are sold to cover the tax, the sales proceeds are used to fund the tax obligation. When shares are withheld to cover the tax, the company withholds a sufficient number of shares equal to the required tax withholding, and the company remits cash to the taxing authorities from company funds. However, a large number of RSAs and RSUs vesting in a single day can result in a large number of shares being sold on one day to fund the payroll tax or the company having to remit a significant amount of cash to pay the tax obligation to the taxing authorities.

1.6.7 Deductions

As discussed for calendar-year companies in section 1.4.3.5 of this chapter, a corporate tax deduction may be claimed when the RSA or RSU is taxable for federal income tax purposes to the employee, provided the company has reported the income on a Form W-2 (or the appropriate Form 1099 for nonemployees). For noncalendar fiscal year companies, however, the timing of a company's tax deduction may differ between RSAs and RSUs. When a company transfers unvested shares to an employee, as in the case of an RSA, a deduction is allowed only for the taxable year of the company in which or with which ends the taxable year in which the amount is included in the employee's gross income. Where the company transfers vested stock to the employee, as in the case of an RSU, the deduction is generally allowed in the employer's year that the shares were transferred.

For example, a company with a September 30 fiscal year end grants an employee an equal number of RSAs and RSUs that vest on January 1, 2025. The company may claim a deduction for the compensation related to the RSAs on its tax return for the fiscal year ended September 30, 2026, since December 31, 2025 (the last day of the employee's year in which the vesting occurs) falls within the fiscal year beginning October 1, 2025, and ending September 30, 2026. The company may claim a deduction for the compensation related to the RSUs on its tax return for the fiscal year ended September 30, 2025, since the vest/issuance date of January 1, 2025, falls within the fiscal year beginning October 1, 2024, and ending September 30, 2025.

1.7   Conclusion

Administering an employee stock plan in today's complex regulatory environment can be a challenging proposition. In addition to the tax, securities, and accounting rules that must be observed, a significant number of procedural matters must also be considered. A company adopting a stock plan for its employees is well-advised to establish formal policies and procedures to ensure that all of the applicable legal and other requirements are satisfied. This includes guidelines for disseminating information and materials about awards granted to employees and for processing the conversion of the awards to stock and, ultimately, to cash. Additional procedures can be implemented for addressing a variety of other common situations that may arise during the term of the plan. If these policies and procedures are implemented and consistently followed, the company can be assured that its program will serve its primary objectives and that a high level of employee satisfaction can be achieved.

Companies seeking to avoid potential problems should ensure that they have implemented and adhere to well-designed policies and procedures for their employee stock plans.

2

Federal Securities Law Considerations for Equity Compensation Plans

Eric Orsic

CONTENTS

Author's note regarding citations: The federal securities law statutes and related SEC rules and forms referred to here may be found on the SEC's website at http://www.sec.gov/, and the federal case law and SEC no-action letters may be found on the Internet using Google or another search engine.

For a variety of reasons, company stock continues to be one of the more popular forms of compensation. Most public companies maintain some form of stock benefit plan for their directors, officers, and key employees. In addition, many public companies are granting stock benefits at multiple levels within the organization, with some offering stock benefits to all full-time employees. Equity compensation plans are not, however, exclusive to public companies. In order to attract and retain talented individuals, many privately held entities and foreign issuers with operations in the United States are offering stock benefits to their key employees.

In recent years, the most common practice has been to adopt an omnibus-type equity compensation plan that covers not only stock options but also restricted stock (including restricted stock units and deferred stock units), stock appreciation rights, performance shares, and cash awards. This chapter will focus on the securities law aspects of the foregoing benefits payable in stock.

Although equity compensation plans are exempt from the burdensome requirements of the Employee Retirement Income Security Act of 1974 (ERISA), there are still a number of important rules and regulations that apply. In particular, equity compensation plans maintained by public companies are subject to the Securities Exchange Act of 1934 (the "1934 Act"), which imposes various reporting requirements and restricts transactions in issuer securities by, among others, designated officers, directors, and persons with material non-public information. In addition, all equity compensation plans are subject to the Securities Act of 1933 (the "1933 Act"), which requires registration of offers to sell securities unless a specific exemption from registration is available.

This chapter focuses on compliance with the federal securities laws rather than enforcement. Suffice it to say that noncompliance can result in serious penalties and liabilities, including fines, forfeiture of profits, treble damages, and federal criminal prosecution, not to mention the adverse publicity and embarrassment to the corporation and the individuals involved. State securities laws must also be considered, but they are beyond the scope of this chapter.

This chapter does not focus on Section 409A of the Internal Revenue Code of 1986, as amended, and its related IRS regulations, which may have a substantial impact on stock options, restricted stock, and all forms of deferred compensation for public and private companies.

2.1 Impact of the 1934 Act on Equity Compensation Plans

2.1.1 In General

An equity compensation plan maintained by a public company must be administered in light of Section 16 of the 1934 Act and the rules promulgated thereunder (the "Section 16 rules"). The Section 16 rules essentially consist of two parts. The first part is Section 16(a) and its related rules, which require directors, certain officers, and principal shareholders of public companies to report to the Securities and Exchange Commission (SEC) all transactions in the issuer's securities.[1] The second part is Section 16(b) and its related rules, which require such persons to disgorge any "short-swing profits" received from transactions in the issuer's securities.[2]

2.1.2 Definition of "Public Company"

As indicated above, the Section 16 rules apply only to "public companies."[3] For these purposes, a "public company" includes any corporation whose stock is listed on a national securities exchange, including NYSE and Nasdaq, but excludes a "foreign private issuer" as described below. A public company can also include non-listed companies. Specifically, if a U.S. corporation has more than $10 million in assets and 2,000 or more shareholders (or 500 or more shareholders who are nonaccredited investors), it will be considered a public company subject to the Section 16 rules, regardless of whether its stock is listed on a national securities exchange or traded over-the-counter. The shareholder count excludes employees who received unregistered equity securities through an employee compensation plan.

"Accredited investors" include executive officers, directors, and individuals meeting specified income or net worth tests.

Becoming a public company due to size and the number of shareholders is an important consideration for non-listed companies. If a corporation becomes a public company under the 2,000 holder/$10

---

1. 1934 Act, § 16(a) and Rules 16a-1 to 16a-13.

2. 1934 Act, § 16(b) and Rules 16b-1 to 16b-8.

3. 1934 Act, §§ 12(a) and 12(g)(1).

million asset value rule, it must comply with the registration requirements under Section 12(g) of the 1934 Act, as well as the 1934 Act's
proxy solicitation, periodic reporting, and short-swing trading provisions.

The Jumpstart Our Business Startups Act of 2012 (JOBS Act)
created an interim category of company called an "emerging growth
company." This designation applies to private companies and newly
public companies that have total annual gross revenues of less than $1
billion.[4] These companies must follow the registration requirements
of Section 12(g), but they are not subject to as many disclosure rules
as other public companies.

2.1.3 Options as Equity Securities

Prior to passage of the JOBS Act, the SEC took the position that an
option (but not a stock appreciation right) was an equity security for
purposes of the then-500-holder test. This meant that, absent an available exemption, a private company could find itself subject to the 1934
Act if it granted options to 500 or more employees and consultants
(and had more than $10 million in assets). However, the JOBS Act
both raised the shareholder threshold to 2,000 (or 500 nonaccredited
investors) and definitively stated that unregistered shares granted under
an "employee compensation plan" would not be counted toward that
limit. The SEC adopted final rules implementing these provisions of
the JOBS Act in 2016.

2.1.4 Foreign Private Issuers

Publicly listed securities of a foreign private issuer, as defined in SEC
Rule 3b-4(c), are exempt from Section 16 pursuant to Rule 3a12-3(b)
under the 1934 Act.[5] The term "foreign private issuer" is defined in
Rule 3b-4(c) to mean any foreign issuer *except* an issuer meeting the
following conditions:

---

4. This designation does not apply to companies that registered shares on or before
   December 8, 2011.

5. The exemption in Rule 3a12-3(b) under the 1934 Act reads as follows:

   Securities registered by a foreign private issuer, as defined in Rule 3b-4, shall be
   exempt from sections 14(a), 14(b), 14(c), 14(f) and 16 of the Act.

1. More than 50% of the outstanding voting securities of such issuer are held of record either directly or through voting trust certificates or depositary receipts by residents of the United States; and

2. Any of the following:

    (a) The majority of the executive officers or directors are United States citizens or residents,

    (b) More than 50% of the assets of the issuer are located in the United States, or

    (c) The business of the issuer is administered principally in the United States.

For these purposes, the term "resident," as applied to security holders, means any person whose address appears on the records of the issuer, the voting trustee, or the depositary as being located in the United States.

Note that there is no exemption for shareholders of foreign private issuers from the reporting obligations under Regulation 13D-G or for liability under Rule 10b-5, as described below.

2.1.5   Definition of "Reporting Persons"

The Section 16 reporting and short-swing profit rules do not apply to all transactions in issuer securities. Rather, only transactions by those individuals who are either "officers" of the public company[6] or members of its board of directors[7] (collectively "reporting persons") are subject to the information reporting requirements and short-swing trading restrictions contained in Section 16 of the 1934 Act.[8]

"Officers" for these purposes includes only those officers of the issuing corporation with certain high level, policy-making responsibilities who are designated as such by the corporation's board of directors (or a committee thereunder) and are listed each year in the issuer's Form

---

6.   1934 Act, § 16(a), Rule 16a-1(f).

7.   1934 Act, § 3(a)(7).

8.   See section 2.1.7 of this chapter for a brief discussion of the application of the Section 16 rules to beneficial owners of more than 10% of any class of equity securities and who are neither officers nor directors.

10-K (annual report).[9] For purposes of the Section 16 rules, an "officer" has been judicially defined as "a corporate employee performing important executive duties of such character that he would be likely, in discharging these duties, to obtain confidential information that would aid him if he engaged in personal market transactions."[10] Merely having the title of an officer does not, by itself, cause an individual to become an "officer" for purposes of the Section 16 rules. Instead, the determining factor is whether the individual's duties are commensurate with those of a policy-making position. The persons who are considered "officers" for Section 16 purposes are often the same persons whose beneficial ownership is required to be reported in the proxy statement under the heading "all directors and executive officers as a group" in the Beneficial Ownership of Management table.[11]

The term "officer" includes the following positions: president; principal financial officer; principal accounting officer (or if there is no such accounting officer, the controller); any vice-president in charge of a principal business unit, division, or function; and any other officer or other person who performs a significant policy-making function. This can include officers of a parent or subsidiary corporation if they perform a policy-making function for the entity that issues the stock in question.[12] The issuing corporation should notify every director or designated officer who becomes subject to the Section 16 rules of his or her status as a Section 16 reporting person. The definition of "officer" in Rule 16a-1(f) contains a footnote instruction that has been interpreted to mean that, if the board of directors adopts a resolution naming its Section 16 officers, the list will be presumed exclusive and correct. Many public companies, as a matter of best practice, will have their boards of directors review and confirm the list of "officers" annually. In addition, if an individual is promoted into an "officer" role

---

9. Rule 16a-1(f).

10. *Colby v. Klune*, 178 F.2d 872, 873 (2d Cir. 1949).

11. The one notable exception is the principal accounting officer, if this position is held by someone other than the chief financial officer. The principal accounting officer is, by definition, an "officer" for Section 16 purposes but not necessarily an executive officer whose beneficial ownership needs to be reported in the proxy statement.

12. Rule 16a-1(f).

or newly hired into such a position, the board may make an interim determination that such person is an "officer" for Section 16 purposes.

2.1.6 Beneficial Ownership

It is important to note that in most circumstances, a reporting person is presumed to be the owner of all securities in which the reporting person has a "pecuniary interest"—that is, the opportunity to profit or share in any profit, either directly or indirectly.[13] This includes securities held by a spouse, children, grandchildren, parent, grandparent, sibling, and other relatives *sharing the same household*, including step-, in-law, and adoptive relationships, and children living away from home while attending college ("household relatives").[14] For example:

> Officer "B" has a daughter who is in college, is financially dependent on "B," and owns Company X stock. "B's" daughter sells her stock. "B" must report the daughter's sale to the SEC on "B's" Form 4 within two business days of the sale.

Even if the reporting person and a relative are not sharing the same household, the reporting person will be deemed the beneficial owner of securities if he or she actually controls the purchase and sale of securities owned by the relative or if the relative is a minor child.

A reporting person may also be deemed to be the beneficial owner of any stock held by a trust, corporation, partnership, or other entity over which he or she has a controlling influence.[15] Special rules exist for trustees and trusts in which the reporting person acts as trustee and a member of his or her family (even if such person does not reside in the reporting person's household) has a pecuniary interest in the securities held by the trust.[16]

The potential application of the Section 16 rules to shares held by household relatives and entities over which the reporting person has a controlling influence needs to be closely monitored to avoid inadvertent violation of the Section 16 rules. If a question exists as to whether the

---

13. Rule 16a-1(a)(2).

14. Rule 16a-1(a)(2)(ii)(A), Rule 16a-1(e).

15. Rule 16a-1(a)(2)(ii)(B), (E), and (F).

16. See Rule 16a-8.

individual is a beneficial owner of certain stock, a statement similar to the following can be included on the SEC stock ownership forms: "Reporting person expressly disclaims beneficial ownership of these shares. Reporting person cannot profit, directly or indirectly, from transactions in these securities." In many instances, it is preferable to resolve doubts as to beneficial ownership in favor of reporting beneficial ownership of the shares and including the disclaimer as a matter of full disclosure.

2.1.7 Ten Percent Shareholders

Any beneficial owner of greater than 10% of a class of equity securities registered under Section 12 of the 1934 Act is also subject to the Section 16 rules. Ten percent beneficial owners are subject to the Section 16 rules because, at that level of ownership, they are presumed to have access to inside information (whether or not they in fact have such access) and are therefore prohibited from profiting from short-swing trading. For determining whether the 10% ownership threshold has been crossed, equity securities include not only common stock and options exercisable within 60 days but also may include warrants, convertible preferred stock, and convertible notes. Beneficial ownership for this purpose is based on Section 13(d) of the 1934 Act and the related rules, which provide that a person beneficially owns those securities as to which that person has or shares voting or investment power, including securities such person has a right to acquire within 60 days. "Investment power" is defined in those rules as "the power to dispose [of] or to direct the disposition of such security." Thus, a person may be a 10% shareholder (and required to file a Form 3 to so indicate), but reporting and liability under Section 16 will be based on that person's "pecuniary interest" in such securities, which may be different than the shareholder's "beneficial interest."

A person must file a Form 3 within 10 days after reaching the 10% ownership threshold. The transaction that results in such a person becoming a 10% shareholder is not subject to Section 16(a) or Section 16(b), and a 10% shareholder need not report, and is not liable for, that transaction and prior transactions unless the person is already otherwise an insider by virtue of being a director or officer. Likewise, a 10% shareholder need not report and is not liable for transactions occurring after a reduction in beneficial ownership to 10% or less unless the person continues to be subject to Section 16 by virtue of director or officer status. However, the transaction that reduces a 10% shareholder's ownership to 10% or less must be reported under Section 16(a) on the appropriate form and is subject to Section 16(b). Unless a 10% shareholder is also a director or executive officer, the 10% shareholder will typically not receive equity compensation awards and, as a result, the balance of this chapter will focus on the Section 16 implications for reporting persons who are directors and officers (and not 10% shareholders). In addition, in many instances, 10% shareholders who are not also directors or officers will handle their own Section 16 filings.

2.2 Reporting Requirements Under Section 16(a) of the 1934 Act

All transactions (with certain limited exceptions) in company stock must be reported to the SEC within two business days of the date of the transaction. As described below, reporting persons must file three kinds of SEC stock ownership forms:

- Initially, a statement of beneficial ownership of issuer stock when the person first becomes subject to Section 16 (Form 3);

- Periodic, as-needed, statements of changes in beneficial ownership (Form 4); and

- Annual statements of changes in beneficial ownership, if needed (Form 5).

Directors and officers are responsible for filing their own Forms 3, 4, and 5. However, as an accommodation, most issuers will handle these filings on behalf of their directions and officers to ensure they are completed correctly and in a timely manner. Nonetheless, the responsibility for these filings ultimately rests with the directors and officers, who would be subject to possible penalties if their filings are not accurate and timely, notwithstanding that the issuer was handling these filings on their behalf.

In late 2014, the SEC announced charges against 13 directors and officers of public companies for violating the reporting requirements under Section 16(a) of the 1934 Act. The SEC also charged six public companies for contributing to the filing failures by insiders or for failing to report their insiders' filing delinquencies as required. Although the SEC has not pursued violations of the Section 16(a) reporting requirements aggressively in the past, this SEC enforcement activity signals a new level of scrutiny by the SEC, and the SEC has made it clear that the failure to timely file a required Form 3, 4, or 5, even if inadvertent, constitutes a violation of these rules.

2.2.1 Form 3

A reporting person must file a statement of beneficial ownership of issuer stock on Form 3 when the person first becomes a director or designated officer of the issuer.[17] If the issuer is already a "public company," a Form 3 must be filed within 10 calendar days after appointment or designation of the individual as a director or designated officer. Otherwise, a Form 3 must be filed on or before the date the issuer becomes a public company. A Form 3 must be filed within these time frames even if a director or officer does not beneficially own any shares of the issuer. In this case, the Form 3 would indicate that no shares were beneficially owned by the reporting person. In certain situations, a reporting person might receive a reportable grant or award at the time the Form 3 filing obligation is triggered (such as a grant or award to a new hire). The SEC has informally taken the position that grants issued at the time an individual becomes subject to Section 16 should not be included in the insider's holdings reported on Form 3 but should instead be reported on a Form 4. In this situation, the deadline for filing the Form 4 for the grant or award (2 business days) would occur before the deadline for filing the Form 3 (10 calendar days). The SEC encourages filing both the Form 3 and the Form 4 by the due date of the Form 4, but this is not required; it is permissible to file the Form 4 first, within the applicable 2-day deadline, and file the Form 3 subsequently, provided it is filed within the applicable 10-day deadline. The same guidance applies to any other Form 4 reportable transactions (e.g., open market purchases and sales) the insider engages in for which a Form 4 would be due before the date by which the insider's Form 3 must be filed.

---

17. 1934 Act, § 16(a), Rule 16a-3.

2.2.2   Forms 4 and 5

A reporting person is also required to file periodic statements of changes in beneficial ownership of issuer securities on Form 4 or Form 5, as applicable. Form 4 reports must be filed within two business days after the occurrence of the transaction resulting in a change in the reporting person's beneficial ownership (unless Form 4 is being used on a voluntary basis, as described below).[18] This would include changes in direct ownership of issuer securities, as well as changes in beneficial ownership by reason of transactions involving household relatives or entities over which the reporting person has a controlling interest.

A Form 5 must be filed by a reporting person within 45 calendar days after the end of the issuer's fiscal year and must report (1) transactions or changes in beneficial stock ownership not required to have been reported earlier on Form 4, and (2) transactions or changes that should have been reported earlier on Form 4 but were not ("delinquent filings").[19] A Form 5 would not be required from a reporting person who had no reportable transactions during the preceding year.[20] Any transaction normally reportable on Form 5 at year-end may be voluntarily reported on an earlier Form 4 filed at any time before the due date of the Form 5, and the filing of the voluntary Form 4 would relieve the reporting person of the obligation to file the Form 5.[21] To avoid confusion and the risk of late or non-filing, it is a best practice to file transactions that are reportable on the year-end Form 5 as soon as possible on a voluntary Form 4 using the "V" code. Even filings past due should be reported on Form 4 as soon as discovered. In other words, do not wait to file on Form 5.

SEC Staff Position Regarding Aggregate Section 16 Reporting. In June 2008, the SEC issued a no-action letter to the Society of Corporate Secretaries and Governance Professionals that permits Section 16 reporting persons to report same-day, same-way open market purchases or sales on an aggregate basis. This was a reversal of a previous position that had the effect of requiring filers to report on multiple lines of Form

---

18. Rule 16a-3(a).

19. Rule 16a-3(f)(1)(ii).

20. Rule 16a-3(f)(2).

21. Rule 16a-3(g)(5).

4 purchases or sales that occurred on a single day pursuant to a single market order (e.g., an order to sell 5,000 shares of stock at the market price), solely because the trade was executed at multiple prices that may have been as little as a fraction of a penny apart. The no-action letter is considered "global," and thus the relief it provides is available to all Section 16 reporting persons.

The no-action letter permits aggregate reporting as follows:

- The transactions reported on an aggregate basis must be effected through a broker-dealer on the open market and must occur on the same day.

- Purchases may only be aggregated with purchases, and sales may only be aggregated with sales.

- Each form of ownership must be reported separately, so that transactions in direct holdings may not be aggregated with transactions in indirect holdings, and each form of indirect holdings must be reported separately.

- The prices must be within a one-dollar range so that if, for example, a filer sold 1,000 shares in 20 separate trades at prices ranging from $16.50 to $17.49 a share, and another 500 shares in 10 separate trades at prices ranging from $17.50 to $17.75 a share, all of the transactions could be reported on two separate lines, showing the weighted average price for the transactions in each line.

- A footnote to each line must indicate the range of prices and include an undertaking to provide on request detailed breakouts in order that the SEC staff, the issuer, or any security holder of the issuer can receive full information regarding the number of shares purchased or sold at each separate price. The footnote may be worded as follows: "Weighted average from multiple transactions with prices ranging from $ _____ to $ _____. Upon request by the Commission staff, the issuer or a security holder of the issuer, the reporting person will undertake to provide full information regarding the number of shares purchased at each separate price."

The filer must maintain copies of the detailed reports of all the trades described in the report.

2.2.3 Electronic Filing of Section 16 Reports

The SEC has emphasized the importance of timely filing stock ownership forms. All Section 16 filings must be made electronically via the SEC's Electronic Data Gathering, Analysis, and Retrieval (EDGAR) system. In most instances, the filing must be made no later than 10 p.m. Eastern time on the second business day after the date of the transaction. To become fully versed in the electronic filing process, the following steps should be taken:

1. *Determine whether the Section 16 reporting persons already have EDGAR access codes, and if not, apply for them immediately.* An issuer's Section 16 reporting persons are not likely to have obtained SEC access codes through another source except for directors and the CEO or CFO, who may be serving on other companies' boards of directors that have already obtained the access codes. It is important not to apply for a second set of access codes for any reporting person who has already obtained an access code. Obtaining new codes will deactivate previous codes. Once the list of persons needing access codes has been obtained, prepare a Form ID for each insider. The Form ID must be filed electronically. A signed and notarized copy of the Form ID must also be filed electronically with the SEC's Filer Management website. Turnaround time can be up to one week. The SEC responds by email with the CIK code. One uses the CIK code and the passphrase, which is created during the electronic Form ID process, to electronically generate the remaining access codes.[22]

2. *Determine which electronic filing system will be used.* Filings can be submitted directly to EDGAR using the SEC's OnlineForms Management website at no cost and without the use of third-party software, but there are a number of third-party systems available to assist with Section 16 filings that have features companies find helpful. Examples of these systems include the Romeo & Dye Section 16 Filer and Equity Edge. In addition, the major financial printers all offer web-based systems for specific fees. The third-party and financial printer systems both allow the continuing storage and retrieval of

---

22. Additional information and filing instructions are available at https://www.filermanagement.edgarfiling.sec.gov.

information about the issuer and the reporting persons and a general body of footnotes. The SEC's online system does not allow for the storage and retrieval of past information. This means that in the SEC's system, you start from scratch each time you use it.

3. *Conduct test filings immediately.* Once a particular system has been selected, the person designated as the Section 16 filing agent for a particular company should begin test filings immediately to work out the bugs contained in all of these systems with respect to the reporting of different types of ownership, the reporting of different classes of stock, and the use of footnotes and exhibits.

2.2.4 Website Posting of Section 16 Reports

The SEC has mandated (Rule 16a-3(k)) that all Section 16 reports must be posted on the websites of public issuers that maintain websites (Release No. 34-47809). Failure to comply with these requirements could result in civil penalties under the general remedies provisions of Section 21 of the 1934 Act. The SEC has indicated three compliance options:

1. Direct posting on the issuer's website. Most companies have set up separate sections of their websites to hold just their Section 16 reports.

2. Linking to a third-party website. This can be accomplished as long as it contains all of the forms in segregated fashion and gives free access.

3. Linking directly to the SEC's website.

The instructions to Forms 3, 4, and 5 require that these forms must also be filed with the stock exchange on which the issuer's securities are listed, if any. Because they are required to be filed electronically, they are deemed filed with the exchanges without any additional filings.[23]

2.2.5 Reportable and Non-Reportable Transactions

Before the Sarbanes-Oxley Act, Forms 3, 4, and 5 were last revised in 1996, and the exemptions to such filings were broadened substan-

---

23. This relief comes from SEC staff no-action letters to the exchanges dated July 22, 1998, and a no-action letter issued to Nasdaq dated August 1, 2006.

tially. The Sarbanes-Oxley Act retained all of the exemptions from Section 16(b) liability but greatly shortened the Section 16(a) reporting process to require the filing of Section 16 reports for most transactions (regardless of whether the transaction is exempt from Section 16(b)) within two business days of the date of the transaction. The following will serve as a general guide for reporting transactions in issuer stock that may arise pursuant to a typical equity compensation plan.[24] Appendix C to this chapter provides more information on how common stock plan transactions should be reported.

Transactions Required to Be Reported on Form 4 (Within Two Business Days):

- Grant or exercise of a stock option or stock appreciation right.

- Grant of stock awards in the form of restricted stock or deferred stock units.

- Grant of restricted stock units. Restricted stock units are derivative securities and should be reported as derivative securities on Form 4, unless the restricted stock units are payable solely in stock (i.e., not cash-settled) in which case they may be reported as the acquisition of common stock. Vesting of restricted stock units reported as derivative securities must be reported on Form 4 within two business days, while vesting of restricted stock units reported as the acquisition of common stock is not required to be reported.

- Grant of performance shares. Where vesting is based on the market price of the issuer's stock, the award is considered acquired when approved by the board of directors (or properly authorized designee) and is reported at that time. Where vesting is not based on the market price of the issuer's stock, the award is not considered acquired until the performance condition has been satisfied and is not reported until then.

- Delivery of stock to issuer to pay for exercise price of an option (i.e., pursuant to a stock-for-stock exercise) or to pay taxes.

- Material amendment of a stock option or stock appreciation right. The SEC is of the view that certain types of amendments may

---

24. Rule 16a-4.

constitute such a material change in the terms of an outstanding award that the amendment itself should be treated as the functional equivalent of cancelling an outstanding award and replacing it with a new one. Examples of material amendments would include a repricing and an amendment that extended the term of an option beyond its original expiration date.

- Withholding of stock by the issuer to satisfy taxes required to be withheld on the exercise of an option or a stock appreciation right, or upon the vesting of a stock award or performance share award.

- Sale of stock acquired pursuant to the exercise of a stock option or stock appreciation right into the open market, including the sale of stock pursuant to a "cashless" option exercise arrangement.[25]

- Sale of stock received in connection with a stock award or a performance share award.

- Cancellation of stock options or stock appreciation rights where consideration is received by the reporting person (Rule 16b-3(e).

- Open market purchases and sales.

- Transactions pursuant to a contract, instruction, or written plan for the purchase or sale of issuer equity securities that satisfies the affirmative defense conditions of Rule 10b5-1(c) (i.e., a Rule 10b5-1 plan) under which the date(s) of execution are specified (such as the first date of each month).

- Any of the foregoing transactions by a reporting person's spouse or other "household relatives," or by an entity over which the reporting person has a controlling interest.

Transactions Required to Be Reported on Form 4 Within Five Business Days:

The SEC has adopted special limited deferred reporting rules (up to five business days depending upon circumstances) for the following transactions:

---

25. A "cashless exercise" is an arrangement under which a stock brokerage firm agrees to pay the issuer the funds required for the exercise of a stock option. The broker provides the funds either in the form of a loan to the option holder from a margin account in which the shares acquired are held as collateral or as an advance on the proceeds from the sale of some or all of the shares acquired on the exercise. Most brokers offer this service. See the discussion of cashless exercises in appendix A.

- Transactions pursuant to a contract, instruction, or written plan for the purchase or sale of issuer equity securities that satisfies the affirmative defense conditions of Rule 10b5-1(c) (i.e., a Rule 10b5-1 plan) under which the date(s) of execution are not specified (e.g., the trade will occur at a certain stock price).

- Discretionary transactions in a 401(k), profit sharing, pension, or similar retirement plan where the Section 16 reporting person does not select the date(s) of execution.

- Deferred compensation plan investments in a company stock fund, but only if they fall within the scope of a Rule 10b5-1 plan.

- Transactions that occur over more than one day, but only if they fall within the scope of a Rule 10b5-1 plan.

These transactions are subject to reporting on Form 4 within two business days of the "deemed execution" date of the transaction. The deemed execution date of the transaction will be the earlier of (1) the date on which the executing broker, dealer, or plan administrator notifies the Section 16 reporting person of the execution of the transaction, or (2) the third business day following the trade date. (The SEC noted in its release adopting the new rules that a trade confirmation sent through the mail could take several days to arrive, and the SEC would therefore usually expect brokers, dealers, and plan administrators to provide the information needed for Section 16(a) reporting purposes to the Section 16 reporting person either electronically or by telephone.) Rule 10b5-1 plan transactions that occur on preset dates must be reported within two business days of the transaction.

For example, assume that in January, an insider implements a Rule 10b5-1 plan to sell 1,000 shares when the stock price reaches $50 per share. Further assume that the $50 target is achieved on Monday, August 10, and the sale is executed on that day.

- If the broker notifies the insider of the sale before Thursday, August 13 (the third business day following the transaction), the date the notification is received is the deemed execution date, and the sale must be reported within two business days of that date. For example, if the broker notifies the insider of the sale on August 11, the sale must be reported by August 13.

- If the broker notified the insider of the sale on or after Thursday, August 13, the deemed execution date is August 13, and the sale must be reported by the following Monday, August 17.

Also note that if the execution date in the above example had been preset, e.g., if the plan had specified that the shares would be sold on August 10 (rather than specifying a price target), the deemed execution date concept does not apply. In this case, the sale would be reported by August 12.

Transactions Required to Be Reported on Year-End Form 5 or Voluntary Form 4 (the best practice is to file these types of transactions during the fiscal year on a voluntary Form 4 or as a voluntary disclosure on a Form 4 required to be filed to report another transaction):

- Gifts to anyone, including family members, public charities, and private foundations (Rule 16b-5).
- Transfers of stock or options to family members, or to a family-controlled entity for estate planning purposes (Rule 16b-5).
- Small acquisitions (not exceeding $10,000 in market value), but not from the issuer or an issuer sponsored stock benefit plan (Rule 16a-6).

Transactions That Are Not Required to Be Reported:

- Expiration or cancellation of stock options where no consideration is received by the reporting person (Rule 16a-4(d) and Rule 16b-6(d)) (grant or exercise of a stock option or stock appreciation right must be reported within two business days).
- A non-material amendment to a stock option. An amendment that accelerates the vesting of an outstanding option is generally not considered material, nor is an amendment to add a tax withholding feature, an amendment to add a cashless exercise feature, or an amendment to make an option transferable.
- Grant of a performance share award that vests based on a goal that is not related to the company's stock price. These grants are, instead, reported at the time of vesting.

- Vesting of an outstanding stock option, stock appreciation right, or stock award (other than the vesting of a restricted stock unit where the grant of the award was reported as a derivative security).

- Vesting of performance shares where vesting is based on the market price of the issuer's stock.

- Change in beneficial ownership, i.e., from direct to indirect or vice versa (this reporting exemption is strictly construed to require that the person's pecuniary interest does not change; for example, a gift to a minor child is not covered by this exemption even though the reporting person is deemed to have an indirect beneficial interest; such a gift must be reported on a voluntary Form 4 or a mandatory Form 5) (Rule 16a-13).

- Transfer of an option, SAR, stock award (including restricted stock units and deferred stock units), or performance shares pursuant to a domestic relations order, including any order entered pursuant to a divorce decree (Rule 16a-12) (grant or exercise of a stock option or stock appreciation right must be reported within two business days).

- Dividend reinvestment plans or their equivalents, provided the issuer has a dividend reinvestment plan generally available to all its shareholders (Rule 16a-11).

- Transactions in "tax-conditioned plans" (other than "discretionary transactions"), including routine purchases under the payroll deduction provisions of a 401(k) plan, excess benefit plan, employee stock ownership plan (ESOP), or employee stock purchase plan (Rule 16b-3(c)).

- Stock splits, reverse stock splits, and other recapitalizations, including possibly pro-rata distributions from limited partnerships and limited liability companies (Rule 16a-9).

- Dividend reinvestments and other stock activities in a rabbi trust.

Note that while the above-listed events do not have to be reported as transactions on the Section 16 stock ownership forms, the SEC does require that the net result of the transactions (other than transactions in a rabbi trust) be reported in the total ownership column with a footnote explanation on a future Form 4 or Form 5. Failure to do so does not, however, make the reporting person a delinquent filer.

As a general rule, reporting persons should assume that any transaction in issuer stock must be reported to the SEC, even if the transaction is involuntary on the part of the reporting person or, when combined with another transaction, results in no net change in ownership. Because of the two–business day reporting requirement, reporting persons should be counseled to contact a designated representative of the issuer regarding any potential transaction involving the issuer's securities, no matter how minor it may seem, before consummating the transaction, to receive assistance in filing any needed SEC forms, as well as information regarding the potential Section 16(b) implications, which are described below. See the discussion in section 2.6 of this chapter concerning a mandatory pre-clearance policy and appendix A to this chapter for the suggested form of pre-clearance policy.

Also, a reporting person who has retired, terminated employment, or otherwise ceased to be a reporting person continues to have reporting obligations for a limited period following cessation of "insider" status.[26] Such a person is still required to report opposite-way matchable nonexempt transactions that are not exempt from Section 16(b) on a Form 4 when all of the following conditions are met:

- The transaction occurs within less than six months of a transaction that occurred before the individual's cessation of insider status.

- The pre-cessation transaction is also not exempt from Section 16(b).

- The pre-cessation transaction is the "opposite" of the transaction occurring after cessation of insider status (e.g., if the post-cessation transaction is a disposition, the pre-cessation transaction would have to be an acquisition to trigger reporting of the post-cessation transaction).

If a reporting person has not had any transactions that are subject to Section 16(b) for the six months before his or her termination, then no further reporting obligation continues except for possible Form 5

---

26. Rule 16a-2(b).

filing requirements, e.g., a gift made while still employed and deferred to Form 5 reporting will still be required to be filed.

In addition, where transactions following cessation of insider status are reportable, they can be matched (for Section 16(b) purposes) with transactions made while an insider to find short-swing profits owed to the issuer. For example:

> "A" will cease to be a director of Company X on October 1. On September 20, "A" sells Company X stock. "A" not only must report this sale on a Form 4 by September 22 (two business days) but also must continue to file Form 4s to report any purchases that are subject to Section 16(b) and occur before the next March 19, and any such purchases will be matched with the September 20 sale. "A" will not have to report any sales subsequent to ceasing director status on October 1, regardless of whether the sales are exempt from Section 16(b). "A" also will not have to report any purchases subsequent to October 1 that are exempt from Section 16(b).

Opposite-way transactions that are exempt from Section 16(b) and same-way transactions (regardless of whether they are exempt from Section 16(b)) made during the six months following cessation of insider status are not reportable. See appendix B for an explanation of exit strategies and a form of exit memorandum to be given to departing Section 16 reporting persons.

2.2.6   Issuer Reporting of Noncompliance

As indicated above, the SEC is serious about compliance with the Section 16(a) reporting requirements. Accordingly, public companies are required to report any noncompliance pursuant to Item 405 of Regulation S-K.[27] This disclosure is set out in the issuer's proxy statement for its annual meeting under the caption "Delinquent Section 16(a) Reports" and must identify each director, officer, or 10% stockholder that failed to file on a timely basis reports required under Section 16(a) during the most recent year or any prior fiscal years.[28] The disclosure

---

27. Item 405(a)(1), Regulation S-K.

28. The instructions to Item 405 of Regulation S-K provide that an issuer is only required to disclose a failure to file timely once. For example, if in the most recently concluded fiscal year a reporting person filed a Form 4 disclosing a transaction that took place in the prior fiscal year and should have been reported in that year,

must include, for each person, the number of late filings, the number of transactions that were not reported on a timely basis, and any known failure to file a required form. If no disclosure of delinquent filings is required, the SEC has encouraged public companies to exclude this caption from their proxy statements. The Section 16 rules also clarify that the issuer is entitled to rely on the Forms 3, 4, and 5 filed electronically with the SEC, as well as written representations by a reporting person that no Form 5 is required.[29] The SEC can impose fines for late filings or enjoin the late filer from serving as a director or officer of the issuer or other public companies.

The Section 16 rules make it clear that the issuer is obligated to consider the absence of certain forms. Specifically, the absence of a Form 3 filing by a Section 16 reporting person is an indication that disclosure is required. Similarly, the absence of a Form 5 is an indication that disclosure is required, unless the issuer has received a written representation that no Form 5 is required, or the issuer otherwise knows that no such filing is required.[30] A "safe harbor" from disclosure is available for an issuer who receives a written representation from the reporting person that no Form 5 was required.[31] This representation is usually set out in an officers and directors questionnaire, which the issuer should send out annually.

2.2.7 Reporting Recommendations

In light of the complexity of the Section 16 rules, the following recommendations will help in the administration of stock benefit plans (see section 2.6 of this chapter for recommendations covering all types of benefit plans):

* Have a mandatory pre-clearance policy (whereby all transactions in company stock by the Section 16 reporting persons or members

---

the issuer should disclose that late filing and transaction pursuant to Item 405 with respect to the most recently concluded fiscal year, but not in material filed with respect to subsequent years.

29. Item 405(b), Regulation S-K.
30. SEC Release No. 34-37260.
31. Item 405(b), Regulation S-K.

of their immediate family require prior notice to the company) for all transactions as to which the timing is within the control of the Section 16 reporting person.

- Establish a cashless exercise policy for Section 16 reporting persons in which the Section 16 reporting person obtains any credit extension from the broker or other third party of his or her choice (and not the issuer) and results in the issuer being paid the exercise price on the day of exercise. See section 2.6 of this chapter for more information on this subject.

- Educate all Section 16 reporting persons by a memorandum, which they should read, sign, and return.

- Obtain powers of attorney with multiple attorneys-in-fact from all Section 16 reporting persons.

2.3 Six-Month "Short-Swing" Profit Recapture Under Section 16(b) of the 1934 Act

To deter insiders from profiting on short-term trading in the securities of their company, Section 16(b) of the 1934 Act requires a public company to recover from any such person the "statutory profit" realized by him or her in either a purchase and sale, or a sale and purchase (or any number of these transactions) which take place within a six-month period. It is important to note that the actual possession of inside information regarding the issuer is *not* a precondition to the recovery of short-swing profits under Section 16(b). This recoverable profit is not necessarily based on economic realities, and there have been situations where an individual actually lost money on a transaction but was held accountable for the return of "profits."

In determining whether there has been a purchase and sale within the meaning of Section 16(b), it is not necessary to establish that the same shares were purchased and sold, or sold and purchased, within the six-month period. Instead, all that needs to be established is that issuer stock (or warrants or similar rights to buy or sell issuer stock) was either purchased and sold, or sold and purchased, during a six-month period. The identity of the particular shares is irrelevant for determining Section 16(b) liability.

Like the reporting requirement under Section 16(a), Section 16(b) may apply to transactions made after an individual ceases having reporting-person status. That is, a purchase or sale after retirement or termination of employment from the issuer can be matched against any sale or purchase effected less than six months earlier at the time the individual was still a reporting person. See appendix B for more information on this subject.

To compute statutory short-swing profits, the highest sale price and lowest purchase price during the six-month period are matched, regardless of whether the sale and purchase involved the same shares. For a series of transactions, the difference between the highest sale price and the lowest purchase price during the period is computed (regardless of the order in which they occur), then the difference between the next highest sale price and the next lowest purchase price, and so forth. These differences are then totaled to determine the "profit realized" in a series of transactions. If the highest sale price is lower than the lowest purchase price, there is no statutory profit realized by the insider.

As with Section 16(a), the director or officer is considered the beneficial owner of stock held by certain family members for short-swing profit purposes. For example:

> Officer "E" purchased Company X stock in September. His spouse, Mrs. "E," sold some shares of Company X stock in December. Despite the fact that Mrs. "E's" accounts were separate from her husband's, her sale would be matched with his purchase; consequently, Officer "E" is liable for any short-swing profit on the matched transactions.

The recovery for short-swing profits belongs to the issuer and cannot be waived by it. If an issuer fails or refuses to collect or sue a reporting person for short-swing profits within 60 days of demand by a shareholder, the shareholder may bring suit in the issuer's name for recovery. Courts have regularly awarded attorney's fees to the plaintiff's counsel in these actions based upon the amount recovered. As a result, there are "strike lawyers" who carefully review SEC reports for violation of Section 16(b), with the intention of bringing lawsuits against the reporting person or the directors of the issuer if the issuer's directors fail to do so after demand. These lawyers receive a percentage of the recovery (up to 30%, but often less) as a reward for bringing the action and obtaining a recovery for the issuer.

Computation of Six-Month Period. Profits are recoverable under Section 16(b) of the 1934 Act only if the transactions being matched occurred "within any period of less than six months." The computation of this period has been the subject of considerable litigation.

Romeo & Dye's Section 16 Deskbook, which is the standard reference in the field, recommends an approach that looks forward and backward six calendar months minus a day. Using this approach, a purchase on January 1 will not be matched with a sale on June 30 (i.e., January 1 to July 1 minus a day), nor will the sale on June 30 be matched with a purchase on the following December 29 (i.e., June 30 to December 30 minus a day). This topic is thoroughly covered in *Romeo & Dye's Section 16 Deskbook.* It is based on a line of cases beginning with *Stella v. Graham-Paige Motors Corp.*[32]

The date of purchase or sale is based on the existence of an irrevocable commitment (i.e., the trade date), not the formalities of stock transfer, such as the delivery of stock or the payment of the purchase price (i.e., the settlement date).

2.3.1 Section 16(b) Exemptions

Not every transaction in issuer securities is considered a "purchase" or "sale" for purposes of the short-swing trading prohibition. There are several important exemptions from Section 16(b) for certain kinds of stock transactions, which are described below. The exemptions set forth in Rule 16b-3, are designed to facilitate the receipt of stock-based compensation by reporting persons without incurring liability under Section 16(b).[33]

Under Rule 16b-3, a transaction between the issuer and a reporting person that involves issuer equity securities will be exempt from the short-swing profit rules of Section 16(b) if it satisfies the appropriate conditions set forth in one of four categories: (1) tax-conditioned plans; (2) discretionary transactions; (3) grants, awards, and other acquisitions from the issuer; and (4) dispositions to the issuer. The Section 16 rules exempt only transactions between a reporting person and the issuer

---

32. 132 F. Supp. 100 (S.D.N.Y. 1955), *remanded on other grounds,* 232 F.2d 299 (2d Cir.), *cert. denied,* 352 U.S. 831 (1956).

33. 1934 Act, Rule 16b-3.

and not between the issuer and persons who are subject to Section 16 solely because they beneficially own greater than 10% of the issuer's equity securities.

The exemptions for tax-conditioned plans and discretionary transactions (with respect to profit sharing and 401(k) plans) generally are not available for discretionary equity compensation plan transactions and are not described herein. This assumes the option plan is not an employee stock purchase plan that satisfies the relevant provisions of Section 423 of the Internal Revenue Code. Under the tax-conditioned plan exemption, certain transactions in issuer securities in connection with an employee stock purchase plan governed by Code Section 423 are exempt without further condition from Sections 16(a) and 16(b).

The third and fourth exemptions are the ones that provide the relevant exemptions for equity compensation plan transactions and, therefore, are discussed below in greater detail.

Grants, Awards, and Other Acquisitions from the Issuer. Any grant or award of issuer stock from the issuer to a reporting person is an exempt transaction under Section 16(b) if it satisfies any one of the three conditions described below. Grant and award transactions are those that provide issuer stock to participants on a basis that does not require either the contribution of assets or the exercise of investment discretion by participants. Examples of grant and award transactions that are not participant-directed include grants of stock options, stock appreciation rights, restricted stock (including restricted stock units and deferred stock units), or performance share awards. A participant-directed transaction, on the other hand, requires the participant to exercise investment discretion as to either the timing of the transaction or the assets into which the investment is made. Examples of participant-directed transactions include the exercise of an option or stock appreciation right or the sale of shares acquired thereunder. Participant-directed dispositions to the issuer are potentially eligible for the "dispositions" exemption described below.

Any transaction involving a grant, award, or other acquisition by a reporting person from the issuer (other than a transaction meeting the definition of a discretionary transaction) will be exempt from Section 16(b) if any one or more of the following conditions are met:

- The issuer's board of directors or a committee of the board comprised solely of two or more "non-employee directors" approves the acquisition *in advance*;[34]

- The issuer's shareholders approve the acquisition in advance or ratify it not later than the date of the next annual meeting of shareholders;[35] or

- The insider holds the securities acquired for six months following the date of acquisition.[36]

- For these purposes, a "non-employee director" is defined as a director who (1) is not currently an officer or otherwise employed by the issuer, or a parent or subsidiary of the issuer; (2) does not receive compensation directly or indirectly from the issuer, its parent, or subsidiary for services rendered as a consultant or in any capacity other than as a director, except for an amount that does not exceed the dollar amount (currently $120,000) for which disclosure would not be required pursuant to Item 404(a) of Regulation S-K; and (3) does not possess an interest in any other transaction for which disclosure would be required pursuant to Item 404(a) of Regulation S-K.

Thus, exercises of stock options or stock appreciation rights will be exempt from Section 16(b) if approved by the issuer's board of directors, by a committee consisting solely of two or more nonemployee directors, or by the issuer's shareholders.

Note that if an option, SAR, or stock award does not satisfy one of the approval requirements, it may in any event qualify for an exemption from Section 16(b) under the six-month holding period rule. This rule provides that the acquisition of a security will be exempt from Section 16(b) if the security is held by the recipient for six months following the acquisition or, in the case of a derivative security, if the underlying security is held for six months after the acquisition of the derivative security.[37] In the case of a stock option, this means that the grant will be

---

34. 1934 Act, Rule 16b-3(d)(1).
35. 1934 Act, Rule 16b-3(d)(2).
36. 1934 Act, Rule 16b-3(d)(3).
37. Rule 16b-3(d)(3), Note (3).

an exempt *purchase* of issuer securities if the option (or the underlying issuer stock) is held for at least six months from the date of grant. For example, if an option is granted on May 1, and the option is exercised on or after November 1 of the same year, the grant of that option will be exempt and cannot be matched up with any other nonexempt sales. However, if the option is exercised earlier and the underlying stock is sold before November 1 (in this example), the option grant itself can be treated as a nonexempt purchase of issuer stock matchable against the subsequent sale.

The SEC has made clear that the approval requirement relates to each specific transaction and is not satisfied by approval of a plan in its entirety, except for plans where the terms and conditions of each transaction are fixed in advance, such as a formula plan.[38] Where the terms of a subsequent transaction are provided at the time a transaction is initially approved, the subsequent transaction does not require further specific approval. For example, the acquisition of common stock that occurs upon the exercise of a stock option or stock appreciation rights is exempt as long as the exercise is pursuant to the express terms provided for in the option as originally approved. Similarly, if the terms of an award of stock options, as originally approved, provide for a stock-for-stock exercise (a "stock swap"), the disposition of company stock in connection with the exercise would be exempt without further condition if effected pursuant to those terms. Conversely, if a stock swap was not approved at the time of the initial grant, it would require subsequent approval before exercise in order to be exempt from Section 16(b).

Dispositions to the Issuer. In addition to the potential Section 16(b) impact of the grant or exercise of an option, the disposition of shares in connection with an option also must be considered. The issue here is whether or not a disposition of issuer securities in connection with or following the exercise of a stock option will be an exempt or non-exempt sale.

In this regard, all dispositions of issuer securities by a reporting person pursuant to open market transactions will be treated as *non-*

---

38. SEC Release No. 34-37260, Part II, D.

exempt sales that can potentially be matched against any nonexempt purchases occurring within six months of the sale. As a result, sales of issuer securities into the open market pursuant to a "cashless exercise" arrangement with a broker or other third party will result in nonexempt sales of issuer securities by a reporting person.

However, dispositions of issuer securities *back to the issuer* by a director or officer will be exempt if approved in advance by the issuer's board of directors, by a committee of the board comprised solely of two or more nonemployee directors, or by the shareholders.[39] Note that these are the same approval requirements described above in connection with grants, awards, and other acquisitions. Unlike the exemptions for "acquisitions," however, the six-month holding period rule does *not* apply to "dispositions" of issuer securities. Furthermore, the exemption for dispositions to the issuer by directors or officers is available for all shares owned by such persons, and it is not conditioned on the transaction being intended for a compensatory or other particular purpose.

Thus, as long as the approval requirements are met, the Section 16(b) rules will exempt a disposition of issuer stock by a reporting person *back to the issuer* pursuant to (1) the right to have securities withheld, or to deliver securities already owned, either in payment of the exercise price of an option or to satisfy the tax withholding consequences of an option exercise; (2) the expiration, cancellation, or surrender to the issuer of a stock option or stock appreciation right (SAR) in connection with the grant of a replacement or reload option;[40] or (3) the election to receive, and the receipt of, cash in complete or partial settlement of an SAR.[41] Additionally, the Section 16 rules will give the issuer the flexibility to redeem its equity securities from reporting persons in connection with nonexempt replacement grants (e.g., in the context of a repricing) and in discrete compensatory situations such as individual buybacks.

---

39. SEC Release No. 34-37260, Part II, E.

40. A "reload option" generally means an option that is granted in replacement of shares purchased upon the exercise of a prior granted option. Reload option programs generally work in tandem with a stock-for-stock exercise feature. If the optionee exercises his or her option by delivering previously owned issuer shares, the issuer may grant a new option replacing the number of shares delivered to exercise the prior option.

41. SEC Release No. 34-37260, Part II, E.

For issuers that intend to provide reporting persons with the ability to engage in stock-for-stock exercises or the delivery of issuer securities to satisfy tax withholding, it is recommended that these features be included in the original option grant so as to avoid the need for additional approval of the disposition of securities at the time of option exercise. Also, it is important to note that the sale of shares to pay the exercise price of an option under a cashless exercise program will be exempt from Section 16(b) *only* if the issuer is the purchaser, and not if the shares are sold on the open market by a broker or other third party. Note that an issuer has no tax withholding obligation with respect to its nonemployee directors. Customarily, the option grant to a nonemployee director should not contain a tax withholding obligation on the part of the issuer or a corresponding ability to use share withholding to pay taxes on the part of the nonemployee director. If such a provision is in the option grant, it could cause disclosure requirements under S-K Item 404(a). See the further discussion at Section 2.6.2 below.

Merger No-Action Letter. In 1999, the SEC issued a no-action letter setting forth how shares acquired by officers and directors of a public company within six months of that company being acquired for cash or stock in a merger can be protected from the short-swing profit recapture under Section 16(b) pursuant to the exemption in Rule 16b-3.[42] This no-action letter has become the standard under which these transactions are being conducted. It relies on the exemption for dispositions to the issuer in Rule 16b-3(e). Language should be put in merger documents to protect the directors and executives of public target companies referencing the procedures in this no-action letter.

Drafting and Other Considerations. Under the Section 16 rules, it is not necessary that an employee benefit plan be in writing or that the plan receive shareholder approval in order to qualify for the Rule 16b-3 exemptions. The shareholder approval element of the Section 16 rules relates to each individual option grant rather than the plan in its entirety and therefore is not needed. As a result, most issuers will rely on the board of directors' or the committee's approval to satisfy an ex-

---

42. See *Skadden, Arps, Slate, Meagher & Flom,* SEC No–Action Letter (April 28, 1999).

emption under Section 16(b). However, most issuers seek shareholder approval of their equity compensation plans to satisfy other requirements, such as requirements of the stock exchanges (including NYSE and Nasdaq), state corporate law, or Internal Revenue Code Section 422 (which requires shareholder approval of an equity compensation plan that allows for the grant of incentive stock options). Most equity compensation plans are required to be shareholder-approved under NYSE and Nasdaq rules.

Transaction Review and Assistance. Because of the complexities involved in reporting under Section 16(a) and the danger of short-swing recapture under Section 16(b), most companies have developed programs to assist directors and officers in complying with these federal statutes. The compliance program usually consists of the following:

- All directors and designated officers must contact the issuer's designated compliance officer before they, a family member, or a trust or other entity which they control engage in any transactions in company stock, including gifts, purchases, sales, etc.

- The designated compliance officer usually prepares the Section 16 reports and files them with the SEC.

- All directors and designated officers are requested to execute a power of attorney enabling the designated compliance officer to sign and file the necessary forms with the SEC.

- Brokers representing directors and designated officers are informed of the company's policies concerning insider trading and Section 16 reporting.

See the model pre-clearance policy included as appendix A to this chapter.

2.4 Trading While in Possession of Inside Information

As a general rule, any person with material non-public information about the issuer is obligated under Rule 10b-5 under the 1934 Act to refrain from purchasing or selling stock until such information has been released into the marketplace. Also, the Insider Trading and Securities Fraud Enforcement Act provides civil penalties for insider trading in the amount of the greater of $1 million or three times the profit gained or loss avoided. It also prescribes criminal penalties of a maximum 10-year jail term and a maximum fine of $1 million for individuals. Although stock options and stock appreciation rights may be exercised at any time even if the holder has material non-public information about the issuer, such person is obligated under Rule 10b-5 to refrain from selling the shares acquired upon exercise of an option or stock appreciation right until the material non-public information has been released into the marketplace. Stock swaps, net exercises, and the use of share withholding to pay taxes should be carefully considered while the reporting person is in possession of material non-public information because such transactions go beyond the scope of mere exercises of stock options or stock appreciation rights. See the discussion below under the caption "Stock Transactions During Closed Trading Windows."

To be found liable for insider trading, the reporting person must have benefited from material, non-public information in connection with a purchase or sale of a security. (Using material, non-public information to refrain from a purchase or sale does not violate Rule 10b-5.) Information is considered "material" for these purposes if there is a substantial likelihood that a reasonable investor would consider it important in arriving at a decision to buy, sell, or hold stock of the issuer. Examples of inside information that might be deemed material include:

- Actual or projected sales or earnings (including changes of previously announced estimates).

- Actual or projected significant capital expenditures.

- Actual or projected significant borrowings.

- Public or private sale of a significant amount of additional securities of the company, or major financings or refinancings.

- Non-business matters affecting the market for company securities (such as upcoming research, brokerage firm recommendations, or the intention of parties to buy or sell an abnormal amount of securities).

- A proposed merger, acquisition, joint venture, or disposition of stock or assets, or a tender offer for another company's securities.

- Any action or event that could have a significant effect on annual sales or earnings.

- Any action or event that may result in a special or extraordinary charge against earnings or capital, or significant changes in asset values or lines of business.

- A significant change in capital investment plans.

- Major new products, discoveries, or services.

- A call of securities for redemption or a program to repurchase company shares.

- A change in control or significant management changes.

- Significant litigation and changes in pending litigation.

- Significant changes in operating or financial circumstances.

- Significant labor disputes or other pay-related issues.

- Significant actions by regulatory bodies.

- Information regarding other companies learned through special business relationships with them.

- Dividend increases or decreases.

- Rating agency upgrades or downgrades.

The foregoing list is for illustration only and is not exhaustive; other types of information may be material at particular times, depending upon all the circumstances.

Insider Trading Policies. The most risky time to engage in a purchase or sale of issuer stock is shortly in advance of the public release by the issuer of important financial information, such as quarterly or year-end results, or other important news. Most companies impose trading windows on their officers and directors, with closed trading windows typically beginning at least 10 days before the end of the quarter or fiscal year and ending 1 or 2 days after the release of earnings. The safest time to engage in purchases or sales is the period—commonly referred to as an open trading window—shortly following the release and publication of such information. However, even engaging in transactions during an open trading window presumes that the person is not aware of any other material information which has not been made public. After any such information has been released, it is important to be sure that sufficient time has elapsed to enable the information to be disseminated to and considered by investors.

Stock Transactions During Closed Trading Windows. Insider trading policies generally prohibit cashless exercises of stock options (involving open market sales through a broker or other third party) while in possession of material non-public information, but they generally do not prohibit cash exercises, stock-for-stock exercises, or share withholding to pay taxes where the issuer is the purchaser. These transactions are with the issuer, which is the ultimate insider and is presumed to have full knowledge. If the issuer is holding back on "good news," these transactions will be at a bargain price to the issuer and will not create insider trading liability as long as the person exercising the option has full knowledge of the "good news." If the issuer is holding back on "bad news," the person exercising the option by the delivery of previously owned shares is getting the benefit of too high a price for those shares, but once again this should not create insider trading liability. At worst, it creates a claim of corporate waste by the shareholders if they become aware of the transaction. This claim should be defended against on the basis of the "business judgment rule" that it was in the best interest of the company to permit the transaction. Given the shareholder and SEC activity in the area of option exercises, the more prudent practice would be to prohibit cash exercises, stock-for-stock exercises, and share withholding to pay taxes during the company's traditional black-out periods. Insiders may alleviate some of the hardship that may arise as result of such a prohibition (e.g. where an insider has restricted stock that vests during a closed trading window) by adopting a 10b5-1 plan during an open trading window under which the stock-for-stock exchange or share withholding would be pre-arranged. (See the discussion below.) Note that transactions under these plans are matchable for the purposes of the short-swing profits rules under Section 16(b) of the Exchange Act.

In a 2005 SEC investigation involving Analog Devices, Inc. (NYSE: ADI), the SEC appeared to be concerned about a company granting stock options to its directors and executive officers immediately before the announcement of good news. In connection with the settlement, ADI consented to a cease-and-desist order under Section 10(b) of the Securities Exchange Act and Rule 10b-5 thereunder, paid a civil money penalty of $3 million, and repriced options granted to the CEO and other directors in certain years. Options granted to all other employees were excluded from the repricing. The CEO consented to a cease-and-desist order under Sections 17(a)(2) and (3) of the Securities Act, paid a civil money penalty of $1 million, and made a disgorgement payment with respect to options granted in certain years.

Taking this SEC concern to the next level could lead one to conclude that the SEC would be equally concerned with a company permitting the delivery of previously owned shares to pay the exercise price of a stock option or related taxes at a time when the company was in a closed trading window involving the nondisclosure of material adverse information. In light of the SEC's activity in this area, it may be sensible for a public company's insider trading policy to prohibit the delivery of shares to pay the exercise price or related taxes during closed trading windows.

2.4.1 Backdating of Stock Option Grants

In recent years, many corporations have been involved in investigations concerning the timing of stock option grants made to senior executives. These investigations—which have been separately pursued by the SEC and the U.S. Department of Justice (DOJ)—have prompted financial restatements by some corporations.

The issue catalyzing these investigations is whether corporations used stock option grants to improperly enrich their senior executives. These investigations focus on two main issues:

- Whether options were "backdated," or retroactively granted on a date when the stock price was low in order to build in a profit for the executives.

- Whether the options were "spring-loaded," or granted immediately before corporate announcements that were likely to increase the price of the shares.

The options backdating investigations raise both civil and criminal issues for corporations and their executives. The SEC has investigated whether companies backdated options to provide undisclosed compensation to senior executives and whether the failure to disclose this practice constituted securities fraud. These investigations have focused on how companies report and disclose backdated options for financial and tax reporting purposes.

Similarly, the DOJ has reviewed these cases from a criminal standpoint, i.e., was there fraud? Were documents altered or misdated as a part of the fraud? Finally, were shareholders told the truth about the option grants and the compensation of corporate officials? The corporations and executives involved in improperly backdating options may face securities, mail, and wire fraud charges as well as tax charges. Private civil litigation involving these same issues also has been filed against some companies.

Because of the potential civil and criminal liability that companies and their officers may face, corporations suspecting they may have problems relating to the backdating of options need to evaluate a number of possible compliance issues and should consult counsel. In some instances, corporations acting through special committees of the board of directors may want to seek independent counsel to investigate such problems.

It should be noted that options backdating can occur without any intentional wrongdoing merely due to failures in corporate procedures. Even though such inadvertent errors are uncommon, the consequences can be serious.

The current executive compensation rules discussed below address this issue of option backdating in a disclosure manner. If the options are not granted at the "closing market price" (last sales price), an extra column must be added in the proxy statement in the table disclosing option grants showing the difference between the grant price and the closing market price. Some omnibus plans have a definition of fair market value related to the average of the high and low prices on either the date of grant or the date preceding the date of grant. This definition will trigger the disclosure discussed above. Many public companies have either amended their plans or adopted resolutions to provide that options will only be granted at the closing market price (the last sales price) on the date of grant. This concept of last sales price is also applicable to any use of fair market value for equity compensation plans; i.e., for the delivery of previously owned shares to pay the exercise price or for share withholding to pay taxes.

2.5 1933 Act Registration Requirements; Resales by Plan Participants

The 1933 Act makes it unlawful for any person to sell or to offer to sell any security unless a registration statement has been filed and declared effective with respect to such security or the offer or sale is pursuant to an available exemption from registration.[43] The purpose of the 1933 Act is to ensure that adequate disclosure of all material facts is made to potential investors at the time they are making an investment decision with respect to the securities. The 1933 Act adopts a philosophy of disclosure; the SEC does not review the merits of a particular investment, but rather it polices the adequacy of the disclosure made by the issuer to potential investors. Unless an exemption is available, the process of registration involves the preparation of a registration statement that includes a prospectus containing copious amounts of information about the issuer. The preparation of a registration statement can be costly and time-consuming; therefore, identifying an available exemption from registration for a particular transaction is important. There are a number of exemptions from the registration rules listed below that may be available for stock issued pursuant to an employer-sponsored equity compensation plan. Failure to comply with the registration requirements may give the purchaser of securities a rescission right.[44] To allow for marketability of shares acquired in connection with an equity compensation plan, it is important to make sure the shares have been properly registered or an exemption from registration is available.

2.5.1 Registration Requirements

Section 5 of the 1933 Act provides that it is unlawful for any person, directly or indirectly, to use any form of interstate transportation or

43. 1933 Act, § 5.

44. 1933 Act, § 12.

communication or the mails to offer a security for sale unless a registration statement has been filed with respect to such security or to sell, carry, or deliver for sale any security unless a registration statement is in effect for such security.[45] Thus, in implementing an equity-based compensation arrangement, an employer must consider whether the arrangement involves the issuance of a security and, if so, whether the security to be issued under such plan should be registered pursuant to the provisions of the 1933 Act, or whether one or more exemptions from registration may be available.

Even if an exemption from registration is available, the employer should also consider whether participants in the plan are free to sell securities received under such a plan without violation of the federal securities laws.

Registration on Form S-8. If an issuer is subject to the reporting requirements of the 1934 Act—that is, the issuer is a "public company" (including, in this instance, a foreign private issuer)—registration of stock to be issued to officers, directors, and employees under any employee benefit plan of the employer can be accomplished very simply by filing a Form S-8 with the SEC.[46] The Form S-8 must be on file with the SEC before any shares of stock are issued to participants under an employee benefit plan. The Form S-8 consists of a prospectus and a registration statement. This registration statement registers a fixed number of shares for use with respect to the benefit plan. When those shares are used up, a new registration statement should be filed for any additional shares allocated to the plan. The registration statement incorporates by reference the employer's current and future 1934 Act reports, including certain information incorporated into such reports to satisfy certain Form S-8 updating requirements and, as a result, it is a fairly abbreviated form. The prospectus includes, among other things, general plan information, a description of the securities being offered, and information regarding the tax consequences of participating in the plan. The prospectus is not filed with the SEC. Thus, the registration statement can remain "alive" for a number of years (until the registered

---

45. 1933 Act, § 5(a)(1).

46. SEC Release No. 33-6188, Part VI, A, as well as 33-6281.

shares are used up) without any need to rewrite and redistribute the prospectus. Most changes to the information in the prospectus can be made by means of a prospectus supplement or appendix. Not only does registering the stock on Form S-8 satisfy the employer's requirements under Section 5 of the 1933 Act, it also permits all plan participants, except "affiliates," to sell stock received under the registered plan freely and immediately once any vesting restrictions have lapsed.

- *Sales by Affiliates.* An "affiliate" is defined as any person in a re-lationship of control with the issuer, such as a director, executive officer, or large shareholder. The question of which persons are in a relationship of control such that they should properly be considered affiliates is a fact-specific inquiry that should be addressed by each company and its counsel. As a result of their control relationship with the employer, affiliates may be deemed to be acting as the cor-porate issuer when they sell the issuer's stock. Thus, although stock issued pursuant to an equity compensation plan may be registered on Form S-8, an affiliate may not freely sell such stock unless an exemption applies or unless the affiliate's sale itself is registered.[47] In most cases, resales by affiliates are made pursuant to the exemption from registration provided by SEC Rule 144.[48] If the shares being sold by the affiliate have been registered under the 1933 Act (on Form S-8, for example), the six-month holding period requirement of Rule 144 does not apply. However, the other conditions of Rule 144 continue to apply.

  As an alternative to Rule 144, an affiliate's shares can be reg-istered for resale, either by means of a separate registration state-ment or by means of a resale prospectus filed together with the plan's registration statement on Form S-8. A resale prospectus filed with Form S-8 may under certain circumstances be prepared in accordance with the requirements of Form S-3, even though the issuer is not otherwise eligible to use that abbreviated form. Most companies do not use this resale prospectus because of the nega-tive impact it has on the trading market for the stock: the public

---

47. SEC Release No. 33-6188, Part VI, A, as well as 33-6281.

48. For a more detailed discussion of Rule 144, see "1933 Act Registration Require-ments; Resales by Plan Participants—Sales Under Rule 144" below.

shareholders could construe it as a vote of no confidence by the company's affiliates since the resale prospectus facilitates insiders exiting their investment in company stock.

Finally, an affiliate may be able to sell stock received under a stock plan in a privately negotiated transaction. However, the various considerations that apply to such sales under the securities laws are complex, and careful consultation with counsel is recommended before any such transaction is undertaken.

Issuance of Stock Without Registration. In certain instances, stock can be issued pursuant to an equity compensation plan without registration of the stock or the plan. However, under most of the available exemptions from registration, the participant will receive stock that is not freely tradable. Some of the exemptions from registration do not require the employer to provide specified information; nevertheless, sales under any of these exemptions will remain subject to the antifraud provisions of the 1933 and 1934 Acts. Several of the commonly used exemptions from registration for equity compensation plans are briefly described below.

- *Non-public Offering.* Section 4(a)(2) of the 1933 Act provides an exemption for a "private placement" of securities, which is an offering of stock to a limited number of investors who have access to the same information normally provided in a public offering *and* who are sophisticated enough both to assess and bear the risks of investing in the issuer's securities. No specific information is required to be disclosed to purchasers, but their access to information about the employer is generally considered to be an element of the exemption. This exemption may be available for the issuance of stock to the employer's top executives, but it is less likely to be available for a broad-based stock compensation program.

- *Regulation D Offerings.* Regulation D contains two (formerly three) alternative exemptions from registration under Section 3(b) of the 1933 Act, set forth as Rules 504 and 506.[49] In October 2016, the SEC adopted amendments to Regulation D that as of early 2017

---

49. 1933 Act, Rules 504 and 506.

increased the limit under Rule 504 and removed a third exemption, Rule 505.[50] The limit under Rule 504 was subsequently increased in November 2020. The Regulation D exemptions require the filing of a relatively simple form with the SEC.

Rule 504 exempts an offering of up to $10 million of stock in any 12-month period. (The limit was formerly $1 million but was increased to $5 million effective as of January 20, 2017, and subsequently increased to $10 million effective as of March 15, 2021.)[51] Note that the $10 million limit during any such 12-month period is reduced by the amount of any other offerings exempt under Section 3(b) of the 1933 Act. The Rule 504 exemption does *not* require that offerees be sophisticated or knowledgeable about the issuer or that specific information about the issuer be disclosed. However, the former $1 million limitation of Rule 504 could be a significant problem in the case of a stock option plan because the offering is deemed to be continuing for the entire period during which the options are exercisable; this is eased under the new $10 million limit.

Rule 506 does not limit the size of the offering or the number of purchasers that are "accredited investors" (see below), but instead limits the number of nonaccredited purchasers to 35 and requires that such nonaccredited purchasers, either alone or with a financial advisor, be capable of evaluating the investment. Under Rule 506, specific, detailed disclosures are required unless the offering is made exclusively to "accredited investors."

- *Rule 701.* Rule 701 (as described in greater detail below) can also exempt sales under compensatory benefit plans if certain conditions are met.[52] This exemption is nonexclusive and can be used

---

50. SEC Release Nos. 33-10238; 34-79161 (Oct. 26, 2016). Rule 505, which under the October 2016 SEC amendments was removed effective May 22, 2017, provided an exemption for offerings of up to $5 million in any 12-month period to as many as 35 nonaccredited investors and an unlimited number of accredited investors, reduced by the amount of any other offerings exempt under Section 3(b) of the 1933 Act.

51. SEC Release Nos. 33-10238; 34-79161 (Oct. 26, 2016) and SEC Release Nos. 33-10884; 34-90300 (Nov. 2, 2020).

52. 1933 Act, Rule 701.

in conjunction with Regulation D and other exemptions. In the author's view, an exemption under Rule 701 is preferable to Regulation D, and in many cases an exemption under Regulation D is a fallback to qualifying under Rule 701.

2.5.2   Rule 701

For certain compensatory issuances of stock or stock options to employees and other service providers, Rule 701 provides an exemption from the registration requirements of the 1933 Act for offers and sales of securities. The primary features of Rule 701 are as follows:

*   The purpose of the issuance must be compensation. If the purpose of the plan is to circumvent registration requirements and is not for compensation purposes, then the exemption is not available.

*   Rule 701 is an exemption from federal securities laws and does not provide an exemption from applicable state securities laws. Many states, however, have adopted equivalent exemptions that either specifically provide for issuances made pursuant to Rule 701 or generally exempt issuances that are made for compensatory purposes.

*   The issuer cannot be a reporting company under Section 13 or 15(d) of the 1934 Act nor an investment company required to be registered under the Investment Company Act of 1940. However, a privately held subsidiary of a publicly held parent may rely on Rule 701 and may issue securities to its employees, directors, officers, general partners, trustees (if the issuer is a business trust), or consultants and advisors as well as those of its publicly held parent or other majority-owned subsidiaries of its parent.[53]

*   The participants may be employees, directors, officers, general partners, trustees (if the issuer is a business trust), or consultants and advisors, and their family members who acquire such securities through gifts or domestic relations orders. Former employees, directors, general partners, trustees, officers, or consultants and

---

53. *American Bar Association*, SEC No-Action Letter [1999–2000 Transfer Binder] Fed. Sec. L. Rep. (CCH) ¶ 77,604 at 76,132 (Aug. 3, 1999).

advisors can participate only if they were employed by or provided services to the issuer at the time the securities were offered. Further limitations on the participants are detailed below.

- Limitations are imposed on the sales price or amount of securities that can be issued pursuant to Rule 701. Basically, the limitation is that during any 12-month period the aggregate sales price or amount of securities sold in reliance on Rule 701 cannot exceed the greatest of (1) $1 million, (2) 15% of the total assets of the issuer, or (3) 15% of the outstanding amount of the class of securities being offered and sold in reliance on Rule 701. Further details are provided below.

- Although this is an issuer-only exemption, Rule 701 also provides special rules for resale after the company has gone public. Further resale details are provided below.

- No SEC notice is necessary for an issuance pursuant to Rule 701. Notice requirements, however, exist under some state securities regulations.

- The issuance must be made pursuant to a written compensation contract or written compensatory plan.[54]

- Disclosures must be provided. The issuer must deliver to investors a copy of the benefit plan or contract. If the aggregate sales price or amount of securities sold exceeds $10 million in a consecutive 12-month period, then certain other disclosures (including U.S. GAAP financial statements of a U.S. issuer or International Financial Reporting Standards (IFRS) for a qualified foreign private issuer) must be made within a reasonable period before the date of sale, as detailed below.[55]

---

54. A compensatory benefit plan is defined as any purchase, savings, option, bonus, stock appreciation, profit sharing, thrift, incentive, deferred compensation, pension, or similar plan.

55. The threshold for providing the additional disclosures was increased from $5 million to $10 million effective July 23, 2018. SEC Release No. 33-10520 (July 18, 2018).

- Rule 701 transactions are not integrated with other exempt transactions.[56]

- Rule 701 is not exclusive, so that other exemptions may be claimed.

Participants. As noted above, the participants may be employees, directors, general partners, trustees (if the issuer is a business trust), officers, or consultants and advisors, and their family members who acquire such securities through gifts or domestic relations orders. In a 1999 amendment of Rule 701, the SEC significantly restricted the definition of "consultants and advisors" who may participate in a Rule 701 issuance and harmonized the Rule 701 interpretation of the phrase with the Form S-8 interpretation.[57] Consultants and advisors must be natural persons and provide bona fide services to the issuer, its parents, or their majority-owned subsidiaries.

In addition to the above basic requirements to be a consultant or advisor, securities promoters may not participate under the exemption because they do not qualify as consultants or advisors. This exclusion covers people whose services are inherently capital-raising or promotional, such as brokers, dealers, those who find investors, those who provide shareholder communications services, and those who arrange for mergers or take the company private. Business advisors whose activities are not inherently capital-raising or promotional would be allowed to participate in an offering under Rule 701.

Independent agents, franchisees, and salespersons that do not have an employment relationship with the issuer are also not within the scope of "consultant or advisor." A person in a *de facto* employment relationship with the issuer, however, such as a nonemployee providing services that traditionally are performed by an employee, with compensation paid for those services being the primary source of the person's earned income, would qualify as an eligible person under the exemption. Other persons displaying significant characteristics of "employment," such as the professional advisor providing bookkeeping

---

56. A general solicitation in connection with a Rule 701 transaction, however, may cause an integration problem with respect to exemptions that do not permit general solicitation.

57. SEC Release No. 33-7646 (April 7, 1999).

services, computer programming advice, or other valuable professional services may qualify as eligible consultants or advisors, depending upon the particular facts and circumstances.

The term "employee" specifically includes insurance agents who are exclusive agents of the issuer, its subsidiaries or parents, or derive more than 50% of their annual income from those entities.

Limitations on Issuances. During any 12-month period the aggregate sales price or amount of securities sold in reliance on Rule 701 cannot exceed the greatest of (1) $1 million, (2) 15% of the total assets of the issuer (or of the issuer's parent if the issuer is a wholly owned subsidiary and the parent fully and unconditionally guarantees the obligations of the issuer), or (3) 15% of the outstanding amount of the class of securities being offered and sold in reliance on Rule 701. Both the total assets and outstanding amount of securities are measured at the issuer's most recent balance sheet date, if it is no older than its last fiscal year end.

The aggregate sales price means the sum of all cash, property, notes, cancellation of debt, or other consideration received or to be received by the issuer for the sale of the securities. Non-cash consideration must be valued by reference to bona fide sales of the consideration made within a reasonable time or, in the absence of such sales, on the fair value as determined by an accepted standard. The value of services exchanged for securities issued must be measured by reference to the value of the securities issued. Thus, compensatory arrangements for consultant and employee services must be valued, and they cannot be valued at "zero" or as a gift. Options must be valued based on the exercise price of the option, and if options are subsequently repriced, then a recalculation of the aggregate sales price under Rule 701 must be made. The aggregate sales price of options is determined upon the grant of the options, regardless of when the options become exercisable or are exercised. Restricted stock and restricted stock units are valued based on their fair market value at the time of grant. Deferred compensation and similar plans are measured as of the date an irrevocable election to defer compensation is made. The aggregate sale price of other securities not mentioned above is determined on the date of sale.

The total assets of the issuer for the 15%-of-total-assets test are determined by using the calculation of assets on the balance sheet of the issuer. While not specifically mandated by the SEC, in pursuing an exemption under Rule 701, companies use the assets total from their balance sheets.

The amount of outstanding securities for the 15%-of-the-outstanding-class-of-securities test is calculated by including all currently exercisable or convertible options, warrants, rights, or other securities. This amount does not include options, warrants, or rights that are not presently exercisable, and it also does not include presently nonconvertible securities.[58] The amount of outstanding securities does not include securities issuable pursuant to Rule 701. That is, the amount of outstanding securities does not include exercisable options, warrants, or rights issued pursuant to Rule 701 that have not yet been exercised.

In relation to the 15%-of-outstanding-class-of-securities test, for the purposes of determining the number of outstanding shares of a class, separate classes of common stock may be considered as a single class if the rights of such separate classes are nearly identical.[59]

Disclosures. If the aggregate sales price or amount of securities sold exceeds $10 million in a consecutive 12-month period, then certain other disclosures must be made within a reasonable period before the date of sale. These are in addition to the disclosure of the written benefit plan or contract. These additional disclosures include (1) if the plan is subject to ERISA, a copy of the summary plan description required by ERISA, or, if the plan is not subject to ERISA, a summary of the material terms of the plan; (2) information about the risks associated with investment in the securities sold pursuant to the compensatory benefit plan or compensation contract; and (3) U.S. GAAP or IFRS financial statements as of a date no more than 180 days before the sale of securities in reliance on Rule 701. If the issuer relies on its parent's total assets to determine the amount of securities that may be sold, the parent's financial statements, which must meet certain standards if the parent is a reporting company under Section 13 or 15(d) of the 1934 Act, must be delivered. If the sale involves a stock option or other

---

58. *American Bar Association Subcommittee on Employee Benefits and Executive Compensation*, SEC No-Action Letter, LivEDGAR (September 6, 1988).

59. *Osler Health, Inc.*, SEC No-Action Letter (February 11, 1998).

derivative security, the issuer must deliver disclosures a reasonable period of time before the date of exercise or conversion.

Resale Limitations. Securities issued under Rule 701 are "restricted securities" as defined in Rule 144. Resales of securities issued pursuant to Rule 701 must be in compliance with the registration requirements of the 1933 Act or an exemption from those requirements, such as Rule 144. However, with respect to Rule 144, Rule 701 provides that certain Rule 144 requirements for resale fall away 90 days after the issuer becomes subject to the reporting requirements of Section 13 or 15(d) of the 1934 Act,[60] as in the case of an initial public offering. Thus, following an initial public offering, securities issued under Rule 701 may be resold by nonaffiliates pursuant to Rule 144 without having to meet the holding period and public information requirements of Rule 144 (note that the seller must have been a nonaffiliate for the three months ending on the date of sale). With respect to post-initial public offering resales by affiliates of securities issued under Rule 701, only the holding period requirement falls away. Rule 144's other requirements for resales by affiliates and nonaffiliates are set forth below.

Proposed Rules. In November 2020, the SEC proposed certain amendments to Rule 701 and Form S-8. The proposed amendments are designed to modernize the Rule 701 exemption and Form S-8 registration statement requirements in light of the significant evolution in compensatory offerings since the SEC last substantively amended these regulations, consistent with investor protection. Overall, the proposed amendments are intended to expand the availability of Rule 701 and Form S-8.

With respect to Rule 701, the SEC proposed a number of amendments, including to raise two of the three alternative regulatory ceilings that cap the overall amount of securities that an issuer may sell pursuant to Rule 701 during any consecutive 12-month period. Under the proposed rules, the limitation on the amount of securities that could be sold under Rule 701 would increase (1) from 15% of the total assets of the issuer to 25% and (2) from $1 million to $2 million. The limitation of 15% of the outstanding amount of the class of securities

---

60. See Rule 701(g)(3).

being offered and sold in reliance on Rule 701 remains unchanged. The proposed amendments revise the additional disclosure requirements for Rule 701-exempt transactions exceeding $10 million, including how the disclosure threshold applies, the type of financial disclosure required, and the frequency with which it must be updated. The proposed amendments also make the Rule 701 exemption available for offers and sales of securities under a written compensatory benefit plan (or written compensation contract) established by the issuer's subsidiaries, whether or not majority-owned.

With respect to Form S-8, the SEC proposed a number of amendments, including to clarify the ability to add multiple plans to a single Form S-8. In addition, issuers may file an automatically effective amendment to a previously filed Form S-8 to add employee benefit plans and register additional shares. The proposed amendments clarify that issuers are not required to allocate registered securities among incentive plans. For issuers using this flexibility, the initial registration statement would be required to list the types of securities covered by the registration statement and identify the plan or plans pursuant to which the issuer intendeds to issue securities. The registration statement would not need to assign or allocate the securities to particular incentive plans. In this way, the form may be used to create a pool of registered shares that may be issued under the issuer's various incentive plans as necessary. However, issuers would need to track their offers and sales of securities to ensure they have sufficient capacity registered to fulfill the needs of the various incentive plans identified on the form. These clarifications and amendments are intended to facilitate the use of a single Form S-8 to cover all compensatory benefit plans, should an issuer decide to do so, thereby promoting efficiency and flexibility.

With respect to both the Rule 701 exemption and the Form S-8 registration statement, the proposed amendments extend consultant and advisor eligibility to entities meeting specified ownership criteria designed to link the securities to the performance of services. In particular, the SEC proposed expanding consultant and advisor eligibility to an entity, subject to the following conditions: (1) substantially all of the activities of the entity involve the performance of services and (2) substantially all of the ownership interests in the entity are held directly by: (a) no more than 25 natural persons, of whom at least 50% perform such services for the issuer through the entity, (b) the estate of such natural persons, and (c) any natural person who acquired ownership interests in the entity by reason of the death of such natural persons. The SEC believes the proposed amendments strike a balance between, on the one hand, allowing service providers flexibility to obtain the legal benefits of organizing as entities and, on the other hand, preventing securities from being issued to passive investment vehicles in reliance on Rule 701 or under Form S-8.

2.5.3 Sales Under Rule 144

U.S. securities laws start from the premise that every person who wants to sell a security must establish an exemption from applicable federal and state securities law registration requirements or must comply with such registration requirements. When a normal investor wishes to resell registered securities, he or she can rely on the exemption in Section 4(a)(1) of the 1933 Act, which exempts from further registration any transaction by a person other than an issuer, underwriter, or dealer. However, that exemption is not available for sales of unregistered securities ("restricted securities") acquired by nonaffiliates from the issuer or an affiliate of the issuer, and it is not available for sales of issuer securities by affiliates of the issuer no matter how acquired ("control stock"). The applicable exemption from registration for such securities is provided by Rule 144 promulgated under the 1933 Act. Rule 144 serves as a safe harbor, allowing directors and officers to sell securities without complying with the SEC's registration requirements, provided that certain specific conditions are met.

As stated above, "restricted securities" are securities acquired from the issuer or an affiliate of the issuer in a transaction *not* involving a public offering. Thus, shares of common stock issued upon exercise of compensatory stock options that have not been registered under the 1933 Act on a Form S-8 are restricted securities. No restricted securities may be sold unless either the sale of such securities is registered with the SEC or the sale is exempt from the registration requirements, as in the case of a sale that falls within the provisions of Rule 144. Rule 144 is not the only exemption available. Private sales in particular may be eligible for other exemptions. However, Rule 144 provides essentially the only way to sell restricted securities in the public market.

In general, "affiliates" are persons in a relationship of control with the issuer, such as a director, executive officer, or large shareholder.[61] In 1997 the SEC proposed a bright-line test for the definition of affiliate that would indicate that a person would not be deemed to be an affiliate if the person is not (1) a 10% owner, (2) a Section 16 reporting person, or (3) a director of the issuer. While this proposal has not been enacted, it is generally accepted as indicative of the SEC's perspective on the issue.[62]

Affiliates usually sell issuer securities in a Rule 144 transaction, which is an unsolicited broker's transaction on a stock exchange (including NYSE and Nasdaq). Before such a transaction can occur, Rule 144 requires that the issuer be current in its filings with the SEC, and it limits the amount to be sold in any three-month period. Certain Rule 144 transactions also require the advance filing of SEC Form 144, which remains valid for three months after filing.

As indicated above, a designated officer or director of the issuer is considered an "affiliate" of the issuer. All issuer stock held by affiliates is deemed "control stock," which generally can be sold only (1) pursuant to a 1933 Act registration statement (as a "selling shareholder"), (2) pursuant to the private placement exemption, or (3) pursuant to Rule 144. If an affiliate received the stock from the issuer or another affiliate in other than a registered transaction, the shares are both "control stock" and "restricted securities" under Rule 144. Shares received through the exercise of a registered stock option are not restricted securities. Such shares are, however, considered "control stock." This definition of "control stock" should not be confused with the definition of "control stock" in the business world, in which context control stock means stock owned by major shareholders with a significant degree of control or stock with superior voting rights. For purposes of this chapter, "control stock" is used in a securities law context, and the term applies to stock held by affiliates as defined here.

Under Rule 144, stock held by any household relative of an affiliate, as well as any stock held by a corporation or trust in which an affiliate has a 10% ownership or beneficial interest, is attributable to the affili-

---

61. See http://www.sec.gov/investor/pubs/rule144.htm.

62. SEC Release No. 33-7391 (February 20, 1997) (10% ownership creates a rebuttable presumption of affiliate status).

ate, and the holder of such stock must also comply with Rule 144 in connection with its sale. Stock received by others by gift or bona fide pledge from an affiliate or a household relative retains its restrictions and must be sold under Rule 144 by the donee or pledgee, except that all Rule 144 restrictions lapse in the hands of the donee or pledgee once the holding period has passed since the date of acquisition of the stock by the affiliate.

Rule 144 essentially does two things. First, it sets forth the circumstances under which restricted securities may be sold, and second, it sets forth the circumstances under which affiliates may sell *any* shares of common stock (whether restricted securities or control stock). Non-affiliates (meaning persons who have not been affiliates during the three months preceding the given sale) may freely sell restricted securities under Rule 144 once the restricted securities have been held for the requisite holding period. (The requisite holding period is determined using the rules described below.) Unlike sales by affiliates and sales of restricted securities held for less than the requisite holding period, these sales may be made *without* complying with the other requirements of Rule 144 described below, and the shares need not bear a restrictive legend.

Restricted securities and any stock held by affiliates may be sold under Rule 144 pursuant to the following requirements:

Availability of Current Public Information. In the case of an issuer that has been subject to the reporting requirements of Section 13 of the 1934 Act for a period of at least 90 days ending on the day before the date of sale, such an issuer must have filed the SEC reports required of it for at least 12 months before the sale of securities (or for such shorter period as the issuer was required to file such reports).[63] Potential sellers are entitled to rely on a statement made on the facing sheet of the most recent Form 10-Q or Form 10-K to the effect that required reports have been filed, or upon a written statement from the issuer that all reporting requirements have been met, unless they know or have reason to know that the issuer has not complied with such requirements. If the issuer is not subject to the reporting requirements of Section 13 of the 1934 Act, there must be publicly available the information concerning the

---

63. 1933 Act, Rule 144(c)(1).

issuer specified in paragraphs (a)(5)(i) to (xiv), inclusive, and paragraph (a)(5)(xvi) of C.F.R. § 240.15c2-11.[64]

This requirement always applies to affiliates, and applies to nonaffiliates who have held the stock for less than one year.

Holding Period for Restricted Securities. Restricted securities must have been "beneficially owned" for at least six months (one year if the issuer is not a reporting company).[65] (Affiliates selling control stock are not subject to this requirement.) To be beneficially owned, restricted securities that were purchased (rather than obtained, e.g., by gift) must have been fully paid for. Securities received in certain stock splits, stock dividends, recapitalizations, and conversions are deemed to have been acquired when the underlying securities were acquired, but securities received upon exercise of warrants are generally deemed to be acquired when the warrants were exercised and the exercise price paid. Securities being sold by a bona fide pledgee, donee, trust, or estate will in certain circumstances be deemed to have been held from the dates of acquisition by the pledgor, donor, settlor, or decedent, as the case may be. Each share held by a given shareholder must be analyzed separately to determine when it is eligible for sale under Rule 144.

This requirement applies to affiliates and nonaffiliates and increases to one year if the issuer is not a reporting company.

Quantity. Rule 144 also places an upper limit on the amount of securities that may be sold by an affiliate in any three-month period.[66] The maximum number of shares that may be sold is limited to the greater of (1) 1% of the total number of shares of common stock outstanding as last reported or (2) the average weekly reported volume of trading in the issuer's common stock during the four calendar weeks preceding notice of the sale. Sales of this amount may be made in successive three-month periods. For an affiliate these limitations apply to total sales of *both* restricted securities and control stock.

---

64. 1933 Act, Rule 144(c)(2).

65. 1933 Act, Rule 144(d)(1).

66. 1933 Act, Rule 144(e).

In determining amounts that may be sold by an affiliate, sales by the following persons are deemed made by the affiliate:[67] (1) relatives living in the same home, (2) trusts or estates in which the shareholder or such relatives collectively have 10% or more of the beneficial interest or act as trustee or executor, and (3) corporations and other organizations in which the shareholder or such relatives collectively own 10% or more of any class of equity securities. In addition, in determining amounts that may be sold by a bona fide pledgee, donee, estate, or trust, sales by the pledgor, donor, decedent, or settlor during the same three-month period must be included if the securities being sold were acquired by the pledgee, donee, estate, or trust within six months (or one year if the issuer is not a reporting company) before the date of the intended sale. Persons agreeing to act in concert for the purpose of selling stock in the issuer must aggregate their sales in determining whether or not the quantity limitations are met. Stock sold pursuant to a registration statement or another exemption is not aggregated.

The volume limitations apply only to affiliates.

Manner of Sale. Sales by affiliates can be made only in "brokers' transactions," i.e., transactions in which the broker merely executes an order to sell without compensation exceeding normal brokers' commissions.[68] The seller may not solicit orders for the stock or make payments to any person other than the broker. The broker may not solicit or arrange for the solicitation of orders to buy in connection with the transaction. In addition, the broker must satisfy himself or herself after reasonable inquiry that the sale is being made pursuant to the provisions of Rule 144. *This requirement applies only to affiliates.*

Notice. Notices of intended sales by affiliates must be filed with the SEC and the relevant stock exchange, except for transactions that do not exceed 5,000 shares or $50,000 in proceeds during any three-month period.[69] Three copies of a notice on Form 144 must be transmitted to the SEC concurrently with the placing of an order with a broker to ex-

---

67. 1933 Act, Rule 144(a)(2) and Rule 144(e)(3).

68. 1933 Act, Rule 144(f).

69. 1933 Act, Rule 144(h).

ecute a sale under Rule 144. Typically, the broker will prepare the Form 144, obtain the necessary signatures, and submit the filing to the SEC. In June 2022, the SEC adopted rules that require Form 144 to be filed electronically with the SEC as opposed to historical filings that could be made in paper format. *This requirement applies only to affiliates.*

Departing Director or Executive Officer. A departing director or executive officer should be guided by Section 16, insider trading, and Rule 144 considerations, as more fully explained in appendix B, which contains a memorandum on exit strategies, a sample exit memorandum, and a Rule 144 summary. As to Rule 144: (1) control stock can be sold immediately after the person ceases to be an affiliate, subject to insider trading considerations (Rule 10b-5); (2) for restricted securities, a departing director or executive officer who is considered an affiliate (the CEO, COO, and CFO are presumed to be affiliates) needs to sell under the conditions of Rule 144 for three months and then can use Rule 144(b)(1) as to restricted securities held for at least one year. Rule 144(b)(1) permits the sale of restricted securities without compliance with any of the other conditions of Rule 144 as long as the stock has been held for one year and the seller has not been an affiliate for three months. If the restricted securities have been held for less than one year but more than six months, some Rule 144 conditions must be satisfied. If the restricted securities have been held for less than six months, no sales may be made. (These rules apply to any holder of restricted securities.)

As a general rule, it is suggested that the departing director or executive officer comply with the issuer's insider trading policy for three months after departure to allow his or her insider knowledge to go stale. The three-month period is based on analogy to the three-month period in Rule 144(b)(1).

2.5.4   Sales Under Regulation S

Regulation S is technically not an exemption from registration under the 1933 Act, but rather a clarification of the territorial approach to the registration requirements of Section 5 of the 1933 Act. The SEC adopted Regulation S in 1990 to clarify when offers and sales will be deemed to take place outside the United States and, therefore, not be subject to the registration requirements of the 1933 Act.

Rule 904 provides a safe harbor for determining when resales by any person other than the issuer, a distributor, or any of their respective affiliates (except any officer or director who is an affiliate solely by virtue of holding such position) will be deemed to occur outside the United States. To fall within the Rule 904 safe harbor, the offer or sale must take place in an "offshore transaction," and "no directed selling efforts" may be made in the United States. Special additional conditions apply to resales by dealers, persons receiving selling commissions, and certain affiliates (any officer or director of the issuer who is an affiliate of the issuer solely by virtue of holding such position). Each one of these terms is defined in Rule 902. An accurate summary of them would be almost as long as the regulation itself.

This exemption is useful for U.S. issuers with employees outside the United States and for foreign private issuers with employees in the United States. If the foreign private issuer is registered under the 1934 Act, then Form S-8 is available, and there is no need to look to Regulation S; however, if the foreign private issuer is not registered under the 1934 Act, then it will need to use Rule 701 or Regulation D to make offers and sales to its U.S. employees. Those exemptions will result in the purchase of restricted securities that cannot be sold in the United States without further exemptions. In addition, there is probably no trading market in the United States for such securities. To cover that situation, Rule 904 of Regulation S will allow for sales outside the United States without having to comply with any other U.S. exemptions. For further discussion of Regulation S, see SEC Release No. 33-7505.

2.6   The Sarbanes-Oxley Act of 2002: Impact on Executive Compensation Plans

The Sarbanes-Oxley Act of 2002 (the "Sarbanes-Oxley Act") made far-reaching changes in federal regulation applicable to corporate America and its executives, auditors, and advisers. In addition to corporate governance and accounting reforms, the Sarbanes-Oxley Act made several changes that immediately affected many executive compensation arrangements (including stock benefit plans) and their administration, including the following:

- Prohibition on personal loans to directors and executive officers
- Accelerated Section 16 filing deadlines
- Forfeiture of executive pay due to accounting restatements
- Restrictions on stock transactions during retirement plan closed trading windows

2.6.1 Prohibition on Personal Loans to Directors and Executive Officers

Section 402 of the Sarbanes-Oxley Act amended Section 13 of the 1934 Act to prohibit publicly held U.S. and non-U.S. companies from making or extending personal loans to directors and executive officers.

General Loan Prohibition Under Section 402. Section 402 states that "[i]t shall be unlawful for any issuer (as defined in Section 2 of the Sarbanes-Oxley Act), directly or indirectly, including through any subsidiary, to extend or maintain credit, to arrange for the extension of credit, or to renew an extension of credit, in the form of a personal loan to or for any director or executive officer (or equivalent thereof) of that issuer." As a result, issuers are prohibited from extending a personal loan in any manner to a director or executive officer. The breadth of the personal loan prohibition has led public companies to avoid transactions that may be considered extensions of credit to directors and executive officers.

Cashless Stock Option Exercises Under Section 402. The loan prohibition under Section 402 has led to the common practice of "broker-assisted" cashless exercises of stock options. In a "broker-assisted" cashless exercise, the option holder instructs a brokerage firm to sell a sufficient number of the shares being acquired by the option exercise to satisfy the option exercise price and any applicable withholding taxes. The broker sells the shares and remits the exercise price and any taxes required to be withheld to the company, with any balance remitted to the option holder. The company delivers the requisite number of shares to the broker and the balance to the option holder.

2.6.2 Accelerated Section 16 Filing Deadlines

General. As a result of the Sarbanes-Oxley Act, all transactions by an issuer's directors and executive officers that are reportable on a Form 4 must be reported to the SEC no later than 10 p.m. Eastern time on the second business day following the transaction date. Under the prior rules, transactions only needed to be reported monthly and filings could have been made in paper form.

Recommendations. The following recommendations should be considered in order to comply with the Section 16 reporting requirements:

- Have a mandatory pre-clearance policy for all transactions as to which the timing is within the control of the Section 16 reporting person. Appendix A provides a suggested form of such pre-clearance policy.

- For transactions as to which timing is outside the control of the Section 16 reporting person, require brokerage firms conducting transactions for the Section 16 reporting person to provide promptly upon trade execution, and certainly by the third business day, the information needed for Section 16(a) reporting purposes to the Section 16 reporting person either electronically or by telephone.

- Review and update the procedures for discretionary transactions under benefit plans to ensure that the Section 16 reporting person receives timely notification (no later than three business days) of execution of the transaction from the plan administrator.

- Educate all Section 16 reporting persons by a memorandum that they should read, sign, and return.

- Establish a cashless exercise policy for Section 16 reporting persons in which the Section 16 reporting person obtains any credit extension from the broker or other third party of his or her choice and (not the issuer) and results in the issuer being paid the exercise price on the day of exercise.

- Obtain powers of attorney with multiple attorneys-in-fact from all Section 16 reporting persons.

- Apply for EDGAR access codes for all Section 16 reporting persons. Section 16 reporting persons can obtain a Form ID for obtaining EDGAR access codes from the SEC.

2.6.3 Clawback of Executive Compensation

Section 304 of the Sarbanes-Oxley Act requires forfeiture of certain bonuses and profits realized by the CEO and CFO of a company that is required to prepare an accounting restatement due to the company's "material noncompliance, as a result of misconduct, with any financial reporting requirement under the securities laws." Specifically, the CEO and CFO must reimburse to the company any bonus or other incentive or equity-based compensation received, and any profit realized from the sale of the company's stock sold, during a specified recapture period. Reimbursement is required whether or not the CEO or CFO engaged in or knew of the misconduct. The "recapture period" is the 12-month period following "the first public issuance or filing with the SEC (whichever first occurs) of the financial document embodying such financial reporting requirement."

In July 2015, the SEC proposed rules under the Dodd-Frank Wall Street Reform and Consumer Protection Act of 2010 directing national securities exchanges (including NYSE and Nasdaq) to establish listing standards that require executive officers of public companies to pay back incentive-based compensation that they were awarded erroneously. The comment period for the proposed rules was reopened in October 2021 and again in June 2022. In October 2022, the SEC adopted its final clawback rules. Under new Rule 10D-1, public companies will be required to develop and enforce recovery policies that, in the event of an accounting restatement, "claw back" from current and former executive officers incentive-based compensation they would not have received based on the restatement. Recovery will be required without regard to fault. The new rules will also require disclosure of public companies' recovery policies, and their actions under those policies.

Under the new rules, the listing standards will apply to incentive-based compensation that is tied to accounting-related metrics, stock price, or total shareholder return. Recovery will apply to excess incentive-based compensation received by executive officers in the three fiscal years preceding the date that the company is required to prepare an accounting restatement.

Each public company will be required to file its recovery policy as an exhibit to its 10-K. In addition, a public company will be required to disclose its actions to recover in its 10-K and any proxy statement that requires executive compensation disclosure if, during its last fiscal year, a restatement requiring recovery of excess incentive-based compensation was completed, or there was an outstanding balance of excess incentive-based compensation from a prior restatement.

Although, as of the time of this writing, the NYSE and Nasdaq have not yet adopted the listing standards required under the new rules, many public companies have begun to review their existing clawback policies to evaluate the changes that will be required once the exchange listing standards are adopted.

2.6.4   Insider Trades During Pension Fund Closed Trading Windows

Section 306(a) of the Sarbanes-Oxley Act makes it unlawful for any director or executive officer of an issuer of any equity security (other than an exempted security), directly or indirectly, to purchase, sell, or otherwise acquire or transfer any equity security of the issuer (other than an exempted security) during any pension plan closed trading window ("blackout period") with respect to such equity security, if the director or executive officer acquires the equity security in connection with his or her service or employment as a director or executive officer. This provision equalizes the treatment of corporate executives and rank-and-file employees with respect to their ability to engage in transactions involving issuer equity securities during a pension plan closed trading window if the securities were acquired in connection with their service to, or employment with, the issuer.

Regulation BTR (Blackout Trading Restriction), originally adopted to clarify the scope and operation of Section 306(a) of the Sarbanes-Oxley Act and to prevent evasion of the statutory trading restriction, defines terms used in Section 306(a), including the term "acquired in connection with service or employment as a director or executive officer." Under this definition as originally adopted, one of the specified methods by which a director or executive officer directly or indirectly acquires equity securities in connection with such service is an acquisition "at a time when he or she was a director or executive officer, as a result of any transaction or business relationship described in paragraph (a) of Item 404 of Regulation S-K."

2.7 Schedule 13D and Schedule 13G

Beneficial owners of more than 5% of any registered class of a public company's shares are subject to special reporting and disclosure requirements under regulations commonly referred to as the Williams Act. Such owners are required to make certain disclosures by filing with the SEC either a Schedule 13D or Schedule 13G. These disclosures are designed to ensure that market-sensitive information concerning an issuer's significant shareholders is promptly made available to the issuer and the public. The test of beneficial ownership for purposes of the Williams Act is different from the test of beneficial ownership for purposes of reporting and liability under Section 16 of the Exchange Act in that pecuniary interest is not a factor in the determination of beneficial ownership for purposes of the Williams Act. Beneficial ownership for purposes of the Williams Act is based on Section 13(d) of the 1934 Act and the related rules, which provide that a person beneficially owns those securities as to which that person has or shares voting or investment power, including with respect to securities such person has a right to acquire within 60 days. "Investment power" is defined in those rules as "the power to dispose [of] or to direct the disposition of such security." Under these principles, the shares of common stock underlying a performance share award are not beneficially owned until the performance condition is satisfied and the shares are actually delivered since, until such time, the recipient of the award does not have voting or investment power with respect to the underlying shares. Beneficial ownership may be acquired either individually or as a group. If two or more persons agree to act together to acquire or vote shares, a group is considered to have acquired the shares of each member of the group as of the date of that agreement. The share ownership of group members is aggregated in applying the test of beneficial ownership under the Williams Act. In such circumstances, each member of the group must file either a Schedule 13D or Schedule 13G or the group members may agree to file one such form on behalf of the group.

While both Schedule 13D and Schedule 13G require disclosure of the identity and background of the reporting person or group, the class of equity securities and beneficial ownership, the disclosures required under the short-form Schedule 13G are less extensive than those required under Schedule 13D. Schedule 13D requires certain additional information concerning the source and amount of funds used to acquire the securities, the purpose for which the securities were acquired, and any agreements between the person making the filing and the issuer or otherwise relating to the shares owned. Whether a Schedule 13D or Schedule 13G is required depends upon such factors as the nature of the investor (i.e., individual or institutional investor), the intent of the investor (i.e., active or passive investor) and the nature of the transaction. Generally, a passive investor (an investor that has not acquired the securities with the purpose of changing or influencing control of the company) owning 20% or less of the issuer's common stock and who has no intent to acquire or influence control of the issuer may use the abbreviated Schedule 13G. Depending on future circumstances, such as a change from passive investment intent to active, an investor may lose Schedule 13G eligibility, and a Schedule 13D would be required.

A Schedule 13D must be filed with the SEC and sent to the issuer within 10 days of a triggering acquisition. Amendments must be filed to reflect changes in beneficial ownership of 1% or more or other material changes in previously reported facts. A Schedule 13G must be filed within 45 days after the end of the calendar year in which a report on Schedule 13D would have been required. Amendments to Schedule 13G must be filed by February 14th of each succeeding year to reflect any changes as of the most recent year end, subject to certain exceptions that may require earlier filing. Shareholders who file Schedule 13Ds or Schedule 13Gs and who are not also directors or officers will typically handle their own filings.

2.8   Conclusion

As reflected by the above discussion, the federal securities laws issues attributable to an equity compensation plan are numerous and complex. Many times, compliance problems are attributable to a failure by the issuing corporation to either (1) adequately communicate the various securities law reporting and trading restrictions governing the purchase and sale of employer securities by its directors and officers or (2) provide sufficient support to enable such persons to comply with these rules. Companies offering stock options and other equity compensation, particularly public companies, are well advised to provide directors and officers with a summary description of the relevant securities laws and to establish a program for assisting directors and officers in complying with these laws. Along these lines, most companies establish (1) a "code of business conduct" prohibiting insider trading by their employees and establishing closed trading windows during which company stock may not be traded by officers, directors, and other reporting persons possessing material information about the company and (2) a preclearance policy.

To avoid noncompliance problems, broad assistance should be provided to directors and officers to make sure they understand and comply with trading and reporting restrictions.

APPENDIX A

Section 16 Mandatory Pre-clearance Policy

(As Authorized by the Board of Directors of the Company)

To: Section 16 Insiders (all directors and executive officers)

The Sarbanes-Oxley Act amended Section 16(a) of the Securities Exchange Act of 1934 to accelerate the reporting by Section 16 Insiders of all transactions involving the Company's stock. Section 16 Insiders are required to report changes in beneficial ownership involving the Company's stock within two business days of the transaction. Failure to file on a timely basis will result in the person being named as a delinquent filer in the Company's proxy statement. Repeated failure to file on a timely basis can result in civil actions against the individual by the SEC, which has the power to seek fines for delinquent filings and bring injunctive actions against delinquent filers. Under the Securities Enforcement Remedies and Penny Stock Reform Act of 1990, the SEC is also empowered to seek removal of an officer or director from office and to ban such persons from future service as an officer or director of a public company.

The Board of Directors believes that the only way to assure timely compliance is to impose a mandatory pre-clearance policy for all transactions by Section 16 Insiders and members of their immediate family involving the Company's stock. Transactions covered by this policy include, without limitation, stock option grants and option exercises, stock awards and stock equivalent awards, purchases and sales publicly or privately, gifts, and transfers in or out of trusts or limited partnerships or any other estate planning devices.

Accordingly, all Section 16 Insiders and members of their immediate family may not engage in any transactions involving the Company's stock without first notifying the Vice President-Chief Financial Officer *and* the [Vice President-General Counsel and Secretary]. This notice must be given in writing to the designated persons at least three business days before the proposed transaction. Failure to comply with this Policy will result at a minimum in embarrassment to the Company and the Section 16 Insider. It also can expose the Section 16 Insider to the civil actions and penalties discussed above.

If you have any questions about the pre-clearance policy, please contact the [Vice President-General Counsel and Secretary].

APPENDIX B-1

Memorandum to Company Regarding Continuing Reporting Obligations with Respect to a Departing Officer or Director of the Company

MEMORANDUM

Confidential

Attorney-Client Privilege

Date:

To:

cc:

From:

Re: Continuing Reporting Obligations Applicable to a Departing Executive Officer or Director of the Company

This Memorandum discusses the continuing reporting obligations and transaction restrictions after an executive officer or director of the company ("Section 16 Reporting Person") ceases to be a Section 16 Reporting Person by resigning as an executive officer or director of the company.

Attached is a sample memorandum for departing Section 16 Reporting Persons [appendix B-2]. This memorandum can be used to cover Section 16 reporting obligations as well as insider trading restrictions under Rule 10b-5.

Section 16 Reporting Obligations

A Section 16 Reporting Person has an obligation to file Section 16 reports (Form 4s) for six months after that person's status as a Section 16 Reporting Person is terminated, but only with respect to nonexempt transactions that are matchable with nonexempt transactions that occurred while the person was a Section 16 Reporting Person. For example, if a Section 16 Reporting Person had an open market purchase three months prior to his or her termination of Section 16 reporting status, that person would have to report all open market sales for the three months following his or her termination, and the purchases and sales would be matchable for Section 16(b) purposes.

Option exercises, vesting of restricted stock, and gifts are all examples of exempt transactions that would not have to be reported. To carry this example further, if the option exercise was done by the delivery to the company of previously owned company shares, that transaction would likewise be exempt and not reportable. The same would be true if shares were delivered to the company to pay taxes. If, however, the departing Section 16 Reporting Person uses a cashless exercise method (sale of stock by a broker to pay the exercise price), the sale is not exempt and must be reported and potentially matched if there were opposite-way purchases within the same six-month period while the person was a Section 16 Reporting Person. [Finally, we understand that the company's 401(k) plan has a company stock fund. The transfer out of that fund after termination of Section 16 reporting status is reportable only if there has been a transfer into the stock fund within six months while the person had Section 16 reporting obligations. This is considered a "discretionary transaction" and involves very arcane concepts. As a general rule, a departed Section 16 Reporting Person should pre-clear all discretionary transactions with the General Counsel's Office before they are entered into.]

In addition, if the Section 16 Reporting Person has had a transaction while he or she was a Section 16 Reporting Person that was deferred until the Form 5 was due (such as a gift), that transaction should be reported either on a voluntary Form 4 or a mandatory Form 5 within 45 days of the end of the company's fiscal year. We recommend reporting it on a voluntary Form 4 to get it out of the way. We understand that is the company's present policy.

Rule 10b-5 Insider Trading Restrictions

In addition to Section 16, the departing Section 16 Reporting Person has to be guided by the company's insider trading policy for some period of time after cessation of Section 16 reporting status to allow his or her knowledge about the company with respect to non-public material information to go stale. As a guideline, we recommend that the former Section 16 Reporting Person follow the company's insider trading policies for at least three months after termination of Section 16 reporting status. After that, it is highly likely that the Section 16 Reporting Person's knowledge would be stale. Note that the departing Section 16 Reporting Person can remain employed beyond the date of his or her termination of Section 16 reporting status. As long as the former Section 16 Reporting Person is not performing activities that would cause him or her to continue to be a Section 16 Reporting Person, the three-month period should run from his or her termination of Section 16 reporting status.

Rule 144

It is our understanding that no person at the company has restricted securities within the meaning of SEC Rule 144. By "restricted" we mean securities that have been obtained from the issuer not in a registered public offering. If you wish more information on restricted securities and control securities, involving Rule 144, we will be glad to give you a more detailed analysis. Attached for your reference is a brief outline of Rule 144 requirements [appendix B-3].

Proxy Statement Disclosure

Regulation S-K Item 405 would still apply to the departing Section 16 Reporting Person and would require disclosure in the proxy statement of any delinquencies in that person's filings.

Any special compensation arrangements for a departing Section 16 Reporting Person may have to be disclosed in the company's proxy statement for the ensuing year, depending on whether that person fits the definition of "named executive officer" in S-K Item 402.

APPENDIX B-2

Exit Memorandum

MEMORANDUM

[DATE]

TO: [Name of Departing Section 16 Reporting Person]

FROM: [Name of Section 16 Compliance Person]

RE: Continuing Reporting Obligations and Transaction Restrictions Applicable to a Departing Executive Officer or Director of the Company

With respect to your recent resignation as a[n] [executive officer/director], I am writing to remind you that any person who ceases to be an executive officer or director of the company continues to have certain obligations under the federal securities laws as follows:

Rule 10b-5 Trading Restrictions. Rule 10b-5 states that you may not buy or sell securities of the company on the basis of material non-public information obtained from the company or any party associated with the company. In addition, you may not furnish material non-public information about the company to any person who might trade on the information. We suggest that you follow these rules and the company's insider trading policy for three months from the termination of your [executive officer/director status].

Short-Swing Profit Rule Applies up to Six Months After Termination. Section 16(b) provides for the disgorgement of profits on any sale and purchase of company common stock within a six-month period. It continues to apply to open market purchases or sales that occur within less than six months of an opposite-way, open market purchase or sale that took place while you were subject to Section 16.

For example, if you bought stock in the open market three months before you terminated your status as a Section 16 Reporting Person, any open market sales you make for three months after you have terminated your status will be reportable on a Form 4 within two business days and potentially matchable with the purchase you made while you were a Section 16 Reporting Person. Stock option exercises, however, are treated as exempt purchases and need not be reported regardless of the transactions that occurred while you were a Section 16 Reporting Person. This is equally true with respect to the delivery of previously owned shares to pay the exercise price or to pay taxes on the vesting of restricted stock. However, a cashless exercise in which you sell stock in the open market to pay the exercise price is reportable and matchable if you have had an open market purchase within six months while you were a Section 16 Reporting Person. [With respect to any proposed transactions involving the company's common stock in the company's 401(k) plan, you should consult with me or an attorney in my office before changing your investments in the company stock fund. Any other transactions involving the 401(k) plan need not be pre-cleared.]

Form 4. You must file a Form 4 to report any open market purchases or sales in company stock after you cease to be a Section 16 Reporting Person that occurs within six months of any opposite-way, open market purchase or sale that took place while you were a Section 16 Reporting Person. Form 4 must be filed with the SEC by the second business day after the date of execution of the transaction. Please notify us so we may do the filing for you.

Form 5. You must file a Form 5 [within 45 days after the issuer's fiscal year-end] to report any pre-resignation transactions and any reportable post-resignation transactions not previously reported on Form 4. For example, a gift made while you were a Section 16 Reporting Person and not reported on a voluntary Form 4 needs to be filed on a voluntary Form 4 or mandatory Form 5. (It is the company's policy to report all gifts on a voluntary Form 4, so this should not be a problem unless we were not told of the gift.) If you have no transactions requiring a Form 5, we may ask you to so certify to the company in writing prior to the printing of the company's proxy statement to avoid being named in the company's proxy statement for failing to file a Form 5.

Exit Box. On each Form 4 or Form 5 you file after your resignation, the "exit" box in the upper left hand corner of the form should be checked.

SEC Enforcement. There may be significant civil and criminal penalties if you fail to comply with the above requirements.

Because the Section 16 reporting requirements are extremely complex, the company recommends that you consult with [Section 16 compliance person], when preparing any Form 4 or Form 5, or if you have any questions regarding the reporting requirements.

Rule 144. [Our records indicate that you do not have any restricted securities.] If you have "restricted" securities, they need to be sold under Rule 144 for at least three months after your cessation of Section 16 status, provided that you have held the restricted securities for at least six months. After three months (and after satisfying the six-month holding period), you may sell the securities free of any Rule 144 restrictions.

APPENDIX B-3
Summary of Rule 144 Under Current Rules

Rule 144 is a safe harbor exemption for sales of restricted securities and control stock. Restricted securities are shares acquired from the issuer without registration of those shares. Control stock means stock held by an affiliate regardless of source, i.e., bought from the issuer or in the open market. The requirements for sale under Rule 144 are:

1. Current public information about the company must be available.
    Affiliates: Always applies
    Nonaffiliates: Stock held for less than one year

2. If the shares are restricted securities, they must be held for six months before sale; unrestricted control stock does not have to be held for any period.

3. The amount to be sold during any three-month period is limited to the greater of (1) one percent of the total number of outstanding shares, or (2) the average weekly trading volume for the four calendar weeks preceding the filing of Form 144 *(applies only to affiliates)*.

4. The stock must be sold in unsolicited brokers' transactions (any responsible broker will know how to do a 144 transaction) - *applies only to affiliates*.

5. Form 144 must be filed with the SEC before the sale occurs if greater than 5,000 shares or $50,000 *(applies only to affiliates)*.

Notes:

Rule 144(b)(1) (previously, Rule 144(k)) permits sales of restricted securities free from the requirements of Rule 144 by persons who have been nonaffiliates for at least three months after a one-year holding period.

If the reporting person is an affiliate, sales must be reported on SEC Form 4 no later than the second business day following the sale and are matchable against any nonexempt purchases made by the reporting person six months before or after the sale.

APPENDIX B-4
Rule 144

Topic	Current Rule 144
Resales of Restricted Securities by Nonaffiliates Under Rule 144	–Unlimited resales after holding restricted securities of Exchange Act reporting companies for six months if they have not been affiliates during the prior three months, except that such resales would be subject to the current public information requirement between the end of the six-month holding period and one year after the acquisition date of the securities. –Unlimited resales after holding restricted securities of non-reporting companies for one year if they have not been affiliates during the prior three months. –Specific provision tolling the holding period when engaged in certain hedging transactions. Maximum one-year holding period.
Resales by Affiliates Under Rule 144	–Limited resales after holding restricted securities of Exchange Act reporting companies for six months. –Limited resales after holding restricted securities of non-reporting companies for one year. –Specific provision tolling the holding period when engaged in certain hedging transactions. Maximum one-year holding period.
Manner of Sale Restrictions	–Would not apply to resale of debt securities by affiliates or to any resale by nonaffiliates.
Form 144	–With respect to affiliates, filing threshold at 5,000 shares or $50,000. –No Form 144 filing required for nonaffiliates.

APPENDIX B-5
SEC Summary of Rule 144 from Final Release

The final conditions applicable to the resale under Rule 144 of restricted securities held by affiliates and nonaffiliates of the issuer have been summarized by the SEC in Release 33-8869 as follows:

	Affiliate or Person Selling on Behalf of an Affiliate	Nonaffiliate (and Has Not Been an Affiliate During the Prior Three Months)
Restricted Securities of Reporting Issuers	*During six-month holding period*—no resales under Rule 144 permitted. *After six-month holding period*—may resell in accordance with all Rule 144 requirements, including: • Current public information, • Volume limitations, • Manner of sale requirements for equity securities, and • Filing of Form 144.	*During six-month holding period*—no resales under Rule 144 permitted. *After six-month holding period but before one year*—unlimited public resales under Rule 144 except that the current public information requirement still applies. *After one-year holding period*—unlimited public resales under Rule 144; need not comply with any other Rule 144 requirements.
Restricted Securities of Non-reporting Issuers	*During one-year holding period*—no resales under Rule 144 permitted. *After one-year holding period*—may resell in accordance with all Rule 144 requirements, including: • Current public information, • Volume limitations, • Manner of sale requirements for equity securities, and • Filing of Form 144.	*During one-year holding period*—no resales under Rule 144 permitted. *After one-year holding period*—unlimited public resales under Rule 144; need not comply with any other Rule 144 requirements.

APPENDIX C

Reporting Procedures for Common Stock Plan Transactions

The table below describes the reporting requirements for common stock plan transactions. All transactions except open-market sales via a broker are assumed to be exempt from the short-swing profits recovery provisions of Section 16(b). All transactions that are reportable must be reported on a Form 4 within two business days.

TRANSACTION	REPORTING PROCEDURES
Stock Options and SARs	
Grant of stock option or SAR	Stock options and SARs are reported as an acquisition of a derivative security.
Vesting of stock option or SAR	Because stock options and SARS are considered to be acquired at the time of grant, vesting of options and SARs is generally considered a non-event for Section 16 purposes and, as such, is not reportable.
Cash exercise of stock option	The SEC views the exercise of a stock option as two transactions: the first transaction closes out the option position, and the second transaction is the acquisition of the common stock underlying the option. Thus, an exercise is reported as two transactions: 1. Disposition of derivative security (to close out the option position). 2. Acquisition of common stock.
Broker-assisted cashless exercise of stock option or SAR	A broker-assisted cashless exercise involves the same two transactions as a cash exercise, but also involves a third transaction, which is the disposition on the open market of the common stock acquired upon exercise.
Stock-for-stock exercise	A stock-for-stock exercise involves the same two transactions as a cash exercise, but also involves a third transaction, which is a disposition representing the tender of shares to the company to cover the option exercise price (and shares tendered or withheld to cover taxes, if applicable).

TRANSACTION	REPORTING PROCEDURES
Net exercise	The SEC views a net exercise as the acquisition of the full number of shares underlying the option and a disposition of the shares withheld by the company to cover the option exercise price and/or taxes. Thus, a net exercise is reported in three transactions: 1. Disposition of derivative security for the full number of shares exercised (to close out the option position). 2. Acquisition of common stock for the full number of shares exercised. 3. Disposition of common stock for the shares withheld to cover option exercise price (and shares withheld to cover taxes, if applicable).
Exercise of an SAR settled in cash	The SEC views the exercise of a cash-settled SAR as an acquisition of the full number of shares underlying the SAR and the liquidation of the shares for cash in a disposition to the company. Thus, the exercise is reported in three transactions: 1. Disposition of derivative security for the full number of shares exercised (to close out the SAR position). 2. Acquisition of common stock for the full number of shares exercised. 3. Disposition of the full number of shares of common stock acquired upon exercise (to report the liquidation of the shares for cash).
Exercise of an SAR settled in stock	The exercise of a stock-settled SAR is reported in the same manner as the exercise of a cash-settled SAR, except that the number of shares in the third transaction are just those sufficient to cover the price of the SAR (and taxes due, if applicable).
Expiration or forfeiture of stock option	Expiration or forfeiture of a stock option for no consideration is not reportable.
Cancellation of an option for cash or other compensation	Cancellation of an option for cash or other compensation is viewed as a sale of the option back to the company. It is reported as a disposition of a derivative security.

TRANSACTION	REPORTING PROCEDURES
Repricing of a stock option or SAR	A repricing is treated as a cancellation of the original option or SAR in exchange for the grant of a new option/SAR. It is reported in two transactions: 1. Disposition of a derivative security (to report the cancellation of the original option/SAR). 2. Acquisition of a derivative security (to report the grant of the new option/SAR).
Restricted Stock (Time-Based)	
Grant of restricted stock	The grant of restricted stock is reported as an acquisition of common stock. If desired, note in a footnote that the acquired shares are non-transferable and subject to forfeiture until vested.
Vesting of restricted stock	Because restricted stock is considered to be acquired at the time of grant, vesting of restricted stock is generally considered a non-event for Section 16 purposes and, as such, is not reportable.
Withholding of stock to pay taxes	Withholding of shares to cover the tax payments due at vest is reported as a disposition of common stock.
Forfeiture of restricted stock	Report as a disposition of common stock. Note, however, that forfeitures that occur after an individual is no longer considered an insider are not reportable.
Restricted Stock Units/Phantom Stock (Time-Based)	
Grant of restricted stock unit/phantom stock payable only in stock	For Section 16 purposes, restricted stock units and phantom stock payable in stock on a one-for-one basis are considered to be the economic equivalent of restricted stock, and as such, can be reported in the same manner (i.e., as an acquisition of common stock at grant). Alternatively, the grant of an RSU or phantom stock can be reported as an acquisition of a derivative security. (Note that a provision on the award that allows for payout in cash in the event of a change in control does not prohibit reporting the award in the same manner as a grant of restricted stock.)
Vesting of restricted stock unit/phantom stock payable only in stock	Because the award is considered acquired at grant, vesting of awards of RSUs or phantom stock is generally considered a non-event and is not reportable (unless the grant was reported as an acquisition of a derivative security, in which case the vesting will need to be reported).

TRANSACTION	REPORTING PROCEDURES
Payout of restricted stock unit/phantom stock payable only in stock	The reporting procedures for the payout of RSUs and phantom stock payable only in stock will vary based on how the original grant was reported. Where the original grant was reported as an acquisition of common stock, it is not necessary to report the payout event. Where the original grant was reported as an acquisition of a derivative security, it is necessary at payout to report the closing out of the derivative position and the acquisition of common stock. This is reported in two transactions: 1. Disposition of the derivative security (to close out this position). 2. Acquisition of common stock.
Grant of restricted stock unit/phantom stock payable in either stock or cash or cash only	The grant of RSUs or phantom stock that can or must be settled in cash is reported as the acquisition of a derivative security.
Vesting of restricted stock unit/phantom stock payable in either stock or cash or cash only	Because the award is considered acquired at grant, vesting of awards of RSUs or phantom stock is generally considered a non-event and is not reportable.
Payout in cash of restricted stock unit/phantom stock payable in either stock or cash	Where RSUs and phantom stock that are payable in either cash or stock are paid out in stock, the payout is viewed as two transactions: the first transaction closes out the derivative position, and the second transaction is the acquisition of the common stock underlying the award. Thus, the payout is reported as two transactions: 1. Disposition of derivative security (to close out the derivative position). 2. Acquisition of common stock. Note that where shares will be withheld to cover the taxes due at payout, the acquisition should be for the full number of shares paid out, and a third transaction, for the disposition of the shares withheld, is reported.

TRANSACTION	REPORTING PROCEDURES
Payout of restricted stock unit/phantom stock in cash	The SEC views the payout of RSUs and phantom stock in cash as the acquisition of the full number of shares underlying the award and the simultaneous liquidation of these shares in a disposition to the company. Thus, the payout is reported in the following three transactions: 1. Disposition of derivative security for the full number of shares exercised (to close out the derivative position). 2. Acquisition of common stock for the full number of shares underlying the payout. 3. Disposition of the full number of shares of common stock acquired as a result of the payout (to report the liquidation of the shares for cash).
Withholding of stock to pay taxes	Withholding of shares to cover the tax payments due at payout is reported as a disposition of common stock.
Forfeiture of restricted stock unit/phantom stock (regardless of payment method)	Forfeitures of RSUs and phantom stock are generally not reported, regardless of payout method and regardless of how the grant was originally reported.

Performance Awards (Vesting Contingent on Targets Other than Stock Price)	
Grant of performance award	Where vesting of a performance award is contingent on goals other than the targets tied to the company's stock price, the grant is considered a non-event and is not reportable. For purposes of Section 16, the award is not considered acquired until vested. Note: • In contrast to the accounting treatment of TSR awards, for Section 16 purposes, absolute TSR is considered to be the equivalent of a stock price target only if the company does not pay dividends or pays only a de minimis dividend. Relative TSR is never considered the equivalent of a stock price target for Section 16 purposes because it encompasses the stock price of the company's peers as well as the company's own stock price. • Where vesting is contingent on multiple metrics, including both a stock price target and targets that are not tied to stock price, the award is treated as an award in which vesting is contingent on targets other than stock price.

TRANSACTION	REPORTING PROCEDURES
Vesting of performance award	Where vesting of a performance award is contingent on goals other than the targets tied to the company's stock price, the vesting event is considered to be the acquisition of the award. Assuming the award is paid out at that time, the vesting event is reported as an acquisition of common stock.
	If the award is paid out in cash, a second transaction, in the form of a disposition of the common stock acquired as a result of the payout, is reported to reflect the liquidation of the stock for cash.
	If the award is paid out in stock but shares are withheld to cover the taxes due at payout, a second transaction, for the disposition of the shares withheld, is reported.
	If the award is not paid out at vesting, the vesting event is reported as the acquisition of a derivative security. The eventual payout will be reported in the same manner as the payout of an RSU that is payable in cash or stock. Alternatively, where the award is payable in stock only on a one-for-one basis, the vesting event can be reported merely as an acquisition of common stock. Where this approach is used, it is not necessary to report the eventual payout.
Forfeiture of award	Because a performance award contingent on goals other than the targets tied to the company's stock price is not reported until vested, it is not necessary to report forfeitures prior to vesting.

Performance Awards (Vesting Contingent on Stock Price Targets)

Grant of performance award	Grant of an award that is contingent solely on stock price targets is reported as an acquisition of a derivative security.
	The SEC has not addressed the question of whether the reported acquisition should be for the maximum number of shares payable under the award or the target number of shares. As a conservative approach, we recommend reporting the maximum shares.
Vesting of performance award	Because an award that is contingent solely on stock price targets is considered acquired at the time of grant, no further reporting is required to reflect the vesting event.
Forfeiture of performance award	Forfeiture of a performance award that is contingent solely on stock price targets is not reportable.

TRANSACTION	REPORTING PROCEDURES
Payout of performance award	Payout of a performance award that is contingent solely on stock price targets is viewed as two transactions: the first transaction closes out the derivative position, and the second transaction is the acquisition of the common stock underlying the award. Thus, the payout is reported as two transactions: 1. Disposition of derivative security (to close out the derivative position). 2. Acquisition of common stock. If the award is paid out in cash, a third transaction, in the form of a disposition of the common stock acquired as a result of the payout, is reported to reflect the liquidation of the stock for cash. If the award is paid out in stock but shares are withheld to cover the taxes due at payout, a third transaction, for the disposition of the shares withheld, is reported.

CHAPTER

3

State Securities Law Considerations for Equity Compensation Plans

Joseph Phelps

CONTENTS

The term "blue sky laws" refers to state statutes that prescribe the methods by which stock and other securities may be sold or offered for sale within a state. They are known as "blue sky" laws

Portions of this chapter were originally written by Matthew Topham, Rumei Mistry, Gene Hwang, and Kristy Harlan.

because many of the business deals that these laws were intended to address were so questionable they had no more substance to them than "air" or "blue sky."[1] As with the federal securities laws, these statutes generally prohibit companies and shareholders from selling (or offering to sell) securities unless the sale is registered with the state's securities commission or fits into one of the exemptions from registration provided by the state's blue sky laws. In most states, these exemptions parallel or complement many of the federal exemptions.[2] However,

---

1. See, e.g., *Hall v. Geiger-Jones Co.*, 242 U.S. 539, 550, 37 S. Ct. 217, 220–21, 61 L. Ed. 480, 489 (1917) ("The name that is given to the law indicates the evil at which it is aimed—that is, to use the language of a cited case, 'speculative schemes which have no more basis than so many feet of blue sky;' or, as stated by counsel in another case, 'to stop the sale of stock in fly-by-night concerns, visionary oil wells, distant gold mines, and other like fraudulent exploitations.'"). See also Paul G. Mahoney, "The Origins of the Blue Sky Laws: A Test of Competing Hypotheses," University of Virginia School of Law, December 2001.

2. It is important to note that certain employee benefit plan securities, which are exempted from federal registration requirements by § 3(a)(2) of the Securities Act of 1933, are also preempted from state regulation (except for enforcement actions with respect to fraud), under the National Securities Markets Improvement Act of 1996, Pub. L. No. 104-290, 110 Stat. 3416 (1996). Section 3(a)(2) exempts, among other things:

   any interest or participation in a single trust fund, or in a collective trust fund maintained by a bank, or any security arising out of a contract issued by an insurance company, which interest, participation, or security is issued in connection with (A) a stock bonus, pension, or profit-sharing plan which meets the requirements for qualification under section 401 of Title 26, (B) an annuity plan which meets the requirements for the deduction of the employer's contributions under section 404(a)(2) of Title 26, (C) a governmental plan as defined in section 414(d) of Title 26 which has been established by an employer for the exclusive benefit of its employees or their beneficiaries for the purpose of distributing to such employees or their beneficiaries the corpus and income of the funds accumulated under such plan, if under such plan it is impossible, prior to the satisfaction of all liabilities with respect to such employees and their beneficiaries, for any part of the corpus or income to be used for, or diverted to, purposes other than the exclusive benefit of such employees or their beneficiaries, or (D) a church plan, company, or account that is excluded from the definition of an investment company under section 3(c)(14) of the Investment Company Act of 1940 [15 U.S.C.A. § 80a-3(c)(14)], other than any plan described in subparagraph (A), (B), (C), or (D) of this paragraph (i) the contributions under which are held in a single trust fund or in a separate account maintained by an insurance company for a single employer and under which an amount in excess of the employer's contribution is allocated to the purchase of securities (other than interests or

this chapter does not discuss exemptions from federal securities laws, which must also be considered before offering or selling securities (see chapter 2 for a discussion of federal securities law issues).

In many cases, in order to qualify for an exemption under state blue sky laws, the issuer must take certain steps before issuing the security. In the case of securities granted or sold pursuant to employee stock option, stock purchase, or other benefit plans, these steps may include filing the relevant plan with the state securities administrator or including specific provisions in the plan. Failure to comply with these steps could render an exemption unavailable and leave the issuer with no alternative but to register the security before it is either offered or sold. Therefore, it is critical for issuers to plan ahead and evaluate possible exemptions from registration, preferably at the time the plan is being drafted and certainly before any securities are issued. To demonstrate how this process might work, this chapter uses a fictitious company, Sample Corporation, to show how blue sky laws apply in several different states.

3.1 Identifying the Relevant Blue Sky Laws and Related Regulations

3.1.1 Determining the Relevant Jurisdiction

The first step in the process of seeking a valid exemption from registration for the grant of a stock option, the issuance of stock upon the exercise of the option, or the sale of stock pursuant to an employee

---

participations in the trust or separate account itself) issued by the employer or any company directly or indirectly controlling, controlled by, or under common control with the employer, (ii) which covers employees some or all of whom are employees within the meaning of section 401(c)(1) of Title 26 (other than a person participating in a church plan who is described in section 414(e)(3)(B) of Title 26), or (iii) which is a plan funded by an annuity contract described in section 403(b) of Title 26 (other than a retirement income account described in section 403(b)(9) of Title 26, to the extent that the interest or participation in such single trust fund or collective trust fund is issued to a church, a convention or association of churches, or an organization described in section 414(e)(3)(A) of Title 26 establishing or maintaining the retirement income account or to a trust established by any such entity in connection with the retirement income account).

This chapter presumes that the securities in question do not fall within the exemption set forth in § 3(a)(2) and are not preempted from state regulation.

stock purchase plan is identifying which blue sky laws apply. Most states require registration of securities that are offered for sale or sold in their jurisdiction. In addition, some blue sky laws treat an offer to sell as occurring in both the place from which the offer originates as well as the place where the employee receives the offer. If the issuer of the securities and employee are located in the same state, then the issuer need only be concerned with the blue sky laws of that one state. If, however, the issuer is located in one jurisdiction and the employee is located in another, then the issuer may be required to comply with the blue sky laws of both jurisdictions.

As a hypothetical example, take Sample Corporation, a Delaware corporation that has its headquarters in Seattle, Washington, and has operations in Washington, Nevada, and Texas. Sample adopted an equity incentive plan that allows for the grant of incentive stock options, nonqualified stock options, restricted stock, and restricted stock units to employees, consultants, and directors. The plan is administered by a committee of Sample's board of directors, which includes Sample's president, who is located in Washington. After awards under the plan have been approved by the committee, Sample's president will either contact the recipient directly to make the offer or will instruct Sample's senior vice president in Nevada or senior vice president in Texas, depending upon which region the person receiving the award will be supporting, to make the offer. Sample would like to hire a software engineer who lives in Palo Alto, California, to support Sample's Nevada operations. The software engineer will telecommute from Palo Alto. After the committee approves a compensation package for the software engineer, Sample's president instructs the senior vice president in Nevada to make the offer. The senior vice president in Nevada calls the California engineer at home and offers her a job with Sample with a compensation package consisting of a salary of $15,000 per month and a stock option to purchase 100,000 shares of Sample common stock at a price of $1 per share subject to time-based vesting. The California employee accepts this offer.

Under the circumstances described in the hypothetical, which state's blue sky law will apply to the offer and issuance of the stock option? To answer this question, it is necessary to analyze where the acts essential to the offer or sale of the stock option took place. Where all acts essential to a sale or transfer of securities take place in one state only, the transaction is governed by the securities laws of that state; however, where the acts are performed in several different states, it is necessary to apply conflict of law principles to determine which state's securities law will control.[3] This analysis must be made on a case-by-case basis and will depend on the specific facts. Where there is some territorial nexus to a securities transaction, laws of two or more states may simultaneously apply without presenting a conflict of laws question.[4] Thus, issuers may be required to comply with the blue sky laws of multiple states in connection with the same transaction.

Companies should be aware that this analysis will often require the company to make a judgment call as to whether the blue sky laws of a specific state apply, particularly if there are some states that have a very limited nexus to the transaction. If after making a thorough analysis, which may include discussing the issue on an anonymous basis with the relevant state securities administrator, reasonable doubt exists as to whether a given state's blue sky laws apply, the author recommends taking a conservative position in favor of compliance with each potentially applicable state's laws. Below is a sample analysis based on the hypothetical facts set forth above. This analysis reflects the author's views, and different practitioners may reach a different conclusion with respect to the applicability of the blue sky laws in one or more of these states.

Four states must be analyzed in connection with the transaction described in the example above: Delaware, Washington, Nevada, and California.

Delaware blue sky law provides that it is unlawful for any person to offer or sell any security in Delaware unless it is registered under the Delaware securities act, the security or transaction is exempted under Section 73-207 of the Delaware securities act, or it is a federal covered security for which a notice filing has been made.[5] In the example, the only nexus between Delaware and the offer of the stock option is the fact that Sample was incorporated in Delaware and that if the stock

---

3. 79A C.J.S. Securities Regulation § 476.

4. See *Barnebey v. E.F. Hutton & Co.,* 715 F. Supp. 1512, 1533-1536 (M.D. Fla. 1989); *Lintz v. Carey Manor Ltd.,* 613 F. Supp. 543, 550 (W.D. Va. 1985).

5. Del. Code Ann. tit. 6, § 73-202.

option is exercised, the underlying stock will be issued under Delaware law. Neither Sample nor the employee is located in Delaware, and none of the communications relating to the transaction occurred or originated in Delaware. As a general rule, a transaction involving corporate stock, such as a sale, issuance, or transfer, is not governed by the securities act of the state where the corporation is organized if the transaction occurs in another state.[6] Here, the transaction occurred outside of Delaware, and the Delaware blue sky law should not apply.

Washington blue sky law provides that it is unlawful for any person to offer or sell any security in Washington unless the security is registered by coordination or qualification under the Washington securities act, the security or transaction is exempted under Wash. Rev. Code Section 21.20.310, .320, or .880, or the security is a federal covered security and, if required, a notice filing is made and fee is paid.[7] An "offer to sell" under the Washington blue sky law includes every attempt or offer to dispose of, or solicitation of an offer to buy, a security or interest in a security for value.[8] Based on the facts in the example, there is a reasonable possibility that the Securities Division of the Washington Department of Financial Institutions would take the position that an offer to sell occurred in Washington because the offer originated in Washington, although the offer was communicated to the employee by the vice president in Nevada and is being made to an employee who will be based in California. There may be some debate as to whether the offer of the stock option in exchange for employment was "for value" for purposes of the Washington blue sky law. Although there is no Washington case law directly on point, there is authority in other jurisdictions that supports the position that when an employee bargains for compensation that includes stock or stock options, the employee has provided value for the securities.[9]

---

6. See *Guynn v. Shulters*, 223 Miss. 232, 78 So. 2d 114, *error overruled*, 223 Miss. 232, 78 So. 2d 793 (1955).

7. Wash. Rev. Code § 21.20.140.

8. Wash. Rev. Code § 21.20.005(14).

9. When an individual "commits herself to employment by a corporation in return for stock or the promise of stock," she will be considered by the court to be an investor worthy of protection under federal securities laws. See *Yoder v. Orthomolecular Nutrition Inst., Inc.*, 751 F.2d 555, 560 (2d Cir. 1985). Where a plaintiff accepted

Even if the stock options were not considered to have been offered for value under Washington law, the offer of the stock option also included the offer to sell the underlying stock at $1 per share, which is probably sufficient to satisfy the requirement that the offer be for value for purposes of Washington blue sky law.[10] It should be noted that it is not certain that the Securities Division of the Washington Department of Financial Institutions would take any enforcement action under the circumstances described in the example because the transaction does not involve an offer to a Washington resident. However, because significant acts relating to the offer of the option

---

employment with an issuer in return for an annual salary of $40,000 plus options to purchase up to 30,000 shares of the issuer's stock, the plaintiff was found to have 'purchased' the options. Id. at 560. Similarly, in *Rudinger v. Insurance Data Processing, Inc.,* the plaintiff bargained for and received an employment contract wherein he was entitled to receive a certain number of stock options in addition to an annual salary of $100,000 and other substantial benefits. 778 F. Supp. 1334, 1338-39 (E.D. Pa. 1991). The court held that "[a]n agreement exchanging a plaintiff's services for a defendant corporation's stock constitutes a 'sale' under the terms of the Securities Exchange Act." Id.; see also *Campbell v. National Media Corp.,* No. 94-4590, 1994 WL 612807 (E.D. Pa. Nov. 3, 1994) (holding that a grant of options to purchase 50,000 shares in an executive's employment agreement was a purchase of securities); *Collins v. Rukin,* 342 F. Supp. 1282, 1289 (D. Mass. 1972) (agreeing with plaintiff's claim that stock options were a "quid pro quo offered to induce plaintiff to enter into the employ of [the issuer]"). In addition, *In re Cendant Corp. Securities Litigation,* 76 F. Supp. 2d 539, 544 (D.N.J. 1999) cited the cases above and stated that "[t]hese cases indicate that where a potential employee acquires the right to options as part of his or her bargained-for compensation, courts will infer that the employees made an intentional decision to 'purchase' the options."

The cases cited above were decided by federal courts and considered issues based on federal securities laws. Therefore, these decisions do not create binding authority in most states. But these cases do indicate that at least some courts treat an agreement to work in exchange for securities as a purchase of such securities for value. Note, however, that under some circumstances courts have held that interests in stock-related benefit plans do not constitute a "security." See, e.g., *Childers v. Northwest Airlines, Inc.,* 688 F. Supp. 1357, 1363 (D. Minn. 1988) (holding that employees' participation in an employee stock ownership plan could not be characterized as a "purchase" of a security since the participating employees did not furnish value). Therefore, the question of whether securities issued in connection with employment have been acquired for value should be considered carefully on a case-by-case basis.

10. Wash. Rev. Code § 21.20.005(14).

occurred in Washington, as a precautionary measure, the author would recommend that Sample comply with Washington blue sky law.

Nevada blue sky law provides that it is unlawful for a person to offer to sell or sell any security in Nevada unless the security is registered or the security or transaction is exempt under the Nevada securities act.[11] The Nevada blue sky law's definition of "offer to sell" is similar to the definition under Washington blue sky law.[12] Based on a strict reading of the statute, the actions of Sample's Nevada vice president could be interpreted to constitute an offer of a security to the California employee. Sample could argue that the Nevada vice president was simply following instructions and did not have the authority to approve or make the offer, which originated in Washington. This is a reasonable argument, and given the limited nexus between Nevada and the transaction, the author believes it is unlikely that the Securities Division of the Office of the Nevada Secretary of State would take the position that Sample is required to comply with Nevada blue sky law in connection with the offer. However, Sample must accept that there is a risk that the Securities Division could take that position; therefore, Sample should evaluate the requirements of Nevada blue sky law to determine how onerous compliance would be. As explained below, Nevada blue sky law has a self-executing exemption from registration, so complying with Nevada blue sky law will not impose any additional burden on Sample. In other states, compliance may not be this simple, and it will be more difficult to decide whether it is worthwhile to undertake the burdens associated with compliance where there is a very limited nexus with the state in question. This example illustrates one reason why many issuers may only allow offers of stock options or other equity incentives to be made from a single location, such as corporate headquarters. By inserting additional jurisdictions into the offer process, the issuer expands the list of blue sky laws that must be analyzed and creates unnecessary risk.

California blue sky law treats an offer to sell as occurring in both the location where the offer originates and the location where the

---

11. Nev. Rev. Stat. § 90.460.
12. Nev. Rev. Stat. § 90.280[1].

offeree receives the offer.[13] The definition of an "offer to sell" under California blue sky law is similar to the definition under Washington and Nevada blue sky laws.[14] In addition, under California blue sky law, every sale or offer of a right to purchase another security includes an offer and sale of the other security at the time of the offer of the right to purchase such other security.[15] This means that the offer of the stock option included the offer and sale of the underlying stock. And because this offer was directed to and received by the employee in California, Sample should comply with the California blue sky law in addition to the Washington blue sky law and Nevada blue sky law (since it does not impose any additional burdens in this case) with respect to the stock option grant.

3.1.2 Reviewing the Relevant Blue Sky Laws

Once the issuer has determined the relevant jurisdictions, the next step is to review the blue sky laws for those jurisdictions. The blue sky laws for a particular state are typically contained in the state's securities act (the exact title of the securities act will vary from state to state). Each state's securities act contains a section dealing with exemptions. In some states, all of the exemptions are contained in a single section, while in other states there are separate sections for exempt securities and exempt transactions. It is not sufficient to review only the exemptions listed in the state securities act. In many cases, the legislature delegates the authority to the state securities administrator to create additional exemptions beyond or to further qualify those listed in the securities act. Therefore, the issuer must also review the regulations, if any, promulgated under the securities act as well as any decisions, comments, no-action letters, or other interpretive guidance published by the state securities administrator. It should be noted that the responsibility for administering the state securities laws varies from state to state and may rest on the department of financial institutions,

---

13. Cal. Corp. Code § 25008(b) ("An offer to sell or to buy is made in this state when the offer either originates from this state or is directed by the offeror to this state and received at the place to which it is directed.").

14. Cal. Corp. Code § 25017(b).

15. Cal. Corp. Code § 25017(e).

a securities commission, or some other department or agency. This chapter refers to the applicable agency or department generally as the "state securities administrator."

Continuing with the example of Sample Corporation, Sample should start by reviewing the Washington State Securities Act, which is contained in Title 21 of the Revised Code of Washington. However, Sample should also review Title 460 of the Washington Administrative Code, which contains rules and regulations governing the offer and sale of securities that have been adopted by the Washington Department of Financial Institutions pursuant to statutory authority. Sample should also review the Nevada Uniform Securities Act, which is contained in Chapter 90 of the Nevada Revised Statutes, and the related regulations contained in Chapter 90 of the Nevada Administrative Code. Finally, Sample should also review the California Corporate Securities Law of 1968, which is contained in Sections 25000 through 25707 of the California Corporations Code. In addition, California has blue sky regulations contained in Title 10 of the California Code of Regulations.

3.2 Identifying Applicable Exemptions

A stock option and the stock underlying the option are separate securities. Therefore, in the case of stock option plans, the issuer must have an exemption for both the grant of the stock option and the issuance of the underlying stock. In many cases, the exemption that covers the grant of a stock option will also cover the issuance of stock upon the exercise of that option. However, an issuer should not presume this will be the case and should confirm the existence of a valid exemption for both the grant of the option and the issuance of the stock upon exercise ahead of time. This issue does not arise in connection with employee stock purchase plans because issuers typically sell shares of common stock and not derivative or convertible securities under such plans.

Several states have broad exemptions either for securities or transactions relating to employee benefit plans, which are referred to in this chapter generally as "blanket exemptions." These blanket exemptions, as well as other exemptions and the requirements to qualify for those exemptions, are outlined below.

3.2.1 Stock Option Grants and Sales Under Stock Purchase Plans

Exempt Securities. A number of state blue sky laws specifically exempt from registration securities issued in connection with certain employee benefit plans, specifically including stock option plans.[16] Other blue sky laws exempt investment contracts or securities issued in connection with an employee's stock purchase, savings, pension, profit-sharing, or similar benefit plan, without specifically mentioning stock option plans.[17] The state securities administrators in many of the states with an exemption of the latter type (i.e., exemptions that do not specifically mention stock option plans), treat stock option plans as a "similar benefit plan" for purposes of the exemption. However, the issuer should confirm that this is the case with the state securities administrator before issuing stock options.[18]

Even if exemptions related to employee benefit plans apply, most attach additional requirements or conditions to that exemption. For example, some blue sky laws require that the issuer submit a plan to the state securities administrator within a set number of days before or after issuing securities under that plan or that the content of the plan include certain substantive provisions. What follows are some of the most common requirements contained in blanket exemptions for exempt securities issued in connection with employee benefit plans.

1. *Securities must be issued in connection with a plan that meets the requirements for qualification under the Internal Revenue Code.*

---

16. See, e.g., Ark. Code § 23-42-503(a)(8); Conn. Gen. Stat. § 36b-21(a)(11); 815 Ill. Comp. Stat. 5/3 [N]; Ky. Rev. Stat. Ann. § 292.400(11); N.C. Gen. Stat. § 78A-16(11); Nev. Rev. Stat. § 90.520[2](l); 70 Pa. Cons. Stat. § 1-202; R.I. Gen. Laws § 7-11-401(12); Utah Code Ann. § 61-1-14(1)(g).

17. See, e.g., Ala. Code § 8-6-10(10); Alaska Stat. § 45.55.900(a)(5); Colo. Rev. Stat. § 11-51-307(1)(i); Del. Code Ann. tit. 6, § 73-207(a)(11); Md. Code Ann., Corps. & Ass'ns § 11-601(11); Mass. Gen. Laws ch. 110A, § 402(a)(11); Mont. Code Ann. § 30-10-104(10); N.J. Stat 49:3-50(a)(11); N.Y. Gen. Bus. Law § 359-f.[2](e); Or. Rev. Stat. § 59.025(13); Va. Code Ann. § 13.1-514[A][10]; Wash. Rev. Code § 21.20.310(10).

18. Essentially every state's blanket exemption for securities issued in connection with employee benefit plans specifically lists stock purchase plans.

One common requirement contained in exemptions for securities issued in connection with benefit plans is that the applicable benefit plan must qualify under certain sections of the Internal Revenue Code of 1986. For example, Washington blue sky law provides an exemption for:

> Any security issued in connection with an employee's stock purchase, savings, pension, profit-sharing, or similar benefit plan if: (a) The plan meets the requirements for qualification as a pension, profit sharing, or stock bonus plan under section 401 of the internal revenue code, as an incentive stock option plan under section 422 of the internal revenue code, as a nonqualified incentive stock option plan adopted with or as a supplement to an incentive stock option plan under section 422 of the internal revenue code, or as an employee stock purchase plan under section 423 of the internal revenue code; or (b) the director is notified in writing with a copy of the plan thirty days before offering the plan to employees in this state.[19]

The referenced sections of the Internal Revenue Code contain requirements that must be satisfied in order for the plan to be qualified under those sections. For example, Section 422, which governs incentive stock options, includes requirements, among others, relating to exercise price, expiration, and transferability. In order for a plan to qualify under Section 422, it must include these provisions. Section 423 imposes requirements on employee stock purchase plans relating to eligibility, shareholder approval, purchase price and duration of the right to purchase. If an issuer intends to rely on an exemption such as Wash. Rev. Code Section 21.20.310(10)(a), it must satisfy the applicable requirements from the Internal Revenue Code. In the example above, Sample's equity incentive plan provides for the issuance of incentive stock options, nonqualified stock options and restricted stock grants. Although it is possible that the Washington state securities administrator might conclude that this plan would qualify as a "nonqualified incentive stock option plan adopted with or as a supplement to an incentive stock option plan under section 422 of the [I]nternal [R]evenue [C]ode" for purposes of Wash. Rev. Code Section 21.20.310(10) (a), there is no interpretive guidance that supports this conclusion. Therefore, Sample should not rely on Wash. Rev. Code Section

---

19. Wash. Rev. Code § 21.20.310(10).

21.20.310(10)(a) and should instead submit the plan to the director of the Washington Department of Financial Institutions in accordance with Wash. Rev. Code Section 21.20.310(10)(b) at least 30 days before offering securities under the plan to employees in Washington.[20]

2. *Securities must be issued in connection with a plan that has been submitted to the state securities law administrator.* Several jurisdictions require the issuer to submit any plan or a description of the plan to the state securities law administrator before any securities are issued pursuant to such plan.[21] Other jurisdictions have exemptions, such as the Washington statute cited above, that require the issuer to submit the plan only if it does not qualify under certain sections of the Internal Revenue Code.[22] The state securities administrator typically has a certain number of days after receipt of the plan to disallow or deny the exemption.

3. *Securities must be issued pursuant to a plan that only applies to employees and directors.* Most exemptions for securities issued pursuant to benefit plans refer specifically to plans for employees. However, issuers frequently adopt stock option plans that provide for grants to directors and consultants as well as employees. The question is whether securities issued to directors and consultants under such plans qualify for the blanket exemption for employee benefit plans. Some state blue sky laws specifically provide that the exemption applies to directors and consultants as well as employees. In other states, the state securities administrator takes the position that the exemption only applies to consultants to the same extent Rule 701 of the Securities Act of 1933 (the "Securities Act") applies to consultants. Rule 701 is the federal law exemption covering offers and sales of securities under a written compensatory benefit

---

20. A problem may arise if the issuer issues the securities before sending the director notice and a copy of the plan. In that situation, the issuer must apply to the director, which can grant relief from the failure to meet the 30-day pre-filing requirement for good cause upon finding that it is in the public interest to grant such relief.

21. See, e.g., Mass. Gen. Laws ch. 110A, § 402(a)(11); Minn. Stat. § 80A.46(21).

22. See, e.g., Ark. Code § 23-42-503(a)(8); Ky. Rev. Stat. Ann. § 292.400(11); Md. Code Ann., Corps. & Ass'ns § 11-601(11); Wash. Rev. Code § 21.20.310(10).

plan. Rule 701 specifically allows for grants to officers, directors, consultants and advisors, but it imposes certain requirements on consultants and advisors. For example, consultants and advisors must be natural persons (i.e., individual human beings as opposed to corporations, limited liability companies, trusts, etc.) and must provide bona fide services that are not in connection with the offer or sale of securities in a capital-raising transaction and do not directly or indirectly promote or maintain a market for the issuer's securities. The issuer should research any interpretive guidance provided by the state securities administrator on whether the blanket exemption for employee benefit plans applies to securities issued to consultants and directors under such plans and, if so, whether there are any restrictions with respect to such persons, such as those contained in Rule 701. If the issuer cannot find any written guidance on this issue, the issuer should contact the state securities administrator directly.

Exempt Transactions. Unlike the state blue sky laws described above that treat securities granted in connection with certain employee benefit plans as exempt *securities,* some state blue sky laws treat the issuance of securities in connection with an employee benefit plan as an exempt *transaction.*[23] Several of these blue sky laws require that in order for the transaction to be exempt, either the plan must be qualified under certain provisions of the Internal Revenue Code or the sale of securities under the plan must meet the exemption contained in Rule 701. An example of this requirement is contained in the Ohio blue sky law, which provides the following:

> (5)　The sale of any security pursuant to a pension plan, stock plan, profit-sharing plan, compensatory benefit plan, welfare plan, or similar plan is exempt pursuant to division (V) of section 1707.03 of the Revised Code if:

23.　See, e.g., Ariz. Rev. Stat. § 44-1844[A][14]; Cal. Corp. Code § 25102(o); Fla. Stat. § 517.061(15); Ga. Code Ann. § 10-5-11(21); Haw. Rev. Stat. § 485A-202(a)(21); Idaho Code § 30-14-202(21); Ind. Code § 23-19-2-2(21); Iowa Code § 502.202 [21]; Kan. Stat. Ann. § 17-12a202(21); La. Rev. Stat. Ann. § 51:709(9)(c); Me. Rev. Stat. Ann. tit. 32, § 16202[22]; Mich. Comp. Laws (Ann) § 451.2202(1)(u); Minn. Stat. § 80A.46(21); Miss. Code § 75-71-202(21); Mo. Rev. Stat. § 409.2-202(21); N.M. Stat. Ann. § 58-13C-202[U]; N.D. Cent. Code § 10-04-06[11]; Ohio Admin. Code § 1301:6-3-03(E)(5); 71 Okla. Stat. § 1-202[22]; Tex. Rev. Civ. Stat., Art. 581-5[I] (b).

(a) The security is sold pursuant to a plan qualified under sections 401 to 425 of the Internal Revenue Code of 1986, 26 U.S.C. 1, as amended;

(b) The sale of the security is exempt from the provisions of section 5 of the Securities Act of 1933, 15 U.S.C. 77a, as amended, because it meets the exemption set forth in rule 701 of the Securities Act of 1933, 15 U.S.C. 77a, as amended, and any commission, discount or other remuneration paid or given for the sale of the security in this state is paid or given only to dealers or salespersons licensed by the division;

(c) The security is effectively registered under sections 6 to 8 of the Securities Act of 1933, as amended, and is offered and sold in compliance with the provisions of section 5 of the Securities Act of 1933 as amended; or

(d) The security is sold pursuant to a contributory employee welfare benefit plan and trust that are qualified under section 501(c)(9) of the Internal Revenue Code of 1986, 26 U.S.C. 1, as amended.[24]

In jurisdictions such as Ohio that have a blanket exemption based on Rule 701, the issuer must comply with the requirements of Rule 701 (unless the plan qualifies under an appropriate section of the Internal Revenue Code), discussed above, in order to qualify for the state blue sky law exemption.

California blue sky law contains a transaction-based blanket exemption for an offer or sale of any security pursuant to an option plan or agreement where the security at the time of issuance is exempt from registration under the Securities Act pursuant to Rule 701, provided that the terms of the option plan or agreement comply with Sections 260.140.41, 260.140.45, and 260.140.46 of Title 10 of the California Code of Regulations and the issuer files a notice of transaction with the state securities administrator and pays a filing fee no later than 30 days after the initial issuance of any security under that plan.[25] Section 260.140.41 requires the plan to contain specific provisions, such as restrictions on the maximum exercise period. Sections 260.140.45 and 260.140.46 contain requirements relating to the maximum number of securities issuable under a plan and the delivery of financial statements to security holders, respectively, but neither of these sections

---

24. Ohio Admin. Code § 1301:6-3-03(E)(5).

25. Cal. Corp. Code § 25102(o).

applies to a plan or agreement that complies with all conditions of Rule 701. This California exemption highlights the importance of planning ahead to make sure that the necessary provisions are included in the option plan or agreement. A company such as Sample, which is based in Washington but may periodically grant options to employees in California, should consider adding a separate section to its option plan that contains the language required by Sections 260.140.41, 260.140.45, and 260.140.46 and applies only to options granted to California employees, officers, directors, advisors, or consultants. Alternatively, Sample could leave these provisions out of the plan and handle grants to California employees, officers, directors, advisors, and consultants through separate agreements that contain the required language.

Limited Offering Exemptions. In the event the issuer does not qualify for a blanket exemption of the type described above, another alternative is to issue the stock options under a private offering exemption. Because these exemptions typically limit the number of purchasers to somewhere between five and thirty-five persons, they are not a practical alternative for an issuer seeking an exemption for the issuance of stock options to a large number of people. However, these exemptions are useful in situations where the issuer only plans to issue options to a few key executives or wants to grant options without a written plan or agreement that qualifies for the blanket exemption. These exemptions may require providing advance notice to the state securities administrator and generally have specific restrictions that may include limitations on the number of offerees, the number of purchasers, the aggregate value of securities sold, the number of shareholders after the offering, and written material that must be provided to offerees. Therefore, as is the case with the blanket exemptions, it is imperative that the issuer research the exemption before the offering.

One limited offering exemption that is important to mention in this context is Rule 506(b) of Regulation D, which was adopted pursuant to the Securities Act. Although Rule 506(b) is a federal law exemption, it is relevant in the context of a chapter on state blue sky laws because, pursuant to the National Securities Markets Improvement Act of 1996, offers and sales under Rule 506(b) are exempt from state blue sky laws with the exception of notice requirements in certain jurisdictions.

Some of the advantages of Rule 506(b) over state law limited offering exemptions are (1) Rule 506(b) does not limit the dollar amount of securities that can be offered; (2) if the offering is only made to "accredited investors" as defined in Rule 501 of Regulation D, then the issuer is not required to provide the participants with any specific disclosure materials; and (3) the number of purchasers is limited to 35, but accredited investors do not count against this number (i.e., there can be an unlimited number of accredited investors). The definition of "accredited investor" includes, among others, (1) any corporation, partnership or limited liability company not formed for the specific purpose of acquiring the securities offered, with total assets in excess of $5,000,000; (2) any director, executive officer, or general partner of the issuer of the securities being offered or sold, or any director, executive officer, or general partner of a general partner of that issuer; (3) any natural person whose individual net worth, or joint net worth with that person's spouse, at the time of his or her purchase exceeds $1,000,000, excluding the value of the primary residence of such person; and (4) any natural person who had an individual income in excess of $200,000 in each of the two most recent years or joint income with that person's spouse in excess of $300,000 in each of those years and has a reasonable expectation of reaching the same income level in the current year.

Including nonaccredited investors in a Rule 506(b) offering destroys much of the benefit the rule provides because issuers must provide nonaccredited investors who participate in a Rule 506(b) offering with comprehensive disclosure. In some cases, this disclosure is comparable to what would be required in a registration statement. Rule 506(b) offerings are frequently used for sales to institutional investors or high net worth individuals. However, because the definition of accredited investor includes executive officers and directors, Rule 506(b) can be an effective tool for issuing stock options or selling stock to officers and directors before a benefit plan has been established or outside of a plan that does not have enough shares available.[26]

---

26. Rule 506(c) of Regulation D is also available to issuers. Unlike Rule 506(b), Rule 506(c) does not limit general solicitation in connection with offers of securities. However, sales of securities may be made to accredited investors only, and the issuer must take reasonable steps to verify the purchaser's accredited investor status.

3.2.2 Issuance of Stock Upon Exercise of Options

As discussed above, the stock issued upon exercise of a stock option is a security distinct from the option itself and must either be registered or exempt from registration. In general, if a stock option was granted pursuant to a valid exemption, then there will be a valid exemption for the issuance of stock upon the exercise of that stock option. This chapter presumes that, as is typically the case, employee stock purchase plans only involve the sale of common stock and do not involve the sale of any derivative or convertible security that can subsequently be exercised for or converted into common stock. Accordingly, this section does not address employee stock purchase plans.

Blanket Exemptions. Although some of the blanket exemptions referenced above specifically cover the issuance of stock upon the exercise of stock options that were granted pursuant to the exemption,[27] most of the blanket exemptions refer broadly to any securities issued in connection with particular types of benefit plans. The question is whether this language is broad enough to cover stock issued upon the exercise of a stock option that was granted pursuant to an employee benefit plan. In order to answer this question in a particular jurisdiction, the issuer should review any regulations or interpretive guidance created by the applicable state securities administrator. If these sources do not provide an answer, the issuer should contact the state securities administrator directly and confirm that the exemption covers both the grant of the stock option and the issuance of stock upon the exercise of the option. In all likelihood the state securities administrator will confirm such is the case, but it is best to clarify this in advance.

For example, as discussed above, Wash. Rev. Code Section 21.20.310(10) exempts "[a]ny security issued in connection with an employee's stock purchase, savings, pension, profit-sharing, or similar benefit plan." The Washington state securities administrator has issued interpretive guidance clarifying that this language covers both the stock option and the stock issued upon exercise of the option. Therefore, the issuance of stock upon the exercise of Sample's stock options granted

---

27. See La. Rev. Stat. Ann. § 51:709(9)(d).

pursuant to the plan should be exempt pursuant to Wash. Rev. Code Section 21.20.310(10).

Section 90.520[2](l) of the Nevada Revised Statutes provides an exemption for "[a] security issued in connection with an employees' stock purchase, savings, option, profit-sharing, pension or similar employees' benefit plan." The Securities Division of the Nevada Secretary of State has not issued written guidance clarifying whether this exemption covers the issuance of the underlying stock. However, even if this section does not cover the issuance of the underlying stock, Section 90.530[14] of the Nevada Revised Statutes provides an exemption for a transaction pursuant to an offer to sell to existing security holders of the issuer (subject to satisfaction of certain conditions), which should cover the issuance of stock upon the exercise of a stock option.

As already noted above, California blue sky law treats the grant of a stock option as a sale of the underlying stock at the time the option is granted.[28] Therefore, assuming the grant of the options was exempt pursuant to Cal. Corp. Code Section 25102(o), Sample does not need to find a separate exemption for the issuance of the stock upon exercise because the issuance of that stock does not constitute a separate offer or sale for purposes of California blue sky law.

Exemption for Transactions Pursuant to an Offer to Existing Security Holders. In the event that a blanket exemption is not available to cover the issuance of stock upon the exercise of a stock option, the issuer should research whether the applicable blue sky laws provide an exemption for transactions with existing security holders, such as the Nevada statute referenced above. This is a common exemption that is generally appropriate for the issuance of a security upon the exercise or conversion of an already outstanding security, such as a warrant or a convertible security (for example, preferred stock). In most states, this

---

28. See Cal. Corp. Code § 25017(e) ("Every sale or offer of a warrant or right to purchase or subscribe to another security of the same or another issuer, as well as every sale or offer of a security which gives the holder a present or future right or privilege to convert the security into another security of the same or another issuer, includes an offer and sale of the other security only at the time of the offer or sale of the warrant or right or convertible security; but neither the exercise of the right to purchase or subscribe or to convert nor the issuance of securities pursuant thereto is an offer or sale.").

exemption requires that either no commission or other remuneration is paid or given directly or indirectly for soliciting any security holder in the state or the issuer must first file a notice specifying the terms of the offer and the state securities administrator does not disallow the exemption within a set number of days, which ranges from thirty days to five business days, depending on the jurisdiction.[29]

Limited Offering Exemption. If a blanket exemption or an exemption for transactions with existing security holders is not available, the issuer should research whether a limited offering exemption is available. As discussed above, limited offering exemptions are subject to a variety of qualifications, which the issuer must carefully research before relying upon the exemption. If the issuer is unable to find a valid exemption, then the issuer must consider registration, which is discussed below.

Additional Exemptions Available for Public Companies. In addition to the exemptions above, which are available for both public and private companies, the blue sky laws of most states contain an exemption that may cover the issuance of stock of public companies upon the exercise of stock options. This exemption is for securities that are listed, or authorized for listing, on the New York Stock Exchange, the Nasdaq Stock Market, or any successor to such entities. This exemption does not apply to the grant of the stock options themselves because the stock options are not listed on any exchange or the national market system. However, this exemption would apply to listed stock issued upon the exercise of stock options.

3.3 Registration

If an issuer is unable to find an applicable exemption for granting stock options, issuing stock upon the exercise of stock options, or selling

---

29. See, e.g., Alaska Stat. § 45.55.900(b)(7); Colo. Rev. Stat. § 11-51-308(1)(l); Conn. Gen. Stat. § 36b-21(b)(12); Del. Code Ann. tit. 6 § 73-207(b)(11); Fla. Stat. § 517.061(6); Haw. Rev. Stat. § 485A-202(a)(14); Idaho Code § 30-14-202(15); 815 Ill. Comp. Stat., 5/4[B]; La. Rev. Stat. Ann. § 51:709(8); Mass. Gen. Laws, ch. 110A, § 402(b)(11); N.M. Stat. Ann. §58-13C-202[O]; 70 Pa. Cons. Stat. § 1-203(n); Tex. Rev. Civ. Stat., Art. 581-5[E]; Utah Code Ann. § 61-1-14(2)(j); Va. Code Ann. § 13.1-514[B][8]; Wash. Rev. Code § 21.20.320(11).

stock pursuant to an employee stock purchase plan, then the issuer must register the securities that the issuer intends to offer (i.e., stock options or stock). Registration is typically done through coordination or qualification and involves the filing of a registration statement with the state securities administrator. The registration statement generally includes information about the issuer, its subsidiaries, officers and directors, capitalization, kind and amount of securities to be offered, anticipated proceeds from the offering and use of the proceeds, a copy of any prospectus or offering circular to be used in connection with the offering, an opinion of counsel as to the legality of the security being registered, and financial statements meeting specified requirements. In many states, registration by coordination is available only if the issuer has already filed a registration statement with respect to such securities under the Securities Act. Registration by coordination generally requires filing with the state securities administrator a copy of the documents filed pursuant to the Securities Act and an abbreviated registration statement as compared to what is required for registration by qualification.

3.4   Conclusion

While blue sky laws vary from state to state and can cause confusion about whether an issuer needs to register securities, in most cases companies can qualify for an exemption for the offering and sale of stock options or stock under employee benefit plans. Working with an experienced attorney who thoroughly understands and can carefully review blue sky laws in the state in which the issuer is based (as well as in those states in which the issuer's employees participating in the plan might reside and any other potentially relevant states), companies should be able to avoid the time and expense of registration.

CHAPTER

4

Preparing for an Initial Public Offering

Jacobin Zorin

CONTENTS

For many companies, an initial public offering (IPO) of securities is a significant measure of the success of the enterprise. There are several reasons for conducting an IPO. The most frequently cited motive is to raise additional capital for the business. Other rea-

Portions of this chapter were originally written by Mark A. Borges.

sons include enhancing the image of the company, spreading the risk of future development activities, and providing an avenue to liquidity for the company's founders and other shareholders.

The IPO process can be quite complex and involves the combined efforts of many parties: the company's management; the underwriters for the transaction; and the company's attorneys, accountants, and other professional advisors. If the company maintains an employee equity plan, several issues related to the IPO must be included in the preparations. Identifying and preparing for these issues will greatly ease the transition from a privately held business to a public reporting company.

In addition, administering the employee equity plan in an environment where there is a public market for the company's securities is significantly more sophisticated than when a company is privately held. Exercises of outstanding stock options are common and more complex. Often other equity vehicles will be offered to employees, officers, and directors. Officers and directors are subject to a multitude of restrictions on their ability to trade in the company's securities, which affect their participation in employee equity plans. Regulatory compliance increases, particularly as it relates to the public disclosure of plan activity. It becomes imperative to have a knowledgeable and engaged equity plan administrator to manage these increased responsibilities.

This chapter summarizes the key issues involving a company's equity plan before an IPO. While it is intended to provide a checklist of matters that a company should consider in connection with its IPO, it is not exhaustive. Because the requirements for conducting an IPO are revised from time to time and the regulatory considerations affecting employee equity plans are constantly changing, a company should consult its professional advisors to ensure the appropriate application of the rules discussed here to its particular situation.[1]

4.1 Overview of the IPO Process

While a comprehensive discussion of the IPO process is beyond the scope of this chapter, it is helpful for the equity plan administrator to have a basic understanding of the regulatory framework in which the offering takes place.

---

1. See chapter 5 for a discussion of post-IPO issues.

Generally, an IPO represents a company's first sale of securities to the general public. Typically, the company engages one or more investment banks to "underwrite" the offering; that is, to act as intermediaries for the distribution of the securities to public investors.

Any offering of securities in the U.S. is subject to compliance with the Securities Act of 1933 (the "Securities Act"), the basic purpose of which is to ensure that complete and accurate information about the securities being offered to the public and the company offering them is available to prospective investors. To meet this objective, the Securities Act requires that the offering either be registered with the Securities and Exchange Commission (SEC) or satisfy the conditions of an appropriate exemption from the registration requirement. Because an IPO is aimed at reaching a broad audience of prospective investors, it is almost always conducted as a registered transaction with the SEC.

One common misconception regarding an IPO is that it registers all of a company's securities. In fact, registration under the Securities Act covers only the specific securities actually being offered (typically, common stock) and only for the specific purposes of the offering described in the registration statement. While the securities sold in the IPO are previously authorized but unissued shares of common stock of the company, frequently the founders and other shareholders of the company also sell some of their shares in the offering. These are called selling shareholders.

In addition to complying with the Securities Act, the company must satisfy the securities laws in each state in which the shares of stock will be offered. For most IPOs, this means compliance with the securities laws of virtually all 50 states. Fortunately, most states have specific exemptions that can be used to avoid the registration process in those states. For example, most state securities laws provide exemptions for securities that are listed or approved for listing on a national securities exchange or quoted for trading through a national securities association. Other states exempt sales of securities to registered broker-dealers or financial institutions.

The securities offered in the IPO also must be designated for trading on a stock market—either an "exchange" market such as the New York Stock Exchange (NYSE) or the Nasdaq Stock Market (Nasdaq), or the "over-the-counter" (OTC) market. Unless and until a company can meet the stringent listing requirements of an exchange, its securities will be traded on the OTC market. Listing on an exchange requires, among other things, agreement by the company to observe the market's corporate governance requirements, which reflect minimum standards for conducting its internal corporate affairs. The Financial Industry Regulatory Authority (FINRA) regulates all securities firms doing business in the U.S. FINRA performs market regulation under contract for Nasdaq, the International Securities Exchange, the NYSE, and other industry utilities.

4.2 Planning Considerations

A number of matters involving the company's employee equity plans require the attention of the company's management before an IPO.

4.2.1 Amending the Equity Plan

While an equity plan, in most material respects, operates similarly whether a company's securities are privately held or publicly traded, there will be some features of the plan that company management should consider modifying before the company's IPO. Some of these changes may require shareholder approval, either for regulatory purposes or as required by the plan itself. Preplanning is desirable because it is generally easier to obtain shareholder approval while the company's securities are still privately held. Typical amendments to consider include the following:

Increase Plan Share Reserve. Company management should review the plan share reserve to ensure there is a sufficient number of shares available to cover projected future equity awards for a predetermined period of time (often, one, two, or three years). In addition, company management may seek to add an "evergreen" provision to the plan. Generally, an "evergreen" provision automatically adds a formulaically determined number of shares (typically expressed as a percentage of the total outstanding shares) to the plan share reserve each year for a specified number of years (often up to 10 years). The presence of such a provision will relieve a company from having to seek shareholder approval of a plan share reserve increase following the IPO for the duration of the provision.

Revise Plan Eligibility Criteria. The equity plan administrator should review the plan eligibility provision to determine whether the plan permits grants to the appropriate categories of individuals. For example, if the company has not provided for grants to nonemployee consultants and advisors in the past, it may be desirable to expand the category of eligible participants to include such individuals. Conversely, if the company has granted equity compensation to consultants and advisors in the past but now plans a shift in philosophy as a public company, the plan can be amended to restrict future awards to such individuals. Finally, the company should determine how the participation of the members of its board of directors, including nonemployee directors, will be handled after the IPO, either under the general equity plan or through a separate directors' equity plan.

Include Additional Equity Compensation Vehicles. To ensure flexibility to support the needs of a public company, the company may want to add additional equity compensation vehicles to its existing equity plan. For example, many pre-IPO companies draft their plans to include only stock options and/or restricted stock awards. However, the company may want to add the ability to grant restricted stock units (RSUs), stock appreciation rights (SARs), performance shares, performance units, or other equity alternatives when amending the equity plan.

Limit Individual Grants. The company may want to consider specifying a maximum per-individual share limit on the number of shares that can be granted pursuant to the equity plan to an individual in a single year. Before 2018, such a per-employee limit was required under Section 162(m) of the Internal Revenue Code if the company wanted to take advantage of an exception to the annual deduction limit of $1 million per senior executive officer for so-called "performance-based" compensation (that is, compensation granted pursuant to a shareholder-approved equity plan that satisfied several other conditions). This exception was eliminated by the Tax Cut and Jobs Act of 2017 for taxable years beginning on or after January 1, 2018. Nonetheless, some practitioners believe that a limit or "ceiling" on the size of the grants that may be made to an individual in a single year represents a good corporate governance practice and, therefore, should be considered. Another consideration is that shareholder advisory firms are more likely to recommend voting for equity plans that contain a per-person grant limit. Accordingly, company management, in consultation with the company's professional advisors, should determine whether a limit is appropriate and, if so, select an amount that will act as the maximum number of shares subject to an equity award that can be granted under the plan during a specified period to any individual.

Eliminate Certain Contractual Restrictions. The equity plans of most privately held companies impose certain contractual restrictions on the ability of a participant to sell or otherwise transfer company shares following the exercise of a stock option or vesting of an equity award. Typically, these restrictions take the form of a right of first refusal (on third-party transactions), a vested share repurchase option, or a similar arrangement. To the extent that such provisions do not automatically terminate upon the IPO, they should be deleted from the plan. Another contractual change to be considered is removing the use of promissory notes to pay the exercise price of a stock option. At the very least, use of promissory notes should not be allowed to be used by executive officers or directors, in accordance with Section 13(k) of the Securities Exchange Act of 1934 (the "Exchange Act").

Revise Exercise Payment Methods. In anticipation of the establishment of a public market for the company's common stock, management should consider expanding the range of permissible payment methods under the equity plan. To the extent that the equity plan does not expressly permit broker-assisted same-day exercise and sale transactions, such a provision should be added to the equity plan.

As permitted under Regulation T, a securities brokerage firm may advance funds to an optionee to cover the exercise price and any associated withholding taxes upon the exercise of a stock option, provided the optionee has delivered to the firm an executed notice of exercise and a copy of irrevocable instructions from the optionee directing the company to deliver the option shares to the firm. The instructions must designate the account into which the option shares are to be deposited (either a margin account or a cash account). Where the option shares are to be immediately sold by the firm, a cash account will be designated from which the sale proceeds will fund the exercise. To execute a same-day exercise and sale, most securities brokerage firms use websites, rendering signed paper instructions unnecessary.

Regulation T covers any receipt of securities pursuant to an employee benefit plan under which shares are registered with the SEC on Form S-8. This allows a securities brokerage firm to advance funds in connection with the exercise of stock options held by consultants and nonemployee directors in addition to employees. However, if the shares underlying an equity plan are not registered on a Form S-8, then the options held by nonemployees may not be exercised under Regulation T.

While it is not required, the company may find that it is more expedient to amend its equity plan to permit this type of exercise. This will provide the company with more flexibility in structuring its same-day exercise and sale arrangements with one or more securities brokerage firms. The company will also want to consider any applicable tax, securities law, and accounting issues that may be associated with amending the equity plan to add this provision.

Under Section 13(k) of the Exchange Act, public companies are prohibited from making personal loans, or facilitating the extension of credit, to their executive officers and members of their board of directors. It is unclear whether a stock option exercise by an executive officer or director using a broker-assisted same-day exercise and sale program constitutes a prohibited loan under this section. Consequently, a company should consult its professional legal advisors when amending a plan to establish a broker-assisted same-day exercise and sale program to determine whether the program may be extended to its executive officers and members of its board of directors. Note there is not a prohibition on credit vehicles not made directly by the company.

Finally, company management should consider whether it is appropriate to amend outstanding stock options to add a brokers' same-day exercise and sale provision to those options. Once again, applicable legal and accounting implications should first be considered before taking such action.

Composition of Plan Administration Committee. Typically, an equity plan will identify the body authorized to administer the plan and will also set forth certain guidelines for the committee's composition and operation. Most equity plans provide that the company's board of directors or a committee of the board, such as the compensation committee, is responsible for administering the plan. While it may not require a formal plan amendment, company management should seek to coordinate the composition of the plan administration committee to comply with the conditions of the Exchange Act Rule 16b-3 exemption and, if the company is to be listed on the NYSE or Nasdaq, the applicable corporate governance listing standards for director and (where applicable) compensation committee member independence.

For purposes of Exchange Act Rule 16b-3, stock option grants may be approved by a committee of two or more "nonemployee" directors. For purposes of the NYSE and Nasdaq corporate governance listing standards, the compensation committee of the board of directors must be comprised solely of "independent" directors. The definition of a "nonemployee" director varies, in several ways, from the "independence" definitions contained in the NYSE and Nasdaq corporate governance listing standards. Further, in response to Section 10C of the Exchange Act and Exchange Act Rule 10C-1, the national securities exchanges have adopted revisions to their listing standards to prohibit the listing of any company that does not have a compensation committee comprised only of members of the board of directors of the company, all of whom meet the requirements for "independence" as set forth in the listing standards.

Under Exchange Act Rule 16b-3, a "nonemployee director" is an individual who is not currently an officer or otherwise employed by the company or a parent or subsidiary company; does not receive compensation, directly or indirectly, from the company or its parent or subsidiary companies for services rendered as a consultant or in any capacity other than as a director (except for an amount for which disclosure would not be required under the "related-person transaction" rules of SEC Regulation S-K); does not possess an interest in any other transaction for which disclosure would be required under the "related-person transaction" rules of Regulation S-K; and is not engaged in a business relationship with the company for which disclosure would be required under the "related-person transaction" rules of Regulation S-K.

For purposes of the NYSE corporate governance listing standards, a director is "independent" if the board of directors affirmatively determines that the director has no "material relationship" with the listed company (either directly or indirectly), and, within the past three years, the director is or has not:

- been an employee, or had an immediate family member who is or was an executive officer, of the listed company;
- received, or had an immediate family member who is an executive officer of the company who received, during any 12 month period during the past three years more than $120,000 in direct compensation from the listed company (other than director and committee fees, and pension or other deferred compensation for prior service);
- been a current partner or employee of a firm that is the listed company's internal or external auditor, been an immediate family member who is a current partner of such a firm, been an immediate family member who is a current employee of such a firm and personally works on the listed company's audit, or been the director or an immediate family member who was within the last three years a partner or employee of such a firm and personally worked on the listed company's audit within that time;
- been employed, or had an immediate family member who is or was employed, as an executive officer of another company where any of the listed company's present executive officers at the same time serves or served on that company's compensation committee; or
- been an employee, or had an immediate family member who is a current executive officer, of a company that made payments to, or received payments from, the listed company for property or services in an amount which, in any single fiscal year, exceeded the greater of $1 million or 2% of such other company's consolidated gross revenues.

For these purposes, a "material relationship" includes commercial, industrial, banking, consulting, legal, accounting, charitable, or familial relationships.

In addition, to comply with Section 10C of the Exchange Act, the listing standards of the NYSE provide that, for purposes of serving on the compensation committee of the board of directors, the listed company's board of directors must make an affirmative determination of each committee member's independence, taking into consideration all factors specifically relevant to determining whether the director has a relationship with the company that is material to his or her ability to be independent from management in acting on executive compensation matters, including, but not limited to, (1) the source of the director's compensation, including any consulting, advisory or other compensatory fee paid by the company to the director, and (2) whether the director is affiliated with the company or any of its subsidiaries or affiliates.

Nasdaq corporate governance listing standards provide a similar, although not identical, definition of "independence." To comply with Section 10C of the Exchange Act, the listing standards of Nasdaq provide that all listed companies appoint a standing independent compensation committee of its board of directors. In addition, Nasdaq listing standards provide that compensation committee members meet the exchange's general standards for director independence. In making an independence determination, the board of directors also needs to consider (1) the source of the director's compensation, including any consulting, advisory, or other compensatory fee paid by the company, and (2) whether the director is affiliated with the company or any of its subsidiaries or affiliates, and whether this affiliation would impair the director's judgment in serving on the compensation committee.

Once the company has determined its strategy for complying with Exchange Act Rule 16b-3 and the applicable corporate governance listing standards, if applicable, it should identify the appropriate directors to serve on the compensation committee of the board of directors. It may be necessary to add individuals to the board of directors to ensure that the Exchange Act Rule 16b-3 exemption will be available for future transactions and periods and that the applicable listing standards are satisfied. Company management should review the equity plan to determine whether any coordinating amendments are required.

Other Amendments. Because of limitations on the ability of the company's officers and directors to obtain liquidity for their shares due to federal and state insider trading restrictions, company management may want to consider amending the equity plan to permit participants subject to Section 16 of the Exchange Act to tender shares of stock to satisfy any income tax withholding obligations that arise in connection with the exercise of their stock options and/or the vesting of their other equity awards.

Management should also review the "change of control" provisions in the equity plan and outstanding equity and employment agreements, if any, for consistency and to ensure that future equity grants will contain features that ensure the desired treatment in the event of a change of control and for the impact, if any, of Sections 280G and 4999 of the Code (the "golden parachute" provisions). In addition, the company's accountants should be consulted to consider the effect that the change of control provisions and any contemplated changes may have on the accounting treatment of a future acquisition of the company.

Finally, the company may want to consider changing the standard form of employee stock option grant from a statutory (incentive) stock option to a nonstatutory (nonqualified) stock option. Generally, this change does not require a formal amendment to the equity plan; instead, it requires a change to the company's philosophy for equity compensation. If the company anticipates that most employees will use a broker-assisted same-day exercise and sale procedure to exercise their stock options, it may find that, for practical purposes, nonstatutory stock options are preferable because they are simpler to administer and ensure that the company will receive a corporate income tax deduction upon exercise of the options.

4.2.2 Adoption of Employee Stock Purchase Plan

Concurrent with an IPO, some companies implement a broad-based employee stock purchase plan. Often, this plan supplements the company's equity plan. Occasionally, the plan substitutes for an equity plan where the company believes that it may no longer be possible to grant stock options or other equity awards in meaningful amounts to all employees. For a discussion of broad-based employee stock purchase plans, see chapter 11 of this book.

4.2.3   Adoption of Directors' Equity Plan

The company may want to consider adopting a separate equity plan for the members of its board of directors. While it is quite common to grant stock options or other equity vehicles (such as restricted stock and RSU awards) to nonemployee directors out of the company's primary equity plan while the company is privately held, separate arrangements are sometimes implemented after an IPO.

Historically, such plans were "formula" plans under which eligibility was limited to nonemployee directors; the plan, by its terms, specified the amount, price, and timing of option grants or other equity awards; and the company's ability to amend these plan provisions more than once every six months was limited. These formula plans played an important role in ensuring that a company could provide stock options and other equity awards to its nonemployee directors without jeopardizing their "disinterested" status for purposes of administering the company's discretionary equity plans. Under current SEC rules, "disinterested" status is no longer needed to ensure that grants or awards to officers and employee-directors under a company's discretionary equity plans are exempt from the "short-swing profits" recovery provisions of Section 16(b) of the Exchange Act. Just the same, some companies continue to use formula plans as a way of minimizing conflict-of-interest issues that might arise where nonemployee directors are both administrators and beneficiaries of a company's equity program. This has become particularly important in recent years where some shareholders have challenged the equity awards granted to nonemployee directors on a discretionary basis by a subcommittee of the board of directors, alleging that the directors were paying themselves excessive compensation. In fact, in the past few years, where equity awards are granted to directors on a discretionary basis (either through a separate employee equity plan or the general employee equity plan), it is becoming more common for companies to seek to minimize the risk of litigation over "excessive compensation" by adding a "meaningful" limit to the plan on the aggregate number of shares of stock that may be granted to an individual director in any one year.

Exchange Act Rule 16b-3 does not prohibit nonemployee directors (or the full board, for that matter) from awarding themselves grants of the company's securities or stock options on those securities. Nor does it automatically subject these transactions to shareholder scrutiny. Instead, such transactions will be subject to state laws governing corporate self-dealing. As a result, companies must decide whether to use a separate plan or to simply include them as participants in their general employee equity plan. For shareholder relations purposes, as well as to maintain the objectivity and impartiality of the nonemployee directors and limit potential liability, a company may find that it is still prudent to implement a separate director formula plan.

If the company is to be listed on the NYSE or Nasdaq, the plan will need to be submitted to the company's shareholders for their approval.

4.2.4 Assisting Employees in the Disposition of Their Equity

Tax Considerations. Once the company's employees are informed of the impending IPO, most individuals will have questions concerning the impact of the transaction on their outstanding stock options or other equity awards. Some employees will seek counseling concerning their equity and may look to the equity plan administrator to advise them on how to proceed. While the equity plan administrator should avoid giving individual tax and financial advice, it may be prudent to schedule one or more informational meetings for employees to provide them with basic information about their equity and outline the key planning considerations they should address with their own financial advisors.

Securities Law Restrictions. In addition, it will be helpful to educate employees on the resale limitations imposed contractually and under the federal securities laws that will affect their ability to sell their equity following the IPO.

Generally, an employee who has acquired shares of stock under the company's equity plan will hold "restricted securities." For purposes of the federal securities laws, "restricted securities" are securities acquired from a company in a transaction, or series of transactions, that has not been registered under the Securities Act. Under the Securities Act, any proposed sale of shares must either be registered or exempt from registration.

Securities Act Rule 144 provides an exemption from the registration requirement of the Securities Act for a person seeking to resell "restricted securities." To sell restricted securities in reliance on Rule 144, several conditions must be satisfied. First, the company must be subject to the reporting requirements of the Exchange Act and must be current in meeting its reporting obligations. Next, the securities to be sold must have been fully paid for and held for a specified minimum period (currently six months). Third, the amount of securities that can be resold during any three-month period must not exceed the greater of (1) 1% of the outstanding stock of the company or (2) the average weekly trading volume of the company's stock during the four calendar weeks preceding the date of the proposed sale. Fourth, all sales must be made in unsolicited brokers' transactions or directly to market makers. Finally, a notice of the proposed sale, on Form 144, must be filed with the SEC (and any national securities exchange on which the securities are admitted for trading) before or concurrently with the sale if the proposed sale involves more than 5,000 shares or has an aggregate sale price over $50,000.

For purposes of Rule 144, the specified holding period is measured from the date that the securities are paid for in full. Payment with a promissory note that is essentially financed by the company does not constitute full payment unless the note is a full-recourse obligation and is collateralized by property other than the shares of stock being purchased, which property has a fair market value at least equal to the total purchase price of the shares. In addition, the promissory note must be repaid in full before the sale of the restricted securities.

In addition to transactions in restricted securities, Rule 144 is the primary exemption from the registration requirements of the Securities Act for resales of securities by "affiliates" of the company. For purposes of the federal securities laws, an "affiliate" includes any person directly controlling or controlled by the company or any person under direct or indirect common control with the company. While the determination of affiliate status ultimately depends on the facts and circumstances of each individual case, the officers, members of the board of directors, and principal shareholders of a company generally are considered affiliates of the company.

Rule 144 applies to any sale of securities by an affiliate (whether of registered securities or restricted securities). The conditions of the rule to be satisfied in the case of an affiliate transaction depend on the nature of the securities to be resold. If the securities are restricted securities, all of the conditions of Rule 144 described above must be met. If the securities have previously been registered, then all of the conditions of Rule 144, other than the holding period condition, must be met.

Most of the time securities will be issued in electronic form known as "book entry," either through the Depository Trust Company's direct registration system (DRS) or through being held in "street name" by a brokerage firm. Electronic issuance eliminates the need to transfer certificates upon purchase or sale; instead, entries are merely changed in the books of the transfer agent. For electronic shares with restrictions on sale, the transfer agent will typically require direction from the company to allow onward transfer. These directions may be in the form of legal opinions, including blanket opinions, letters of instruction, and similar guidance. When a company issues physical stock certificates, it typically places a restrictive legend directly on the certificate for shares of stock that are either restricted securities or held by an affiliate. This legend is intended to alert the company's transfer agent and/or a stock brokerage firm assisting with a proposed sale to the fact that the shares are subject to the conditions of Rule 144. In all cases, the company may issue "stop transfer" instructions to its transfer agent as a precaution against inadvertent sales that do not comply with Rule 144.

Rule 144 is applicable to resales of restricted securities and securities held by affiliates, however, regardless of whether or not a legend appears on the certificate or stop-transfer instructions have been issued. Following the IPO, unless an employee's equity acquired before the offering are first registered with the SEC, such shares may only be sold in reliance on Rule 144. There is a significant exception to this requirement, however. If equity was granted under the exemption provided by Securities Act Rule 701 for employee benefit plans, a special resale provision in the rule will be triggered following the IPO. While option shares and other types of equity acquired pursuant to Rule 701 are deemed to be restricted securities for resale purposes, 90 days after the company becomes subject to the reporting requirements of the Exchange Act, nonaffiliates may sell their Rule 701 shares without regard to Rule 144 (other than the manner-of-sale condition) and affiliates may sell their Rule 701 shares pursuant to Rule 144 (but without regard to the holding period).

Contractual Restrictions. Notwithstanding compliance with applicable securities laws, employees may still be restricted contractually from selling their equity immediately following an IPO. Frequently, the underwriter for the offering will require the officers, directors, and principal shareholders of the company to agree not to sell any shares of stock in the public market for a specified period of time following the IPO (often for a period of up to 180 days). This is done primarily to ensure stabilization of the market price for the company's stock during the post-IPO period. This restriction is often called the "underwriters' lockup" or "market standoff" requirement.

Where there are a large number of stock options or other equity outstanding at the time of the IPO, it is not uncommon for the underwriters to request that each individual holding equity awards agree to be bound by the lockup provision. This may require the equity plan administrator to obtain written agreements from each individual, agreeing to the applicable restrictions. Consequently, many companies include a contractual lockup provision in their standard equity agreements to avoid having to obtain lockup agreements individually in connection with an IPO. An explanation of these provisions and their applicability should be included in the information provided to the employees about the IPO.

4.3   Regulatory Considerations

4.3.1   "Cheap" Stock

Before an IPO, management should closely monitor the prices at which the company grants stock options to its employees. The SEC will scrutinize the methodology used to set the exercise price for these stock options to ensure that the company has not issued "cheap" stock, that is, stock issued at prices below the stock's true market value. The SEC may presume that stock options granted during the period immediately before an IPO involve cheap stock unless the options were granted at the offering price and will require the company to record a compensation expense for these stock options to the extent that the exercise price is less than the offering price. Disputes are common in which a company and the SEC disagree about whether stock options were properly valued and accounted for in the company's financial statements.

Where the SEC presumes that stock options were not priced at fair market value at the time of grant, it will require the company to record a compensation expense for the "discount" reflected in the stock options. Such a result can both delay the offering (as the parties wrangle over the proper valuation for the stock options) and change the financial statements, altering investors' views of the company and the proposed offering. As discussed below, such a result may also raise issues under Section 409A of the Code.

To minimize potential problems, the company should begin documenting the methodology employed to price its stock option grants during the 12- to 18-month period before the IPO. Important factors in responding to an SEC inquiry include the number of months between the stock option grant and the IPO, the difference between the exercise price and the offering price, and whether significant changes in the company's business prospects have taken place since the grant date. An often-persuasive factor is whether the company engaged the services of an independent professional appraiser in setting the stock option exercise price. Many companies retain an independent appraiser to assist in the stock option valuation process during the months before the offering.

The possibility that stock options were not priced at fair market value at the time of grant may also raise issues under Section 409A of the Code. Section 409A governs the federal income tax treatment of nonqualified deferred compensation (NQDC). A discount stock option, i.e., an option with an exercise price that is less than the fair market value of the granting company's stock on the date of grant, is considered to involve a deferral of compensation and is subject to Section 409A. (Where an option is determined to involve a deferral of compensation, Section 409A requires that the optionee make an advance election as to when to exercise the option.) A stock option that has an exercise price that is not less than the fair market value of the granting company's stock on the date of grant is not subject to Section 409A.

Stock valuation will be important for purposes of determining whether outstanding stock options must comply with the restrictions governing NQDC under Section 409A. For the stock of a privately held company, fair market value may be determined using any reasonable valuation method that takes into account a number of specified factors (such as the value of the company's assets or the present value of its cash flows) and is consistently applied. Under Internal Revenue Service (IRS) regulations, the following valuation methods will be presumed to be "reasonable":

- appraisals that satisfy the Code's requirements for the valuation of employee stock ownership plan (ESOP) stock (which will be presumed to be reasonable for a one-year period after the appraisal unless new information becomes available);

- formula valuations based on non-lapse restrictions as defined in Section 83 of the Code (for example, a permanent requirement that an optionee sell the option shares back to the company at a formula price), but only if the valuation method is used consistently for both compensatory and noncompensatory purposes; and

- for illiquid stock of a "start-up corporation," special valuations that meet the following requirements: (1) the company is in its first 10 years of active trade or business, (2) it has no readily traded securities, (3) it does not anticipate a change in control or initial public offering within a specified period after the valuation, and (4) it applies the valuation to stock that is not subject to a put or call or repurchase obligation.

The potential for cheap stock determination and application of Section 409A are key reasons why a company will want to closely monitor the prices at which it grants stock options and the valuation methodologies used. A valuation method is considered to be consistently used if it is used for all equity awards and for all terms of an award.

4.3.2 Section 16

The officers, members of the board of directors, and principal shareholders of any company that has a class of equity securities registered under Section 12 of the Exchange Act are subject to the provisions of Section 16 of the Exchange Act. Generally, registration of a class of securities is required under Section 12(b) of the Exchange Act where a company elects to have equity securities listed for trading on a national securities exchange or under Section 12(g) of the Exchange Act where the company has 2,000 or more holders of record (or 500 or more "non-accredited investors") and total assets exceeding $10 million as of the end of the company's fiscal year. For purposes of this calculation under Section 12(g), it is permissible to exclude persons who received their securities under an employee compensation plan in a transaction that was exempt from the Securities Act. A company may also voluntarily register a class of its equity securities under Section 12(g).

Under Section 16 of the Exchange Act, officers, members of the board of directors, and beneficial owners of more than 10% of the class of equity securities registered under the Exchange Act must disclose their holdings of, and transactions involving, the equity securities of the company and further must return to the company any profits that they realize in the event of any "short-swing" trading in such securities.

Determination of Insiders. Initially, the equity plan administrator must assist in the determination of who will be subject to Section 16 as a result of the Section 12 registration. Section 16 applies to officers and directors of a Section 12 company, as well as any beneficial owner of more than 10% of the company's registered equity securities. The determination of directors subject to Section 16 is generally straight-forward: it includes each member of the company's board of directors. The determination of officer status for purposes of Section 16 can be more challenging.

The rules under Section 16 contain a specific definition of who is to be considered an "officer" for purposes of Section 16. A Section 16 officer includes a company's (1) president; (2) principal financial officer; (3) principal accounting officer (or, if there is none, the controller); (4) any vice president in charge of a principal business unit, division, or function (such as sales, administration, or finance); (5) any other officer performing a significant policy-making function; and (6) any other person performing a significant policy-making function. A Section 16 officer may also include an officer of the parent or a subsidiary company who is performing policy-making functions for the company.

The rules under Section 16 make it clear that function, rather than title, will be determinative of officer status. In establishing whether an individual is to be treated as a Section 16 officer, the policy-making responsibilities of the individual will be a key factor. The rules further provide that if a company identifies an individual as an "executive officer" (in its proxy statement or annual report on Form 10-K), a presumption will arise that the board of directors made this judgment and that the individual is therefore a Section 16 officer. Consequently, once the initial group of Section 16 officers has been identified, the company's board of directors should formally confirm this status. Thereafter, the board of directors should consider taking action annually to review and confirm the identities and titles of its officers subject to Section 16.

Section 16 Reporting. An insider must prepare and file an initial report concerning the insider's holdings of equity securities of the Section 12 company on Form 3, the initial statement of beneficial ownership of securities. Generally, a Form 3 must be filed with the SEC within 10 days after the insider first becomes subject to Section 16, listing the insider's holdings of equity securities as of that date. In the case of a company registering a class of equity securities under Section 12 for the first time, however, a Form 3 must be filed with the SEC for each insider by the effective date of the Section 12 registration. Where Section 12 registration is being made concurrent with the IPO, such filings must take place by the effective date of the IPO. The Form 3 must list and describe all of the equity securities of the company beneficially owned by the insider before the effective date of the Section 12 registration. A Form 3 must be filed whether or not the insider owns any equity securities of the company. The Form 3 must be filed electronically with the SEC on its Electronic Data Gathering and Retrieval (EDGAR) system.

An insider must prepare and file subsequent reports concerning changes to the insider's holdings of equity securities on either Form 4 or Form 5 within the prescribed deadlines set forth in the applicable Exchange Act rules as discussed in chapter 5 of this book. These forms must also be filed electronically with the SEC on EDGAR.

Special "Lookback" Rule. Before an IPO, a privately held company may grant stock options and otherwise issue shares of stock to its officers and members of its board of directors. In addition, such individuals may have other transactions involving the company's equity securities during the pre-IPO period.

To discourage officers and members of the board of directors of pre-public companies from using their knowledge of the impending offering for their own economic advantage, Exchange Act Rule 16a-2 provides that purchase and sales of the company's equity securities during the six-month period preceding the IPO are subject to Section 16 if carried out by officers or directors who become subject to Section 16 solely as a result of the IPO.

This means that any pre-IPO purchase or sale must be disclosed if it occurs within six months of any Form 4 reportable transaction taking place after the IPO. Likewise, such pre-IPO transactions can be matched for purposes of the Section 16(b) "short-swing profits" recovery provision with any IPO sale of securities or any post-IPO transaction that takes place within a six-month period. Consequently, it is important for the equity plan administrator to ensure that any pre-IPO equity awards under an equity plan comply with the applicable conditions of the Exchange Act Rule 16b-3 exemption (as discussed in chapter 5).

4.3.3   Preparing the Registration Statement

The purpose of a formal registration statement is to ensure that complete and accurate information is available about the company and the securities to be offered to the public. The registration statement contains certain detailed information as required by the Securities Act and the SEC rules and forms.

Generally, a registration statement contains two parts: (1) the "prospectus," which must be furnished to each prospective and ultimate purchaser of the securities, and (2) "Part 2," which is filed with the SEC and is available to the public. The basic registration form is Form S-1, which must be used in any offering of securities for which no other form is authorized or prescribed.

Under the SEC's "integrated disclosure system," the basic disclosure requirements for all Securities Act and Exchange Act documents are set forth in a series of SEC regulations. The required disclosures with respect to the company's financial statements are set forth in Regulation S-X. The textual disclosures for the registration statement itself are contained in Regulation S-K. The requirements under the SEC's

EDGAR system, which prescribes electronic filing of all required disclosure documents, are set forth in Regulation S-T.

Compliance with these requirements results in a disclosure document that is both comprehensive and complex. While most of the registration statement will be prepared by the company's corporate securities attorneys, there are certain portions of the document that require detailed disclosure of the company's equity compensation plans and arrangements and other related information. This includes certain information about the company's executive compensation program in both narrative and tabular format as more fully described in chapter 5, as well as a Principal Shareholders table, Shares Eligible for Future Sale table, and, if individuals will be participating in selling their shares during the IPO process, a Selling Shareholder table.

4.3.4   Shares Eligible for Future Sale

The registration statement must disclose, with specificity, the number of shares of stock of the company that are eligible for future sale following the IPO. This discussion typically sets forth the source of these shares of stock, the basis for such future sales, and any contractual or securities law restrictions on such sales. To the extent that the company intends to register its employee equity plans following the IPO, disclosure of these plans is required. This information provides prospective investors with a complete description of the potential dilutive effect that sales of these shares of stock could have once any restrictions on resale have lapsed.

4.3.5   Financial Statement Disclosures

Stock Option Valuation. All companies, including privately held companies, must estimate and recognize a compensation expense for their employee equity awards using the "fair value" method of accounting under ASC 718. An option's "fair value" is to be determined using an option-pricing model, such as the Black-Scholes or a binomial model, that takes into account, as of the grant date, (1) the option price, (2) the expected life of the option, (3) the current price of the underlying shares of stock, (4) its expected volatility, (5) expected dividends on the stock, and (6) the risk-free interest rate for the expected option term.

Under ASC 718, both privately held and public companies are generally subject to the same rules for valuing stock options and other equity awards that are classified as equity instruments. The most challenging aspect of valuation for privately held (or, as they are designated under ASC 718, "nonpublic" companies) is estimating stock price volatility—a required assumption in option-pricing models. Public companies typically estimate volatility using their historical volatility or, if available, the implied volatility of their stock derived from publicly traded options or other derivative securities. These sources are generally unavailable to nonpublic companies. Another difficult input is the current price of the underlying shares of stock. The Financial Accounting Standards Board (FASB) issued ASU 2021-07 in October 2021 to assist nonpublic companies with this complicated input. ASU 2021-07 provides that private companies "may use a value determined by the reasonable application of a reasonable method." It states several factors to be considered for a reasonable valuation. Note this is for accounting purposes only, not for tax or gain calculations.[2]

In addition, the IPO may result in a large number of stock option exercises related to the offering. These transactions should be given less weight in the evaluation of the company's historical data for purposes of establishing the expected option life assumption because the economic conditions that influenced the exercise decisions are not likely to be duplicated in the near future.

Some nonpublic companies may be able to estimate volatility based on the internal market for their shares, private sale transactions, or issues of new equity securities. Alternatively, some nonpublic companies may be able to estimate volatility by using the volatilities of the companies in their performance or compensation peer groups. If volatility cannot be estimated using this type of information ASC 718 prescribes the use of a "calculated value" method. (Under this methodology, a company substitutes the historical volatility of an appropriate industry sector index for its own stock price volatility in the option-pricing model.) In the rare circumstance in which a privately held company cannot estimate either fair value or calculated value because of the

---

2   For an in-depth discussion of ASU 2021-07, see Barbara A. Baksa, *Accounting for Equity Compensation*, 19th ed. (NCEO, 2023)

complexity of an award's terms, the award's intrinsic value must be used and be remeasured at each reporting date.

Detailed descriptions of the disclosure requirements are discussed in chapter 5.

4.3.6 Securities Ownership

When a company goes through an IPO, it will disclose its beneficial ownership in the registration statement. This information includes identities and certain related data concerning beneficial ownership of the company's securities, including equity awards, by certain principal shareholders (primarily those owning 5% or more of the company's outstanding equity), members of management and the board of directors, and any selling shareholders.

4.3.7 Emerging Growth Companies

In April 2012, the Jumpstart Our Business Startups (JOBS) Act was signed into law. Aimed at stimulating capital-raising transactions by small, developing businesses, the JOBS Act contains provisions that simplify the executive compensation compliance and disclosure requirements for certain growth-oriented companies with annual gross revenues of less than $1.07 billion[3] in the previous fiscal year. Companies that fit this description are called "emerging growth companies."

Among other things, an emerging growth company is permitted to file its offering documents with the SEC confidentially, is allowed to communicate with certain investors and other parties while still in the registration process, is exempt from certain of the financial disclosure requirements under Regulation S-X, and is permitted to phase in the requirement for a public company's auditors to provide an attestation report on its internal controls.

Of immediate importance, an emerging growth company is permitted to comply with the executive compensation disclosure requirements by disclosing the same information as a "smaller reporting company" (that is, a company with a common equity "public float" of less than $250 million or that had annual revenues of less than $100 million

---

3. This limit is subject to inflation adjustment every five years.

and either (1) no public float, or (2) a public float of less than $700 million). Specifically, an emerging growth company (as well as a smaller reporting company) need only provide:

- A Summary Compensation table, but covering only three, rather than five, NEOs (including the chief executive officer, but not necessarily the chief financial officer) and limited to two (rather than three) fiscal years' information;

- An Outstanding Equity Awards at Fiscal Year-End table;

- A Director Compensation table; and

- Certain limited narrative disclosure about the employment agreements, post-employment compensation arrangements, and recent equity awards of its NEOs.

An emerging growth company is not required to prepare a Compensation Discussion & Analysis. While emerging growth companies and smaller reporting companies are not required to quantify the potential payments that would be received by their named executive officers (NEOs) in the event of a termination of employment or change in control of the company, they must provide a narrative description, to the extent it is material, of the material terms of each retirement plan that applies to the NEOs and the material terms of each contract, agreement, plan, or arrangement that provides for payment(s) to an NEO at, following, or in connection with the resignation, retirement, or other termination of employment, change in control of the company, or a change in the NEO's responsibilities following a change in control of the company. Another item not required of Emerging Growth Companies is the nonbinding shareholder advisory vote on named executive officer compensation discussed in the following chapter.

4.4 Conclusion

While the reasons for an IPO can be compelling, companies often underestimate the amount of work involved in getting ready to "go public." A fundamental understanding of the process and adequate advance preparation are essential to a successful offering. Because the company's employee equity plan may be the primary source of equity for the company's employees before and after the IPO, it is important to understand both the impact the plan will have on the offering and the impact the offering will have on the plan. In addition, administering the equity plan following an IPO can be very complex and challenging. The equity plan administrator must have a thorough familiarity with the applicable legal regulations and other requirements to ensure a smooth transition from a privately held to a public company.

CHAPTER

5

Executive and Equity Compensation Considerations After an IPO

Jacobin Zorin

CONTENTS

Portions of this chapter were originally written by Mark A. Borges.

Following the initial public offering (IPO) process discussed in the previous chapter, many opportunities and obligations await the newly public company. Some of the types of information required in the registration statement for the IPO are also seen again after the IPO in the public company's regular filings with the Securities and Exchange Commission (SEC). This chapter will discuss some of the disclosure requirements for a public company, along with certain obligations placed on its directors, officers and shareholders, many of which will be monitored and/or maintained by the equity plan administrator.

Public companies are subject to the Securities Exchange Act of 1934 (the "Exchange Act"). Among other things, the Exchange Act imposes certain disclosure and reporting requirements on public companies, prohibits the use of fraudulent and deceptive or manipulative practices in connection with trading in securities, restricts the trading activities of certain corporate insiders, and regulates the use of credit in connection with the purchase of securities.

5.1   Certain Post-IPO Considerations

As discussed in the previous chapter, Section 12 of the Exchange Act requires companies to register a class of equity securities with the SEC if the class is listed for trading on a national securities exchange (Section 12(b)) or if the company has 2,000 or more holders of record (or 500 or more "non-accredited investors") and total assets exceeding $10 million as of the end of the company's fiscal year (Section 12(g)). For purposes of this calculation under Section 12(g) of the Exchange Act, it is permissible to exclude persons who received their securities under an employee compensation plan in a transaction that was exempt from the Securities Act of 1933. In addition, a company may voluntarily register a class of its equity securities under Section 12.

Under Section 13(a) of the Exchange Act, any company that has registered a class of equity securities under Section 12 must file periodic reports with the SEC. These reports include a quarterly report on Form 10-Q, an annual report on Form 10-K, and current reports on Form 8-K.

In addition, the company is subject to the proxy rules of Section 14 of the Exchange Act, and the officers, members of the board of directors, and principal shareholders of the company must file reports and conduct their trading activities in accordance with the requirements of Section 16 of the Exchange Act. Further, except as noted in the following sentence, under Section 14A of the Exchange Act, the company must conduct a shareholder advisory vote on the compensation of its named executive officers in connection with its initial annual meeting of shareholders following its IPO, as well as a shareholder advisory vote to ascertain the preference of its shareholders for the frequency of future shareholder advisory votes on named executive officer compensation (that is, every year, every two years, or every three years). An emerging growth company is not required to conduct these shareholder advisory votes while it maintains that status.[1]

Even if a company has not registered a class of equity securities under Section 12, Section 15(d) of the Exchange Act requires companies with an effective registration statement under the Securities Act that are not otherwise subject to the registration requirements of Section 12 to comply with the reporting requirement of Section 13(a) until such time as they have fewer than 300 shareholders of record at the beginning of any subsequent fiscal year.

Some of the more prominent compliance requirements under the Exchange Act that affect administration of the company's equity plan are discussed below.

5.1.1 Form S-8 Registration

Following the IPO, a company will need to ensure that the securities issued to employees under its equity plans satisfy the requirements of federal and state securities laws. Generally, securities cannot be issued under an equity plan unless a registration statement is in effect or an exemption from registration is available.

---

1.   See chapter 4 for a discussion of emerging growth companies.

Form S-8 is a simplified registration statement that may be used by a company subject to the reporting requirements of the Exchange Act to register the securities to be offered and sold pursuant to the company's equity plan for purposes of the federal securities laws. Form S-8 reflects an abbreviated disclosure format and incorporates by reference information contained in the company's other publicly available documents.[2]

Unlike other registration statements, Form S-8 does not require the preparation and distribution of a formal prospectus. Instead, under Section 10(a) of the Securities Act, the company need only deliver to participants certain required information about the equity plan and a statement of the documents that are available upon request to participants. This information can be provided separately or integrated into the company's customary employee communications. The information must be identified as comprising part of the Form S-8 "prospectus," which is accomplished by including a specific legend at the beginning of each document that contains the required equity plan information.

A company is eligible to use a Form S-8 at any time after becoming subject to the reporting requirements of the Exchange Act. In addition, a Form S-8 must be filed before any option shares are issued to participants and becomes effective immediately upon filing with the SEC.

Form S-8 covers offers and sales of securities under an equity plan to consultants and advisors, as well as to employees,[3] officers, and directors. Transactions by former employees are also covered in certain

---

2. In November 2020, the SEC proposed changes to Form S-8 that among other things, include the ability to include multiple plans as well as the allocation of securities among multiple incentive plans on a single Form S-8; permit the addition of securities or classes of securities by filing an automatically effective post-effective amendment to a previously filed Form S-8; include improvements to simplify share counting and fee payments; and eliminate the requirement to describe tax effects of plan participation on the issuer.

3. A separate set of changes, also proposed by the SEC in November 2020, concerns the temporary rule provision that, for five years, an issuer would be able to use Form S-8 to register offerings of securities to its platform workers, defined as workers who provide services through the issuer's internet-based marketplace platform or other widespread, technology-based system.

instances.[4] Form S-8 applies to transactions pursuant to individual written compensatory contracts, as well as actual equity plans.

Option shares acquired under a Form S-8 registration statement may be resold by nonaffiliates without restriction. Affiliates may sell their Form S-8-registered option shares pursuant to Securities Act Rule 144, but without regard to the holding period condition.

5.1.2 Establishing a Same-Day Exercise and Sale Program

As noted in the previous chapter, once public, the company will probably elect to establish a broker-assisted same-day sale program to provide optionees with an efficient means to finance the exercise of their stock options. A same-day sale exercise is a process by which an employee can finance the exercise of a stock option by immediately selling through a securities brokerage firm that number of option shares, from the stock option being exercised, necessary to satisfy the payment of the total option price for the option shares being purchased plus any withholding taxes due.

The company may elect to make formal arrangements with one or more securities brokerage firms to facilitate these transactions. Not only do such arrangements, sometimes referred to as "captive broker" programs, simplify the administration of these programs, they also enable the transactions to be completed efficiently. The company will keep the firm or firms updated on outstanding stock options, thereby enabling optionees to contact the firm directly when they want to exercise their stock options. To further simplify the administration of these transactions, some companies will establish an "omnibus" account with one or more firms and transfer a block of shares to the account for the purpose of ensuring sufficient shares are available to deliver upon the settlement of the sale.

Under Section 13(k) of the Exchange Act, reporting companies are prohibited from making personal loans or facilitating the extension of credit to their executive officers and members of the board of directors. It remains unclear whether stock option exercises by an executive of-

---

4. The proposed changes also include expanding eligibility to former employees, allowing companies to issue awards following termination as compensation for services rendered during the employment period.

ficer or member of the board of directors using a broker-assisted same-day exercise and sale program constitute prohibited loans under this section. Consequently, a company should consult its professional legal advisors when establishing a broker-assisted same-day exercise and sale program to determine whether the program may be extended to its executive officers and members of its board of directors. Note there is not a prohibition on credit vehicles not made directly by the company.

5.1.3   Form 8-K

In addition to the quarterly report on Form 10-Q and the annual report on Form 10-K, the SEC has identified a series of events that must be reported on a current report on Form 8-K to effect real-time disclosure of important company information. These disclosure items cover a range of significant corporate events, such as the departure of a director or principal officer and an amendment to the company's articles of incorporation or bylaws. They also include some events that are potentially applicable to the administration of a company's equity plan, such as the entry into a definitive material agreement involving a compensatory arrangement.

Currently, a publicly traded company must file a Form 8-K for compensation-related transactions and events in the following instances:

•   where a director resigns or refuses to stand for reelection to the board of directors because of a disagreement with the company that is known to at least one of the company's executive officers on any matter involving the company's operations, policies, or practices, or if a director is removed for cause;

•   where the company's principal executive officer, president, principal financial officer, principal accounting officer, or principal operating officer, or any person performing similar functions (principal officer), or any named executive officer (NEO)[5] whose compensation must be disclosed in the proxy statement, retires, resigns, or has his or her employment terminated, or if a director retires, resigns, is removed, or refuses to stand for re-election (except because of a disagreement, as noted above);

---

5.   For more detail, see section 5.3.4.3.

- where the company appoints a new principal officer (in this case, the required disclosure must describe any material plan, contract, or arrangement to which the covered officer is a party or in which he or she participates that is entered into or material amendment in connection with the triggering event, and any grant or award made to the officer or modification thereto, under the plan, contract, or arrangement in connection with such event);

- where the company elects a new director at a time other than in connection with an annual or special meeting of shareholders (in this case, the required disclosure must briefly describe any material plan, contract, or arrangement to which the director is a party or in which he or she participates that is entered into or material amendment in connection with the triggering event, and any grant or award made to the director or modification thereto, under the plan, contract, or arrangement in connection with such event); and

- where the company enters into, adopts, or otherwise commences a material compensatory plan, contract, or arrangement in which the company's principal executive officer, principal financial officer, or an NEO participates or is a party, or such compensatory plan, contract, or arrangement is materially amended or modified, or a material grant or award under any such plan, contract, or arrangement to any such person is made or materially modified (in this case, the required disclosure must briefly describe the terms and conditions of the plan, contract, or arrangement and the amounts payable to the officer thereunder).

In the case of this last disclosure trigger, a Form 8-K need not be filed in the case of grants or awards (whether involving cash or equity) that are materially consistent with the previously disclosed terms of such plan, contract, or arrangement, provided the company has previously disclosed such terms and the grant or award is subsequently included in the company's proxy disclosure about executive compensation. In addition, a company does not need to file a Form 8-K regarding a plan, contract, or arrangement that does not discriminate in scope, terms, or operation in favor of executive officers or directors and that is available generally to all salaried employees.

It is important to note that this Form 8-K filing requirement is in addition to an individual executive's obligation to file a Section 16(a) insider report within two business days of the receipt of an equity award from the executive's company (as discussed below).

A Form 8-K must be filed with the SEC within four business days of a triggering event. Sometimes companies will need to file a Form 8-K (to meet the four-day filing deadline) when all of the details about the disclosure may be unclear. The rules contain a limited "safe harbor" from liability under the federal anti-fraud rules solely for situations where the company adopts a new material compensation plan or makes a material grant or award under such a plan or arrangement. For example, if a company does not make a required Form 8-K filing for the grant of an equity award (because it originally believed the award was not material), it will not be subject to possible anti-fraud liability as long as the award is disclosed in its next required quarterly or annual report.

5.2 Section 16 and Insider Trading

Assuming a company has registered a class of its equity securities with the SEC under Section 12 in connection with its IPO, the officers and members of the board of directors of the company will be subject to Section 16 following the offering. Section 16 governs reporting obligations and regulates the trading activities of the officers, members of the board of directors, and principal shareholders of public companies in the equity securities of their own companies. Specifically, officers and members of the board of directors of a company that has a class of equity securities registered under the Exchange Act and beneficial owners of more than 10% of the class of equity securities so registered (often called "insiders") must disclose their holdings of, and transactions involving, the equity securities of their company, and further must return to the company any profits that they realize in the event of any "short-swing" trading in such securities.

5.2.1 Section 16 Reporting and Matching

Under Section 16(a) of the Exchange Act, an insider must file reports with the SEC (which reports are available to the public) disclosing their holdings of, and transactions involving, the equity securities of the insider's company. This reporting is required for any equity securities that the insider beneficially owns. Although the reporting obligation technically falls to the insider, the equity plan administrator or other designated individual is typically responsible for assisting the company's officers and directors in complying with their filing obligations. All Section 16(a) reports must be filed electronically with the SEC on its Electronic Data Gathering and Retrieval (EDGAR) system.

The filing of a Form 3, an initial statement of beneficial ownership of securities, in connection with an IPO is discussed in the previous chapter. For companies that are already public, each time an individual joins the company as an officer or director, or is promoted to officer or director status, a Form 3 must be filed with the SEC by the new insider within 10 calendar days of becoming an insider.

With limited exceptions, a Form 4, the statement of changes in beneficial ownership of securities, must be filed with the SEC within two business days after the date of execution of a transaction that results in a change in the insider's beneficial ownership of the company's equity securities that is not otherwise eligible for deferred reporting under a specific SEC rule. In other words, a Form 4 must be filed within two business days whenever there is an acquisition or disposition of equity securities by an insider, such as an open-market purchase or sale, including any exercise or conversion of a derivative security, such as an employee stock option. Under the Section 16 rules, any transaction that may be reported on a deferred basis on Form 5 may be reported voluntarily on an earlier filed Form 4.

Generally, a Form 5, the annual statement of changes in beneficial ownership of securities, must be filed with the SEC within 45 days after the end of the company's fiscal year to report any change in the insider's beneficial ownership of the company's equity securities that is otherwise eligible for deferred reporting. In other words, a Form 5 must be filed whenever there is an acquisition or disposition of equity securities by an insider (such as a bona fide gift) that is eligible for deferred reporting and that has not been previously reported on a Form 4. See chapter 2 for more specific details on these reporting requirements.

"Short-Swing Profits" Liability. Under Section 16(b) of the Exchange Act, a public company may recover from an insider any profits that

are realized as a result of the purchase and sale, or sale and purchase, of the company's equity securities within a period of less than six months. Section 16(b) imposes strict liability on an insider who meets the required elements of the provision. In other words, disgorgement of any profits realized from the "short-swing" transactions is required whether or not the insider actually used material nonpublic information to conduct the trades. Moreover, Section 16(b) may operate to require that the insider forfeit "short-swing profits" to the company even where the insider has, in fact, realized no economic gain from the transactions.

For purposes of Section 16(b), the terms "purchase" and "sale" are interpreted broadly and may include acquisitions and dispositions involving derivative securities as well as acquisitions and dispositions arising in connection with a merger or other corporate transaction. Certain types of transactions, however, such as a bona fide gift, are exempt from "purchase" or "sale" status by virtue of a specific SEC rule and thus are outside the scope of Section 16(b). In addition, under the broad definition of "beneficial ownership," transactions by other persons can be attributed to an insider for purposes of Section 16(b). For example, in certain situations, the equity securities held by relatives of an insider will be deemed to be beneficially owned by the insider. Thus, a purchase or sale of the securities by a member of an insider's immediate family may be matched with a sale or purchase by the insider that occurs within the same six-month period to trigger short-swing profits recovery.

Where short-swing trading has occurred, the amount of "profits" recoverable by the company is to be determined by pairing the insider's transactions within the six-month period so as to match the transaction with the highest sale price and the transaction with the lowest purchase price. It does not matter whether the purchase or the sale occurred first, and it is not necessary for the same securities to have been involved in each of the matched transactions. The sum of the profits from these matched purchases and sales is the amount that the insider must turn over to the company. As previously noted, because gains are not offset by losses, it is possible for an insider to realize profits for purposes of Section 16(b) even though the insider actually lost money from the trading activities.

Typically, the equity plan administrator assists a company's officers and members of its board of directors in avoiding the operation of Section 16(b) when planning and executing their transactions involving the company's equity securities. In addition, the equity plan administrator should ensure that transactions involving the company's equity plans satisfy an appropriate exemption under Exchange Act Rule 16b-3 so as to ensure that such transactions are not considered to involve either a purchase or a sale for purposes of Section 16(b). Under Rule 16b-3, a transaction between a company (including an employee benefit plan sponsored by the company) and its officers and members of its board of directors is exempt from the short-swing profits recovery provisions of Section 16(b) if it satisfies the applicable conditions of the exemption.

Routine, non-volitional transactions pursuant to a "tax-conditioned plan" (which generally encompasses most Section 401(k) plans, tax-qualified profit-sharing plans, and Section 423 employee stock purchase plans) are typically exempt from the operation of Section 16(b) without having to satisfy any specific conditions. Fund-switching transactions or volitional cash withdrawals from an employer securities fund in an employee benefit plan will be exempt if the election to engage in the transaction is at least six months after the last "opposite way" (purchase vs. sale) transaction under any company plan.

Other acquisitions of a company's equity securities by an officer or member of the board of directors from his or her company, including grants of stock options and other equity vehicles, are exempt from the operation of Section 16(b) if the transaction is approved by the company's board of directors, approved by a committee of two or more "nonemployee directors" (as defined under the rule), approved or ratified by the company's shareholders, or a six-month holding period requirement is satisfied. While these conditions make it much easier to qualify an award of a company's equity securities, including stock option grants, for exemptive treatment, the equity plan administrator must make sure that the required approval has been obtained for each award to an insider.

Proxy Statement Disclosure. A public company is required by Item 405(a)(1) of Regulation S-K to disclose in its annual proxy statement and annual report on Form 10-K under the caption "Delinquent Section 16(a) Reports" a list of any insiders who have been delinquent in filing or failed to file the required Section 16(a) reports with the SEC during the last completed fiscal year. This disclosure is to include: (1) the name of the insider who failed to file reports on a timely basis during the fiscal year, (2) the number of late reports by the insider, (3) the number of transactions not reported on a timely basis, and (4) any known failures to file a required report. If there are no late filings, no disclosure is required.

This disclosure is based solely on the information contained in the reports furnished to the company during the fiscal year and any written representations delivered to the company by insiders stating that no Form 5 was required. The company may rely on a written representation from an insider that no Form 5 was required if the company maintains a file of such representations for two years and makes copies available to the SEC upon request.

5.2.2   Insider Trading

Under the federal securities laws, any person, including an insider, possessing "material" nonpublic information about a company must refrain from engaging in transactions in the company's securities until adequate public disclosure of this information has been made. The penalties for trading in securities while in the possession of material nonpublic information are severe and include injunctive actions or actions for civil penalties that may be brought by the SEC, actions for monetary damages that may be brought by private parties, and criminal penalties. The federal securities laws also prohibit persons, including insiders, from "tipping" third parties, either by disclosing confidential information to such persons or by making trading recommendations based on such information.

Of the various antifraud provisions found in the federal securities laws, Section 10(b) of the Exchange Act has enjoyed the broadest application. Generally, Section 10(b) makes it unlawful for any person, directly or indirectly, to use or employ, in connection with the purchase or sale of a security (whether or not registered on an exchange), "any manipulative or deceptive device or contrivance" which contravenes such rules and regulations as the SEC may adopt.

Pursuant to this authority, the SEC has adopted Exchange Act Rule 10b-5, which states that it is unlawful for any person, directly or indirectly, to employ any "device, scheme or artifice to defraud," to make any untrue statement of a material fact, to omit to state a material fact necessary to make statements not misleading, or to engage in any "act, practice or course of business which operates" as a fraud or deceit upon any person.

One of the primary uses of Rule 10b-5 over the years has been to prohibit trading in securities by persons having knowledge of material, undisclosed information, thereby promoting full and fair disclosure of material information to all investors. This prohibition on "insider trading" is applied broadly by the courts and covers not only officers, members of the board of directors, and principal shareholders of the company, but essentially anyone who comes into possession of confidential information and has a duty to disclose (or to abstain from trading), including an insider's spouse and immediate family members. The prohibition covers trading in the equity, debt, and derivative securities of the company.

"Material" Information. While there is no specific definition of what constitutes material information for purposes of the insider trading prohibitions, at least two standards are commonly applied to determine the "materiality" of specific information. First, if the information would be expected to significantly affect the market price of the company's stock, then it is probably material. Alternatively, if the information would influence or affect the investment decisions of a reasonable investor, then, once again, it is probably material. Typical examples of material information might include a company's quarterly and annual financial results (or components thereof); major proposed or pending transactions; changes in a company's capital structure; research and development projects or plans; pricing, sales, or market plans or projections; management or other key personnel changes; and litigation developments.

Nonpublic Information. Generally, information is considered to be "nonpublic" until it has been disseminated throughout the securities markets. As construed by the courts, this means that the information must have first been distributed through the media of widest circulation. Typically, this is accomplished by disclosure of the information in one or more of the company's periodic reports or filings under the federal securities laws or through the issuance of a press release.

The prohibitions against insider trading not only restrict a person from making use of the confidential information but also prohibit "tipping," which means passing the information on to another person who then trades on the basis of the information (where the person could have reasonably foreseen that the recipient would make use of the information).

Trading Policies. Because of the difficulties associated with determining the materiality of undisclosed information, many companies maintain internal trading policies to prevent inadvertent violations of the insider trading prohibitions. A typical trading policy will restrict transactions in the company's stock to certain designated periods following the release of quarterly financial information about the company. These trading periods are commonly referred to as "window" periods. (Similarly, the periods when trading is not permitted are commonly referred to as "closed trading windows.") In addition, the company may designate an employee, usually a member of management, to act as a compliance officer. In this capacity, the compliance officer must clear in advance any trade in the company's stock by an employee or other individual subject to the policy.

At a minimum, corporate trading policies will be applied to its officers, members of its board of directors, and other insiders. Some companies extend the policy to several additional levels of employees, while others apply the policy to all employees. Even where a company limits its trading policy to insiders, most companies take steps to ensure that, at a minimum, all employees are aware of their obligations under the federal securities laws.

Rule 10b5-1. Under Exchange Act Rule 10b5-1, for purposes of Section 10(b), an individual will be considered to have traded "on the basis of" material non-public information if he or she was aware of the information at the time he or she made the subject purchase or sale of securities. However, the rule goes on to provide an affirmative defense to this "awareness" standard for determining insider trading liability. If an individual has (1) entered into a binding contract to purchase or sell a security, provided instructions to another person to purchase or sell a security for the instructing person's account, or adopted a written plan for trading securities before becoming aware of the material nonpublic information; (2) the binding contract, instructions, or written plan expressly provides (by amount or formula) the amount, price, and date of the transaction (and does not permit the individual to exercise any subsequent influence over how, when, or whether to effect purchases or sales); and (3) demonstrated the transaction in question was pursuant to the binding contract, instructions, or written plan, then the binding contract, instructions, or written plan will act as an affirmative defense to a claim of insider trading. Note, however, that a transaction (that is, a purchase or sale) conducted pursuant to a binding contract, instructions, or written plan will still be subject to short-swing profits liability under Section 16(b) if it is an opposite-way transaction from a separate nonexempt sale or purchase of securities that takes place within a period of less than six months either before or after such transaction.

Because a written program for trading securities may cover any securities owned by an individual, many officers and members of boards of directors of public companies have taken to adopting written trading plans as a means for implementing liquidity strategies for their companies' equity. Unlike a trading window instituted to ensure compliance with Rule 10b-5, a trading plan does not permit any discretion on the part of the individual adopting the plan. It does, however, permit trading at any time, as long as all criteria for trading were established at a previous time when the individual was not aware of any material nonpublic information about the company. If a trading plan involves the disposition of "restricted securities" for purposes of Rule 144, the parties must ensure compliance with the resale conditions of that rule.

Insider Trading Prohibition During Pension Fund Closed Trading Windows. Section 306(a) of the Sarbanes-Oxley Act prohibits executive officers and members of the board of directors of public companies from, directly or indirectly, purchasing, selling, or otherwise acquiring or transferring any equity security of the company during a pension plan closed trading window that prevents plan participants or beneficiaries from engaging in equity security transactions, if the equity security was acquired in connection with the executive officer or director's employment or service as an executive officer or member of the board of directors. In addition, the company must provide timely notice to its executive officers and members of its board of directors, as well as to the SEC, of an impending closed trading window.

The SEC has adopted Regulation BTR, which contains rules that clarify the application of this insider trading prohibition, including rules that define when an equity security is acquired "in connection with" employment or service as an executive officer or member of the board of directors. Generally, these rules provide that equity securities, including equity awards, acquired under an equity plan maintained by the company are to be considered acquired in connection with employment or service. Accordingly, companies will need to assist their executive officers and directors in identifying the equity securities that are subject to the trading prohibition and in monitoring any pension plan closed trading windows to avoid violations of the prohibition.

Where an executive officer or director engages in a prohibited transaction, he or she is subject to possible enforcement action by the SEC. In addition, the company may recover from the executive officer or director any profits that are realized as a result of the purchase, sale, acquisition, or transfer that occurred during the closed trading window. Similar to Section 16(b), Section 306(a) imposes strict liability on an executive officer or director who violates the trading prohibition. In other words, disgorgement of any profits realized from the prohibited transaction is required whether or not the executive officer or director intended to trade in violation of the statutory provision.

Certain Insider Trading Statutory Provisions. Over the past 40 years, the existing body of insider trading law has been supplemented by a number of statutory provisions. The adoption of these provisions has been frequently cited as a significant influence in the development of insider trading policies and other internal controls by many publicly held companies. For example, in the mid-1980s, the Insider Trading Sanctions Act of 1984 was enacted by Congress. Among other things, the Act authorized the SEC to seek civil penalties of up to three times the profit gained or the loss avoided where a person purchased or sold securities while in possession of material nonpublic information.

In 1988, Congress enacted the Insider Trading and Securities Fraud Enforcement Act, which added Section 21A to the Exchange Act. Among other things, Section 21A authorizes the SEC to seek civil penalties against employers and other controlling persons who "knew or recklessly disregarded" the fact that a controlled person was likely to engage in insider trading and failed to take appropriate steps to prevent such act before it occurred. While the Exchange Act does not define what constitutes appropriate steps, most companies have concluded it is necessary to communicate regularly with all employees, especially those most likely to have access to confidential information, about their responsibilities under the federal securities laws and to establish some control over trading by directors and officers.

Section 21A retained the civil remedy established by the Insider Trading Sanctions Act against primary traders. In addition, it authorized the imposition of a penalty against controlling persons of the greater of $1 million or three times the profit gained or loss avoided as a result of the controlled person's violation.

In 1990, the Securities Enforcement Remedies and Penny Stock Reform Act (SERPSR) was enacted. This substantially increased the enforcement powers of the SEC for violations of the federal securities laws. Among the remedies available under the SERPSR, the SEC has the authority to issue both permanent and temporary cease-and-desist orders to enforce the various federal securities laws, the power to seek in federal district court monetary penalties ranging from $5,000 to $500,000 for securities law violations, and the ability to seek to have individuals who have violated specific provisions of the federal securities laws barred from serving as a director or officer of a public company.

5.3 Annual Disclosures

A company is required to disclose much detailed information annually in its SEC filings. Between the annual report on Form 10-K and the proxy statement, certain information will be provided in each document, or may be incorporated by reference in one or the other document. Form 10-K gives a comprehensive summary of a company's history, business and financial performance, organizational structure, and audited financial statements, among other information. The Form 10-K is distinct from the annual report to shareholders, which a company must send when it holds an annual meeting to elect directors and transact other annual business. Today many companies combine the annual report to shareholders and the Form 10-K into one document, typically called a "Form 10-K wrap."

Generally, a proxy statement is a document required when a company wishes to solicit votes from its shareholders. The SEC requires that shareholders of a company whose securities are registered under Section 12 of the Exchange Act receive a proxy statement before a shareholder meeting, whether it is an annual or special meeting. The information contained in the proxy statement must be filed with the SEC before soliciting a shareholder vote on the election of directors and the approval of other corporate actions, such as the approval or amendment of an equity plan. Solicitations, whether by management or shareholders, must disclose all important facts about the issues on which shareholders are asked to vote. Typically, the equity plan administrator is involved in providing some of the information disclosed in the proxy statement.

This section discusses some of the information included in the proxy statement and certain other required disclosures.

5.3.1 Shareholder Approval of Equity Plans

Companies that are listed on the NYSE or Nasdaq must obtain shareholder approval of their equity plans and material revisions or amendments to such plans, subject to the limited exemptions discussed below.

Under the NYSE listing standards, an "equity compensation plan" is a plan or other arrangement that provides for the delivery of shares (either newly issued or treasury shares) of a listed company to any employee, director, or service provider as compensation for services, including a compensatory grant of options or other equity securities that is not made under a formal plan. Certain plans are not considered equity compensation plans for purposes of the standard, including:

- Plans that provide for the payment of cash based on the value of shares, rather than for the delivery of actual shares;

- Plans that are made available to shareholders generally (such as a typical dividend reinvestment plan); and

- Plans that merely allow employees, directors, or service providers to elect to buy shares on the open market or from the listed company for their current fair market value, regardless of whether the shares are delivered immediately or on a deferred basis, or the payments for the shares are made directly or by giving up compensation that is otherwise due (for example, through payroll deductions).

The Nasdaq listing standards do not define the types of plans that must be approved by shareholders. Instead, the standards cover stock option and purchase plans and other equity compensation arrangements pursuant to which options or stock may be acquired by officers, directors, employees, or consultants, except for warrants or rights issued generally to all shareholders, stock purchase plans available on equal terms to all shareholders (such as a typical dividend reinvestment plan), tax-qualified, nondiscriminatory employee benefit plans or parallel nonqualified plans (provided such plans are approved by the company's independent compensation committee or a majority of the company's independent directors), plans that merely provide a convenient way to purchase shares on the open market or from the company at fair market value, plans or arrangements relating to an acquisition or merger as permitted under the listing standards, or "inducement" awards to individuals being hired by the company or being rehired following a bona fide period of interruption of employment (provided such plans are approved by the company's independent compensation committee or a majority of the company's independent directors).

Both standards require shareholder approval of any material revision or amendment of an equity compensation plan, such as a company's equity plan. Generally, a "material revision" or "material amendment" is a modification that expands, rather than curtails, the scope of the equity plan.

The NYSE listing standards do not require shareholder approval for the adoption or amendment of certain specified types of plans and arrangements. These plans and arrangements are exempt, however, only if approved by the listed company's independent compensation committee or a majority of the company's independent directors. In addition, in the case of a listed company, the NYSE must be notified in writing when one of these exemptions is relied upon.

Generally, the exemptions under the NYSE listing standards include:

- "inducement" awards to individuals being hired by the company or being rehired following a *bona fide* period of interruption of employment;

- the conversion, replacement, or adjustment of outstanding options or other equity compensation awards to reflect the terms of a merger or other acquisition transaction;

- post-transaction grants of options and other equity awards of shares under certain pre-existing plans acquired in a corporate merger or acquisition;

- grants and awards pursuant to tax-qualified, nondiscriminatory employee benefit plans (such as Section 401(a) plans and Section 423 plans); and

- grants and awards pursuant to pension plans designed to work in parallel with tax-qualified employee benefit plans that meet certain conditions.

Finally, special rules apply to so-called "formula" and "discretionary" plans, as defined in the relevant listing standard.

5.3.2 Proxy Advisory Firm Review of Equity Plans

In addition to these regulatory requirements, institutional shareholders and their advisors will carefully scrutinize an equity plan as part of their review process before casting their votes at the annual meeting of shareholders at which the equity plan is being submitted for shareholder action. While some of the larger institutional shareholders rely on their own internal policies in evaluating the terms and conditions of the equity plan and the potential dilutive effect that it will have on their interests, many shareholders rely on the analyses of the equity plan conducted by one or more of the major proxy advisory firms (such as Institutional Shareholder Services, Inc. (ISS) and Glass Lewis & Company) before making a voting decision.

Benchmarks. Each year, the shareholder advisory firms update the benchmark policy guidelines they will use in evaluating the matters submitted at the annual meetings of shareholders of the companies in the Russell 3000 and formulating their voting recommendations for their institutional clients.

For example, ISS formulates its recommendations on the approval of an equity plan proposal using a "scorecard" approach (the "Equity Plan Scorecard" or "EPSC"). This approach considers a range of positive and negative factors, rather than a series of pass/fail tests, to evaluate equity plan proposals. Generally, the total EPSC score will determine whether ISS recommends "for" or "against" an equity plan proposal. While some "highly egregious" equity plan features continue to result in "against" recommendations regardless of other factors, vote recommendations are largely based on a combination of factors related to the equity plan's cost, its features, and the company's equity award grant practices. For example, an equity plan where cost is nominally higher than a company's "allowable cap" (as explained below) may receive a favorable recommendation if sufficient positive factors (involving the features of the equity plan and the company's equity award grant practices) are present. Conversely, an equity plan where the cost is nominally lower than the "allowable cap" may ultimately receive an unfavorable recommendation if a preponderance of the scorecard factors are negative.

The EPSC system considers factors that fall under three general categories: plan cost, plan features, and grant practices. Some of the key factors considered under each category are as follows:

Plan Cost. This category evaluates the total estimated cost of a company's equity plans (but excluding employee stock purchase plans) relative to its industry/market cap peers. This cost is determined using the company's estimated "shareholder value transfer" (SVT), as described below (that is, the estimated value being transferred to executives and other employees through the grant of equity) in relation to its peers and considers both:

- SVT based on new shares requested plus shares remaining for future grants, plus outstanding unvested awards and unexercised options (whether vested or unvested); and

- SVT based only on new shares requested plus shares remaining for future grants.

Where an equity plan provides for both option-like and full value awards, unless limits are placed on the number of full-value shares that may be awarded under the equity plan (that is, a "fungible share" provision), ISS will assume that all awards will be granted as full-value awards. An equity plan's SVT will be considered reasonable if it falls below a company-specific "allowable cap." As a matter of policy, ISS does not disclose the relative weightings of these SVT calculations.

Plan Features. The presence or absence of any of the following features in a company's equity plan is taken into consideration:

- Automatic single-triggered award vesting upon a change in control of the company;
- Discretionary vesting authority (without regard to whether there has been a change in control of the company);
- Liberal share recycling on various award types; and
- Minimum vesting period of at least one year for awards made under the equity plan.

Grant Practices. The following award practices are considered:

- The company's value-adjusted burn rate[6] relative to its index group peers, now updated for the 2023 proxy season (previously the three-year burn rate);
- Vesting schedules and performance periods contained in the most recent equity awards granted to the company's chief executive officer during the prior three years;
- The estimated duration of the equity plan based on the sum of shares remaining available for issuance and the new shares requested, divided by the average annual shares granted in the prior three years;

---

6. The value-adjusted burn rate is based on calculations that are based on actual stock prices for full-value awards and Black-Scholes values for stock options.

- The proportion of the chief executive officer's most recent equity awards subject to performance conditions;

- Whether the company maintains a compensation recovery ("clawback") policy that includes equity grants; and

- Whether the company has established post-exercise/post-vesting shareholding requirements.

Each of the three EPSC categories is weighted based on a company's index group. The three groups are: (1) the S&P 500, (2) the Russell 3000, minus the S&P 500, and (3) non-Russell 3000 companies and those companies that have recently gone public.

Finally, ISS will recommend a vote against an equity plan proposal if the combination of above factors indicates that the equity plan is not, overall, in shareholders' interests, or if any of the following apply:

- Equity awards may vest in connection with a liberal change-of-control definition;

- The equity plan permits the repricing or cash buyout of "underwater" stock options without shareholder approval, either by expressly permitting it (for NYSE-listed and Nasdaq-listed companies) or by not prohibiting it when the company has a history of repricing (for non-listed companies);

- The equity plan is a vehicle for problematic pay practices (such as inclusion of a Section 280G excise tax "gross-up" provision for equity plan awards) or a pay-for-performance disconnect;

- Dilution from the company's equity plans exceeds 20% for S&P 500 companies or 25% for Russell 3000 companies; or

- Any other equity plan features are determined to have a significant negative impact on shareholder interests.

Equity Plan Cost. For purposes of establishing the cost of an equity plan, ISS uses a figure expressed as the SVT, which is measured using a binomial option pricing model assessing the amount of shareholders' equity flowing out of the company to the equity plan participants (typically, executives, directors, and employees). SVT is expressed as both a dollar amount and as a percentage of market value, and includes the new shares proposed for issuance under the proposed equity plan, the shares available under existing equity plans, and the shares previously granted but unexercised. For purposes of this calculation, all award types are valued. In the case of an "omnibus" equity plan, unless limits are placed on the number of shares that may be granted as the most expensive types of awards (for example, full-value awards), ISS will assume that all awards to be granted will be the most expensive type.

ISS views a company's SVT as reasonable if it falls below the company-specific "allowable cap." The allowable cap is determined as follows: The top quartile performers in each industry group (using the Global Industry Classification Standard (GICS)) are identified. Benchmark SVT levels for each industry are then established based on these top performers' historic SVT. Regression analyses are run on each industry group to identify the variables most strongly correlated to SVT. The benchmark industry SVT level is then adjusted upward or downward for the specific company by plugging the company-specific performance measures,[7] size, and cash compensation into the industry cap equations to arrive at the company's allowable cap.

Pay-for-Performance Assessment. In the case of the "pay-for-performance" assessment, if a significant portion of the pay of a company's chief executive officer (CEO) is attributed to non-performance-based equity awards (and, therefore, is considered misaligned), and there is an equity plan on the agenda for the annual meeting of shareholders in which the CEO is an eligible participant, ISS will consider (1) the magnitude of this perceived misalignment; (2) the contribution of non–performance-based equity awards to overall pay; and (3) the proportion of equity awards granted in the last three fiscal years concentrated at the NEO level in formulating its voting recommendation on the equity plan proposal.

---

7.   Company-specific performance measures include outstanding grants and shares remaining for future grants, generally reported in the company's annual 10-K or proxy filing. To determine SVT benchmarks, ISS downloads company-specific data points, including option-pricing model inputs, from a third-party vendor four times a year.

Liberal Share Recycling. ISS considers whether a company maintains a "liberal share recycling" provision in its equity plan. For this purpose, an equity plan is considered to have a "liberal share recycling" provision if shares granted and exercised can, under certain circumstances, be added back to the equity plan reserve for future grant. Equity plans with such provisions will receive a more costly valuation in the ISS model as if all shares will be granted as full-value awards. For purposes of the ISS policy, "recycled shares" may include, but are not limited to: (1) shares tendered as payment for an option exercise; (2) shares withheld for taxes; (3) shares added back that have been repurchased by the company using stock option exercise proceeds; and (4) stock-settled awards where only the actual shares delivered with respect to the award are counted against the equity plan reserve.

If there is a stated limit on full-value awards and the equity plan explicitly provides that liberal recycling is only allowed on full-value awards, then ISS will apply the limit accordingly as stated. If liberal recycling is also permitted on other forms of awards (such as stock options), however, then ISS will consider that the recycling feature effectively nullifies the stated limit under the equity plan because of the additional cost attributed to the potential of recycling other types of awards.

Stock Ownership Guidelines. In addition to the above, proxy advisory firms are very interested in the details of any stock ownership guidelines maintained by companies. In recent years, many companies have adopted specific guidelines regarding the required ownership of company stock by certain officers and directors. The board or compensation committee will adopt a guideline that contains a certain number or percentage of stock for each position that must be held by each person, allowing for a period to comply. The basic concept is that each director and officer will hold a meaningful number of shares while at the company, which aligns their economic interests with that of shareholders. Proxy advisory firms consider ownership guidelines part of a good governance structure. Guidelines differ significantly across companies, with some companies allowing a certain percentage of shares to be made up of vested options or unvested restricted stock units (RSUs) as well as stock owned outright. The method of classification and weight given to a company's stock ownership guidelines should be discussed with the company's proxy advisory firm to determine scoring according to its specific guidelines.

5.3.3 Dodd-Frank Executive Compensation Provisions

While largely dealing with regulation of the financial services industry, the Dodd–Frank Act, enacted in 2010, also contains a number of executive compensation-related provisions that apply to publicly traded and/or exchange-listed companies.

Say on Pay. Section 14A(a)(1) of the Exchange Act requires public companies to conduct a nonbinding shareholder advisory vote on the compensation of their named executive officers (as reflected in the executive compensation disclosure in their proxy statements) at least once every three years ("say on pay"). In addition, under Section 14A(a)(2) of the Exchange Act, public companies must conduct a nonbinding shareholder advisory vote at least once every six years on whether to hold a say-on-pay vote annually, every two years, or every three years. Finally, Section 14A(b) of the Exchange Act (Section 14A(b)) requires public companies that are seeking shareholder approval of an acquisition, merger, consolidation, or other proposed sale or other disposition of all or substantially all the assets of the company to (1) disclose any arrangement that the company has with any named executive officer to provide post-employment compensation that is based on or otherwise relates to the transaction, and (2) at the same time, conduct a nonbinding shareholder advisory vote to approve such compensation arrangements (to the extent not previously subject to a say-on-pay vote). The SEC has adopted Exchange Act Rule 14a-21 to set out requirements for the operation of these provisions. These provisions also apply to smaller reporting companies.[8] As previously noted, these provisions do not apply to emerging growth companies while they maintain that status.

The Dodd-Frank Act makes clear that these "advisory" votes are not binding on the company or its board of directors and will not overrule a decision of the company or its board of directors, create or imply any change to the fiduciary duties of the company or its board of direc-

---

8.   See chapter 4 for a discussion of smaller reporting companies.

tors, create or imply any additional fiduciary duties for the company or its board of directors, or limit or restrict the ability of shareholders to submit proposals on executive compensation for inclusion in the company's proxy materials.

Compensation Committee and Advisor Independence. Section 10C(a) of the Exchange Act required the SEC to direct the national securities exchanges to prohibit the listing of any company issuing equity securities (with certain limited exceptions, including controlled companies and certain foreign private issuers) unless all of the members of its compensation committee are directors and meet specific independence standards. These independence requirements went into effect in 2014.

Section 10C(b) of the Exchange Act specifies that the compensation committee of a board of directors may select a compensation consultant, legal advisor, or other advisor only after taking into consideration factors identified by the SEC that affect such advisor's independence. These factors, which are to be competitively neutral, include:

1. the provision of other services to the company by the person that employs the compensation consultant, legal advisor, or other advisor;

2. the amount of fees received from the company by the person who employs the compensation consultant, legal advisor, or other advisor as a percentage of that person's total revenue;

3. the policies and procedures of the person that employs the compensation consultant, legal advisor, or other advisor that are designed to prevent conflicts of interest;

4. any business or personal relationship of the compensation consultant, legal advisor, or other advisor with a member of the compensation committee;

5. any stock of the company owned by the compensation consultant, legal advisor, or other advisor; and

6. any business or personal relationship of the compensation consultant, legal advisor, or other advisor or the compensation consultant, legal advisor, or other advisor's employer with an executive officer of the company.

These requirements became effective in 2013. Section 10C(c)(2) of the Exchange Act requires companies to disclose in their annual meeting proxy statements whether the compensation committee has engaged a compensation consultant, whether the consultant's work has raised any conflict of interest, and, if so, the nature of the conflict and how it was resolved. The SEC adopted rules implementing this provision which were effective for any annual meeting of shareholders at which directors will be elected occurring on or after January 1, 2013. Finally, Section 10C confirms the authority of the compensation committee to retain and oversee the work of a compensation consultant, legal counsel, and other advisors and directs companies to provide appropriate funding for these engagements.

Pay for Performance. Section 953(a) of the Dodd-Frank Act amended Section 14 of the Exchange Act to require public companies to disclose in their annual meeting proxy statements the relationship between the compensation actually paid to their executives and their financial performance, taking into account any change in the value of their shares and any dividends and distributions. This disclosure may be in either graphic or narrative form. The SEC proposed rules to implement this provision in April 2015. The final rules were approved by the SEC in August 2022. Companies must comply with the final rules for fiscal years ending on or after December 16, 2022. These final rules added Item 402(v) to Regulation S-K (see "Pay for Performance Table" below).

Pay Ratio. Section 953(b) of the Dodd-Frank Act directed the SEC to amend its executive compensation disclosure rules to require each public company to disclose in any filing (including registration statements, periodic reports, and proxy statements):

1. the median annual total compensation of all employees (except the CEO),

2. the annual total compensation of the CEO, and

3. the ratio of the median annual total compensation of all employees to the annual total compensation of the CEO.

In August 2015, the SEC adopted Item 402(u) to Regulation S-K to implement this provision, with companies subject to compliance for the first fiscal year beginning on or after January 1, 2017. Accordingly, the initial pay ratio disclosures began appearing in annual reports on Form 10-K and definitive proxy and information statements during the 2018 proxy season. Under the JOBS Act, this provision does not apply to emerging growth companies while they maintain that status.

The key to satisfying the pay ratio rule is developing a process for identifying the company's "median employee" (since that takes the most time and effort) that is reasonable, defensible, and repeatable. To begin, a company must determine the number of workers who performed services for the company in each country where it operated or maintained a business presence for the last completed fiscal year. This will enable the company to determine the employee population from which the "median employee" will be identified. Item 402(u) permits certain categories of workers, including certain non-U.S. employees and employees of certain acquired businesses, to be excluded from the employee population to be used to identify the median employee.

Once the employee population has been determined, a company must evaluate the compensation arrangements of either its entire employee population or, if it opts to use statistical sampling, the sample group or groups to select a compensation measure that best suits its situation to identify the median employee. For this purpose, the company may use the annual total compensation of each employee or any other compensation measure that is consistently applied to all employees included in the calculation, such as information derived from its tax and/or payroll records. For most companies, selecting a specific compensation measure to be applied across the relevant employee pool or group will probably be easier than calculating annual total compensation for every employee. Consequently, the measure may be base salary or wages, total cash compensation, or total direct compensation, depending on the company's specific facts and circumstances, the accessibility of the underlying data, and the overarching requirement that the measure be applied consistently across the company's employee population.

After the compensation measure has been selected, a company is required to convert any amounts paid in a foreign currency to U.S. dollars and may annualize the compensation of permanent employees who worked less than the full year and apply a cost-of-living adjustment, subject to certain requirements, if the median employee is located in a jurisdiction other than that of the CEO.

Once the median employee has been identified, then his or her annual total compensation, along with that of the CEO, must be calculated using the methodology set forth in the SEC's executive compensation disclosure rules for purposes of completing the Summary Compensation table discussed later. These compensation amounts, along with the resulting pay ratio and a brief description of the methodologies used to identify the median employee and calculate annual total compensation, must then be disclosed in the company's annual report on Form 10-K or, alternatively using the SEC's forward incorporation by reference technique, its definitive proxy or information statement. Some local jurisdictions have imposed additional taxes on companies whose pay ratios exceed certain levels.

Clawbacks. In October 2022, the SEC adopted new Exchange Act Rule 10D-1 and amended existing rules to add new clawback requirements and corresponding disclosures in annual reports and proxy statements. Under the timetable set by the SEC for securities exchanges to finalize their listing requirements, issuers will have to comply with the new clawback and disclosure rules by late 2023 or early 2024. Section 954 of the Dodd-Frank Act added Section 10D to the Exchange Act, requiring the SEC to direct the national securities exchanges to prohibit the listing of any company that does not develop and implement certain policies to recover (claw back) excess incentive-based compensation from current and former executive officers in the event of an accounting restatement. Rule 10D-1 implements this requirement, applying whether or not the executive officers were at fault for the restatement. The officers subject to the clawback provision include the president; principal financial officer; principal accounting officer; any vice president in charge of a principal business unit, division or function; and any other officer who performs a policy-making function (including officers of a parent or subsidiary company who perform policy-making functions for the company). Companies that fail to comply with Rule 10D-1's requirements may be delisted. The SEC also added the following disclosure requirements:

- New Item 402(w) to Regulation S-K (Item 402(w)) requires certain disclosures in the proxy statement, annual report, or registration statement if there was a restatement that triggered a clawback pursuant to the company's clawback policy during the last fiscal year, or if there was an outstanding balance of excess incentive-based compensation from a prior restatement.

- New Item 601(b)(97) to Regulation S-K (Item 601(b)(97)) requires the company to file its clawback policy as an exhibit to Form 10-K and to include two new checkboxes on the cover of its annual report indicating whether the filing contains corrections to prior financial statements and whether those corrections resulted in a restatement that triggered the policy's clawback provisions.

Companies subject to Rule 10D-1, with limited exceptions, include all public companies, emerging growth companies, and smaller reporting companies.

The sum to be recovered is the pretax amount in excess of what would have been paid to the executive officer under the restatement. Only incentive-based compensation is included in the calculation.

Hedging Policies. Section 955 of the Dodd-Frank Act added Section 14(j) to the Exchange Act to require the SEC to promulgate rules requiring proxy statement disclosure of whether a company permits its employees or directors to purchase financial instruments (including prepaid variable forward contracts, equity swaps, collars, and exchange funds) that are designed to hedge or offset market declines affecting compensatory equity awards or other equity securities held by the employee or director. In December 2018, the SEC adopted Item 407(i) of Regulation S-K to implement this provision, with most companies subject to compliance with these disclosure requirements for proxy and information statements with respect to the election of directors during fiscal years beginning on or after July 1, 2019.

5.3.4 Compensation Committee Disclosure

The SEC, the New York Stock Exchange, and the NASDAQ Stock market require public companies to have a compensation committee that assumes a number of compensation-related responsibilities. If for some reason (for example, the company is not listed on the NYSE or NASDAQ) a company has chosen not to appoint a standing compensation committee (or a committee performing similar functions), as part of its corporate governance disclosure under Item 407(e) of Regulation S-K it must state the basis for the view of the board of directors that it is appropriate not to have such a committee. In this instance, the company must identify each director who participates in the consideration of executive officer and director compensation.

Under SEC rules, the company must disclose whether or not the compensation committee has a charter and provide certain information about the charter, including whether a current copy is available to shareholders on the company's website. If the charter is unavailable elsewhere, the company must include a copy in an appendix to its proxy statement at least once every three fiscal years, and each year the charter has been materially amended during that fiscal year.

As part of its disclosure relating to its compensation committee, the company must also provide a narrative description of its processes and procedures for the consideration and determination of executive and director compensation, including:

1. the scope of authority of the compensation committee and the extent to which the compensation committee may delegate any authority to other persons (and specifying what authority may be so delegated and to whom);

2. any role of executive officers in determining or recommending the amount or form of executive and director compensation; and

3. any role of compensation consultants in determining or recommending the amount or form of executive and director compensation during the company's last completed fiscal year, identifying the consultant or consultants, stating whether they were engaged directly by the compensation committee or any other person, describing the nature and scope of their assignment, and the material elements of the instructions or directions given to them with respect to the performance of their duties under the engagement.

In addition, with respect to (3) above, if the consultant was engaged by the compensation committee to provide advice or recommendations on the amount or form of executive and director compensation and either it or its affiliates also provided additional services to the company (or its affiliates) in an amount in excess of $120,000 during the last completed fiscal year, the company must disclose the aggregate fees for determining or recommending the amount or form of executive and director compensation and the aggregate fees for such additional services, whether the decision to engage the consultant or its affiliates for these other services was made, or recommended, by management, and whether the compensation committee or the board approved such other services of the consultant or its affiliates. Similarly, if the compensation committee has not engaged a consultant, but management has engaged a consultant to provide advice or recommendations on the amount or form of executive and director compensation and such consultant or its affiliates has provided additional services to the company in an amount in excess of $120,000 during the last completed fiscal year, the company must disclose the aggregate fees for determining or recommending the amount or form of executive and director compensation and the aggregate fees for any additional services provided by the consultant or its affiliates.

Finally, with regard to any consultant identified with respect to (3) above whose work has raised any conflict of interest, the company must disclose the nature of the conflict and how the conflict is being addressed. For this purpose, the company should use the factors listed in section 5.3.3 as the starting point for determining whether a conflict of interest exists.

In connection with the inclusion of the Compensation Discussion and Analysis (CD&A), further discussed below, in the required SEC filing and under the caption "Compensation Committee Report," the compensation committee (or other committee performing equivalent functions or, in the absence of any such committee, the entire board of directors) must state whether the compensation committee has reviewed and discussed the CD&A with management and whether, based on such review and discussion, the compensation committee has recommended to the board of directors that the CD&A be included in the company's annual report on Form 10-K and proxy statement.

Further, the name of each member of the compensation committee (or other committee performing equivalent functions or, in the absence of any such committee, the entire board of directors) must appear below this disclosure. The disclosure need only be provided one time during any fiscal year.

5.3.5 Director Compensation Disclosure

Under Item 402 of Regulation S-K, a company must provide a Director Compensation table that discloses the compensation paid to each member of its board of directors during the last completed fiscal year. This table divides the compensation of the directors into several categories, each of which is reported in a separate column of the table (table 5-1). The amounts to be disclosed for each director include:

- the aggregate dollar amount of all fees earned or paid in cash for services as a director (including annual retainer fees, committee and/or chairmanship fees, and meeting attendance fees);
- the full grant date fair value for equity awards granted during the covered fiscal year in accordance with ASC 718;
- the value of non-equity incentive plan compensation earned for the covered fiscal year;
- the aggregate change in the actuarial present value of the accumulated benefit under all defined benefit and actuarial pension plans (including supplemental plans) during the covered fiscal year, and any above-market or preferential earnings on nonqualified deferred compensation;
- all other compensation for the covered fiscal year that could not be properly reported in any other column of the table (which elements are to be aggregated and reported as a single amount); and
- the total compensation for the covered fiscal year (the sum of all of the columns in the table).

Non-equity incentive plan compensation generally involves performance-based incentive awards that are payable in cash. These awards can be either annual or long-term incentive awards.

Name	Fees earned or paid in cash ($)	Stock awards ($)	Option awards ($)	Non-equity incentive plan compensation ($)	Change in pension value and nonqualified deferred compensation earnings ($)	All other compensation ($)	Total ($)
Director1							
Director2							
Director3							

Table 5-1. Director Compensation

The items to be included in the "all other compensation" category include:

- perquisites and other personal benefits;

- tax "gross-ups" or other reimbursements;

- preferential discounted stock purchases;

- amounts paid or accrued in connection with a termination of employment or a change in control of the company;

- company contributions to defined contribution plans;

- consulting fees earned from, paid, or payable by the company and/ or its subsidiaries;

- the annual cost of payments and promises of payments pursuant to director legacy programs and similar charitable award programs;

- the dollar value of any insurance premiums paid for life insurance for the benefit of a director; and

- the dollar value of any dividends or other earnings paid on equity awards (where those amounts were not factored into the award's grant date fair value).

Perquisites and other personal benefits are reportable where the aggregate amount is $10,000 or more. Each perquisite must be separately identified (for example, in a footnote), and where an individual perquisite exceeds the greater of $25,000 or 10% of the total amount of perquisites reported for a director, that perquisite must be quantified and the valuation methodology described.

5.3.6 Executive Compensation Disclosure

Under Item 402, the company must disclose information concerning the various forms of compensation paid to senior executive officers and members of the board of directors and explain its compensation philosophy and decisions involving senior executive compensation. These disclosure requirements consist of approximately 10 items, which are sometimes grouped into "soft" and "hard" disclosures. The "soft" disclosures include the Compensation Discussion & Analysis (CD&A), the Compensation Committee Report, the Compensation Committee Interlocks and Insider Participation Report, and the narrative to accompany the required tabular disclosure. In addition to this narrative disclosure, extensive tabular disclosure is required covering the actual compensation packages of a company's senior executive officers. The compensation of each of the senior executive officers is highlighted in up to eight separate tables and charts. The equity plan administrator will frequently be called upon to assist with the preparation of the specific tabular disclosures.

The senior executive officers subject to this heightened disclosure are considered the company's "named executive officers" (NEOs). They include:

- all individuals who have served as the CEO of the company (or acted in a similar capacity) during the last completed fiscal year (regardless of the level of compensation paid to the individual during the year),
- all individuals who have served as the CFO of the company (or acted in a similar capacity) during the last completed fiscal year (regardless of the level of compensation paid to the individual during the year),
- each of the company's three most highly compensated executive officers (other than the CEO and CFO) who were serving as execu-

tive officers at the end of the last completed fiscal year whose total compensation exceeded $100,000 for the fiscal year, and

- up to two additional individuals who would have been among the three most highly compensated executive officers but for the fact that the individual was not serving as an executive officer of the company at the end of the last completed fiscal year.

For purposes of determining a company's most highly compensated executive officers, "total compensation" includes all amounts that are included in the Summary Compensation table (as described below) except for the amounts required to be disclosed in the "Change in pension value and nonqualified deferred compensation earnings" column of that table.

Compensation Discussion and Analysis. The Compensation Discussion and Analysis ("CD&A") is the principal narrative discussion of a company's executive compensation program. The CD&A is supposed to set the context for and explain the other required executive compensation disclosures. The CD&A should address the objectives and policies of a company's executive compensation program as well as how that program is implemented. The CD&A is to be a "principles-based" discussion, that is, the company must tailor the disclosure to its own individual situation. To assist in this process, the disclosure requirements provide that the following broad topics be addressed in the CD&A:

- the objectives of the company's compensation programs;
- what each program is designed to reward;
- the different elements of compensation offered by the company;
- why the company chooses to pay each element;
- how the company determines the amount (and where applicable, the formula) for each element;
- how each element and the company's decisions regarding that element fit into the company's overall compensation objectives and affect decisions regarding other elements; and
- how the company has considered the results of the most recent shareholder advisory vote on executive compensation required

by Section 14A(a)(1) in determining compensation policies and decisions and how that consideration has affected the company's executive compensation decisions and policies.

While the company must provide detailed information about the performance measures and target levels that it uses in its performance-based incentive compensation plans and arrangements, it is not required to disclose the specific target levels for these performance measures to the extent that they involve confidential information the disclosure of which would cause competitive harm to the company.

In response to concerns about stock option backdating and the timing of option grants around the disclosure of material nonpublic information, the company is also required to address its equity award grant practices for its executives. This disclosure must describe why the company selects particular dates for granting options and other equity awards and how it sets an option's terms and conditions, including the option exercise price.

Summary Compensation Table. The centerpiece of the tabular disclosure requirements, the Summary Compensation table is designed to provide a comprehensive overview of a company's executive compensation actions and decisions in a single location. This information is intended to enable prospective investors to understand clearly the compensation paid for the prior fiscal year, to evaluate the company's compensation policies and practices in light of its overall performance, and to compare trends in compensation policies and practices between companies.

The Summary Compensation table covers the compensation paid to each of the NEOs during each of the last three completed fiscal years (two years in the case of emerging growth companies and smaller reporting companies). If the company has not been a reporting company under the Exchange Act for the prior three years (due to a recent IPO, for example), the table need only cover the shorter period that the company has been a public company, but it must cover at least the last completed fiscal year.

The Summary Compensation table divides the compensation of the NEOs into several categories, each of which is then reported in a separate column of the table (table 5-2). The amounts to be disclosed for each NEO for each covered fiscal year include:

- base salary earned;

- bonus earned;

- value of stock awards granted;

- value of stock options granted;

- value of non-equity incentive plan compensation earned;

- aggregate change in the actuarial present value of accumulated benefit under all defined benefit and actuarial pension plans (including supplemental plans), and any above-market or preferential earnings on nonqualified deferred compensation;

- all other compensation that could not be properly reported in any other column of the table (which elements are to be aggregated and reported as a single amount); and

- total compensation (the sum of all the columns in the table).

Equity awards or other long-term incentive compensation that is received in lieu of salary or bonus should be reported in the appropriate column for the specific award type and must be included in determining whether a person is an NEO.

The dollar amount reported for stock and option awards is to be based on the full grant date fair value for financial reporting purposes in accordance with ASC 718 for awards made during the covered fiscal year. The calculation of fair value is discussed below.

Non-equity incentive plan compensation generally involves performance-based awards that are payable in cash. These awards can be either annual or long-term incentive awards. Thus, most annual incentive awards that would otherwise be characterized as "bonuses" will be reported in this category when they are subject to the achievement of objective performance criteria that were established at the beginning of the year, were substantially uncertain when established, and were communicated to the NEOs at that time.

The items to be included in the "all other compensation" category include:

Table 5-2. Summary Compensation

Name and principal position	Year	Salary ($)	Bonus ($)	Stock awards ($)	Option awards ($)	Non-equity incentive plan compensation ($)	Change in pension value and nonqualified deferred compensation earnings ($)	All other compensation ($)	Total ($)
CEO									
CFO									
NEO3									
NEO4									
NEO5									

- perquisites and other personal benefits;
- tax "gross-ups" or other reimbursements;
- preferential discounted stock purchases;
- amounts paid or accrued in connection with a termination of employment or a change in control of the company;
- company contributions to defined contribution plans;
- the dollar value of any insurance premiums paid for life insurance for the benefit of the NEO; and
- the dollar value of any dividends or other earnings paid on stock or option awards (where those amounts were not factored into the award's grant date fair value).

Perquisites and other personal benefits are reportable where the aggregate amount is $10,000 or more. Each perquisite must be separately identified (for example, in a footnote), and where an individual perquisite exceeds the greater of $25,000 or 10% of the total amount of perquisites reported for an NEO, that perquisite must be quantified and the valuation methodology described.

Pay for Performance Table. New Item 402(v) requires additional disclosures regarding pay for performance. The final rules set forth a new table that must be included in the proxy disclosures. The new table will be required in proxy statements filed for fiscal years ending on or after December 16, 2022. These include:

- a table of up to five years (only three years for smaller reporting companies) of specific executive compensation alongside company financial performance measures;
- a description of the relationship between company performance and executive compensation, using the information shown in the table (table 5-3); and
- a tabular list of most important performance measures the company used to link executive compensation and company performance.

Reporting companies, including smaller reporting companies, need to include in the new table:

Table 5-3. Pay for Performance

| Year (a) | Summary compensation table total for CEO (b) | Compensation actually paid to CEO (c) | Average summary compensation table for non-CEO NEOs (d) | Average compensation actually paid to non-CEO NEOs (e) | Value of initial fixed $100 investment based on: | | Net income (h) | [Company selected measure] (i) |
					Total shareholder return (f)	Peer group total shareholder return (g)		
Year 1								
Year 2								
Year 3								
Year 4								
Year 5								

- total compensation for the chief executive officer and the average total compensation for NEOs; and

- actual compensation paid for the chief executive officer and NEOs.

The requirements include the use of the table, along with clear descriptions of the relationships between compensation actually paid and the following financial performance measures:

- Cumulative TSR;[9]

- Cumulative peer group TSR;

- Net income; and

- "Company selected measure" other than TSR.

The total compensation in the table should equal the total executive compensation as reported in the Summary Compensation table for the chief executive and the other NEOs. To complicate matters, if a company has more than one chief executive officer during a reporting year, it must disclose details for each separately.

There are significant adjustments required to deduct the equity amounts in the Summary Compensation table, which are beyond the scope of this chapter and will likely involve not only the equity plan administrator but other internal and external advisors. Along with the equity adjustments, the final rules also modify pension disclosures (described further in the Pension Benefits table below).

The final rules require the company to provide detailed descriptions as well as the new table. This discussion must include the relationship of actual executive compensation during the past five years (three for smaller reporting companies) to the company's TSR, and the relationship of the company's TSR to that of its peer group. These relationships

---

9.   Total shareholder return (TSR) is a measure of a company's share performance over time. The final rules clarify that both the TSR and peer group TSR should be calculated based on a fixed investment of $100 at the measurement point. The measurement period is calculated from market close on the last trading day before the company's earliest year shown in the table through, and including, the end of the year in which TSR is being calculated. This will result in cumulative calculations in future years.

may be provided in graphic form, narrative form, or a combination of the two. Regarding important financial performance measures, the company will be required to list three to seven of the most important factors used to link executive compensation to company performance. The list, however, does not need to be ranked. Net income must be calculated according to generally accepted accounting principles (GAAP). The company-selected measure in the table must be financial, but non-financial measures may also be included in additional columns to the table for any other performance measures it may consider important. These additional measures cannot not be misleading and must be labelled as supplemental information.

Emerging growth companies are not subject to the new pay-for-performance disclosure requirement, but smaller reporting companies are subject to less onerous disclosures. Reporting companies will be required to provide only three years of information the first year, with an additional year's disclosure in the two subsequent proxies adding up to five years of disclosure by year three. Smaller reporting companies may provide two years in their first filing, moving to three years in the following year's filing. Note that smaller reporting companies do not have to:

- disclose pension-related amounts in executive compensation actually paid;
- disclose peer group TSR;
- disclose a company-selected measure; or
- provide a tabular list of financial performance measures.

Grants of Plan-Based Awards Table. The Grants of Plan-Based Awards table requires disclosure of supplemental information about the incentive and equity awards granted during the last completed fiscal year to each NEO (table 5-4). Unlike the Summary Compensation table, this disclosure covers only the last completed fiscal year. Each award must be identified and discussed separately in one of four broad categories: (1) non-equity incentive plan awards; (2) equity incentive plan awards; (3) service-based stock awards; and (4) service-based stock option awards.

Table 5-4. Grants of Plan-Based Awards

Name	Grant date	Estimated future payouts under non-equity incentive plan awards			Estimated future payouts under equity incentive plan awards			All other stock awards: number of shares of stock or units (#)	All other option awards: number of securities underlying options (#)	Exercise or base price of option awards ($/Sh)	Grant date fair value of stock and option awards ($)
		Threshold ($)	Target ($)	Maximum ($)	Threshold (#)	Target (#)	Maximum (#)				
CEO											
CFO											
NEO3											
NEO4											
NEO5											

Among other things, this table must include the grant date for each equity award, as well as its full grant date fair value on an award-by-award basis. If the award's grant date differs from the date on which the board of directors or compensation committee took action to grant such awards, a separate, adjoining column must be added to the table showing such date. In addition, in the case of stock options, the per-share exercise price of the option must be disclosed. If the exercise price is less than the closing market price of the company's stock on the grant date, a separate, adjoining column must be added showing the closing market price on the grant date. Whenever the exercise price reported is not the closing market price, the company must describe the methodology for determining its exercise price.

A Grants of Plan-Based Awards table is not required from an emerging growth company or a smaller reporting company.

The company must supplement the Summary Compensation table and the Grants of Plan-Based Awards table with a narrative description of any material factors necessary for understanding the information disclosed in these tables. Such information may include:

• the material terms of each NEO's employment agreement (if any);

• the details of any stock option repricing or the material modification of any equity awards during the last fiscal year;

• the material terms of any award reported in the Grant of Plan-Based Awards table; and

• an explanation of the amount of salary and bonus in proportion to total compensation.

In the case of an emerging growth company or smaller reporting company, this narrative disclosure must supplement the Summary Compensation table and include any material factors necessary for understanding the information disclosed in the table. Such information may include:

• the material terms of each NEO's employment agreement (if any);

• a description of any equity award repricing or material modification that took place during the last completed fiscal year;

- any waiver or modification of any specified performance target, goal, or condition to payout with respect to any amount included in the non-equity incentive plan compensation column of the Summary Compensation table;

- the material terms of each equity award;

- the material terms of any non-equity incentive plan award made to an NEO during the last completed fiscal year;

- the method of calculating earnings on nonqualified deferred compensation plans, including nonqualified defined contribution plans; and

- the identification, to the extent it is material, of any item included under the all other compensation column of the Summary Compensation table.

Outstanding Equity Awards at Fiscal Year-End Table. The Outstanding Equity Awards at Fiscal Year-End table requires disclosure of each equity award outstanding at the end of the last completed fiscal year held by each NEO (table 5-5).

In the case of stock options, which must be disclosed on a grant-by-grant basis, the table must include:

- the number of securities underlying unexercised service-based options that are currently exercisable,

- the number of securities underlying unexercised service-based options that are currently unexercisable,

- the total number of shares underlying unexercised performance-based options that have not been earned,

- the option exercise price, and

- the option expiration date.

Other equity awards may be disclosed on an aggregated basis, and the table must include:

- the total number of unvested shares of stock subject to service-based awards;

Table 5-5. Outstanding Equity Awards at Fiscal Year-End

Name	Option awards					Stock awards			
	Number of securities underlying unexercised options exercisable (#)	Number of securities underlying unexercised options unexercis-able (#)	Equity incentive plan awards: number of securities underlying unexercised unearned options (#)	Option exercise price ($)	Option expira-tion date	Number of shares or units of stock that have not vested (#)	Market value of shares or units of stock that have not vested ($)	Equity incentive plan awards: number of unearned shares, units or other rights that have not vested (#)	Equity incentive plan awards: market or payout value of unearned shares, units or other rights that have not vested ($)
CEO									
CFO									
NEO3									
NEO4									
NEO5									

- the aggregate market value of these unvested shares;

- the total number of unearned shares, units, or other rights subject to equity incentive plan awards; and

- the aggregate market or payout value of these unearned shares.

In the case of performance-based options and RSUs, there may be cases where the performance criteria were met late in the fiscal year, but the actual certification of the performance metrics did not occur until after the fiscal year ended. In such cases, for purposes of this table, many companies will consider these options as unexercised options that are currently exercisable (i.e. vested). Similarly, performance RSUs may be considered vested and would therefore not be included in the total number of unearned shares in the table. However, the equity plan administrator should discuss this situation with their legal counsel. This performance certification issue may require the inclusion of additional footnotes describing the vesting/certification requirements.

Option Exercises and Stock Vested Table. The Option Exercises and Stock Vested table requires disclosure of stock option exercises and exercises of free-standing SARs and the vesting of outstanding restricted stock awards and units that occurred during the last completed fiscal year for each NEO (table 5-6). While this disclosure covers only the last completed fiscal year, unlike the Outstanding Equity Awards at Last Fiscal Year-End table, these transactions may be aggregated and reported as a single amount in each general category.

Among other things, this table must include the number of shares received upon exercise (or, if no shares were received, the number of securities with respect to which the option and/or SAR was exercised) and the aggregate dollar value realized upon exercise. In the case of other equity awards, this table must include the number of shares of stock that have vested and the aggregate dollar value realized upon the vesting of these shares.

An Option Exercise and Stock Vested table is not required from an emerging growth company or a smaller reporting company.

As with the performance-based vesting issues discussed above, the equity plan administrator may encounter reporting issues for the

Option Exercises and Stock Vested table. Performance-based RSUs that vested but were not yet certified at the end of the fiscal year will likely be reported in this table. Again, the equity plan administrator should discuss this particular situation with their legal counsel because additional footnoting may be recommended.

Table 5-6. Option Exercises and Stock Vested				
	Option awards		Stock awards	
Name	Number of shares acquired on exercise (#)	Value realized on exercise ($)	Number of shares acquired on vesting (#)	Value realized on vesting ($)
CEO				
CFO				
NEO3				
NEO4				
NEO5				

Pension Benefits Table. The Pension Benefits table requires disclosure of the potential payments and benefits payable to the NEOs under the company's defined benefit pension plans (both tax-qualified and nonqualified plans).

Among other things, this table must include the name of each plan in which an NEO participates, the number of years of service credited to the NEO under the plan, the actuarial present value of the NEO's accumulated benefit under the plan, and the dollar amount of any payments and benefits paid to the NEO during the last completed fiscal year (table 5-7).

For purposes of computing the present value of the current accrued benefit to be reported in the table, the company must use the same assumptions used by the company for financial reporting purposes, except that retirement age is to be assumed to be the normal retirement age as defined in the plan (or if not defined, the earliest time at which a participant may retire under the plan without any benefit reduction due to age). The company must disclose the valuation method and all material assumptions used in quantifying the present value of the current accrued benefit. If an NEO's years of credited service with re-

		Number of years credited	Present value of accumulated	Payments during last
Name	Plan name	service (#)	benefit ($)	fiscal year ($)
CEO				
CFO				
NEO3				
NEO4				
NEO5				

Table 5-7. Pension Benefits

spect to any plan differ from his or her actual years of service with the company, the disclosure must quantify the difference and any resulting benefit augmentation.

Under new Item 402(v), if a plan is amended during the reporting year, the company needs to add the cost of benefits granted under the plan amendment to the total compensation shown in the Summary Compensation table. If the plan amendment results in a reduction in benefits, the overall amount listed in the Summary Compensation table should likewise be reduced. The company will likely engage an external advisor for assistance with these calculations.

The company must supplement the Pension Benefits table with a narrative description of any material factors necessary to an understanding of the information disclosed in the table. Such information may include:

- the material terms and conditions of payments and benefits available under the plan;

- where an NEO is currently eligible for early retirement under a plan, the plan's early retirement payment and benefit formula and eligibility standards;

- the specific elements of compensation (for example, salary and bonus) included in applying the payment and benefit formula;

- with respect to the NEO's participation in multiple plans, the reasons for each plan; and

- company policies with regard to such matters as granting extra years of credited service.

A Pension Benefits table is not required from an emerging growth company or a smaller reporting company.

Nonqualified Deferred Compensation Table. The Nonqualified Deferred Compensation table requires disclosure of information about each nonqualified defined contribution plan or other nonqualified deferred compensation plan or arrangement (table 5-8).

Table 5-8. Nonqualified Deferred Compensation					
Name	Executive contributions in last fiscal year ($)	Registrant contributions in last fiscal year ($)	Aggregate earnings in last fiscal year ($)	Aggregate withdrawals /distributions ($)	Aggregate balance at last fiscal year end ($)
CEO					
CFO					
NEO3					
NEO4					
NEO5					

Among other things, for the last fiscal year, this table must include the dollar amount of aggregate contributions by an NEO, the dollar amount of aggregate company contributions during the last fiscal year, the dollar amount of aggregate interest or other earnings accrued (all earnings, not just above-market or preferential amounts), the aggregate dollar amount of all withdrawals by and distributions to the NEO, and the dollar amount of the total balance of the NEO's account as of the end of the last fiscal year.

To avoid possible double-counting of this information with amounts that have been previously disclosed, the company must quantify the extent to which amounts reported in the contributions and earnings columns are reported as compensation in the company's Summary Compensation table for the last completed fiscal year and amounts reported in the aggregate balance at the last fiscal year end column previously were reported as compensation to the NEO in the company's Summary Compensation table for previous years.

The company must supplement the Nonqualified Deferred Compensation table with a narrative description of any material factors necessary to an understanding of the information in the table. Such information may include:

- the type(s) of compensation permitted to be deferred, and any limitations (by percentage of compensation or otherwise) on the extent to which deferral is permitted;
- the measures for calculating interest or other plan earnings (including whether such measure(s) are selected by the NEO or the company and the frequency and manner in which selections may be changed), quantifying interest rates and other earnings measures applicable during the company's last fiscal year; and
- the material terms applicable to payouts, withdrawals, and other distributions.

A Nonqualified Deferred Compensation table is not required from an emerging growth company or a smaller reporting company.

Potential Payments Upon Termination or Change in Control. The company must disclose information about each contract, agreement, plan, or arrangement that provides for payment(s) to an NEO at, following, or in connection with any termination of employment, including resignation, severance, retirement, or a constructive termination of employment, a change in control of the company or a change in the NEO's responsibilities following a change in control of the company. While this information need not be provided in tabular form, as a practical matter the company will probably use one or more tables to disclose the required information (table 5-9).

Among other things, the disclosure must describe the specific circumstances that would trigger payment(s) or the provision of other benefits (including perquisites and health care benefits); quantify the estimated annual payments and benefits that would be provided in each covered circumstance (including whether they would or could be lump-sum or annual, disclosing the duration, and by whom they would be provided); explain how the appropriate payment and benefit levels are determined under the various circumstances that trigger payments or provision of benefits; explain any material conditions or obligations that apply to the receipt of payments or benefits (including

			Pension/		Tax		
Name	Cash ($)	Equity ($)	NQDC ($)	Perquisites/ benefits ($)	reimbursement ($)	Other ($)	Total ($)
CEO							
CFO							
NEO3							
NEO4							
NEO5							

Table 5-9. Potential Payments Upon Termination or Change in Control

noncompetition, nonsolicitation, nondisparagement, or confidentiality agreements); and describe any other material factors regarding each contract, agreement, plan, or arrangement.

In calculating the potential payments and benefits that may be received by an NEO, the company is to assume that the triggering event took place on the last business day of the last completed fiscal year, and the price per share of the company's securities is the closing market price as of that date. If uncertainties exist as to the provision of payments and benefits or the amounts involved, the company must make a reasonable estimate (or provide a reasonable estimated range of amounts) of the payment or benefit and disclose the material assumptions used to make such estimates or estimated ranges in its disclosure. Perquisites may be excluded only if their aggregate amount will be less than $10,000. A company need not provide information about contracts, agreements, plans, or arrangements that do not discriminate in favor of the company's executive officers and that are available generally to all salaried employees.

While emerging growth companies and smaller reporting companies are not required to quantify the potential payments that would be received by the NEOs in the event of a termination of employment or change in control of the company, they must provide a narrative description, to the extent it is material, of the material terms of each retirement plan that applies to the NEOs and the material terms of each contract, agreement, plan, or arrangement that provides for payment(s) to a NEO at, following, or in connection with the resignation, retirement, or other termination of employment, or a change in control of the company or a change in the NEO's responsibilities following a change in control of the company.

5.3.7 Equity Compensation Plan Information

A company is required to disclose in tabular form each year in its annual report on Form 10-K, and in its proxy statement in years in which the company is submitting a compensation plan (either cash or equity) for shareholder approval, certain information about the number of securities to be issued upon the exercise of outstanding stock options and other equity vehicles, the weighted-average exercise price of outstanding options, and the number of securities remaining available for future issuance under all of the company's equity plans (table 5-10).

Table 5-10. Equity Compensation Plan Information			
	(a)	(b)	(c)
Plan category	Number of securities to be issued upon exercise of outstanding options, warrants and rights	Weighted-average exercise price of outstanding options, warrants and rights	Number of securities remaining available for future issuance under equity compensation plans (excluding securities reflected in column (a))
Equity compensation plans approved by security holders			
Equity compensation plans not approved by security holders			
Total			

This disclosure is to be made on an aggregated basis in two categories: plans that have been approved by shareholders and plans that have not been approved by shareholders. Individual equity compensation arrangements, such as individual equity awards that have been granted outside a formal plan and equity compensation plans that have been assumed in a merger, consolidation, or other acquisition transaction may be aggregated in the appropriate category with the company's plan disclosure.

In addition, where a company has one or more equity plans that have not been approved by shareholders, the company must disclose the material features of each non-shareholder-approved plan and attach a copy of the plan as an exhibit to the Form 10-K, unless the plan is immaterial in amount or significance.

5.4   Financial Statement Matters

Equity Valuation. The company will need to use the "fair value" method of accounting as set forth in ASC 718 for purposes of calculating the expense associated with its stock option and other equity award programs.

In the case of stock options, fair value is to be determined using an option-pricing model, such as Black-Scholes or a binomial model, that takes into account, as of the grant date, (1) the option price, (2) the expected life of the option, (3) the current price of the underlying shares of stock, (4) the expected volatility of the stock price, (5) expected dividends on the stock, and (6) the risk-free interest rate for the expected option term.

One potential problem in formulating the expected option life assumption can arise if there are differences in the terms and conditions of the stock options being valued and the stock options that will form the basis of the historical information to be analyzed to determine the assumption. Where the terms and conditions of the stock options being valued differ from those of the historical option grants (for example, different vesting schedules), the equity plan administrator will need to decide to what degree the historical data is relevant to determining the expected life of the stock options being valued.[10]

Earnings Per Share. Currently under GAAP, an earnings-per-share (EPS) computation must be presented by publicly held companies.

---

10. For further discussion of these issues, see Barbara A. Baksa, *Accounting for Equity Compensation,* 19th ed. (NCEO, 2023); and Takis Makridis, *Advanced Topics in Equity Compensation Accounting,* 10th ed. (NCEO, 2021).

This information is used by investors to assess the profitability and the performance of the company from period to period and to compare the company to other businesses. Simply put, the EPS computation involves spreading the company's earnings for the period being reported over the number of common equity securities outstanding during such period. For purposes of this computation, the company's shares of stock are weighted for the actual time that such shares were outstanding during the period.

The current requirements for calculating EPS are set forth in ASC Topic 260. The standard requires the presentation of both "basic" and "diluted" EPS. The basic EPS computation does not take into consideration the effects of dilution. It is calculated by dividing the income available to common shareholders for the reporting period by the weighted average number of shares of common stock actually outstanding during that period, without factoring in any potentially issuable securities that could have a dilutive effect on the company's outstanding shares of stock, such as stock options or other equity vehicles. Shares of stock issued during the period and shares reacquired during the period are weighted for the portion of the period that they were outstanding.

The diluted EPS computation reflects the potential dilutive effect of outstanding stock options and other common stock equivalents by treating them as if they were exercised or converted into common stock that then shares in the total income of the company available to shareholders. The calculation of diluted EPS is similar to the calculation of basic EPS except that the denominator is increased to include the number of additional shares of common stock that would have been outstanding if the dilutive potential common shares had been issued. In addition, the calculation does not take into consideration the exercise or conversion of any securities that would have an anti-dilutive effect on EPS (that is, the exercise or conversion would result in an increase to EPS because the acquisition of the shares of stock would result in the payment to the company of more than the current value of the shares). Generally, the dilutive effect of options and warrants is to be reflected in the calculation through the application of the "treasury stock" accounting method. Under this method, (1) the exercise of options and warrants is to be assumed at the beginning of the reporting period (unless actually exercised at a later time during the period) and shares of common stock are assumed to be issued, (2) the proceeds from the assumed exercise are further assumed to be used to repurchase outstanding shares of common stock at the average fair market value of the company's stock for the reporting period, and (3) the incremental shares of common stock (the difference between the number of shares assumed to be exercised and the number of shares assumed to be repurchased) are included in the denominator used in the diluted EPS calculation.[11]

Disgorgement of Bonuses and Profits upon Financial Restatement. Under Section 304 of the Sarbanes-Oxley Act, if a public company is required to restate its financial statements because of the material noncompliance of the company, due to misconduct, with any financial reporting requirements, the company's CEO and CFO are required to return to the company any bonus or other equity or incentive based compensation received from the company during the one-year period following the issuance of the original financial statements (that are now being restated) and any profits realized from any sale of the company's securities during the same one-year period.

5.5   Section 162(m)

Under Section 162 of the Internal Revenue Code (the "Code"), a company is entitled to deduct from gross income all ordinary and necessary expenses paid or incurred during a taxable year in connection with carrying on a trade or business. The expenses contemplated by this provision include a reasonable allowance for salaries or other compensation for personal services actually rendered. Thus, amounts expended by a company to compensate its employees, including equity compensation, are deductible as long as the amounts are "reasonable."

Section 162(m) of the Code contains a limitation on the deductibility of certain executive compensation. Section 162(m) limits the ability of publicly held corporations to deduct from their corporate income taxes compensation in excess of $1 million paid to certain current or

---

11. For further discussion of these issues, see also chapter 10 of Baksa, *Accounting for Equity Compensation*, 19th ed. (NCEO, 2023), and Elizabeth Dodge and Pam Chernoff, section 10.7 in *The Stock Options Book,* 23rd ed. (NCEO, 2023).

former executive officers. While the limit is clearly aimed at limiting the deductibility of cash compensation, such as salary and bonus, it is also potentially applicable to compensation income realized in connection with the receipt of equity under a company's equity plan. For example, the limit would apply in the case of compensation income realized upon the exercise of a nonqualified stock option and upon the vesting of restricted stock or a restricted stock unit award.

The deduction limit of Section 162(m) applies only to "publicly held corporations." For these purposes, a corporation is considered to be "publicly held" if it is an issuer the securities of which are required to be registered under Section 12 or that is required to file reports under Section 15(d). Thus, companies that voluntarily register under Section 12 are not subject to Section 162(m).

The deduction limit of Section 162(m) applies only to the compensation paid to specific "covered employees." An employee is a covered employee if he or she:

1. was the CEO of the company (or the individual acting in that capacity) at any time during the taxable year;

2. beginning with fiscal years beginning on or after January 1, 2018, was the CFO of the company (or the individual acting in that capacity) at any time during the taxable year;

3. was among the three most highly compensated officers for the taxable year (other than the individuals serving as the CEO or CFO), as calculated under the Exchange Act; or

4. was a covered employee of the company for any preceding taxable year beginning after December 31, 2016.

Note that the covered employee definition is not congruent with the NEO group as determined under SEC rules. First, it continues to apply to an individual even after he or she no longer is the CEO, CFO, or one of the three most highly compensated executive officers for a given taxable year. Second, an employee who was an executive officer during the year, but who is no longer employed at the end of such year, will be a covered employee if he or she received compensation during the year that was the third-highest compensation of all the company's executive officers (other than anyone serving as CEO or CFO during the year) who were no longer employed as of the end of the year and higher than the compensation of the three highest-paid individuals (other than anyone serving as CEO or CFO) who were executive officers as of the end of the year and, thus, NEOs for purposes of the company's executive compensation disclosure. In 2027, the definition of covered employees will change to the 10 highest-paid employees, regardless of whether they are executive officers of the company.

For purposes of the deduction limit, "applicable employee remuneration" with respect to any covered employee includes all otherwise deductible remuneration for services performed by the employee (whether or not such services were performed during the taxable year). Thus, covered compensation can include the compensation income recognized upon the exercise of a nonqualified stock option, the disqualifying disposition of an incentive stock option, or the vesting of restricted stock, even if the option or restricted stock was granted in a prior year.

Certain types of compensation are expressly excluded from the deduction limit of Section 162(m) and thus need not be taken into account in determining whether an employee's total compensation for the year exceeds the $1 million threshold. These include (1) certain "fringe" benefits that are not included in the employee's gross income; (2) payments made to or from certain tax-qualified retirement plans; and (3) compensation payable under any written binding contract that was in effect on February 17, 1993 (and which has not been subsequently modified in any material respect). The prior exclusions for compensation payable solely on a commission basis and "performance-based" compensation were repealed by the Tax Cuts and Jobs Act of 2017.

Performance-Based Compensation. As previously noted, the exception for "performance-based" compensation was repealed by the Tax Cuts and Jobs Act of 2017 for taxable years beginning on or after January 1, 2018. Notwithstanding the foregoing, compensation paid in 2018 and thereafter pursuant to a written binding contract that was in effect on November 2, 2017, and that is not subsequently modified in any material respect, will continue to be deductible if it satisfies the conditions of the performance-based compensation exception. To be considered "performance-based," (1) the compensation must be payable solely upon the attainment of one or more performance goals that are determined by a compensation committee of the board of directors comprised solely of two or more "outside" directors; (2) the material terms of the plan or arrangement under which the compensation is to be paid, including the performance goals, must have been disclosed to shareholders and approved by a majority of the vote in a separate shareholder vote before the payment of the compensation; and (3) before the payment of the compensation, the compensation committee must certify that the performance goals and any other material terms of the arrangement were in fact satisfied. In August 2018, the Internal Revenue Service (IRS) published limited initial guidance about the scope of this "grandfather" provision for certain outstanding compensation arrangements that is very narrow in its application.[12] Thus, a company should consult with its professional advisors to determine (1) whether any of its compensation arrangements with its senior executive officers outstanding on November 2, 2017, are eligible for "grandfathering" protection; (2) the rules that will continue to apply to such arrangements for purposes of qualifying for deductibility; and (3) what type of actions or revisions to such arrangements may constitute "material modifications" that will disqualify them from deductibility.

Transition Provision for Privately Held Companies. Unless a company has been publicly held for the entire taxable year, the deduction limit of Section 162(m) does not apply to any compensation plan or agreement that was in effect while the company was privately held, as long as the plans and agreements were adequately disclosed at the time of the company's IPO and were not thereafter materially modified. In other words, the deduction limit would not apply to stock options or certain other equity awards granted under equity plans that were in existence when a company became publicly held—even if made after the IPO, provided that such plans were disclosed as part of the prospectus accompanying the company's IPO. Generally, while the continuation of this transition relief is not entirely free from doubt as a result of the amendments made to Section 162(m) by the Tax Cuts and Jobs Act of 2017, it is believed that this relief applies to stock options, SARs, and restricted stock awards granted until the first meeting of the company's

---

12. See IRS Notice 2018-68.

shareholders at which directors are to be elected that takes place after the end of the third calendar year following the calendar year in which the company completed its IPO (although the relief may end earlier, as noted below). Further, this transition rule applies even if the stock options, SARs, or restricted stock awards are exercised or vest after the post-IPO reliance period has ended.

This exception may be relied upon until the earliest to occur of (1) the expiration or material modification of the plan or agreement, (2) the issuance of all the securities or other compensation that has been allocated under the plan, or (3) the first meeting of shareholders at which the directors are to be elected that occurs after the close of the third calendar year following the calendar year in which the IPO took place. Thus, corporations can rely on the exemption for any compensation received as the result of the exercise of a stock option or the vesting (or receipt) of restricted stock if the grant or award (rather than the exercise or vesting) occurs before the end of the reliance period.

In March 2015, the IRS adopted final regulations under Section 162(m) with important implications for the use of RSUs following an IPO. Previously, there had been a question whether the transition relief described above applied to RSUs and phantom stock arrangements granted during the post-IPO reliance period. These regulations confirm the IRS's position that it does not. In particular, the regulations provide that RSUs (and phantom stock arrangements) granted on or after April 1, 2015, will be exempt from the Section 162(m) deduction limit only if and to the extent they vest and are paid before the end of the post-IPO reliance period. To soften the impact of this result, it is prospective only (that is, it only applies to RSU awards granted on or after April 1, 2015). RSU awards granted before April 1, 2015, and during an existing post-IPO reliance period will continue to be exempt from the Section 162(m) deduction limit regardless of when they vest and are paid. Finally, this position applies only to RSU grants and not to restricted stock awards. Restricted stock awards granted by a newly public company remain eligible for the full exemption from the deduction limit even if they vest after the post-IPO reliance period.

Health Care Providers. In 2010, as part of the Affordable Care Act, Section 162(m) was amended to provide a limitation on the deductibility of compensation for so-called "covered health care providers" or "CHIPs."[13] This limitation is $500,000 rather than $1 million. In addition, this deduction limitation applies with respect to any compensation paid to any officer, director, or employee of a CHIP (or a member of its controlled group) or any other individual who provides services for or on behalf of the CHIP (or a member of its controlled group), rather than just to a covered employee.

5.6 Section 409A

Section 409A of the Code governs the design and operation of plans and arrangements that provide for the deferral of compensation. While the definition of a "deferral of compensation" for purposes of Section 409A is broad enough to encompass employee stock options and other types of equity awards, IRS regulations provide the following guidance:

- Incentive stock options (ISOs) and options granted under employee stock purchase plans that comply with Section 423 of the Code are not subject to Section 409A.

- Nonstatutory stock options are not subject to Section 409A if they can never have an exercise price less than the fair market value of the underlying stock on the grant date, the transfer or exercise of the option is subject to taxation under Section 83 of the Code, and the option does not contain any deferral feature other than the right to exercise the option.

- SARs, whether settled in stock or cash, are not subject to Section 409A as long as (1) the amount payable upon exercise of the SAR does not exceed the difference between the fair market value of the underlying stock on the grant date and the exercise date, (2) the exercise price of the SAR can never be less than the fair market value of the underlying stock on the grant date, and (3) the SAR does not include any deferral feature other than the right to exercise the SAR in the future.

Any stock option or SAR that does not qualify for the exemptive treatment described above is considered to involve a deferral of com-

---

13. See Section 162(m)(6).

pensation and must comply with the requirements of Section 409A—which involve the timing of deferral elections and permissible distribution events—to avoid early inclusion of the award's appreciated value in employees' income, plus a 20% penalty and interest.

To be exempt from Section 409A, a stock option or SAR may only be exercisable for so-called "service recipient stock." The definition of a "service recipient" is defined broadly and includes an employer company; a 50% subsidiary; and, given a legitimate business reason (for example, in some joint ventures), a 20% subsidiary. The IRS regulations also indicate that service recipient stock may include American Depository Receipts (ADRs) and "units" in mutual insurance companies. However, "service recipient stock" is limited to *common stock*. For public companies, the common stock must be readily tradable on an established securities market; for private companies, common stock must be the class of common stock having the greatest aggregate value of all the classes of common stock outstanding.

Because stock options and SARs with an exercise price that is less than the fair market value of the underlying stock on the grant date (discounted options and SARs) are subject to Section 409A, valuation of a company's stock in connection with an option or SAR grant will be a critical aspect of compliance with Section 409A. For stock that is readily tradable on an established securities market (including over-the-counter markets and many foreign markets), the IRS regulations provide that fair market value may be determined using the stock's trading price (using a method that is determined on a reasonable basis using actual market transactions and that is consistently applied).

For the stock of a privately held company, fair market value may be determined using any reasonable valuation method that takes into account a number of specified factors and is applied consistently. The IRS regulations include some valuation methods that will be presumed to be reasonable:

- appraisals that satisfy the Code's requirements for valuation of employee stock ownership plan (ESOP) stock[14];

---

14. ESOPs are retirement plans that are primarily invested in company stock. For information about ESOPs, see Scott Rodrick, *An Introduction to ESOPs*, 20th ed. (NCEO, 2022).

- formula valuations based on non-lapse restrictions as defined in Section 83 of the Code, but only if the valuation method is used consistently for both compensatory and noncompensatory purposes; and

- for illiquid stock of a "start-up corporation," special valuations that meet the following requirements: the company is in its first 10 years of active trade or business, has no readily traded securities, does not anticipate a change in control or initial public offering within a specified period after the valuation, and applies the valuation to stock that is not subject to a put, call or repurchase obligation.

Because the exemption for stock options and SARs is limited to awards that were not granted at a discount *and* do not contain any additional deferral feature, amending an option or SAR may convert an otherwise-exempt award into a discount option or SAR subject to Section 409A. Under the IRS regulations, certain changes to an option or SAR will cause the award to be treated either as a new award on the amendment date (which is then retested for Section 409A compliance) or as an award with an additional deferral feature that is considered to have been subject to Section 409A from the original grant date. This issue exists not only for nonstatutory stock options but also for ISOs and Section 423 ESPP options. Any change in the terms of an award that provide the employee a direct or indirect reduction in the award's exercise price, an additional deferral feature, or an extension or renewal of the award is potentially subject to this principle.

5.7 Conclusion

Public companies have many reporting obligations involving their executive and director compensation and their equity compensation plans and arrangements, as discussed above. Most equity plan administrators will be responsible for contributing to their company's compliance with its quarterly and annual reporting requirements to the extent it involves the items subject to these obligations.

CHAPTER

6

Equity Considerations in Merger and Acquisition Transactions

Sorrell Johnson

CONTENTS

Once a rare occurrence, mergers and acquisitions have become more common in the business landscape. With corporations seeking to consolidate their businesses both horizontally and vertically, equity plan administrators can expect this trend to continue. Unlike other equity compensation topics, very little is written about these corporate events because each transaction is unique and the mechanics can be complicated. However, all involve extensive planning and due diligence, negotiations between the parties, internal and external communication, accounting considerations, taxation considerations (both corporate and personal), executive compensation issues, and equity plan issues. This chapter will discuss the general mechanics of mergers and acquisitions and how the equity plan administrator and award recipients are affected.

6.1   Type of Deal

The first step in understanding the impact of a transaction is understanding the type of deal and the stages of the transaction. There are many types of merger and acquisition transactions, but key to an equity plan administrator is the way in which the equity awards are treated. Equity awards may be cashed out, assumed, converted, or cancelled. The time-line and stages of the transaction also depend on the type of transaction.

6.1.1   Stock Purchase Transaction

In a stock purchase transaction, both the buyer and the seller negotiate and become party to an agreement where all the shares of the seller are sold to the buyer. In this type of transaction, the seller ceases to exist when the buyer purchases every outstanding share of the seller. This type of transaction is most common for private company sellers (which have a limited number of shareholders) and less common for public company sellers. Employees are generally are either integrated into the buying company or terminated.

6.1.2   Merger Transaction

In a merger transaction, an acquisition subsidiary is formed by the buyer. The merger agreement is negotiated between and signed by the buyer, seller, and acquisition subsidiary. The transaction is usually endorsed by both the buyer and seller management as well as both corporations' boards of directors. The buyer and seller both seek approval of the trans-action from their shareholders. If approved, at close of the transaction the seller and the acquisition subsidiary merge. In some instances, the buyer may also merge with the acquisition subsidiary. The seller ceases to exist as an independent entity, and employees are either integrated into the newly created subsidiary, integrated into the buyer, or terminated.

6.1.3   Tender Offer Transaction

Tender offer transactions stand out, not due to the different corporate structure of the transaction, but because of the method the buyer uses to obtain approval. In recent years, many tender offers have become hostile transactions. The seller's management and board are not in-terested in selling the corporation, but the buyer tenders an offer to purchase any outstanding shares directly from the shareholders at an above-market price and appeals to the shareholders directly through publicly filed materials to elect new members to the seller's board of directors. These buyer-nominated board members are in favor of the transaction, and if elected will vote in favor of the transaction. The buyer is successful if it either gains a controlling interest in the company via share purchases or elects new board members who will vote in favor of the buyer in corporate matters. After gaining control, the buyer may complete the transaction much like a merger transaction. The seller no longer exists as an independent entity, and employees are either integrated into the buyer or terminated.

6.1.4   Asset Deal

In an asset deal, the buyer acquires some portion of the seller. This portion may be a business division, intellectual property, or other assets. Both the buyer and seller exist after the close of the transaction. Employees who are affected (if any) are hired by the buyer and terminated by the seller. These employees' equity awards issued by the seller terminate at the close of the deal. If they are hired by the buyer, they become eligible for the buyer's equity award programs. If the buyer is specifically purchasing a business division with the purpose of retaining all of the employees, this is known as an "acqui-hire."

6.2   Stages of Merger/Acquisition Transactions

From start to finish, merger and acquisition transactions have several stages during which key milestones must be met. Some stages may be completed in days, while others take months to complete. During the stages leading up to the closing of the transaction, employees of both the buyer and seller who are aware of the potential transaction are likely be subject to a closed trading window during which they may not trade in either the buyer's or seller's equities, due to the material nature of the transaction. This closed trading window remains in force through, at minimum, the pre-close public announcement of the transaction. It may remain in force until the close of the transaction.

6.2.1   Evaluation Period

At the beginning of the evaluation period, the buyer and seller sign confidentiality agreements to enable the buyer to investigate the seller.

The discussions are conducted at the highest levels of the corporation, with executive officers, the board, and a select few employees aware of the discussions. If successful, the evaluation will result in a letter of intent that outlines the primary terms of the deal, with broad language and little detail.

6.2.2 Due Diligence

Once the letter of intent is signed by both the buyer and seller, the buyer conducts in-depth research while the purchase/merger agreement is drafted. At this stage, more individuals are made aware of the potential transaction, and the closed trading window is expanded to include these individuals. Data is usually shared freely between the buyer and seller, but some employee information may be redacted to protect the seller in the event that the transaction is not completed and to comply with data privacy regulations, such as the European Union's General Data Privacy Regulation (GDPR).

The buyer's equity plan administrators should be included as subject matter experts at this stage to review the seller's equity documents and seek proof of the seller's compliance with legal and tax regulations. There are a number of items and issues to review closely during due diligence, including but not limited to:

- *Plans and agreements.* The buyer's equity plan administrator should review copies of all plans under which equity has been issued by the seller and all agreements under which equity has been granted. Plan definitions of change in control are particularly important to the administrator's work of analyzing the impact the merger or acquisition may have on outstanding equity grants. Also, note that different forms of agreements may exist under these plans. Executives may have special agreements relating to acceleration of vesting upon change in control. These provisions may be contained in their equity agreements or in other agreements, such as offer letters or severance agreements, all of which are important to this analysis and should be provided to the buyer's equity plan administrator.

- *Legal compliance issues.* There are a wide range of legal compliance issues that equity plan administrators may find during due diligence. Are the seller's U.S. and international securities law filings up to date? Are there any unregistered equity offerings that do not qualify for an exemption (e.g., under Rule 701 or Regulation D)? If so, are the exemptions documented in detail? Have data privacy consents been obtained from grantees outside the U.S., or are there data privacy violations? Any instance of non-compliance uncovered should be escalated for review to the legal department for a decision on the materiality of the issue.

- *Tax compliance issues.* Are all grants exempt from or compliant with Section 409A? Are employee elections under Section 83(b) properly documented? Does the seller allow Section 83(i) elections and, if so, are employee elections properly documented? At a taxable event, does the seller properly withhold taxes and report gain to the relevant tax authority? For any tax-favored programs, are all requirements and filings completed in a timely manner? Are mobile employees taxed properly in each jurisdiction?

- *Litigation.* Are there any outstanding claims or lawsuits involving the company's equity compensation? Are the lawsuits related to employee claims or are they family law claims, such as divorce?

Buyers should bear in mind that these issues do not have to kill a deal. They can be remedied by rescission, award cancellation, payment to employees, or corrected securities/tax filings. However, remedies will require additional staff time, research, and money, adding to the overall cost of the deal.

Equity plan administrators may also be asked to make suggestions on post-close treatment of equity compensation and to contribute to the strategic post-close integration planning. (Strategic integration issues that equity plan administrators should consider are discussed below in section 6.3.2.)

6.2.3   Pre-Close

Once due diligence is complete, the transaction enters the pre-close stage. At this point, the announcement of the purchase/merger agreement is disclosed to the public as well as to the buyer and seller's employees. The buyer and seller obtain all necessary consents and approvals from the board, shareholders, and governmental entities. Final due diligence is completed with full disclosure and access to the seller's data. If the buyer requires funding to complete the transaction, money may be raised at this time.

At this point, the buyer and seller also commence employee retention planning. The degree to which the seller is involved will depend on the buyer's preference and the perceived level of power and control the buyer exerts over the planning. Nevertheless, the business objectives should always be the same: retention of executive and non-executive key employees, elimination of duplicate positions/functions, and re-location of employees/jobs to maximize efficiency.

If the equity plan administrator has not previously been aware of the potential transaction, they are informed during the pre-close period. Due diligence may have been conducted by individuals not familiar with equity and the administration thereof during the previous phase. If so, it would behoove the equity plan administrator to conduct their own review of the documents as soon as possible.

Ideally, planning for the close and post-close integration of employees occurs during this stage. On both the buyer and seller side, equity plan administrators and a cross-functional team consisting of members of the legal, human resources, and accounting departments should meet regularly to discuss questions about the resources needed to complete the transaction, impact of the transaction on outstanding awards, and post-close integration of the employees and their awards.

6.2.4   Closing and After

The close of the deal brings an official end to the transaction. At this point, the payment in cash and/or shares is delivered to the seller's shareholders. This is achieved through an exchange agent, possibly a public company transfer agent, who corresponds with shareholders, requesting that they remit the seller's shares and in return receive cash and/or shares of the buyer's stock, pursuant to the terms of the merger or purchase agreement.

At the close of the merger or acquisition, the buyer may adjust the outstanding capitalization via a reverse split of the corporation's shares to minimize the dilutive effects of issuing the buyer's shares to the seller's shareholders.

The transaction is now officially over, but the integration work continues in the post-close period, as the buyer integrates the seller's business assets and employees. Employees who are not integrated into the buyer are terminated at or shortly after the close date. Equity awards are adjusted or cashed out depending upon the details of the transaction agreement and the terms and conditions of the seller's equity plans.

Typically, equity transactions are frozen for employees of the seller shortly before the closing. This allows the seller to provide accurate outstanding award and share details to the buyer in order to complete precise cash-out, substitution, or conversion calculations.

6.2.4.1 Treatment of Equity Awards

Many factors play into the decision regarding the treatment of employee equity at close. For the buyer, cashing out the awards will not raise the buyer's burn rate, and yet it will also provide no incentive for key employees to remain post-close, and cash on hand will be reduced. The cancellation of old grants and substitution with new grants in the buyer's stock or conversion of the seller's grants to buyer stock will help the buyer retain the seller's employees and preserve cash, but these changes will increase the burn rate. Buyers may opt to use a combination of the following methods to best serve their goals.[1]

Acceleration. The seller's equity plans may specify that outstanding grants automatically vest upon the close of the merger or acquisition. The vesting acceleration may apply to all employees or only to executives and may be full or partial. An acceleration of vesting due solely to the close of a corporate transaction is referred to as a "single-trigger" acceleration. If the acceleration of vesting requires not only the close of the transaction but also another event (such as termination of employment), this is referred to as a "double-trigger" acceleration.

Cash-Out of Awards. The buyer may choose to cash out awards under the seller's plans at close. The buyer applies a predetermined formula disclosed in the merger agreement, calculates the value of

---

1. See section 6.3.2.1 for an in-depth discussion of the considerations associated with each approach.

each outstanding equity award, and pays each employee appropriately, essentially cancelling outstanding grants. In most cases, this is a lump-sum payment.

Cancelled and Substituted Awards. In this case, the buyer cancels the outstanding awards issued by the seller and issues new awards in the buyer's stock under the buyer's equity plans. This enables the buyer to ensure that all employee equity awards carry the same terms and conditions.

Assumed and Converted Awards. In this case, the buyer assumes awards outstanding, adjusting only the number of shares and, in the case of stock options, the exercise price, in accordance with a prede-termined formula specified in the merger agreement. In most cases, the buyer does the assumption and conversion under the seller's equity plans and award agreements, meaning all other terms and conditions remain intact for grant recipients who previously worked for the sell-ing company.

Employee Stock Purchase Plans. The seller's employee stock pur-chase plan (ESPP) may purchase one final time any time from a few months to a few days before the close. The seller's ESPP terminates after the final purchase. This is true regardless of whether the ESPP is tax-qualified under Section 423 or nonqualified. The buyer may choose to assume the seller's ESPP, but this is the exception rather than the rule.

6.3 Strategic Equity Considerations for Post-Close Planning

Merger and acquisition transactions are cross-functional events that re-quire a multifaceted approach involving multiple departments working together to solve the unique challenges that arise. A comprehensive dis-cussion of these considerations is outside the scope of this chapter, but common issues that affect equity compensation are discussed below.

6.3.1 Planning Considerations

Normal equity compensation processes involve not only the equity compensation team but also the accounting, legal, human resources, and payroll departments. This also holds true for the buyer and seller sides of merger and acquisition planning. Ongoing meetings with internal stakeholders as a group or individually set at a regular cadence is the best way to ensure that all departments are kept up to date on decisions affecting the transaction and any due dates and deliverables resulting from these decisions. Project plans, whether kept in a simple Excel workbook or using a more complex software solution, are an excellent way of tracking deliverables, deadlines, and responsible parties. Given the breadth of issues and parties involved in a transaction, it might benefit the equity plan administrator to set up separate smaller meetings with specific internal stakeholders on narrower issues in the stakeholder's area of expertise. For example, the human resources department is not likely to contribute in a meaningful way to discussions about the post-close accounting methodology to be used for equity awards, while the accounting department has little to offer regarding the post-close communication schedule for employees.

Equity plan administrators should be mindful of their outside vendors as well. Once a nondisclosure or confidentiality agreement is in place, the outside vendors can be brought up to speed on the transaction. Transfer agents frequently serve as exchange agents in the merger and acquisition process. External legal counsel can assist with securities law filings. Equity plan platform providers can assist with necessary data conversions. It is important to keep all outside vendors, no matter how peripheral a part they may play, involved in planning to ensure a smooth execution.

6.3.2 Equity Administration Considerations

6.3.2.1 Assumption and Conversion of Awards vs. Cash-Out[2]

When negotiating the treatment of equity, the initial question is whether the buyer should cash out or assume and convert the seller's outstanding equity awards. There are advantages and disadvantages to each method (table 6-1).

---

2. As of November 2021, there are changes pending with the Securities and Exchange Commission (SEC) regarding Form S-8 and Rule 701 regarding former service providers and the ability of the issuer to substitute or exchange awards held by this population in a corporate transaction.

Table 6-1. Considerations for Handling Equity Grants		
Corporate or administrative consideration	Assumption and conversion at close	Cash-out at close
Cash burn rate	Little or no reduction of the buyer's cash reserves	Reduction of the buyer's cash reserves
Share burn rate	May increase the buyer's share burn rate if the seller's plans are not assumed	No effect
Potential dilution/ increase of overhang	Increases potential dilution and overhang	No effect
Retention of the seller's employees post-close	Provides retentive power if original vesting schedule is preserved	Provides little retentive power over employees, unless the cash-out is structured over a post-close period (which is unusual)
Non-compatible plan features (early exercise, retirement eligibility, post termination exercise periods)	If the buyer assumes grants under the seller's plans, features can be preserved, but this creates administrative complexity for equity administrators. If the buyer converts grants and issues new ones under the buyer's plan, employees may perceive a loss of benefit	Not applicable
Integration of awards into the equity administration platform, post-close	Equity plan administrator is responsible for conversion and integration of data into the buyer's equity administration platform with tight deadlines	Not applicable if paid in lump sum at close

Table 6-1. Considerations for Handling Equity Grants		
Corporate or administrative consideration	Assumption and conversion at close	Cash-out at close
Complexity of employee communications	Communication will include a large amount of information on a series of topics (see section 6.3.8)	Communications are relatively straightforward, consisting of the cash payment amount calculation and estimated time and method of payment
Form S-8 filings	May be required if assuming the seller's plan or if the buyer requires share increase in current plans to accommodate grants	Not applicable if paid in lump sum at close
Non-U.S. securities law implications: increase in grants under existing exemptions or filings	Filings will be updated to reflect assumed grants; exemptions may be lost due to increased grant or participant numbers	Generally not applicable if paid in lump sum at close
Stock option tax issues	Potential for tax issues and ISO disqualification if economic benefit is not the same (see section 6.3.2.2)	If the options have not yet been exercised, cash payment will be classified as employment income and should be processed through payroll.

6.3.2.2 Stock Options and Code Section 424

If the buyer opts to assume or convert the seller's stock option grants at the close of the transaction, they must be careful to adhere to the terms of Section 424 of the Internal Revenue Code (the "Code") to ensure that the employee does not incur a taxable event. Under Section 424, employee options must meet two criteria:

1. "The excess of the aggregate fair market value of the shares subject to the option immediately after the substitution or assumption over the aggregate option price of such shares is not more than the excess of the aggregated fair market value of all shares subject

to the option immediately before such substitution or assumption over the aggregate option price of such shares," and

2. "The new option or the assumption of the old option does not give the employee additional benefits which he did not have under the old option."[3]

This means the employee must be no better off economically after the assumption and conversion than they were prior. In order to ensure that this does not happen, it is highly advisable to round decimals down on the number of shares and exercise price (if applicable) during the conversion process.

Taxation of Incentive Stock Options. In addition to the rules cited above in this section (6.3.2.2), if the buyer wants to preserve the ISO status of the seller's options, the $100,000 limit per year of exercisable stock must be maintained.

Taxation of Nonqualified Stock Options. If the buyer complies with the rules cited above in this section (6.2.2.2), the taxation treatment of nonqualified stock options will remain the same; namely, the gain at exercise will be taxed as ordinary income.

6.3.2.3 Recordkeeping

Whether opting for an assumption and conversion or cash-out of equity grants, it is imperative to maintain good records for future use. Frequently either the buyer or seller's equity plan administrator departs after the close of the transaction, leaving the remaining equity administrator to answer questions raised by employees. Both equity plan administrators should freely share information. Post-close information and documentation showing conversion calculations, cash payouts, and special exceptions should be preserved in a shared data repository.

6.3.3   Accounting Considerations

The accounting treatment of equity during a merger/acquisition depends upon how the buyer handles the awards. Will they be assumed

---

3.   Code Section 424(a)(1) and (2).

with the current vesting schedule? Will the vesting be accelerated? Will the awards be cashed out, and if so, does the buyer or seller chose to cash them out? A thorough discussion of the accounting and valuation of equity awards during a merger or acquisition depends on these factors, among others, and is beyond the scope of this chapter.[4]

6.3.4 Tax Considerations: Corporate Perspective

For the buyer, there are several corporate tax issues to consider when undertaking a transaction.

6.3.4.1 Capturing Corporate Tax Deductions

If the transaction is structured as a stock purchase or tender offer, the purchase of the outstanding seller shares from employees may result in a tax deduction for the seller entity, now wholly owned by the buyer. In order for the seller entity to claim a tax deduction for shares purchased from employees in the course of the transaction, the purchase must create a disqualifying disposition under Code Sections 422 or 423, and the income resulting from the disposition must be reported on the employee's Form W-2. The buyer should consider this carefully and may want to coordinate the post-close reporting of these dispositions with the seller's brokerage firm.

6.3.4.2 Continuing Tax Reporting Requirements for the Seller

Under Code Section 6039, the seller is required to report any exercises of ISOs and the first transfer of shares under a tax-qualified 423 ESPP for the tax year in which they occur. (The ESPP requirement normally arises when the shares are deposited into the participant's brokerage account.) This obligation does not disappear with the closing of the transaction. The buyer should plan to fulfill the seller's reporting requirements as part of the post-close integration process. If the

---

4. For information regarding this topic, see Takis Makridis and Daniel Hunninghake, "Accounting for Assumed Awards under ASC 805," *Advanced Topics in Equity Compensation Accounting*, 10th ed. (Oakland, CA: NCEO, 2021). See also Accounting Standard Codification Topic No. 805 (ASC 805).

transaction includes the forced exercises of any ISOs at close, these transactions should be included in the seller's final 6039 reporting.

After the closing of the corporate transaction, due dates for 6039 reporting remain the same for the seller's reporting requirements. However, the buyer may elect to make the filings earlier than the scheduled deadline. For example, if the seller's ESPP has a six-month purchase period and one purchase has taken place in the current calendar year at the time of close, the buyer may proceed with making the filing to ensure it is not forgotten during the year-end tasks that occur months later.

6.3.5   Tax Considerations: Employee Perspective

Employees are likely to encounter a taxable event at some point in a merger or acquisition transaction. Corporations should not be reluctant to communicate the basic facts of the transaction to employees; however, tax advice should not be given under any circumstances. The taxable event may occur due to a change in the employees' equity awards or due to their status as a shareholder of the seller.

6.3.5.1   *Employee Equity Award Treatment*

Conversion of Equity Awards. During virtually all transactions, buyers seek to avoid creating income attributable to employees while converting and assuming employee equity awards. While not impossible, it is unlikely that equity awards at close become a taxable event for the employee. If the buyer is contemplating an arrangement that would result in taxable income to employees, extensive employee education is required. Equity plan administrators may need to consult outside advisors for assistance with communications in this instance.

Additionally, if the seller has tax-qualified plans in certain countries, such as Israel or France, and the buyer wants to assume the tax-qualified plan and awards, the buyer and seller should work together to seek approval from the country's tax authority to preserve the tax-qualified status of the existing plan after the close. The tax authority may or may not grant this approval. These approvals often take several months to obtain, so this task should be started early in the merger/acquisition process. *Leaving this task until close may result in the plan being disqualified.* In losing tax qualification, at best the buyer will not be able to use the plan for future awards; at worst, all awards outstanding under the plan will lose their favorable tax status, resulting in higher taxes for both employee and employer.

Cash-Outs of Equity Awards. If the buyer opts to cash out all the seller's employee equity awards, payments are remitted to employees in exchange for their outstanding equity awards, which are cancelled. These payments are taxable income for the employee. These payments may be distributed via the seller's payroll or directly to the employees via their seller-sponsored brokerage accounts. Outside the U.S., countries tax these payments differently, depending on the source distributing the payment, the classification of the payment (employment income vs. capital gains), and local laws. The seller should research and, to the extent possible, distribute payments to employees via the appropriate method to minimize the tax impact. A hybrid approach to payments (via both payroll and the seller-sponsored brokerage account) may be best to accommodate employee needs.

6.3.5.2 Employees as Shareholders

Frequently, employees hold shares of the seller they acquired from a seller-issued equity award transaction (e.g. restricted stock/unit vesting, purchase of shares under an ESPP, or exercise of a stock option). In this instance, employees have an interest not only in what happens to outstanding equity awards but also in the impact of the transaction on shareholders.

Stock Deals. Mergers and acquisitions by U.S. corporations are frequently structured with the intent to be reorganizations under Code Section 368(a).This means U.S. employee shareholders will not recognize any gain or loss on the stock-for-stock exchange, except for any payment made for a fractional share. The payment for any fractional share will result in a gain or loss equal to the difference between the cash received and the shareholder's basis in the fractional share. U.S. employee shareholders should refer to the Form S-4 registration statement, which details the intended structure of the transaction and the tax treatment of the resulting shares.

The S-4 also describes the tax implication if the transaction is not deemed to be a reorganization. In this case, the U.S. employee shareholder would recognize a gain or loss equal to the difference between the fair market value of the stock and cash received and the cost basis of the shares. While it is the intent of both buyer and seller that the transaction qualify under Section 368(a), buyers normally do not seek a binding Internal Revenue Service (IRS) ruling, instead relying on the opinions of legal firms representing either buyer, seller, or both. The IRS is free to challenge the reorganization status of the transaction.

Once the transaction is complete, the buyer will file a Form 8937 with the IRS and/or post the Form 8937 on its corporate website describing the adjustments to the cost basis of the shares due to the transaction. U.S. employee shareholders should carefully review the Form 8937 and adjust their cost basis accordingly or consult a financial advisor regarding this adjustment.

Non-U.S. employee shareholders will likely incur a taxable event at close of the transaction, even if the transaction is a reorganization in the opinion of the IRS. The buyer may want to consider offering transaction-related tax supplements to these employee shareholders to aid understanding of any non-U.S. employee tax obligations.

Stock Purchase/Tender Offer. If the buyer choses to purchase all shares in the seller for cash, employee shareholders are treated in the same way as non-employee shareholders. They receive payment for any seller shares they own. If the shares purchased are the result of an ISO exercise or a purchase under a Section 423 ESPP, sale of shares to the buyer will result in either a qualified or disqualified disposition, depending on whether the employee has held the shares for the statutory holding period of at least two years since the grant date and one year since the exercise or purchase date. These dispositions should be reported on the employee's Form W-2 as required under the Code.

All employees of the seller, regardless of the type of deal or location of residence, should retain any cost basis documents issued by the broker or transfer or exchange agent for shares distributed upon vesting or exercise of their seller-issued equity awards. These brokerage accounts may be decommissioned after the close of the transaction if the awards are canceled and the seller uses a different service provider for its equity compensation plans. The buyer may maintain this information in the equity administration platform but is not required to do so. Employees who do not retain cost basis records may find it difficult to accurately report income to their tax authorities at the time of sale and could essentially be double-taxed as a result.

6.3.6 Executive Compensation Considerations

6.3.6.1 Change in Control Treatment and Acceleration of Vesting

Plan and award documents generally contemplate the treatment of outstanding equity at close of a transaction. However, executives and members of the board of directors may be subject to additional terms and conditions contained in supplemental agreements such as offer letters and change in control agreements. Equity plan administrators should consult these documents and work with both the legal and human resources departments to understand the impact of the transaction on executive equity.

6.3.6.2 Performance-Based Equity Treatment at Close

Many questions arise concerning performance-based equity in a transaction. The equity plan administrator should direct careful attention to the merger agreement, award agreement, and other documents as they apply to changes in control. There are a number of ways in which the transaction may affect any outstanding performance awards. For employees of the seller, the performance measurement period may end on or at the close of the transaction. At that point, the performance criteria and level of achievement may be certified and the award paid out, if goals have been achieved. If the buyer intends to retain key seller executives, the performance awards may be converted and criteria modified to reflect buyer-specific goals.

Generally, only the seller's performance awards will vest at close of the transaction. However, if the merger or acquisition is contemplated in the buyer's performance awards, the closing may trigger certification and vesting of the buyer's awards as well.

6.3.6.3 Payments Under Code Sections 280G and Section 4999

Corporations are generally able to take tax deductions for compensation they pay employees and report as income on the employees' Form W-2. However, there are some limitations on these deductions. During a merger or acquisition transaction the limitation most likely to come into play is Code Section 280G, which disallows a deduction for any payment that qualifies as a "parachute payment." Parachute payments have these characteristics:

- they are of a compensatory nature;
- they are made to a disqualified individual (an officer, director, highly compensated individual or 1% or more shareholder);
- they are contingent on a change in ownership or control of the corporation; and
- they have an aggregate present value of at least three times the individual's base amount (annual income).

Equity compensation-related parachute payments are most likely to occur when an officer or director of the seller is terminated in the course of the transaction and the change in control agreement accelerates the vesting of equity. For executives who receive payments that are considered excess parachute payments under Code Section 280G, Code Section 4999 imposes an additional 20% tax on the payment. Equity plan administrators should closely monitor potential payments to executives upon close and notify their legal and human resources departments. If no agreement is structured to avoid the 20% tax and the corporation will be collecting this amount, the payroll department should be notified in advance of the payment.

6.3.6.4 Section 162(m)

Internal Revenue Code Section 162(m) disallows a deduction by any publicly held corporation for remuneration paid to any covered employee where the employee's remuneration for the tax year exceeds $1 million. A covered employee is any employee who satisfies any one of the following criteria at any time during the year:

1. an employee who was, or acted in the capacity of, the chief executive officer;

2. an employee who was, or acted in the capacity of, the chief financial officer; or

3. any employee who is among the three most highly compensated officers and is required to be reported in the proxy.

Additionally, once an employee becomes a covered employee, they remain so indefinitely. This is a major change, since previously employees were evaluated once yearly to determine who qualified as a covered employee. Covered employee status will continue after a merger, termination, or even death.

Under the American Rescue Plan act of 2021, the definition of a covered employee was amended to include a fourth group containing the next five most highly compensated employees. Employees do not have to be officers or executives to qualify for inclusion in the fourth group. However, these employees are not considered covered employees indefinitely. This change becomes effective with tax years beginning after December 31, 2026.

The only exception to the rules set is in cases of written binding employment contracts in effect on November 2, 2017. These contracts may not be modified in any material respect on or after that date, in order to retain the treatment under the old version of Section 162(m), which exempted qualified performance-based compensation (including performance-based equity awards) from the $1 million calculation.

Additionally, Section 162(m) applies to privately held companies that have registered debt offerings subject to the reporting requirements of Section 15(d) of the Securities Exchange Act and certain foreign private issuers.

6.3.6.5 Retaining Valued Executives: "Re-vesting"?

If the buyer wishes to retain key executives from the seller's organization, the deal negotiations may include a request that executives agree to modification of their outstanding agreements (either equity or cash). Such agreements typically stipulate that grants that would normally be paid out upon closing of the deal instead re-vest over 12,

24, or 36 months after the close. This is also called a "holdback." The buyer's purpose is to retain key executive talent on the seller's side for a smooth integration of the companies. During the pre-close period, equity plan administrators should familiarize themselves with any of these arrangements in preparation for equity award conversion at close.

6.3.7   Legal Considerations

During a merger or acquisition, there are several legally mandated filings under U.S. securities laws and exchange regulations. If corporations have qualified international stock plans, this number only increases. While not all equity plan administrators are a part of the legal department, they may be asked to provide information used in these filings. In order to understand the mechanics of the transaction and plan effectively, equity plan administrators should familiarize themselves with these filings. While table 6-2 lists some of the most common filings, it is not an exhaustive list. Other filings may apply due to special aspects of the transaction or countries where the buyer or seller issues equity. Additionally, after the close, there may be some deregistrations of the sellers' plans in some international locations.

Table 6-2. U.S. Securities Law Filings		
Type of filing/description	Does the buyer file?	Does the seller file?
Form 8-K: A Form 8-K is filed for many reasons, not all of which are transaction related. In reference to a merger or acquisition transaction, a Form 8-K would be filed at several points: announcement of the transaction at signing; status updates on the transaction, appointment, or departure of officers and directors; changes to compensatory arrangements with officers and directors; and the close of the transaction.	Yes	Yes

Table 6-2. U.S. Securities Law Filings

Type of filing/description	Does the buyer file?	Does the seller file?
DEF 14A: If the transaction requires the buyer and the seller to obtain consent from their shareholders via vote, then a Form DEF 14A is filed. Usually both the buyer and the seller will each schedule a special meeting or combine the vote on the transaction with other business at their annual meeting.	Yes	Yes
HSR notice: This filing with the U.S. Federal Trade Commission and the Department of Justice is required under the Hart-Scott-Rodino Act and does not apply to every transaction. The filing is not publicly disclosed, and the primary goal is to ensure the transaction does not adversely affect competition in the buyer and sellers' industry.	Yes	Yes
CFIUS notice: The Committee on Foreign Investment in the United States (CFIUS) requires a notification if the buyer is a foreign-owned or incorporated entity and the seller's products or services are considered key to the national security of the U.S.	Yes	Yes
Form S-4: This registration statement contains material information such as financial information and terms of the potential transaction.	Yes	No
Form 15-12G: This filing certifies the termination of registration of a class of securities, ensuring that no additional filings are required under Sections 13 and 15(d) of the Securities Exchange Act of 1934. The seller files one of these for each class of security outstanding at close of the transaction.	No	Yes

Table 6-2. U.S. Securities Law Filings

Type of filing/description	Does the buyer file?	Does the seller file?
Form S-8: This filing registers shares issued under an employee equity plan. If the buyer assumes the seller's plans, they should file an S-8 registering these shares. The buyer may also have newly approved shares under its own plans to register. An S-8 would also be required for this increase.	Yes	No
Form S-8 POS: This filing deregisters any shares for which a Form S-8 was previously filed. The seller files this form indicating that the seller is terminating all offers of securities under the equity plans.	No	Yes
Form 3: This is the initial statement of beneficial ownership of securities owned by Section 16 insiders of companies whose shares are registered under Section 12 of the Securities Exchange Act of 1934. This filing is required if the buyer is hiring employees from the seller who the buyer designates as Section 16 insiders.	Yes	No
Form 4: This is the statement of changes in beneficial ownership of securities required of Section 16 insiders of publicly traded companies.	Yes, if the buyer is a reporting company and is granting or converting equity.	Yes, if the seller's Section 16 insiders' equity is being assumed, converted, or paid out by the buyer. If the seller's Section 16 reporters are terminated with no compensation for their equity, Form 4 is not required, but is considered by many to be a best practice.

Table 6-2. U.S. Securities Law Filings

Type of filing/description	Does the buyer file?	Does the seller file?
Form 25-NSE: This form is filed to announce the intent to de-list shares from an exchange. Ten days before filing this form with the SEC, the corporation must notify the exchange and issue a press release stating their intention to file this form and delist. The Form 25-NSE becomes effective 10 days after filing. At that point, most filing obligations cease.	No	Yes
Other Filings		
International securities law filings for equity plans: Consult legal counsel for more information regarding international filings.	Yes, if the buyer is assuming and converting the seller's outstanding grants.	Yes, the seller may be required to make a final filing showing that the equity issued is fully vested, cancelled, or no longer outstanding.
Exchange filings: Additional shares	Yes, the buyer may issue new shares in connection with the transaction.	No

6.3.8 Employee Communication Considerations

A transaction creates much uncertainty for employees of both the buyer and the seller and may create unintended employee turnover. Effective communication plans must be developed in the due diligence period and refined and implemented during the pre-close and closing stages of the transaction. Once the transaction is announced and can be discussed publicly, communication is the best way to prevent unfounded employee fears and unnecessary speculation and rumors.

6.3.8.1 Communication Types and Frequency

Companies often wonder whether they over-communicate. This is nearly impossible to do. The seller's employees are nervous about losses of jobs and changes in benefits. The buyer's employees ponder the impact the post-close integration will have on their jobs and the overall structure of the corporation. Companies should not wait until the close of the transaction to start communications with both sets of employees as that is too late in the process. Companies are advised to communicate frequently, in multiple languages, and via various channels.

When drafting a communication plan, companies should consider the locations and demographics of the workforce and not be afraid to send the same information or messages via different channels. For example, if the seller has a large population of manufacturing workers in Malaysia who do not regularly check their corporate email accounts and a large population of administrative workers in the U.S., two different channels of communication in two languages communicating the same message are ideal.

Live or prerecorded meetings may help employees understand the changes that the merger or acquisition will bring. These may solely address equity issues or may involve other benefit administrators as well. Additionally, equity plan administrators may want to consider the use of a special email box specifically for equity-related questions (i.e., mergerequity@seller.com) to handle the flood of questions from employees. Company that rely on social media for other employee communications should consider using this as a platform as well for answering employee questions.

6.3.8.2 Equity-Specific Communication Topics

Employees will seek information regarding the impact to their equity almost the moment the transaction is announced. It is essential that equity plan administrators work with other departments to develop communications regarding the impact on equity at close of the transaction, the loss of equity-related benefits (i.e. discontinuation of early exercise or ESPP), the gain of equity-related benefits (i.e. addition of retirement eligibility), and differences between old and new equity compensation programs and awards.

Many buyers provide the seller's employees with detailed customized statements at close describing the treatment of their equity in detail. These statements frequently present the awards in a table side by side with the "before" and "after" state clearly displayed for each grant.

A cover letter or FAQ document accompanies the statement providing general information about the assumption and conversion or cash-out, such as the conversion ratio or cash-out details. These statements are usually delivered at or before close to aid employee understanding of the transaction's specific impact on their grants as well as timing of any specific equity-related events (i.e., closed trading windows, new grants).

Extensive communication may be required if the buyer's and seller's equity compensation programs are drastically different. For example, if the buyer is a publicly traded corporation that only grants restricted stock units to management-level employees while the seller is a private company granting stock options to all employees, the result can be equity compensation culture shock. If the seller offers a Section 423 tax-qualified ESPP with a 15% discount and look-back, while the buyer only offers a nonqualified ESPP with a 5% discount, employees will be understandably confused and frustrated if they lack the communication and educational resources to clearly understand the new equity compensation programs.

It is likely that every equity plan administrator will encounter a merger or acquisition at some point in their career. A successful transaction depends on understanding the transaction, planning in conjunction with other departments, and robust communication with employees.

7

Handling Death Under an Equity Compensation Plan

Michael J. Album and Steven D. Einhorn

CONTENTS

This chapter has been updated and revised from an earlier published version coauthored by J. Mark Poerio and Donna Yip. The current authors would like to thank the following attorneys at Proskauer Rose LLP for their assistance: Henry Leibowitz, Frank Zarb, Tyler Forni, and Marjorie Hornaday.

While handling the death of a grantee under an equity compensation plan depends largely on the situation at hand, various issues consistently present themselves at both the corporate and individual level. These issues include estate administration, tax consequences, and securities laws. This chapter provides general guidance on these issues. As compensation specialists know, there are many different types of awards that may be granted under an equity plan, including stock options, restricted stock, restricted stock units, and even cash-based awards. The treatment of each type of award upon the death of the grantee varies depending on the nature of the award, but the issues presented in this chapter will provide a general overview and assist compensation specialists in determining what further analysis and action may be necessary in the event that an equity holder dies.

7.1   Estate Administration

A traditional view of estate administration focuses on the management, organization, and disposition of the decedent's estate, including the identification of the various assets held by the estate, probating the will, and distributing the assets to the identified beneficiaries. When evaluating estate administration in conjunction with equity awards held by a decedent, it is clear that a consideration of the equity incentive plan documents (including the plan and individual award agreements) and the involvement of the equity plan administrator are essential to the discussion.

7.1.1   From the Estate Administrator's Perspective

At the estate administration level, one threshold issue is whether the equity plan or an individual award agreement provides for the designation of beneficiaries. Unlike tax-qualified or ERISA-covered retirement plans, there is no legal requirement that the holder's spouse be named as the beneficiary unless the holder's spouse consents otherwise. If the equity award survives the death of the holder and the decedent did not validly designate a beneficiary, then the equity holder's estate would become the beneficiary. In some states, beneficiary designations for equity awards may be invalid. In the event that the holder's designation of a beneficiary is found to be invalid, a dispute may arise as to the rightful beneficiary.

If the decedent has validly designated one or more individuals as beneficiaries of the decedent's interest in the equity plan (hereinafter referred to as "plan beneficiaries"), the decedent's equity interest will pass directly to the plan beneficiaries and will not be subject to probate (the court-supervised process of disposing of the decedent's property as provided under his or her will) or administration (the court-supervised process of disposing of the decedent's property pursuant to the applicable state laws of inheritance if the decedent died without a valid will). A beneficiary designation cannot be changed by will, so it is essential to update the equity holder's plan beneficiaries each time the equity holder changes his or her estate planning documents. The equity holder may also want to revisit his or her beneficiary designations if a plan beneficiary predeceases the equity holder.

If a decedent has not designated a plan beneficiary to receive the decedent's equity plan interest upon death, the decedent's interest in the plan will pass to his or her estate. If the decedent died testate (i.e., with a valid will), the estate (including the equity interest) will be disposed of as provided in his or her will. If the decedent died intestate (i.e., without a valid will), the estate (including the equity interest) will be distributed to the decedent's lawful heirs, as determined by state law.

If the decedent dies testate, the decedent's will must be validated (or "admitted to probate") by the probate court of the jurisdiction in which the decedent died. The probate court will also appoint one or more individuals designated by the decedent in his or her will to act as executor of the decedent's estate. If the decedent dies intestate, the probate court will appoint one or more individuals (typically the surviving spouse, or if none, the decedent's children or another relative) to act as administrator of the estate. The executor or administrator (collectively, the "Representative") of the decedent's estate has the legal authority and responsibility to oversee the disposition of the decedent's estate.

Alternatively, if the decedent transferred any portion of his or her equity interest to a trust during his or her life, the equity interest will be administered by the trustees of the trust, with the disposition of assets in the trust occurring separately from the administration of the estate. It is very important from the outset to understand the context in which ownership and control of the equity interests exists at the time of death.

Upon a decedent's death, the Representative of the decedent's estate is charged with a number of responsibilities concerning the decedent's estate. These responsibilities include but are not limited to: (1) organizing and filing the relevant paperwork surrounding the decedent's estate in the probate court; (2) inventorying and managing the assets of the decedent's estate; (3) taking possession of all of the decedent's property that is subject to probate or administration; (4) filing an inventory of the estate's assets in the probate court; (5) paying the debts, taxes, and liabilities of the estate; (6) if a federal and/or state estate tax return is required to be filed, obtaining appraisals of the decedent's assets, arranging for the preparation of the return, and filing the tax return by the applicable due date (if a federal estate tax return is required to be filed, it is due nine months after the decedent's date of death, subject to being extended); and (7) distributing the remaining assets to the beneficiaries entitled to receive them.

If the decedent's equity interest passes to his or her estate, the Representative's responsibility to inventory and manage the assets of the decedent's estate raises practical issues regarding equity interests. In order to ascertain the types of equity awards that the decedent owned and the general treatment of these awards under the applicable equity plans, the Representative may request from the plan's administrator a copy of all applicable equity documents, which frequently include copies of the actual award agreements, a notice of exercise form, a prospectus, a summary of the decedent's equity grants and exercises, vesting information, and related plan materials. Generally, when the decedent "owns" stock options or unvested restricted stock, the value of these awards must be included in the decedent's gross estate for estate tax purposes,[1] which must be reported on the decedent's federal and/or state estate tax return (if a return is required to be filed for the estate).

Depending on the type of options or equity awards held by the decedent and whether such options or equity awards are transferable

---

1.   Rev. Rul. 53-196, 1953-2 C.B. 178.

to the estate, the Representative may need to determine whether he or she has the authority under both the will and applicable state law to exercise stock options; hold stock; sell stock; or transfer the option, stock, or other equity award. The general tax consequences of these various forms of disposition are discussed below. Other issues may arise, such as whether the Representative has sufficient funds to exercise outstanding options; whether the Representative has the authority to borrow or pledge stock; and, when borrowing funds to exercise options, what restrictions may be imposed upon an institutional fiduciary by Regulation U of the Federal Reserve System Board of Governors.

7.1.2   From an Equity Plan Administrator's Perspective

At the corporate level, the plan administrator often serves as the main contact to interact with the plan beneficiaries, or if none, with the estate's Representative or the trustees of a trust to which equity awards have been transferred. While the estate has the Representative to handle the estate's issues after death, plan administrators themselves must handle various compensation-related issues relating to equity interests for the periods both before and after the death of the equity interest holder.

A prudent equity plan administrator knows that issues relating to the disposition and handling of equity interests in connection with the death of an executive should be dealt with at the design stage, when drafting the terms of an equity plan. In other words, the best time to anticipate and address decisions and accommodations for the various issues that arise in the administration of an equity plan (such as death, retirement, change in control, disability, or termination of employment) is in the design phase of the equity plan.

In the event that an equity holder dies, the equity plan administrator and company's legal counsel should carefully review the terms of all equity plans under which the decedent participated for provisions relating to the treatment of the equity awards in the event of the death of the holder. In connection with this review, each document granting the equity award also must be analyzed, since it is common for individual award agreements to modify or expand relevant plan provisions. In some cases, the relevant equity plan or award agreement may provide that the death of the holder accelerates vesting of some or all of the outstanding awards or results in the proration, through the date of death, of applicable performance-related vesting provisions.

The plan administrator must consider many issues regarding the impact of the holder's death on outstanding equity awards. For example, is the option extinguished, or is it transferable to the plan beneficiaries (e.g., pursuant to the terms of the applicable plan, the holder's will, or the applicable laws of descent and distribution)? Does vesting accelerate on the holder's death? How long are the options exercisable after death? Will the plan beneficiaries or the estate have a right to a prorated portion of the performance cycle in situations where the equity grant covers a performance period that extends beyond the death of the holder?

If an equity plan or an individual award agreement provides for the designation of beneficiaries, any records designating a beneficiary should be examined upon notice of the death of the holder. Unlike tax-qualified or ERISA-covered retirement plans, there is no legal requirement that the holder's spouse be named as the beneficiary. If the equity award survives the death of the holder and the decedent did not validly designate a beneficiary, then the equity holder's estate would become the beneficiary, subject to any specific bequest in the holder's will. In some states, beneficiary designations for equity awards may be invalid. In the event that the holder's designation of a beneficiary is found to be invalid, a dispute may arise as to the rightful beneficiary.

In the event of the death of an equity holder, the equity plan administrator should obtain a copy of the death certificate and contact the plan beneficiaries, if any. If there is no plan beneficiary, the equity plan administrator must correspond and interact with the Representative, who should provide the plan administrator with a copy of the holder's death certificate and the court order appointing the Representative as the executor or administrator of the estate. The equity plan administrator should take prudent steps to ensure that the parties seeking information about the decedent's estate holdings are authorized to do so and to ensure that sensitive information is not inadvertently disclosed to the incorrect parties. For example, in situations where the decedent has been divorced, and the decedent has an ex-spouse and children, the equity plan administrator should take care to ensure that he or she is dealing only with authorized parties.

For additional concerns posed at the equity plan administrator level, please refer to the discussion of tax and securities issues below.

7.2 Tax Consequences

Upon satisfactory resolution of equity plan and estate administration issues relating to the identification and distribution of the equity awards, the Representative, the beneficiaries of the estate, and the former employer must consider the tax consequences associated with the various transactions after the employee's death. These tax consequences vary depending on the underlying equity; the tax discussion below focuses on (1) incentive stock options (ISOs), (2) nonqualified stock options (NSOs), (3) restricted stock, and (4) cash-settled awards.

7.2.1 Incentive Stock Options

An ISO is a special form of option that receives tax-favored treatment by satisfying certain statutory requirements, including employment and holding requirements enumerated in the Internal Revenue Code (the "Code"). For an option to be treated as an ISO, Code Section 422 requires, among other things, that an optionee be an employee of the company granting the option (or an employee of its parent or a subsidiary) at all times during the period beginning on the date of grant through the day three months before exercise. This three-month period is waived in the event of the death of an option holder (thus, delays in exercise following death will not automatically invalidate the ISO). However, most stock option plans or award agreements limit the post-death exercise period associated with an ISO. While the Code also requires that stock acquired through exercise of an ISO be held for at least one year after the date of exercise and that such stock may not be disposed of before two years from the date the ISO was granted, there are again special exceptions to these "holding periods" in connection with options exercised by the executive's plan beneficiaries, his or her estate, or by a person acquiring the option by bequest or inheritance after the death of the original grantee.

The advantage of an ISO is that the holder is not taxed upon the acquisition of the option shares. Instead, the holder will generally not be taxed until the sale of the shares. Additionally, the spread between the option price and sales price will qualify as a long-term capital gain, subject to lower tax rates than the rates that apply to ordinary income. Absent a "disqualifying disposition" of the ISO (i.e., a sale in contravention of the holding requirements) or an acceleration of vesting causing the award to exceed the $100,000 limit on options first exercisable in a single year, the employer will not be entitled to any compensation deduction.[2]

Exercise and Transfer in the Event of Death. While Code Section 422 lays out various rules with respect to the exercise and transfer of an ISO, the transfer of an ISO to a beneficiary or estate is not treated as a modification of the option (although an extension of an exercise period to accommodate an estate or beneficiary will be treated as a modification and will disqualify the ISO), and the transfer of stock to a beneficiary or an estate is not deemed to be a "disqualifying disposition."[3] As noted above, the regular ISO requirement that the option be exercised within three months of the optionee's leaving the company does not apply if an employee dies while in service or up to three months later. However, if the optionee dies more than three months after terminating employment and thereafter the option is exercised by the estate, then the option cannot be treated as an ISO.[4]

If an optionee exercised an ISO before death, the estate may sell the stock acquired by the ISO exercise without satisfying the one- and two-year holding periods generally required for long-term capital gains tax treatment on the post-option grant appreciation.[5] In such a situation, the estate would receive a step-up in basis in the stock equal to its fair market value determined at the date of death of the optionee.[6]

If the optionee has unexercised ISOs at the time of death, the recipient (i.e. the optionee's plan beneficiaries or the optionee's estate and the ultimate beneficiaries of the estate, referred to hereinafter generally

---

2. Code §§ 421(a) and 422(a).

3. Code § 424(c)(1)(A); Treas. Reg. § 1.421-2(b)(2); Code § 421(c)(1); Treas. Reg. § 1.421-2(c)(1); Treas. Reg. § 1.421-2(d).

4. Id.

5. Code § 421(c)(1); Treas. Reg. § 1.421-2(d).

6. Code § 1014(a).

as the "estate") receives a step-up in basis in the option itself. When the option is exercised by the estate, the estate will have a basis in the underlying shares equal to the sum of the exercise price and the fair value of the option, as determined by using a Black-Scholes valuation or a similar valuation method, at the time of the optionee's death.[7] Note that, in this case, the holding period of the option does not "tack" onto (i.e., get the benefit of and get added to) the date that the option was originally granted to the decedent, for purposes of satisfying the one-year holding period for capital gains purposes. Instead, if the estate exercises the ISO, the underlying shares must be held for more than a year to obtain long-term capital gains treatment on the post-grant appreciation.

The Representative should review the ISO award agreements and consult a tax adviser before determining the tax liability relating to the ISO award because there may be further issues to consider based on the particular circumstances of the award. For example, certain award agreements may provide accelerated vesting of all unvested ISOs at the optionee's death. The amount that is accelerated may be greater than the $100,000 annual limit applicable to ISOs under Code Section 422. This accelerating vesting could result in a "disqualifying disposition" that will cause the estate to incur additional federal tax liability and potentially state tax liability as well, depending on the applicable state laws.

Alternative Minimum Tax. The exercise of an ISO may also have consequences that must be considered under the federal alternative minimum tax (AMT) regime. The AMT is determined under a separate tax system originally designed to prevent taxpayers from generating excessive tax deductions and to require taxpayers to pay at least a minimum amount of federal income tax. The taxpayer's federal income tax liability will be the larger of the AMT amount or such taxpayer's "regular tax" liability calculated without regard to the AMT regime. AMT calculations can be quite complex. Generally, the AMT calculation begins by taking a taxpayer's adjusted gross income and reducing it by certain itemized deductions. That amount is increased by the amount of certain deductions that are not permitted to be taken under

---

7. Treas. Reg. § 1.421-2(c)(4)(i); Code § 421(c)(3).

the AMT regime (e.g., income taxes and state and local property taxes) and certain items of income (e.g., ISO spread at exercise) to obtain the taxpayer's alternative minimum taxable income (AMTI). Next, the AMTI amount is reduced by the applicable AMT exemption amount ($70,300 for single filers and $109,400 for married joint filers, adjusted annually for inflation) to obtain the AMT base. The AMTI exemption amount is phased out for high-income individuals by 25 cents for every dollar of AMTI over a specific threshold (for single filers, the exemption begins to be phased out at $500,000 AMTI, and the exemption begins to be phased out at $1,000,000 AMTI for married joint filers). To obtain the amount of AMT owed, apply the 26% AMT rate up to $191,500 of the AMT base ($95,750 for married people filing separately), and apply the 28% AMT rate for amounts above that amount. (The AMT information in this discussion is current as of the time of writing in late 2018.) Often, the exercise of an ISO will cause the employee to pay the AMT because the AMTI base is increased by the amount of the spread but the regular income tax base is not. Thus, if the company's stock has appreciated, the estate may be liable for additional taxes under the AMT regime. In many cases, all or a part of additional taxes owed for the year of exercise of an ISO may be recovered through a tax credit in later tax years when the taxpayer's "regular tax" liability exceeds the AMT liability (but only to the extent of excess). Usually, the bulk of the tax credit cannot be recovered until the sale of the ISO stock.

The forgoing discussion addresses standard AMT issues applicable to taxpayers generally. An estate's inclusion of an ISO raises complicated AMT issues, which should be discussed with a competent tax professional, specifically where an estate exercises an ISO, an estate sells shares acquired through an ISO, or bequests of an ISO by will are concerned.

Additional Employer Considerations. Generally, in employee transactions under a stock option plan, the employer's concerns revolve around withholding and reporting requirements. When administering a stock option plan following the death of a grantee, the employer would not have any withholding obligations upon the exercise of an ISO by the estate or the sale of the underlying stock by the Representative or beneficiary, but the employer must report certain information regarding any ISO exercise to the Representative or beneficiary in January of the following year.[8] Although a stock option plan administrator is generally not involved with the estate tax aspects of an option, it is worth mentioning here that for reporting requirements for estate tax purposes, ISOs are generally given a value equal to the option spread (if any) at date of death.[9]

7.2.2   Nonqualified Stock Options

NSOs are stock options that are not ISOs. Generally, this means that NSOs provide the optionee with more flexibility than that provided by ISOs, but the tradeoff for the optionee is that NSOs do not provide the same tax benefits as ISOs. Generally, the optionee will have no income on the grant of the NSO unless the option is actively traded or has a readily ascertainable fair market value, but both of these situations are rare. Unlike ISOs, no employment or holding requirements generally apply as a matter of law at the time of an NSO grant. Upon the exercise of an NSO, the optionee realizes ordinary income equal to the spread between the fair market value of the stock at the date of exercise and the exercise price.[10] Any gain (or loss) over the optionee's adjusted basis upon disposition (i.e., the price paid plus the amount included in income) is treated as capital gain (or capital loss). The capital gain is given favorable tax treatment as long-term capital gains if the shares are held for more than a year; if the shares are not held for more than one year, then the optionee incurs less favorable short-term capital gains treatment.[11] The employer is entitled to claim a deduction upon exercise equal to the amount that the employee includes in income.[12] The spread at exercise is treated as wages for purposes of federal income tax and FICA withholding, and FUTA.[13]

Unlike ISOs, NSOs exercised after the death of the optionee constitute an item of "income in respect of the decedent" or "IRD" (i.e.,

---

8.   Code § 6039(a).

9.   Rev. Rul. 53-196.

10. Treas. Reg. § 1.83-7(a).

11. Code §§ 1222 and 1(h).

12. Code § 83(h); Treas. Reg. § 1.83-6.

13. Rev. Rul. 78-185, 1978-1 C.B. 304.

an amount that is not includable on the employee/decedent's final tax return as earned compensation but that retains its character as a gross income item in the hands of the recipient).[14] The estate will not be entitled to a step-up in basis on the value of the option.[15] Consequently, the estate or beneficiary must recognize ordinary income in the same manner that the optionee would have if he or she had lived and exercised or disposed of the NSOs (discussed above). The long-term capital gain holding period begins upon the exercise of the option. If the NSO is bequeathed specifically to a beneficiary, the beneficiary obtains the same tax basis as the estate; i.e., there is no step-up in basis. Similarly, the beneficiary would have ordinary income upon exercise of the NSO.[16]

Additional Employer Considerations. The employer is entitled to an income tax deduction equal to the spread upon the NSO exercise. In the case of an NSO exercise following the optionee's death, the employer is not required to withhold for federal income tax purposes regardless of whether the NSO was vested before the optionee's death or became vested due to his or her death.[17] The employer will be required to withhold for FICA purposes if the exercise of the option occurs in the same calendar year as the optionee's death, and the NSO did not vest due to the optionee's death, retirement for disability, or retirement following attaining a retirement age specified in the applicable plan.[18] Alternatively, if a NSO vests due to an optionee's death, retirement for disability, or retirement following attaining a retirement age specified in the applicable plan, the exercise of such option does not impose FICA

---

14. Code § 691(a); Treas. Reg. § 1.691(a)-1; Treas. Reg. § 1.83-1(d).

15. Code § 1014(c).

16. Code § 691(a); Treas. Reg. § 1.83-1(d).

17. Rev. Rul. 86-109, 1986-2 C.B. 196, and PLR 8113058 (December 31, 1980).

18. Code § 3121(a)(13) and (14), Treas. Reg. § 31.3121(a)(13)-1(a), and PLR 8226085 (March 30, 1982). If an NSO was to vest based the satisfaction of time or performance criteria (and not due to the optionee's death, retirement for disability, or retirement following attaining a retirement age), and the NSO was exercised in the year of the optionee's death, then the exercise of such award would impose FICA withholding obligations.

obligations on the employer.[19] Regardless of the reason for vesting, if the option exercise occurs in the calendar year following the optionee's death, the income is not considered to be FICA wages.[20] The employer is required to report income realized by the estate or beneficiary attributable to the exercise of the NSOs on Form 1099-MISC and any FICA or FUTA wages attributable to the exercise of the options during the year of death on the optionee's final Form W-2.[21]

Generally, NSOs are valued for estate tax purposes by reference to the option spread (if any) at the optionee's date of death. However, for vested NSOs of publicly traded companies, the IRS has issued safe-harbor guidance that uses a Black-Scholes valuation model with an additional variable involving the underlying stock's expected dividend yield.[22]

7.2.3 Restricted Stock

Restricted stock is stock that is nontransferable until it is vested. Before it becomes vested, the employee who has been awarded the restricted stock typically has some ownership rights in the stock, such as voting rights or dividend rights, but the stock will be forfeited if the vesting conditions are not satisfied. Upon receipt of the restricted stock, the recipient's basis in the unvested equity is equal to the amount that he or she paid for it (there will be no amount paid for such stock if the employee has been granted the restricted stock, and it vests over time based on continued employment, as is often the case).[23] Once the restricted stock is either no longer subject to forfeiture or freely transferrable, the recipient will recognize as ordinary income an amount equal to the fair market value of the share less the amount paid for such shares, the recipient's basis in the shares will be increased by such amount, and the holding period for the stock will begin (the tax treatment of restricted stock for which an election is made under Code

---

19. Id. See also PLR 8030037 (April 29, 1980).

20. Code §§ 3121(a)(14).

21. Code § 3306(b)(15), Rev. Rul. 86-109.

22. Rev. Proc. 98-34, 1998-1 C.B. 983. Note that this valuation technique is for transfer tax purposes only.

23. Treas. Reg. § 1.83-4(b)(1).

Section 83(b) is discussed below).[24] The employer is entitled to an income tax deduction at the time the recipient recognizes income in an amount equal to the amount of income the recipient recognized.[25]

Upon the death of the recipient of unvested restricted stock, there are no federal tax consequences to the recipient as a result of the recipient's death, but rather the beneficiaries or the estate will generally have income when the restricted stock vests.[26] If the restricted stock never vests and is forfeited, such restricted stock is never included in income (assuming that no election was made under Code Section 83(b), discussed below).

However, if the restricted stock vests upon the recipient's death or is accelerated to vest after the recipient's death, the fair market value of the stock, less any amount paid for it, must be included in income in the year the restricted stock vests. For purposes of the withholding rules, employers are generally required to withhold for federal income tax and FICA purposes at the time the restricted stock vests. However, an employer is not generally required to withhold federal income taxes on amounts includable in the gross income of a deceased recipient's estate or his or her beneficiary if the restricted stock vests as a result of the recipient's death or is accelerated to vest after the recipient's death.[27] The employer will generally be required to withhold for FICA purposes if the restricted stock vests in the year of the recipient's death.[28] In addition to these withholding requirements, the employer is required to report income realized by the estate or beneficiary attributable to the vesting of the restricted stock on Form 1099-MISC and any FICA wages attributable to vesting of the restricted stock during the year of death on the recipient's final Form W-2.[29]

The Code provides for an alternative under which restricted stock could be taxed. To be subject to this alternative regime, the recipient

---

24. Code §§ 83(a) and 83(f), Treas. Reg. § 1.61-2(d)(2) and (6)(i) and Treas. Reg. § 1.83-4(b).

25. Code §§ 83(a) and 83(h).

26. Treas. Reg. § 1.83-1(d).

27. PLR 8117100 (January 29, 1981).

28. Rev. Rul. 86-109.

29. Id.

of the restricted stock award must have made a Section 83(b) election with respect to the award within 30 days of the grant of such award. By making such an election, the recipient of the restricted stock is required to include the fair market value of the restricted stock award, as of the date of the award, less any amount paid for the restricted stock, in his or her income for the year in which such award is made. If a Section 83(b) election is made but the restricted stock never vests and is forfeited, the recipient and his or her estate are not entitled to any tax refund for the taxes that were previously paid. If a Section 83(b) election is made, any subsequent disposition of the stock that was subject to the award is treated as a gain (or loss) from the sale of a capital asset and may be entitled to the favorable long-term capital gain tax treatment discussed with respect to NSOs above. The withholding rules applicable to restricted stock for which a Section 83(b) election has been made are the same as the rules applicable to the restricted stock for which no Section 83(b) election has been made (described above).[30]

7.2.4　Cash-Settled Awards

In the past, some issuers granted stock appreciation rights (SARs), which are cash awards with a payout based on the appreciated value of the issuer's stock over a particular period. More recently, some issuers have begun granting awards under equity plans that are settled in cash but valued based on the issuer's stock. For example, an issuer could grant a fixed number of restricted stock units representing the value of a corresponding number of shares of stock of the issuer that are settled through a cash payment equal in value to the shares of the issuer at the end of the vesting period. If the per-share value of the stock has increased over the vesting period, the cash payout at the time of vesting will have captured the appreciation in value. Upon the death of the grantee, such an award may be either vested in full or subject to special pro-rata vesting rules under the terms of the equity plan. The cash payment associated with such an award will be payable to the plan beneficiary, or, if none, will be an asset of the estate and subject to distribution under the terms of the decedent's will (or, if there is no will, pursuant to applicable intestate distribution rules). Depending on

---

30. General Counsel Memorandum 38069 (August 28, 1979).

the timing of payment and vesting of a cash award, the cash payment may be treated as IRD. Because the IRD rules are extremely complex, if an estate or beneficiary suspects that IRD issues may be raised by any award or payment, the advice of a competent tax professional should be sought.

7.3 General Securities Law Considerations Relating to Equity Grants

Apart from the specific issues that arise when the grantee of an equity award dies, there may be issues of a more general nature involving the federal securities laws. What follows is a short description of issues that may arise under the federal securities laws in connection with securities of an issuer and the death of a grantee. (See chapters 2 and 3 for a more detailed description of securities law issues relating to equity plans.)

7.3.1 Registration

The Securities Act of 1933 (the "1933 Act") requires all "offers" or "sales" of "securities" to be registered by filing a registration statement with the Securities and Exchange Commission (SEC) unless an exemption is available. Generally, an issuer that is publicly reporting can use a short-form registration statement that is relatively easy to prepare and file. Private issuers cannot easily register the issuance of equity, but normally such issuers can use an exemption from registration that the SEC expressly designed for grants under compensation plans. To comply with these SEC requirements, public companies ordinarily register issuances under their stock option plan or restricted stock plan on a short-form Form S-8 registration statement. Consequently, options that are exercised by Representatives and/or the decedent's beneficiaries are covered by the Form S-8 registration statement. The SEC also allows family members to whom options have been transferred before the grantee's death, for tax and estate planning purposes, to exercise such options under a filed Form S-8. It should be noted that companies that are permitted to register equity grants on a Form S-8 are those that also are subject to the additional reporting requirements of the Securities Exchange Act of 1934 (the "1934 Act").

To register a stock option plan or restricted stock plan on Form S-8, the employer must also deliver a description of the plan and its tax consequences (known as a "prospectus") to the eligible employees, together with a copy of the company's latest annual report to stockholders. The employer must advise the plan participants that certain shareholder information is available upon request, and the information provided must be updated periodically. The shares acquired under a plan registered on Form S-8 may be resold without registration or delivery of a prospectus, except that affiliates such as executive officers, directors, and significant equity owners may be subject to certain conditions. Unless the company has included their resales on another registration statement, these "affiliates" may resell only securities in compliance with the applicable limitations of Rule 144 or under another exemption from registration.

Private companies usually rely on Rule 701 for an exemption from the registration requirements for the offer and sale of shares issued for compensatory purposes to officers, employees, or other service providers under a written employment agreement or compensatory plan. Rule 701 imposes limits on the aggregate price and amount of securities that can be issued during a 12-month period. Before a company goes public, securities issued under Rule 701 may be resold only pursuant to registration or an exemption or safe harbor, such as Rule 144; after the company goes public, holders of the securities may resell subject to certain limitations. If equity grants are limited to a small group of highly compensated and sophisticated executives, an employer may elect to rely on the private placement exemption of Section 4(a)(2) of the 1933 Act, or the safe harbor provided by Regulation D, for a registration exemption instead of Rule 701.

7.3.2 Reporting

The transfer of an option or the resulting shares of restricted stock held by an executive to the executive's estate or beneficiary is not reportable per se. Generally, Section 16(a) of the 1934 Act requires "insiders" (generally, officers, directors, and persons who beneficially own more than 10% of any class of securities) of public companies to report various securities transactions. The exercise of a stock option and the sale of the underlying stock by the executive's estate, or the sale of restricted stock by the executive's estate, would not generally be reportable under Section 16 unless the estate is a 10% owner and such transactions occurred more than 12 months after the executive's death.[31] Additionally, an insider who acquires additional shares as a beneficiary of another person's estate must report the acquisition on Form 5 or a voluntary Form 4. Option grants are to be reported on Form 4 by the end of the second business day following the day of grant. Option exercises and resales must be reported on Form 4 by the end of the second business day following the day on which the option is exercised. Form 5 is used to annually report certain other changes in beneficial ownership within 45 days of the end of the company's fiscal year.

7.3.3   Short-Swing Profit Recovery

Any profits resulting from the purchase and sale (or sale and purchase) of stock of a company with a class of securities registered under the 1934 Act within a period of less than six months by any insider may be recovered by an action brought by the company, or on behalf of the company by another stockholder, against the insider under Section 16(b) of the 1934 Act. This disgorgement provision is intended to discourage the unfair use of inside information. Rule 16b-3 provides an exemption for certain transactions involving officers or directors and the company. Option grants and the exercise of options are exempt from the matching of purchases and sales if the grants are authorized by the company's board of directors or by a committee composed of two or more nonemployee directors.[32] Sales of stock acquired by exercises of options can be matched with other purchases.

An executive or director ceases to be an insider upon death. Thus, the transfer of an option or the resulting shares held by an executive to an insider's estate or beneficiary is not subject to short-swing profit recovery. The exercise of a stock option and the sale of the underlying stock by the insider's estate would not be subject to Section 16(b) of the 1934 Act if it occurs during the first 12 months after the insider's

---

31. Rule 16a-2(d).

32. Rule 16b-3(d)(1).

death. Thereafter, such sales would be subject to Section 16 only if the estate is a 10% owner or the Representative is an insider.[33]

If an heir is already an insider, the acquisition of shares as a beneficiary is not deemed to be a purchase for purposes of Section 16(b) of the 1934 Act.[34] If a beneficiary is an insider or receives sufficient stock to become an insider following the executive's death, then the individual would be required to comply with Section 16 following the transfer.

7.4   Section 409A Considerations

Code Section 409A regulates nonqualified deferred compensation arrangements. If a nonqualified deferred compensation arrangement falls under Code Section 409A but does not comply with Code Section 409A in both form and operation, the amount deferred under the arrangement will become immediately taxable, and the employee or grantee will incur an additional 20% income tax on the amount deferred under the arrangement, along with interest and penalties. The treatment of equity awards under Code Section 409A varies depending on the nature and structure of the award. ISOs are exempt from Code Section 409A. For NSOs and SARs based upon service recipient stock, where the exercise price is equal to or greater than the fair market value of the shares at the time of grant, Code Section 409A restrictions will not generally apply. If, however, an option or SAR is granted with an exercise price below fair market value, then Code Section 409A exercise-related restrictions must apply to the exercise of the option, and the holder will lose the flexibility to exercise the option whenever market conditions warrant. Instead, the option or SAR will have to be structured with a limited Code Section 409A-compliant exercise date, which would include fixed exercise dates or exercise upon the death of the holder. Code Section 409A payment restrictions will apply also to restricted stock units that are not settled within a defined time period after vesting (i.e., the "short-term deferral" period under Code Section 409A). Generally, the death of the grantee is a permissible payment event for these types of Code Section 409A-covered arrangements.

---

33. Rule 16a-2(d); see also SEC No-Action Letter, American Soc. of Corp. Secretaries (Dec. 11, 1996).

34. Rule 16b-5.

All of these Code Section 409A rules are fraught with complexity and place a premium on careful planning because of the additional income tax exposure associated with any violation of Code Section 409A.

7.5   Section 162(m) Considerations

Employers can generally deduct reasonable compensation paid to their employees as an ordinary and necessary business expense. However, Code Section 162(m) limits the deductibility of annual compensation paid to certain "covered employees" by a public company to $1 million per year for each covered employee.[35] The tax reform legislation enacted on December 22, 2017, frequently referred to as the Tax Cuts and Jobs Act of 2017, significantly amended Code Section 162(m). Code Section 162(m) does not raise estate issues, but it does raise potential issues to an employer regarding the tax deductibility of certain payments.

Before the Tax Cuts and Jobs Act, Code Section 162(m) defined a "covered employee" as any employee of a corporation, as of the close of the taxable year, who is the chief executive officer or who is acting in such capacity, or any employee whose total compensation is required to be reported to shareholders in the annual proxy statement under the Securities Exchange Act of 1934 because such employee is among the four highest compensated officers for the taxable year (other than the chief executive officer). The Tax Cuts and Jobs Act expanded the definition of a "covered employee" so that it generally includes (1) the chief executive officer and the chief financial officer (or anyone acting in such capacity), (2) the three other most highly compensated executive officers for the year, and (3) anyone who was a covered employee of the employer for any taxable year beginning on or after January 1, 2017.[36] Thus, once an employee qualifies as a covered employee, he or she will continued to be treated as a covered employee indefinitely. These changes to Code Section 162(m) will likely disallow some public companies from taking a tax deduction for payments in excess of $1 million per year to deceased executives.

---

35. Code § 162(m)(1).

36. Code § 162(m)(3) and Internal Revenue Service Notice 2018-68.

7.6   Spousal Rights

Many qualified retirement benefit plans (such as pension plans and 401(k) plans) designate the decedent's surviving spouse as the default beneficiary of the plan upon the decedent's death. In addition, in many cases under a qualified retirement plan, the spouse's written consent is required in order to designate an individual other than the spouse as the beneficiary of such retirement benefits. Before *Obergefell v. Hodges*,[37] the 2015 Supreme Court case declaring unconstitutional state laws not recognizing valid marriages between same-sex spouses, a decedent's same-sex spouse would not have had this marital entitlement if the state law of the decedent's residence did not recognize same-sex marriage. Following *Obergefell*, every state is now required to recognize marriages between same-sex and opposite-sex individuals as equal. Equity grants, however, are often exempt from the marital entitlement restrictions to which many qualified retirement benefits are subject, meaning that spousal consent is typically not required in order to designate an individual other than the spouse as plan beneficiary under the applicable equity incentive plan.

---

37.   135 S. Ct. 2584 (2015).

Evergreen Provisions for Equity Compensation Plans

Thomas LaWer

CONTENTS

Stock award and employee stock purchase plans (throughout this chapter, these will be referred to as "stock plans" or "plans") typically reserve a fixed number of shares for issuance under the plan. To add more shares to a plan, the company's board of directors must amend the plan, and in most cases, the company's shareholders must approve the amendment. If a publicly traded company's stock award or employee stock purchase plan runs out of shares, there is often significant time, expense, and uncertainty involved in receiving shareholder approval of share increases.

To avoid the issues involved with frequent shareholder approval of share increases, a company can incorporate an automatic replenishment feature (commonly referred to as an "evergreen" provision) into its stock plans. An evergreen provision automatically increases the number of shares reserved under the company's stock plans at regular intervals. The evergreen provision can eliminate the expense and difficulty of seeking frequent shareholder approval of a plan share increase. In addition, a company may plan its stock awards for several years with greater certainty because it has a reliable supply of reserved shares. Finally, the evergreen provision detaches equity compensation strategies from the vagaries of the company's stock price. Publicly traded companies may have a more difficult time obtaining shareholder approval for share reserve increases when the stock has performed poorly. Because employers often need to motivate people more in a downturn, this can be the worst time for a company to curtail its stock award grants.

This chapter discusses the issues involved with designing and implementing an evergreen provision.

8.1   Evergreen Design

The simplest evergreen provision annually increases the number of shares reserved under the stock plan by a percentage of the outstanding shares of the company on the date of increase. (See example 1 below.) This evergreen provision allows the stock plan to continue to grow as the company's outstanding capital stock increases. Unfortunately, this design does not meet the tax law requirements for incentive stock options (ISOs) and tax-qualified employee stock purchase plans (ESPPs). However, a "percentage of the outstanding" evergreen provision does work for nonemployee director plans and for stock plans that grant equity awards other than ISOs, such as non-qualified stock options and restricted stock units (but see example 6 below for a hybrid model that can achieve the same objective).

> *Example 1.* The maximum number of shares reserved for issuance under the Plan is 1,000,000 shares, plus an annual increase to be added on each anniversary

date of the adoption of the Plan equal to four percent (4%) of the outstanding Common Stock on such date.

To qualify for preferential tax treatment, ISOs and ESPPs must comply respectively with the requirements of Sections 422(b) and 423(b) of the Internal Revenue Code of 1986, as amended (the "Code"). One of the conditions for preferential tax treatment is that the option must be granted under a plan specifying "the aggregate number of shares which may be issued."[1] The maximum aggregate number of shares that may be issued under a plan must be determinable at the *time the plan is adopted.* That is, on the date the board of directors adopts the plan, the total number of shares that can possibly be granted under the plan must be calculable. The use of a "percentage of the outstanding" as in example 1 does not meet this requirement because we do not know the number of shares outstanding on the dates of the future shares increases.[2] For companies that wish to grant ISOs or have an ESPP, this requirement may limit the flexibility of the evergreen provision. The evergreen provision must provide for periodic increases of a fixed number of shares (see Example 2 below).

> *Example 2.* The maximum number of shares reserved for issuance under the Plan is 1,000,000 shares, plus an annual increase to be added on each anniversary date of the adoption of the Plan equal to 400,000 shares.

However, many companies would prefer to add an amount determined as a percentage of the outstanding shares on a specified date each year, such as each anniversary date of the plan adoption. By adding a percentage of the outstanding shares, the evergreen provision is more likely to remain useful for a longer period of time because it will grow along with the company (and the company's shares outstanding, which also tend to increase over time). As discussed above, such a provision, by itself, violates the requirement of the ISO and ESPP rules for a determinable number of shares. One possible way to remedy this problem is to draft a tiered evergreen provision that provides that the

---

1. Section 422(b)(1) of the Code, Treasury Regulation ("Treas. Reg.") §§ 1.422-2(b)(3) and 1.423-2(c)(3).

2. Treas. Reg. § 1.422-2(b)(3)(ii).

number of shares to be added each year is equal to the lesser of (1) a fixed number of shares or (2) a percentage of the outstanding shares on each anniversary of the plan adoption.[3] (See example 3 below.) In drafting this provision, it is important to select as the fixed number of shares an amount that is significantly greater than the anticipated percentage of the outstanding shares. Otherwise, if there is rapid growth in the number of company shares outstanding, the provision can quickly be constrained by the fixed limit. In the example, the tiered evergreen provision satisfies the maximum-determinable-number-of-shares condition because the maximum number of shares reserved under the plan is equal to the initial reservation of 1,000,000 shares plus 1,000,000 (the fixed number to be added each year) multiplied by the term of the plan.

> *Example 3.* The maximum aggregate number of shares reserved for issuance under the Plan is 1,000,000 shares, plus an annual increase to be added on each anniversary date of the adoption of the Plan equal to the lesser of (1) 1,000,000 shares, and (2) four percent (4%) of the outstanding shares on such date.

A company may retain even greater control over the number of shares being added to the plan by adding to the formula a third variable, the ability of a company's board of directors to provide for a lesser amount each year, to the tiered evergreen provision described above. (See example 4 below.) If either the fixed number of shares or the number of shares equal to a percentage of the outstanding shares provides more generous benefits than is required or appropriate, this refinement lets the board of directors limit the number of shares that would otherwise be added to the plan.

> *Example 4.* The maximum aggregate number of shares reserved for issuance under the Plan is 1,000,000 shares, plus an annual increase to be added on each anniversary date of the adoption of the Plan equal to the least of (1) 800,000 Shares, (2) four percent (4%) of the outstanding shares on such date, and (3) an amount determined by the Board.

---

3. See PLR 9531031, which specifically approves this design structure for an automatic replenishment feature.

Another variation is to reload the option grants made in the prior year (a "top-up" evergreen provision). The number of shares to be added to the plan is still determinable: it is the number of shares reserved under the plan, multiplied by the number of years in the plan term. In example 5 below, the evergreen provision will add the number of shares granted in options in the prior year up to the maximum number of shares reserved under the plan of 400,000. If the plan in example 5 had a five-year term, then the maximum number of shares issuable under the plan would be 2,000,000. There are many variations possible for the top-up provision. However, in all these variations, the basic concept of the top-up is the same.

> *Example 5.* The maximum aggregate number of shares that may be optioned and sold under the Plan is 400,000 shares, plus an annual increase to be added on each anniversary date of adoption of the Plan equal to the lesser of (1) the number of shares of common stock subject to options granted in the immediately preceding year and (2) an amount determined by the Board.

A final variation used in omnibus equity compensation plans (i.e., plans that permit the grant of incentive stock options, nonqualified stock options, restricted stock, stock appreciation rights, phantom stock, and other equity awards) is to combine the use of a fixed share reserve for the grant of incentive stock options with the evergreen provision described in example 1. The ISO regulations finalized in 2004 permit this approach.[4] This allows a company to get the full benefit of an uncapped evergreen provision for all award types except incentive stock options. Example 6 below provides that 4% of the outstanding shares as of the anniversary of the adoption of the plan will be added to the reserve each year, provided that the maximum number of shares that may be granted as incentive stock options is limited to 2,000,000.

> *Example 6.* The maximum number of shares reserved for issuance under the Plan is 1,000,000 shares, plus an annual increase to be added on each anniversary date of the adoption of the Plan equal to the lesser of (1) four percent (4%) of the outstanding Common Stock on such date and (2) an amount determined by the Board. Notwithstanding the foregoing, the aggregate maximum number of shares that may be issued as Incentive Stock Options shall be 2,000,000 shares.

---

4.   Treas. Reg. § 1.422-2(b)(3)(i) and Treasury Decision 9144, Aug. 2, 2004, p. 4.

8.2 Shareholder Approval Considerations

Shareholder approval is required in most circumstances to add an evergreen provision to a stock plan. The shareholder requirements vary based on the type of plan and the specific situation of the company.

8.2.1 Tax Law Requirements

For a stock plan that issues ISOs or for a tax-qualified employee stock purchase plan, shareholder approval is required to add an evergreen provision. The shareholder approval requirement for an evergreen provision is the same as is required for any increase in the shares reserved under such a stock plan.

8.2.2 Stock Exchange Requirements

For both Nasdaq-listed and New York Stock Exchange (NYSE)-listed companies that do not meet one of the respective exchanges' exceptions to shareholder approval,[5] shareholder approval will be required to add an evergreen provision to a stock plan, whether or not the stock plan will issue ISOs. In addition, both Nasdaq and the NYSE limit the term of a shareholder-approved plan that has an evergreen provision to 10 years. If a plan with an evergreen provision has a term longer than 10 years, then Nasdaq will require shareholder approval of the plan every 10 years, and the NYSE will require shareholder approval for each increase in the share reserves from the evergreen provision. Stock plans approved by the shareholders before a company goes public and is listed on the NYSE or Nasdaq generally will be considered to have met the NYSE's and Nasdaq's listing requirements for shareholder approval. (See the discussion below in section 8.2.4 regarding the possibility that when the company seeks shareholder approval for Section 162(m) purposes, institutional investors will withhold approval unless the company drops its evergreen provision.)

---

5. Rule 4350(i)(1)(A) of the *NASD Manual for The Nasdaq Stock Market*. Rule 4350(i)(1)(A) provides an exemption from shareholder approval for the compensatory grant of stock in very limited circumstances. Rule 312.03(a) of the *NYSE Listed Company Manual*. Rule 312.03(a) provides an exemption from shareholder approval for the compensatory grant of stock in very limited circumstances.

8.2.3   Securities Law Requirements

Generally, the securities laws do not require shareholder approval of stock plans for any reason. However, companies granting stock awards in California that are not exempt from California's securities laws[6] will need to obtain shareholder approval of an evergreen provision to the same extent shareholder approval would be required for any increase in the shares reserved under a plan.[7]

It is unusual for a private company to adopt an evergreen provision, because the shareholders of a private company are usually very involved with the management of the company and generally prefer to keep tight control over the dilution of their positions. The only exception to this practice is when a private company is on the eve of having an initial public offering. At this time, private company shareholders generally have been willing to approve stock plans containing an evergreen provision that are effective only after the company's IPO when the company is public.

8.2.4   Shareholder Reaction

Currently, institutional investors rarely vote in favor of evergreen provisions in public company stock plans. Institutional investors want to retain control of any increases in the shares reserved under the stock plans and thereby limit the dilution of their ownership. Before the end of the technology bubble in 2000, there were examples of institutional investors approving evergreen provisions that caused limited dilution. However, in the current business environment, it is extremely unlikely that an institutional investor will vote in favor of an evergreen provision. Historically, there appears to be less resistance from institutional investors for approving evergreen provisions in (1) employee stock purchase plans, which by their broad-based, nondiscretionary nature appear to require less shareholder oversight, and (2) not surprisingly, for companies whose stock price has performed well.

---

6. Companies that are listed for trading on the NYSE, the Nasdaq National Market, and certain other U.S. stock exchanges are exempt from registration under California's securities laws. California Corporations Code § 25100(o) and California Code of Regulations §§ 260.004 and 260.101.2.

7. California Code of Regulations §§ 260.140.41 and 260.140.42.

One of the ways Institutional Shareholder Services (ISS), an important proxy adviser to institutional investors, judges stock plans is based on the shareholder value transfer (the estimate of the cost of the shareholder's equity transferred to stock award recipients).[8] For purposes of these calculations, the maximum number of shares that would be available under the evergreen provision is used without taking into account the timing of the share increases. For example, if the proposal for the evergreen provision is to add 100,000 shares per year for 10 years, ISS would consider the proposal to be a request for an additional 1,000,000 shares. By increasing the number of shares reserved under a plan based on the maximum potential increase, an evergreen provision significantly increases the cost of the stock plan under this ISS calculation. Therefore, by increasing the potential dilution from the stock awards, an evergreen provision will usually make a stock plan too "expensive" to the shareholders, in ISS's opinion. This would result in ISS recommending that shareholders vote against a stock plan with an evergreen provision.

In the past few years, ISS has further increased its resistance to evergreen provisions by recommending against any proposed stock plan amendments where it considers the share reserve in the stock plan to be too expensive.

In the past, to make an evergreen provision more palatable to institutional investors, a company would limit the evergreen provision to a specified period of years. For example, the evergreen may last for three or four years, after which it expires and the company must go back to the shareholders for any further increase in the shares reserved under the plan (see example 8 below). This tactic somewhat undercuts the purpose of the evergreen by limiting the number of shares that can be added to the plan.

> *Example 8.* The maximum aggregate number of shares that may be optioned and sold under the Plan is 1,000,000 shares, plus an annual increase to be added on each anniversary date of the adoption of the Plan for the next three years beginning in the year 2006 equal to the lesser of (1) 800,000 Shares, (2) four percent (4%) of the outstanding shares on such date, or (3) a lesser amount determined by the Board.

---

8. ISS Proxy Voting Manual, Chapter 10.

In the current business environment, it is rare for public companies to propose any type of evergreen provision because their chances of approval are slim or what could receive shareholder approval is unappealing. Currently, the most common time for a company to add an evergreen provision to its stock plans is while the company is still private but on the eve of an initial public offering. At this time, private company shareholders are usually willing to approve the evergreen provision, and institutional investors have not objected to the potential dilution caused by a stock plan in the initial public offering context. This is likely because the decision on whether to purchase stock in an IPO is determined by the persons at the institutional investors who are concerned whether the company's stock price will appreciate and not by the persons responsible for determining how to vote on proxies of companies in which the institutions have already invested.

8.2.5 Voting Issues

For public companies, the NYSE and Nasdaq broker voting rules limit when a broker may vote for a stock plan proposal. Under the 2003 revision of these rules, shares held in street name (i.e., shares owned by a client of the broker but registered under the broker's name to facilitate trading) may not be voted by the broker on stock plan proposals without instructions from the beneficial holders. Where a retail investor throws away his or her proxy, his or her shares cannot be voted on stock plan proposals. In the past, when brokers were able to vote these shares, the likelihood of approval of stock plan proposals was greater, since the brokers generally voted in favor of company proposals. These broker voting rules increase the power of the institutional investors because, unlike individual investors, institutional investors almost always vote. As discussed above, since institutional investors generally do not favor evergreen provisions, these voting rules make it even more difficult for a public company to obtain shareholder approval of an evergreen provision.

8.3 Federal Securities Law Issues

Each year, when the evergreen provision replenishes the stock plan, the S-8 registration statement under which the stock plan shares are registered must be amended to register the increase. This is an important administrative matter that needs to be completed in a timely fashion after the increase and before any shares are issued to participants to ensure that shares issued under the stock plan are registered and tradable.

8.4   Stock Splits, Dividends, and Tracking Stock

The stock award or employee stock purchase plan should contain a provision to adjust the shares reserved under the plan, including the evergreen provision, for any stock split or stock dividend, or for the creation of different classes of stock or tracking stock. With such a provision incorporated into the plan at the time the evergreen provision is adopted, the evergreen provision can automatically be adjusted for the split, dividend, or change in class of shares without any concern about obtaining shareholder approval.

8.5   Conclusion

An evergreen provision can be a useful tool for a company. It reduces the administrative expense involved with adding shares to a stock plan and provides a company with a reliable supply of reserved shares for stock awards. Since 2000, however, unfavorable shareholder reaction to an evergreen provision has generally prevented the adoption of an evergreen provision by most publicly traded companies, except for companies that adopt an evergreen provision in connection with an initial public offering.

Repricing Underwater Stock Options

Colin Diamond and Henrik Patel

CONTENTS

At the height of the last economic downturn, a significant number of publicly traded companies had underwater stock options. (A stock option is considered to be "underwater" when its exercise price is higher than the market price of the underlying stock.) For example, by mid-December 2008, 72% of Fortune 500 companies were reported to have underwater options.[1] Almost 100 companies repriced underwater options from 2008 through March 2009, including a number of high-profile companies, such as eBay, Google (now called Alphabet), Intel, Motorola, Starbucks, and Williams-Sonoma.[2] Between 2004 and 2009, there were a total of 264 stock option repricings announced.[3] As a result of that wave of repricings and improved market conditions, the specter of underwater stock options as a widespread problem has, at the moment, largely receded. For example, three option repricings were announced in 2014, seven option repricings were announced in 2015 and in 2016, and ten option repricings were announced through September of 2016.[4] Very few repricings were reported in 2017, although Fitbit implemented a stockholder-approved option exchange program in which eligible employees could exchange underwater stock options for RSUs.[5]

---

1.   See Phred Dvorak, "Firms Jump to Salvage 'Underwater' Stock Options," *Wall Street Journal*, December 22, 2008, http://online.wsj.com/article/SB122990523912125271.html.

2.   See Tomoeh Murakami Tse, "Firms Refloat Underwater Stock Options," *Washington Post*, March 7, 2009, http://www.washingtonpost.com/wp-dyn/content/article/2009/03/06/AR2009030603384.html.

3.   See David F. Larcker, Allan L. McCall, and Gaizka Ormazabal, "Proxy Advisory Firms and Stock Option Repricing," *Journal of Accounting and Economics* 56 (November–December 2013): 149–169.

4.   See Alix Stewart, "Firms Jump to Salvage 'Companies Move to Reprice Employees' Stock Options," *Wall Street Journal*, September 13, 2016, https://www.wsj.com/articles/companies-move-to-reprice-employees-stock-options-1473721243.

5.   See Schedule TO filed June 21, 2017, https://www.sec.gov/Archives/edgar/data/1447599/000144759917000044/fitbitschedto-i002.htm.

Indeed, Institutional Shareholder Services (ISS), a leading proxy advisory firm, noted in 2014 that "[w]ith the market rebound, fewer companies are seeking shareholder approval for option exchange programs."[6] Nevertheless, experience shows that the need to reprice underwater options arises from time to time as general market conditions fluctuate or due to the situation of a particular company. Under those circumstances, one of the most important strategic issues companies can face is how to address the fact that their stock option plans, which are intended to incentivize employees, can lose a critical element—incentive. For example, according to one survey of equity plan proposals submitted between 2007 and 2012, approximately 4,800 equity plan proposals have been submitted to shareholders of Russell 3000 Index companies. Of the 54 equity plan proposals that failed, one-third failed because they were inconsistent with ISS's repricing policy.[7]

There are many methods for addressing the problem of underwater options, each with its own benefits and drawbacks. The most common method traditionally was to "reprice" the options by lowering their exercise price. As discussed below, repricings now generally take the form of a wide variety of different exchange programs, including programs that involve the issuance of different forms of equity compensation, such as restricted stock or restricted stock units (RSUs), in exchange for underwater options. What all repricings have in common is the goal of reestablishing an incentive component for continued hard work and commitment, as well as restoring the retention capability of an employer's equity compensation plan.

The issue of option repricings increases in importance as companies consider items for inclusion in annual proxy statements. If shareholder approval is required to undertake a repricing (as is generally the case), a company will need to consider its strategy for addressing this challenge in connection with its annual meeting, as it would be extremely uncommon to hold a special meeting to approve a repricing.

---

6. Institutional Shareholder Services, *2014 Comprehensive US Compensation Policy, Frequently Asked Questions*, March 28, 2014, http://www.issgovernance.com/file/2014_Policies/ISSUSCompensationFAQs03282014.pdf.

7. Alliance Advisors, *Equity Plan Proposal Failures: 2007–2012*, https://www.exqty.com/Media/Publications/EP%20Proposal%20Failures%202007-2012_20130107.pdf.

Sufficient time should be allowed to obtain advice from compensation consultants, advance review of option repricing proposals by proxy advisors, and requisite compensation committee and board approvals. Companies may also want to consider how to address underwater options so that they can condition their grants of options (or other securities) on employees relinquishing their underwater options. This approach will not remove the need for shareholder approval (if required) and a tender offer as described below, but it will likely reduce the compensation expense associated with the annual grant and will likely result in a larger number of underwater options being canceled.

Finally, the last two waves of repricings in 2001–2002 and 2009 were both followed by significant rebounds in stock prices. Many of the market and regulatory developments that took place after 2001–2002 resulted in part from a perception that some companies implemented option repricing programs too quickly after stock price declines. By mid- to late 2010, the share price of a large number of companies that exchanged options in 2009 had rebounded to levels above the exercise price of the exchanged options. While it is easy to second-guess the decision to reprice after the fact, there seems little doubt that this experience will cause other companies and investors to view future repricings with greater skepticism.

9.1 Structuring Repricings

9.1.1 One-for-One Exchanges

Option repricings were traditionally effected by lowering the exercise price of underwater options to the then-prevailing market price of a company's common stock. Mechanically, this result was achieved either by amending the terms of the outstanding options or by canceling the outstanding options and issuing replacement options. The majority of repricings that occurred during the 2001 and 2002 market downturn were one-for-one option exchanges. At that time, the majority of new options had the same vesting schedule as the canceled options, and only a minority of companies excluded directors and officers from repricings.

Two subsequent developments have made one-for-one option exchanges the exception rather than the norm:

• In 2003, the New York Stock Exchange (NYSE) and the Nasdaq Stock Market adopted a requirement that public companies must seek shareholder approval of option repricings. As a result, companies must now ask (often unhappy) shareholders to provide employees with a benefit that the shareholders themselves will not enjoy. This development, coupled with the significant influence exerted on shareholder votes by institutional investors and proxy advisors, has made it almost impossible for companies to gain shareholder approval of a one-for-one option exchange due to perceived unfairness to shareholders.

• Before Financial Accounting Standards Board Accounting Standards Codification Topic 718 (ASC 718) and its predecessor (Statement of Financial Accounting Standards No. 123(R)) became effective for years beginning on or after December 15, 2005, stock option grants were not accounted for as an expense on a company's income statement. As a result, provided a company waited six months and one day, there was a limited accounting impact from a significant grant of replacement stock options, giving stock options a distinct advantage over other forms of equity compensation. ASC 718 now requires the expensing of employee stock options over the implied service term (the vesting period of the options). As a result, ASC 718 increased the accounting cost of a one-for-one option exchange.

9.1.2 Value-for-Value Exchanges

Companies seeking to reprice their options now generally undertake a "value-for-value" exchange.[8] A value-for-value exchange affords option

---

8. A one-for-one exchange may still be appropriate under certain circumstances. For example, the board of VMware, Inc., which undertook the largest IPO by a technology company in 2007, approved in August 2008 an exchange offer for the options it granted after its IPO. The exchange ratio for U.S. employees was one-for-one. The plan called for non-U.S. employees to receive RSUs in exchange for their options. Similarly, Google's exchange program in February 2009 enabled a one-for-one exchange of underwater options for new options with extended vesting provisions. While directors and executive officers were excluded from the VMware exchange program, executive officers were permitted to participate in the Google exchange program. However, as discussed below in section 9.2.2, a

holders the opportunity to cancel underwater options in exchange for an immediate regrant of new options at a ratio of less than one-for-one with an exercise price equal to the market price of such shares.

Value-for-value exchanges are more acceptable to shareholders and proxy advisors than one-for-one exchanges. A value-for-value exchange results in less dilution to public shareholders than a one-for-one exchange because it allows the reallocation of a smaller amount of equity to employees, which shareholders generally perceive as being fairer under the circumstances. In addition, the accounting implications of a value-for-value exchange are significantly more favorable than a one-for-one exchange. Under ASC 718, the accounting cost of new options (amortized over their vesting period) is the fair value of those grants less the current fair value of the canceled (underwater) options. As a result, companies generally structure an option exchange so that the value of the new options for accounting purposes—based on Black-Scholes or another option pricing methodology—approximates or is less than the value of the canceled options, thereby making it "value-neutral." If the fair value of the new options exceeds the fair value of the canceled options, that incremental value is recognized as an expense over the remaining service period of the option.

9.1.3   Use of Restricted Stock or RSUs

A common variation of the value-for-value exchange is the cancelation of all options and the grant of restricted stock or RSUs with the same or a lower economic value than the options canceled. Restricted stock is stock that is subject to a substantial risk of forfeiture at grant but vests upon the occurrence of continued employment. Restricted stock is nontransferable while it is forfeitable. RSUs are economically similar to restricted stock but involve the promise to issue the shares or an equivalent cash value at a time that is concurrent with or after vesting.

The U.S. tax rules applicable to restricted stock are different from those applicable to RSUs. Although the taxation of restricted stock is generally postponed until the stock becomes vested (with the grantee treated as receiving ordinary income equal to the fair market value

---

one-for-one exchange is an adverse factor that affects whether not proxy advisors will recommend in favor of an option exchange program.

of the underlying stock on the vesting date), the grantee of restricted stock may elect to be taxed in the year of grant rather than waiting until vesting. If this election is made pursuant to Section 83(b) of the Internal Revenue Code (the "Code"), the grantee is treated as receiving ordinary income equal to the fair market value of the underlying stock on the date of the grant, rather than on the date of vesting. Future appreciation is taxed as capital gain (rather than as ordinary income) when the grantee disposes of the shares after vesting. There is no ability to make Section 83(b) elections with respect to the grant of RSUs, which are taxed upon delivery of the shares following vesting of the RSUs. Outside the United States, many companies grant RSUs to their non-U.S. employees because RSUs generally permit deferral of taxation until delivery of shares of stock underlying the RSU, whereas there may be different tax consequences for restricted stock in non-U.S. jurisdictions upon grant.

One benefit of both restricted stock and RSUs is that such awards ordinarily have no purchase or exercise price and provide immediate value to the grantee. Consequently, the exchange ratio will generally result in less dilution to existing stockholders than an option-for-option exchange. In addition, at a time when institutional investors and proxy advisors may advocate greater use of restricted stock and RSUs, either alone or together with stock options and stock appreciation rights (SARs),[9] such an exchange can be part of a shift in the overall compensation policy of a company. Finally, because restricted stock and RSUs ordinarily have no exercise price, there is no risk that they will subsequently go underwater if there is a further drop in a company's stock price. This is an important consideration in a volatile market.

Income that certain officers recognize from the new restricted stock and RSU grants will be subject to the annual deduction limit of Section 162(m) of the Code, to the extent applicable. Section 162(m) in general terms limits to U.S. $1 million per year the deductibility of

---

9.   SARs are essentially net options, and provide for the delivery, in cash or shares (as applicable), of an amount equal to the spread (i.e., the excess of fair market value of the stock over exercise price) upon exercise. Broker-assisted cashless exercises of options have an economic effect similar to that of SARs but technically involve the payment of the exercise price to the issuer with a loan or other assistance from the broker.

compensation to a public corporation's CEO, CFO, and the next top three highest-compensated officers who served at any time during the corporation's taxable year, as well as employees who were subject to Section 162(m) in a tax year beginning after 2016.[10]

9.1.4   Repurchase of Underwater Options for Cash

Instead of an exchange, a company may simply repurchase underwater options from employees for an amount based on Black-Scholes or another option pricing methodology. The repurchase of underwater options generally involves a cash outlay by the company, the amount of which will vary based on the extent that the shares are underwater and to the extent that such repurchase is limited to fully vested options. Such a repurchase would reduce the number of options outstanding as a percentage of the total number of common shares outstanding (referred to as the "overhang"), which is generally beneficial to a company's capital structure. If a company repurchases its underwater options for cash rather than replacing them with other equity awards, the company will also need to consider how to provide future retention value to the employees.

9.1.5   Treatment of Directors and Officers

Due to the guidelines of proxy advisors and the expectations of institutional investors, directors and executive officers are often excluded from participating in repricings that require shareholder approval. Nevertheless, because directors and executive officers often hold a large number of options, excluding them can undermine the goals of the repricing and may lead to executive retention and motivation issues. As an alternative to exclusion, companies could permit directors and

---

10. Before the enactment of the Tax Cut and Jobs Act of 2017 (the "2017 Tax Act"), "covered employees" subject to Section 162(m) included a public corporation's CEO and its three highest-paid officers (other than the CEO and CFO) who were serving as of the last day of the tax year. The 2017 Tax Act expanded the group of covered employees and provided that for tax years beginning on or after January 1, 2018, covered employees include the CEO, CFO, the three highest-paid officers serving at any time during the tax year, and any employee who was a covered employee for a tax year beginning after 2016. The 2017 Tax Act also eliminated the performance-based compensation exemption for equity awards granted after November 2, 2017.

officers to participate on less favorable terms than other employees and could consider seeking separate shareholder approval for the participation of directors and officers to avoid jeopardizing the overall program. Where the method of repricing or the intention behind the implementation of a new program reflects a shift in the overall compensation policy of a company, such as the exchange of options for restricted stock or RSUs, proxy advisors and institutional investors are more likely to acquiesce in the inclusion of directors and executive officers.

9.1.6 Key Repricing Terms

The following are key terms that a company conducting a repricing will need to consider. It is advisable to retain a compensation consultant to assist with these matters and implementation of the program:

Exchange Ratio. The exchange ratio for an option exchange represents the number of options that must be tendered in exchange for one new option or other security. This must be set appropriately to encourage employees to participate and to satisfy shareholders. In order for a repricing to be value-neutral, there will usually be a number of exchange ratios, each addressing a different range of option exercise prices.

Option Eligibility. The company must determine whether all underwater options, or only those that are significantly underwater and/or were granted before a certain date, are eligible to be exchanged. This will depend on shareholder perceptions as well as the volatility of the company's stock and on the company's expectations of future increases in share price. In addition, if employees in countries other than the U.S. hold underwater options, the company will need to consult with its advisors to determine if there are any issues (e.g., adverse tax consequences to either the company or the employee) that would result if such employees were eligible to participate in the exchange, and it may elect to exclude employees in certain non-U.S. countries.

New Vesting Periods. A company issuing new options in exchange for underwater options must determine whether to grant the new options based on a new vesting schedule, the old vesting schedule, or a schedule that provides some accelerated vesting between these two alternatives.

9.2   Shareholder Approval

9.2.1   NYSE and Nasdaq Requirements

Under NYSE and Nasdaq rules requiring shareholder approval for any material amendment to an equity compensation program, a company listed on the NYSE or Nasdaq must first obtain shareholder approval of a proposed repricing unless the equity compensation plan under which the options in question were issued expressly permits the company to reprice outstanding options.[11] NYSE and Nasdaq rules define a material amendment to include any change to an equity compensation plan to "permit a repricing (or decrease in exercise price) of outstanding options... [or] reduce the price at which shares or options to purchase shares may be offered."[12] A plan that does not contain a provision that specifically permits repricing of options will be considered to prohibit repricing for purposes of the NYSE and Nasdaq rules.[13] Therefore, even if a plan itself is silent as to repricing, any repricing of options under that plan will be deemed to be a material revision of the plan requiring shareholder approval. In addition, shareholder approval is required before deleting or limiting a provision in a plan prohibiting the repricing of options.[14]

The NYSE and Nasdaq define a repricing as involving any of the following:[15]

1.   lowering the strike price of an option after it is granted;

2.   canceling an option at a time when its strike price exceeds the fair market value of the underlying stock, in exchange for another option, restricted stock or other equity, unless the cancelation and

---

11.   The New York Stock Exchange Listed Company Manual, Section 303A.08; Nasdaq Stock Market Listing Rules, Rule 5635(c); and Nasdaq Interpretive Material IM-5635-1. See also the NYSE MKT LLC Company Guide Section 711 and related commentary.

12.   Id.

13.   Id.

14.   Id.

15.   The New York Stock Exchange Listed Company Manual Section 303A.08; Nasdaq OMX Listing Center, Nasdaq "Frequently Asked Questions," https://listingcenter. nasdaqomx.com/MaterialHome.aspx?mcd=LQ.

exchange occurs in connection with a merger, acquisition, spin-off or other similar corporate transaction; and

3. any other action that is treated as a repricing under generally accepted accounting principles.

It should be noted that neither the NYSE nor Nasdaq rules prohibit the straight repurchase of options for cash. Nasdaq has provided an interpretation stating that the repurchase of outstanding options for cash by means of a tender offer does not require shareholder approval even if an equity compensation plan does not expressly permit such a repurchase.[16] In reaching this conclusion, Nasdaq noted that the consideration for the repurchase was not equity. As noted below, however, some proxy advisors still require shareholder approval for a cash repurchase program.

Shareholder approval of a repricing will likely be required for most domestic companies listed on the NYSE or Nasdaq since few companies' equity incentive plans expressly permit a repricing. A discussion regarding the exception available to foreign private issuers is provided below.

9.2.2　Proxy Advisors and Institutional Investors

Leading proxy advisors, such as ISS and Glass, Lewis & Co. ("Glass Lewis"), have taken a clear position on repricing provisions in equity compensation plans. The detailed voting guidelines published by ISS and by Glass Lewis have remained stable over the last several years with respect to option repricings. ISS uses an "equity plan scorecard" model that considers a range of positive and negative factors to evaluate equity incentive plan proposals.[17] Under this approach, ISS will recommend a case-by-case vote on equity plans, depending on a combination of certain plan features and equity grant practices. However, the ISS guidelines indicate that certain "egregious" features will trigger an outright

---

16. Nasdaq Staff Interpretive Letter 2004-21, available at https://listingcenter.nasdaqomx. com/Material_Search.aspx?cid=71&mcd=SI&sub_cid=114,109,101,97,103.

17. Institutional Shareholder Services, *United States Proxy Voting Guidelines Updates, Benchmark Policy Recommendations,* January 4, 2018, https://www.issgovernance. com/file/policy/active/americas/US-Voting-Guidelines.pdf.

negative recommendation on the plan. Specifically, it will recommend a vote against a proposal if the plan would permit the repricing or cash buyout of underwater options without shareholder approval, either by expressly permitting it (for NYSE and Nasdaq listed companies) or by not prohibiting it when the company has a history of repricing (for non-listed companies).[18] ISS considers the following to constitute a repricing: (1) the amendment of outstanding options or SARs to reduce the exercise price of such outstanding options or SARs; (2) the cancellation of outstanding options or SARs in exchange for options or SARs with an exercise price that is less than the exercise price of the original options or SARs; (3) the cancellation of underwater options in exchange for stock awards; or (4) cash buyouts of underwater options. ISS will recommend against the equity plan if the company undertakes such arrangements without shareholder approval. Glass Lewis will consider the company's past history of option repricings and express or implied rights to reprice when making its voting recommendations in connection with an equity plan and will recommend a vote against all members of a company's compensation committee if the company repriced options without shareholder approval within the past two years.[19] Against this background, it is likely that most companies will seek shareholder approval for a repricing even if it is not required under their equity compensation plans.

Glass Lewis explicitly notes that it has great skepticism with respect to option repricings, indicating that a repricing or option exchange program may only be acceptable if macroeconomic or industry trends, rather than specific company issues, cause a stock's value to decline dramatically, and the repricing is necessary to retain and motivate employees. In such a circumstance, Glass Lewis will support a repricing if:

• Officers and board members cannot participate in the program;

• The stock decline mirrors the market or industry price decline in terms of timing and approximates the decline in magnitude;

---

18. Id.

19. Glass Lewis & Co, *Proxy Paper Guidelines, 2018 Proxy Season, An Overview of the Glass Lewis Approach to Proxy Advice, United States,* http://www.glasslewis. com/wp-content/uploads/2018/01/2018_Guidelines_UNITED_STATES.pdf.

- The exchange is value-neutral or value-creative to shareholders using very conservative assumptions and with a recognition of the adverse selection problems inherent in voluntary programs; and

- Management and the board make a cogent case for needing to motivate and retain existing employees, such as being in a competitive employment market.[20]

Similarly, ISS indicates that an option exchange "creates a gulf between the interests of shareholders and management, since shareholders cannot reprice their stock" and therefore it "should be the last resort for management to use as a tool to re-incentivize employees."[21] According to ISS, only deeply underwater options should be eligible for an exchange program.[22] Therefore, as a general matter, the threshold exercise price for eligible options should be the 52-week high for the stock price.[23] ISS cautions that this general rule should be considered along with other factors, such as the timing of the request, whether the company has experienced a sustained stock price decline that is beyond management's control, whether grant dates of surrendered options are far enough back (e.g., two to three years) so as not to suggest that a repricing is being done to take advantage of short-term price declines, and the company's current stock price, among other factors.[24]

9.2.3 Treatment of Canceled Options

Upon the occurrence of a repricing, equity compensation plans generally provide for one of two alternatives: (1) the shares underlying repriced options are returned to the plan and used for future issuances or (2) such shares are redeemed by the company and canceled so as to no longer be available for future grants. A company's equity compensation plan should make clear which alternative it will use. In the case

---

20. Id.

21. See note 6 above.

22. Id.

23. Institutional Shareholder Services, *United States Proxy Voting Guidelines Updates, Benchmark Policy Recommendations, January 4,* 2018, https://www.issgovernance.com/file/policy/active/americas/US-Voting-Guidelines.pdf.

24. Id.

of an option repricing that results in the return of canceled shares to a company's equity incentive plan, ISS considers the total cost of the equity plan and whether the issuer's three-year average burn rate is acceptable in determining whether to recommend that shareholders approve the repricing.[25]

9.2.4 Proxy Solicitation Methodology

Companies seeking shareholder approval for a repricing face a number of hurdles, not the least the fact that shareholders have suffered from the same decrease in share price that caused the options to become underwater. It should also be noted that brokers are prohibited from exercising discretionary voting power (i.e., to vote without instructions from the beneficial owner of a security) with respect to implementation of, or a material revision to, an equity compensation plan.[26] Therefore, the need to convince shareholders of the merits of a repricing is magnified, as is the influence of proxy advisors and institutional shareholders.

The solicitation of proxies from shareholders by a domestic reporting company is governed by Section 14(a) of the Securities Exchange Act of 1934, as amended (the "Exchange Act") and the rules thereunder. Item 10 of Schedule 14A contains the basic disclosure requirements for a proxy statement used by a domestic issuer to solicit approval of a repricing. Pursuant to these requirements and common practice, issuers generally include the following items of disclosure:

- A description of the option exchange program, including a description of who is eligible to participate, the securities subject to the exchange offer, the exchange ratio, and the terms of the new securities.

- A table disclosing the benefits or amounts, if determinable, that will be received by or allocated to (1) named executive officers, (2) all current executive officers as a group, (3) all current directors who are not executive officers as a group, and (4) all employees,

---

25. Institutional Shareholder Services, *United States Proxy Voting Guidelines Updates, Benchmark Policy Recommendations,* January 4, 2018, https://www.issgovernance. com/file/policy/active/americas/US-Voting-Guidelines.pdf.

26. See NYSE Rule 452.

including all current officers who are not executive officers, as a group.

- A description of the reasons for undertaking the exchange program and any alternatives considered by the board.

- The accounting treatment of the new securities to be granted, and the U.S. federal income tax consequences.

It is important that companies ensure that their disclosure includes a clear rationale for the repricing to satisfy the disclosure requirements sought by proxy advisors and necessary to persuade shareholders to vote in favor of the repricing.[27]

Rule 14a-6 under the Exchange Act permits a company that is soliciting proxies solely for certain specified limited purposes in connection with its annual meeting (or a special meeting in lieu of an annual meeting) to file a definitive proxy statement with the Securities and Exchange Commission (SEC) and commence its solicitation immediately. The alternative requirement would be to file a preliminary proxy statement first and wait 10 days while the SEC determines whether it will review and comment on the proxy statement. While there is some room for interpretation, the authors believe that the better position is that a proxy statement containing a repricing proposal should generally be filed with the SEC in preliminary form and then in definitive form after 10 days if there is no SEC review. This is because the purposes for which a proxy statement can be initially filed in definitive form are limited to the following solely in connection with an annual meeting: (1) the election of directors; (2) the election, approval, or ratification of accountants; (3) a security holder proposal included pursuant to Rule 14a-8; (4) the approval, ratification, or amendment of a "plan"("plan" is defined in Item 402(a)(6)(ii) of Regulation S-K as "any plan, contract, authorization or arrangement, whether or not set forth in any formal document, pursuant to which cash, securities, similar instruments, or

---

27. It is worth noting that Item 402 of Regulation S-K requires that any repricing of an option held by a director or named executive be disclosed in a company's annual proxy statement for the election of directors. See also Securities and Exchange Commission, Division of Corporation Finance, *Current Issues and Rulemaking Projects Quarterly Update* (March 31, 2001), Part II, http://www.sec.gov/divisions/corpfin/cfcrq032001.htm.

any other property may be received"); (5) certain specific proposals related to investment companies and Troubled Asset Relief Program financial assistance recipients, and (6) an advisory vote on executive compensation, or for the vote on the frequency of the advisory vote on executive compensation. Most repricing proposals could be viewed as seeking approval of an amendment to a company's plan to permit the repricing and approval of the terms of the repricing itself. The better interpretation seems to be that approval of the terms of a particular repricing is separate from an amendment to the plan to permit repricing since the repricing terms would generally still be submitted for shareholder approval due to proxy advisor requirements even if the plan permitted repricing. Accordingly, companies should consider initially filing proxy statements for a repricing in preliminary form.

9.3   Tender Offer Rules

9.3.1   Application of the Tender Offer Rules

U.S. tender offer rules are generally implicated when the holder of a security is required to make an investment decision with respect to the purchase, modification, or exchange of that security. One might question why a unilateral reduction in the exercise price of an option would implicate the tender offer rules since there is no investment decision involved by the option holder. Indeed, many equity incentive plans permit a unilateral reduction in the exercise price of outstanding options, subject to shareholder approval, without obtaining the consent of option holders on the basis that such a change is beneficial to them. In reality, however, the likelihood of a domestic company being able to conduct a repricing without implicating the tender offer rules is minimal for the following reasons:

- Because of the influence of proxy advisors and institutional shareholders, most option repricings involve a value-for-value exchange consisting of more than a mere reduction in exercise price. A value-for-value exchange requires a decision by option holders to accept fewer options or to exchange existing options for restricted stock or RSUs. This is an investment decision requiring the solicitation and consent of individual option holders.

• A reduction in the exercise price of an incentive stock option (ISO) would be considered a "modification" akin to a new grant under applicable tax laws.[28] The new grant of an ISO restarts the holding periods required for beneficial tax treatment of shares purchased upon exercise of the ISO. The holding periods require that the stock purchased under an ISO be held for at least two years following the grant date and one year following the exercise date of the option. The resulting investment decision makes it difficult in practice to effect a repricing that includes ISOs without seeking the consent of ISO holders since they must decide if the benefits of the repricing outweigh the burdens of the new holding periods.

The SEC staff has suggested that a limited option repricing/exchange with a small number of executive officers would not be a tender offer. In such an instance, the staff position is that an exchange offer to a small group is generally seen as equivalent to individually negotiated offers, and thus not a tender offer. Such an offer, in many respects, would be similar to a private placement. The SEC staff believes that the more sophisticated the option holders, the more the repricing/exchange looks like a series of negotiated transactions. However, the SEC staff has not provided guidance on a specific number of offerees, so this remains a facts-and-circumstances analysis based on both the number of participants and their positions and sophistication.[29]

Not all equity incentive plans involve issuing ISOs, and thus the attendant ISO-related complexities will not always apply. As a result, foreign private issuers and domestic companies that have not granted ISOs and are simply reducing the exercise price of outstanding options unilaterally may also be able to avoid the application of the U.S. tender offer rules. Foreign private issuers are discussed in more detail below.

---

28. For ISO purposes, a modification is any change in the terms of the option that gives the optionee additional benefits under the option, regardless of whether the optionee actually benefits from such change. Treas. Reg. § 1.424-1(e)(4).

29. American Bar Association, Technical Session Between the SEC Staff and the Joint Committee on Employee Benefits, Question and Answers, May 8, 2001, http://www.thecorporatecounsel.net/member/FAQ/employeebenefits/01_JCEB.htm.

9.3.2 Requirements of the U.S. Tender Offer Rules

The SEC views a repricing of options that requires the consent of the option holders as a "self-tender offer" by the issuer of the options. Self-tender offers by companies with a class of securities registered under the Exchange Act are governed by Rule 13e-4 thereunder, which contains a series of rules designed to protect the interests of the targets of the tender offer. While Rule 13e-4 applies only to public companies, Regulation 14E applies to all tender offers. Regulation 14E is a set of rules prohibiting certain practices in connection with tender offers and requiring, among other things, that a tender offer remain open for at least 20 business days.

In March 2001, the SEC issued an exemptive order providing relief from certain tender offer rules that the SEC considered onerous and unnecessary in the context of an option repricing.[30] Specifically, the SEC provided relief from complying with Rule 13e-4(f)(8)(i) (the "all holders" rule) and Rule 13e-4(f)(8)(ii) (the "best price" rule). As a result of this relief, issuers are permitted to reprice/exchange options for only certain selected employees. Among other things, this exception allows issuers to exclude directors and officers from repricings. Furthermore, issuers are not required to provide each option holder with the highest consideration provided to other option holders.[31]

Pre-commencement Offers. The tender offer rules regulate the communications that a company may make in connection with a tender offer. These rules apply to communications made before the launch of a tender offer and while it is pending. Pursuant to these rules, a com-

---

30. Exemptive Order, Securities and Exchange Act of 1934, "Repricing," http://www. sec.gov/divisions/corpfin/repricing.htm.

31. An issuer must satisfy a number of requirements to be eligible for the relief: (1) the issuer must be eligible to use Form S-8, the options subject to the exchange offer must have been issued under an employee benefit plan as defined in Rule 405 under the Securities Act, and the securities offered in the exchange offer will be issued under such an employee benefit plan; (2) the exchange offer must be conducted for compensatory purposes; (3) the issuer must disclose in the offer to purchase the essential features and significance of the exchange offer, including risks that option holders should consider in deciding whether to accept the offer; and (4) except as exempted in the order, the issuer must comply with Rule 13e-4.

pany may publicly distribute information concerning a contemplated repricing before it formally launches the related tender offer, provided that the distributed information does not contain a transmittal form for tendering options or a statement of how such form may be obtained. Two common examples of company communications that fall within these rules are the proxy statement seeking shareholder approval for a repricing and communications between the company and its employees at the time that proxy statement is filed with the SEC. Each such communication is required to be filed with the SEC under cover of a Schedule TO with the appropriate box checked to indicate that the content of the filing includes pre-commencement written communications.

Tender Offer Documentation. An issuer conducting an option exchange will be required to prepare the following documents:

- The offer to exchange, which is the document pursuant to which the offer is made to the company's option holders and which must contain the information required to be included therein under the tender offer rules.

- The letter of transmittal, which is used by the option holders to tender their securities in the tender offer.

- Other ancillary documents, such as the forms of communications with option holders that the company intends to use and letters for use by option holders to withdraw a prior election to participate.

The documents listed above are filed with the SEC as exhibits to a Schedule TO Tender Offer Statement.

The offer to exchange is the primary disclosure document for the repricing offer and, in addition to the information required to be included by Schedule TO, focuses on informing security holders about the benefits and risks associated with the repricing offer. The offer to exchange is required to contain a "summary term sheet" that provides general information—often in the form of frequently asked questions—regarding the repricing offer, including its purpose, eligibility of participation, duration, and how to participate. It is also common practice for a company to include risk factors disclosing economic, tax, and other risks associated with the exchange offer. The most comprehensive section of the offer to exchange is the section describing the terms of the offer, including the purpose, background, material terms and conditions, eligibility to participate, duration, information on the stock or other applicable units, interest of directors and officers with respect to the applicable units or transaction, procedures for participation, tax consequences, legal matters, fees, and other information material to the decision of a security holder when determining whether or not to participate in such offer.

The offer to exchange, taken as a whole, should provide comprehensive information regarding the securities currently held and those being offered in the exchange—including the difference in the rights and potential values of each. The disclosure of the rights and value of the securities is often supplemented by a presentation of the market price of the underlying stock to which the options pertain, including historical price ranges and fluctuations, such as the quarterly highs and lows for the previous three years. The offer to exchange may also contain hypothetical scenarios showing the potential value risks/benefits of participating in the exchange offer. These hypothetical scenarios illustrate the approximate value of the securities held and those offered in the exchange at a certain point in the future, assuming a range of different prices for the underlying stock. If the repricing is part of an overall shift in a company's compensation plan, the company should include a brief explanation of its new compensation policy.

Launch of the Repricing Offer. The offer to exchange is transmitted to employees after the Schedule TO has been filed with the SEC. While the offer is pending, the Schedule TO and all of the exhibits thereto (principally the offer to exchange) may be reviewed by the SEC staff, who may provide comments to the company, usually within five to seven days of the filing. The SEC's comments must be addressed by the company to the satisfaction of the SEC, which usually requires the filing of an amendment to the Schedule TO, including amendments to the offer to exchange. Generally, no distribution of such amendment (or any amendments to the offer to exchange) will be required.[32] This

---

32. If the terms of the offer change (e.g., the option exchange ratio is changed) or other material changes are made to the disclosure in the offer to exchange, a supplement

review usually does not delay the tender offer and generally will not add to the period that it must remain open.

Under the tender offer rules, the tender offer must remain open for a minimum of 20 business days from the date that it is first published or disseminated. For the reasons noted below, most option repricing exchange offers are open for less than 30 calendar days. If the consideration offered or the percentage of securities sought is increased or decreased, the offer must remain open for at least 10 business days from the date such increase or decrease is first published or disseminated. The SEC also takes the position that if certain material changes are made to the offer (e.g., the waiver of a condition), the tender offer must remain open for at least 5 business days thereafter.[33] At the conclusion of the exchange period, the repriced options, restricted stock, or RSUs will be issued pursuant to the exemption from registration provided by Section 3(a)(9) of the Securities Act of 1933, as amended (the "Securities Act") for the exchange of securities issued by the same issuer for no consideration.

Conclusion of the Repricing Offer. The company is required to file a final amendment to the Schedule TO setting forth the number of option holders who accepted the offer to exchange.

9.4 Certain Other Considerations

9.4.1 Tax Issues

Incentive Stock Options. If the repricing offer is open for 30 days or more with respect to options intended to qualify for ISO treatment under U.S. tax laws, those ISOs are considered newly granted on the date the offer was made, whether or not the option holder accepts the offer.[34] If the period is for less than 30 days, then only ISO holders who

---

may need to be prepared, mailed to stockholders, and filed with the SEC as part of a Schedule TO amendment. This rarely occurs in an option repricing.

33. If such change is made at a time when more than five business days remain before the expiration of the tender offer, no extension of the tender offer would be needed. If such change is made in the five-business-day period preceding the scheduled expiration of the tender offer, an extension would be necessary.

34. Treas. Reg. § 1.424-1(e)(4)(iii).

accept the offer will be deemed to receive a new grant of ISOs.[35] As discussed above, the consequence of a new grant of ISOs is restarting the holding period required to obtain beneficial tax treatment for shares purchased upon exercise of the ISO.[36] As a result of these requirements, repricing offers involving ISO holders should generally be open for no more than 30 days.

To qualify for ISO treatment, the maximum fair market value of stock with respect to which ISOs granted to an employee may first become exercisable in any one year is U.S. $100,000. For purposes of applying this dollar limitation, all ISOs granted to the employee are taken into account, the stock is valued when the option is granted, and ISOs are taken into account in the order in which they were granted. Whenever an ISO is canceled pursuant to a repricing, any options and shares scheduled to become exercisable in the calendar year of the cancelation would continue to count against the U.S. $100,000 limit for that year, even if cancelation occurs before the option actually become exercisable.[37] To the extent that the new ISO becomes exercisable in the same calendar year as the cancelation, this reduces the number of shares that can receive ISO treatment (because the latest grants are the first to be disqualified).[38] Where the new ISO does not start vesting until the next calendar year, however, this will not be a concern.

Section 409A Compliance. If the repricing occurs with respect to nonqualified stock options (i.e., options that are not ISOs), such options need to be structured so as to be exempt from (or in compliance with) Section 409A of the Code. Section 409A comprehensively codifies the federal income taxation of nonqualified deferred compensation. Section 409A generally provides that unless a "nonqualified deferred compensation plan" complies with various rules regarding the timing of deferrals and distributions, all amounts deferred under the plan for the current year and all previous years become immediately taxable, and subject to a 20% penalty tax and additional interest, to the extent

---

35. Id.

36. Treas. Reg. § 1.424-1(e)(2).

37. Treas. Reg. § 1.422-4(b)(5).

38. Treas. Reg. § 1.422-4(b)(3); Treas. Reg. § 1.422-4(d), example 2.

the compensation is not subject to a "substantial risk of forfeiture" and has not previously been included in gross income. Nonqualified stock options are usually structured to be exempt from Section 409A. One of the conditions for this exemption is that the option have an exercise price at least equal to the fair market value of the underlying stock on the option grant date. A reduction in the option exercise price that is not below the fair market of the underlying stock value on the date of the repricing should not cause the option to become subject to Section 409A. Instead, such repricing of an underwater option is treated as the award of a new stock option that is exempt from Section 409A.[39] While foreign private issuers may enjoy certain relief from the U.S. tender offer rules, as described below, there is no similar relief from U.S. tax considerations for U.S. taxpayers. This is most important where a foreign private issuer's home country rules allow for the grant of options with exercise prices below fair market value. In such cases, care should be taken to ensure that grantees who are U.S. taxpayers receive awards that comply with Section 409A.

9.4.2   Plan Grant Limitation

It should also be noted that a repriced option will count against any per-person grant limitations (typically an annual limit on the maximum number of shares that may be granted to an individual) in the applicable equity plan.

9.4.3   Accounting Treatment

Accounting considerations are a significant factor in structuring a repricing. Before the adoption of ASC 718 in 2005, companies often structured repricings with a six-month hiatus between the cancelation of underwater options and the grant of replacement options. The purpose of this structure was to avoid the impact of variable mark-to-market charges. Under ASC 718, however, the charge for the new options is not only fixed upfront but is for only the incremental value, if any, of the new options over the canceled options. As discussed above, in a value-for-value exchange, a fewer number of options or shares of restricted stock or RSUs will usually be granted in consideration for

---

39.   Treas. Reg. § 1.409A-1(b)(5)(v)(A).

the surrendered options. As a result, the issuance of the new options or other securities can be a neutral event from an accounting expense perspective.

9.4.4 Section 16

The replacement of an outstanding option with a new option having a different exercise price and a different expiration date involves a disposition of the outstanding option and an acquisition of the replacement option, both of which are subject to reporting under Section 16(a). However, the disposition of the outstanding option will be exempt from short-swing profit liability under Section 16(b) pursuant to Rule 16b-3(e) if the terms of the exchange are approved in advance by the issuer's board of directors, a committee of two or more nonemployee directors, or the issuer's shareholders. It is generally not a problem to satisfy these requirements. Similarly, the grant of the replacement option or other securities is subject to reporting but will be exempt from short-swing profit liability pursuant to Rule 16b-3(d) if the grant was approved in advance by the board of directors or a committee composed solely of two or more nonemployee directors, was approved in advance or ratified by the issuer's shareholders no later than the date of the issuer's next annual meeting, or is held for at least six months.

9.5 Foreign Private Issuers

9.5.1 Relief from Shareholder Approval Requirement

Both the NYSE and Nasdaq provide foreign private issuers with relief from the requirement of stockholder approval for a material revision to an equity compensation plan by allowing them instead to follow their applicable home-country practices. As a result, if the home-country practices of a foreign private issuer do not require shareholder approval for a repricing, the foreign private issuer is not required to seek shareholder approval under NYSE or Nasdaq rules.

Both the NYSE and Nasdaq require an issuer following its home-country practices to disclose in its annual report on Form 20-F an explanation of the significant ways in which its home-country practices differ from those applicable to a U.S. domestic company. The disclosure can also be included on the issuer's website, in which case, under NYSE rules, the issuer must provide in its annual report the web address where the information can be obtained. Under Nasdaq rules, the issuer is required to submit to Nasdaq a written statement from independent counsel in its home country certifying that the issuer's practices are not prohibited by the home country's laws.

A number of foreign private issuers have disclosed that they will follow their home-country practices with respect to a range of corporate governance matters, including the requirement of shareholder approval for the adoption or any material revision to an equity compensation plan. These companies are not subject to the requirement of obtaining shareholder approval. Companies that have not provided such disclosure and wish to avoid the shareholder approval requirements when undertaking a repricing will need to consider carefully their historic disclosure and whether such an opt-out poses any risk of a claim from shareholders.

9.5.2 Relief from U.S. Tender Offer Rules

Foreign private issuers also have significant relief from the application of U.S. tender offer rules if U.S. option holders hold 10% or less of the company's outstanding options.[40] Under the exemption, assuming the issuer's actions in the United States still constitute a tender offer, the issuer would be required to take the following steps:

1. File with the SEC under the cover of a Form CB a copy of the informational documents that it sends to its option holders. This informational document would be governed by the laws of the issuer's home country and would generally consist of a letter to each option holder explaining why the repricing is taking place, the choices each option holder has, and the implications of each of the choices provided.

2. Appoint an agent for service of process in the United States by filing a Form F-X with the SEC.

3. Provide each U.S. option holder with terms that are at least as favorable as those terms offered to option holders in the issuer's home country.

---

40. 17 C.F.R. § 240.13e-4(h)(8)(i).

A more limited exemption to the U.S. tender offer rules also exists for foreign private issuers where U.S. investors hold 40% or less of the options that are subject to the repricing. Under this exception, both U.S. and non-U.S. security holders must receive identical consideration. The minimal relief is intended merely to minimize the conflicts between U.S. tender offer rules and foreign regulatory requirements and provides little actual relief in the context of an option repricing.

9.6   Alternative Strategies

Microsoft and Google used innovative methods to seek to address the issue of underwater employee stock options, providing a viable alternative to repricing.

In 2007, Google implemented a program that afforded its option holders (excluding directors and officers) the ability to transfer outstanding options to a financial institution through a competitive online bidding process managed by Morgan Stanley. The bidding process effectively created a secondary market in which employees can view what certain designated financial institutions and institutional investors are willing to pay for vested options. The value of the options is therefore a combination of their intrinsic value (i.e., any spread) at the time of sale plus the "time value" of the remaining period during which the options can be exercised (limited to a maximum of two years in the hands of the purchaser). As a result of this "combined" value, Google believed that underwater options would still retain some value. This belief is supported by the fact that in-the-money options have been sold at a premium to their intrinsic value. Google's equity incentive plan was drafted sufficiently broadly to enable options to be transferable without the need to obtain Google shareholder approval to amend the plan. It is likely, however, that most other companies' plans limit transferability of options to family members. Accordingly, most companies seeking to implement a similar transferable option program will likely need to obtain shareholder approval to do so. Note that ISOs become nonqualified stock options if transferred. The only options Google granted following its IPO were nonqualified stock options and, accordingly, the issue of losing ISO status did not arise. Finally, notwithstanding the benefits that Google's transferable option program offers, it did not prevent the company from effecting a one-for-one option exchange and incurring a related stock-based compensation expense of U.S. $460 million over the life of the new options.

In 2003, Microsoft implemented a program that afforded employees holding underwater stock options a one-time opportunity to transfer their options to JPMorgan in exchange for cash.[41] The program was implemented at the same time that Microsoft started granting restricted stock instead of options and was open on a voluntary basis to all holders of vested and unvested options with an exercise price of U.S. $33 or more (at the time of the implementation of the program, the company's stock traded at U.S. $26.50). Employees were given a one-month election period to participate in the program, and once an employee chose to participate, all of that employee's eligible options were required to be tendered. Employees who transferred options were given a cash payment in installments dependent upon their continued service with Microsoft.

The methods used by Google and Microsoft raise a number of tax and accounting questions and require the filing of a registration statement under the Securities Act in connection with short sales made by the purchasers of the options to hedge their exposure. To date, these methods have not been adopted and seem unlikely to be adopted by other companies, and it is to be expected that most companies will continue to conduct more conventional repricings to address underwater options.

9.7 Summary

A significant number of companies effected repricings after the financial crisis of 2008. As a result of that wave of repricings, improved market conditions, and many companies switching their compensation practices to include the grant of more full-value awards (such as restricted stock and RSUs) rather than options, presently the specter of underwater stock options has receded. Nevertheless, experience

---

41. Comcast Corporation implemented a similar program with JPMorgan in 2004. In that case, due to the structure of the option plan, Comcast repurchased the options and issued new options to JPMorgan with exercise prices and times to maturity identical to the repurchased options.

shows that the need to reprice underwater options may arise again as general market conditions fluctuate or due to the circumstances of a particular company.

Equity Awards in Divorce

William Dunn and Jennifer George

CONTENTS

While compensatory equity incentives for which shares have not been issued yet (e.g., stock options, restricted stock units, stock appreciation rights, and rights under employee stock purchase plans[1]) are not considered property for tax purposes, they are generally viewed as assets subject to equitable distribution in matrimonial dissolutions. As a result, property settlements in a divorce often address the treatment of stock options (and other equity incen-

---

1. Note that for restricted stock that is transferred to the NEFS (as defined in section 10.2 of this chapter) after vesting, the NEFS will normally be subject to income tax and Social Security on the fair market value of the shares at vesting.

tives, collectively referred to here as "equity awards") held by one of the spouses. Such treatment generally provides for one of the following outcomes: retention, transfer (or partial transfer), or assignment of proceeds. Each of these scenarios has the potential to produce different tax results. This chapter provides a general overview of these scenarios and their attendant tax consequences. It also briefly addresses some of the specific issues associated with the treatment of equity awards in divorce at the state level.

10.1 Retention

When the employee spouse granted the award retains such grants, but other assets are divided in the divorce, the tax analysis is straightforward. The employee spouse retaining the awards is generally taxed according to the rules applicable to the type of equity grant retained without regard to the divorce. For nonqualified stock options (NSOs) and stock appreciation rights, such a spouse will be taxed upon the exercise/purchase of shares for both income and Social Security tax purposes, subject to the applicable reporting and withholding requirements. In the case of incentive stock options (ISOs), Section 422 of the Internal Revenue Code (the "Code") applies in determining the tax treatment. Assuming the option holder has not sold the stock underlying options for the requisite holding periods (two years from the date of grant and one year from the date of exercise), the option holder will be taxed at capital gain rates upon the sale of the stock underlying the ISOs. If not and a "disqualifying disposition" has occurred, the option holder will be subject to ordinary income tax on the spread associated with the option (the difference between the fair market value of the stock on the date of exercise and exercise price for the option). And for restricted stock units (RSUs), the RSU holder spouse will be taxed at the time of share transfer for both income and Social Security tax purposes.

10.2 Transfer of Equity Awards

Where equity awards are transferred from the employee spouse holding the equity award to the other spouse (i.e., the nonemployee former spouse [NEFS]) in connection with a divorce, the tax analysis is more complicated.

Generally, Treas. Reg. § 1.83-3 provides that grants of equity awards that provide for the future delivery of shares (such as options and RSUs) are not viewed as a transfer of property for purposes of Code Section 83. Instead, the future transfer of the shares constitutes a transfer of property for purposes of Code Section 83 at that time. Unless the shares transferred are subject to a substantial risk of forfeiture, the award holder will recognize ordinary income equal to the difference between the fair market value of that stock received, less the price paid for the shares and the equity award (if any) at the time of receipt of the shares.

An exception to this general rule applies where the equity award is disposed of in an arm's-length sale or other disposition. In this situation, Code Sections 83(a) and (b) apply to tax the transfer of money or other property received in the same manner as such provisions would have applied to the transfer of property pursuant to an exercise (or vesting, depending on the type of equity award). This means for example, that an optionee is taxed on the option disposition date for the consideration received, even though the option was not exercised. However, if the transaction is not viewed to be at arm's length, the compensatory element is held open, and the RSU or option is taxed when it is ultimately settled, even though the employee no longer holds the award.[2]

In the case of a divorce, the distribution of property occurs among adverse parties, and the transfers of any equity awards presumably occur in an arm's-length transaction. Thus, under Code Section 83, the NEFS could potentially recognize income equal to the value of the equity award at the date the property settlement/transfer occurs rather than the date of exercise (or vesting, depending on the type of equity award). Fortunately, the IRS has ruled that the arm's-length disposition rules do not apply to such a transaction. Instead, the IRS has taken the position that the NEFS steps into the shoes of the employee spouse with respect to the taxation of the equity award. This position was first limited to married taxpayers who reside in community property states, but was later expanded to also include those who reside in non-community property states.

In the case of stock options, the IRS determined that an employee who transfers interests in nonstatutory stock options to an NEFS inci-

---

2. The same principles apply to other types of equity awards.

dent to divorce is not required to include an amount in gross income upon the transfer. The IRS also stated that the assignment of income doctrine did not apply to these transfers, and the employee is not required to include in gross income any income resulting from the NEFS's exercise of stock options.[3] Instead, when the options are exercised, the NEFS must include in income an amount determined under Code Section 83(a) as if the spouse were the person who performed the services. Thus, the NEFS, not the original option holder, is required to include an amount in gross income when he or she exercises the stock options.

However, the IRS determined that nonstatutory stock options would be subject to Federal Insurance Contributions Act (FICA) and Federal Unemployment Tax Act (FUTA) taxes at the time of exercise by an NEFS to the same extent as if the options had been retained and exercised by the employee spouse.

To the extent employment taxes apply, the wages are considered the wages of the employee spouse. The employee portion of the FICA taxes are deducted from the payment made to the NEFS, and any FICA withholding from the payments does not reduce the amount includible in the gross income of the NEFS.

Income recognized by an NEFS with respect to the exercise of nonqualified stock options is subject to withholding under Code Section 3402. Amounts distributed to an NEFS from nonqualified deferred compensation plans are also subject to withholding under Section 3402.

When the NEFS exercises a nonqualified stock option, no income tax withholding is required for the employee spouse, but Social Security and Medicare withholding are required. For the employee spouse, this income is reportable on his or her Form W-2, but no amount would be includible in Box 1 (compensation income) and Box 2 (tax withholding amounts). For the NEFS, the income with respect to the exercise of a nonqualified stock option is reportable on a 1099-MISC in Box 3. Income tax withholding for the NEFS is required and is required to be reported in Box 4, "federal income tax withheld," in the 1099-MISC.

Income tax withholding on payments to an NEFS is required to be included on a Form 945 filed by the employer. Social Security tax and

---

3. PLR 200442003, citing Rev. Rul. 2002-22 and *Balding v. Commissioner,* 98 T.C. 368 (1992).

Medicare tax are required to be reported on the employer's Form 941, and FUTA tax is required to be reported on the employer's Form 940.

The same principles and requirements set forth above also apply to stock appreciation rights and RSUs that are transferred to the NEFS.

10.3 Assignment of Proceeds

Where the employee spouse continues to hold the equity awards but is obligated under a divorce decree to pay the NEFS a portion of the value of the equity awards when the employee spouse realizes the benefits (i.e., exercise for options, vesting for RSUs), the outcome is less clear. Because this approach does not involve the actual transfer of equity awards, the favorable precedent found in the rulings cited above is not applicable. Therefore, normal assignment-of-income concepts likely apply to the transaction, meaning that the employee spouse will be taxed on the full spread at exercise for nonstatutory options (normal taxation for other types of equity awards) for both income and Social Security tax purposes, subject to the normal reporting and withholding requirements that apply, while the NEFS will enjoy receipt of his or her share of the proceeds (his or her share will be determined by the apportionment/formula as set out in the divorce decree) without tax consequences.

10.4 Statutory Option Stock (Incentive Stock Options and Section 423 ESPPs)

The above information pertains only to nonstatutory stock options (and other types of equity awards that do not receive special tax treatment). Special tax rules apply to "statutory option stock" as defined by Section 424 of the Code, i.e., those shares acquired through incentive stock options (ISOs) and Section 423 employee stock purchase plan (ESPP) options. Unlike the nonstatutory stock options described above, these options are limited by a transferability condition; i.e., upon transfer, the shares lose their status as statutory qualified shares. Rev. Rul. 2002-22 concluded that the transfer of statutory options to a spouse incident to a divorce results in the disqualification of the options,[4] which would

---

4. Disqualification as an ISO or treatment under a qualified ESPP, as stipulated in Code Sections 422(b) (5) and 423(b) (9) respectively.

result in those shares being subject to nonstatutory stock option tax treatment.

ISOs are statutory options offered by a corporation to certain employees that allow for tax-favored treatment if the requirements in Code Section 422 are met. Generally, to receive tax-favored treatment, ISO shares cannot be sold before two years after grant and one year after exercise. Where such conditions are met, Code Section 421(a)(1) stipulates that "no income shall result at the time of the transfer of such share to the individual upon his exercise of the option with respect to such share."

The Tax Court reaffirmed the findings of Rev. Rul. 2002-22 in 2005,[5] where the petitioners proposed a method of dividing ISOs incident to a divorce and were able to preserve ISO status. During the divorce proceedings, the spouses entered into an agreement to split the grants awarded to the employee spouse proportionally (based on the time of vesting and the date of separation). Pursuant to a court order, the employee spouse would retain all legal and beneficial ownership of the ISOs consistent with the statutory nontransferability, exercise, and holding period rules of Code Section 422. The employee spouse would exercise the NEFS's ISOs only according to the NEFS's written instruction and only on that spouse's paying or making arrangements for the payment of the transaction. Such shares would be transferred immediately, and the NEFS would be subject to all applicable taxes. The Tax Court ruled that such a scheme recognizing community property interest in the ISOs, requiring the employee to exercise ISOs according to the NEFS's instruction, and requiring that the employee designate the NEFS as the beneficiary of the NEFS's pro-rata portion of the ISOs would not violate the statutory nontransferability, exercise, and holding period rules imposed by Code Section 422.

Another common form of stock option available to an employee is delivered through an ESPP. ESPPs allow employees to purchase company stock, generally at a discount to its fair market value. Such grants use payroll deductions to fund the purchase price and use relatively short option periods. Unlike ISOs, ESPPs can be granted with a purchase price that is lower than the stock's value at the date of grant

---

5. Private Letter Ruling 200519011 (Jan. 13, 2005).

(up to a 15% discount is permitted). Purchase periods are usually less than a year, with six months being the most common. Most ESPPs are qualified under Code Section 423 and are similar to ISOs in that both regimes impose no tax at the share purchase date and instead tax the optionee at the time that he or she disposes of the shares received upon exercise of the options. Like ISO shares, Code Section 423 ESPP shares must be held at least two years from grant and one year from exercise to convert pre-exercise appreciation into capital gain. However, any discount that exists at the time the ESPP is granted is treated as ordinary income upon disposition, even if the holding period is met.[6]

Under all Code Section 423 ESPP plans, the option rights cannot be transferred to a spouse during the option period (usually termed the "purchase period"). If a transfer does occur, the Section 423 tax qualification may be lost. Therefore, no divorce issues arise out of the ESPP option itself because the option rights are not transferred, just the shares after purchase. Stock acquired by the employee as a result of his or her ESPP purchase is included in the marital estate and therefore may be transferred in a divorce settlement. Code Section 424(c)(4) provides that in the case of transfers of shares acquired under an ESPP between spouses incident to divorce,[7] the transfer shall not be treated as a disposition for tax purposes, and the recipient shall have the same tax treatment as applied to the optionee. Therefore, the NEFS who receives shares and then subsequently disposes of the shares must follow the ESPP share disposition rules to determine the ultimate tax treatment, and the employee who transferred the shares has no residual tax consequences.

10.5 Securities Law Considerations

For U.S. publicly traded companies, shares to be issued under an employee stock plan usually must be registered before they can be offered to employees. The Securities Act of 1933 (the "1933 Act") requires all "offers" or "sales" of "securities" to be registered by filing a registration statement (called a "Form S-8") with the Securities and Exchange Commission (SEC) unless an exemption is available. Generally, the

---

6. Revenue Act of 1964. P.L. 88-272, Sen. Rprt. No. 88-830. (1964). See also *Kast v. Comm'r*, 78 T.C. 1154 (1982).

7. Transfers described in subsection (a) of Code Section 1041.

grant of equity awards is exempt from registration because employees do not have to make an investment decision at grant (provided the equity awards are granted free of charge), the equity awards are nontransferrable and no shares are issued to employees at the time of grant. (The rule is different if shares are issued at grant, as they are for restricted stock.) Shares issued pursuant to equity awards granted by public companies to an NEFS (and the employee spouse) are covered by a Form S-8 registration statement.

To register an employee stock plan on Form S-8, the offering company must deliver a description of the plan and its tax consequences (known as a "plan prospectus") to the eligible employees, together with a copy of the company's latest annual report to stockholders. The offering company must advise plan participants that certain shareholder information is available upon request. The information provided must be periodically updated. The shares acquired under a plan registered on Form S-8 may be resold without registration or delivery of a prospectus, except that officers, directors, and 10% owners are subject to certain conditions. These "affiliates" may sell securities only in compliance with the applicable limitations of Rule 144 or under another exemption from registration. If an offering company is aware of outstanding unvested equity awards held by an NEFS, then the offering company should deliver a copy of the prospectus and latest company annual report to the NEFS.

Private companies usually rely on Rule 701 for an exemption from the registration requirements for the offer and sale of shares under an employee stock plan. Unless a company goes public, securities issued under Rule 701 may be resold only pursuant to registration or an exemption. Additionally, Rule 701 is available for "family members" who have acquired such securities through a gift or a domestic relations order. Furthermore, if option grants are limited to a small group of executives, an offering company may elect to rely on the private placement exemption of Section 4(2) of the 1933 Act for a registration exemption which exemption could include offerings to the NEFS.

10.6 Section 409A Considerations

Most stock options and ESPPs are exempted from the Section 409A deferred compensation rules. However, Section 409A may affect RSUs, and care should be taken to ensure that if there is a deferral of settlement of RSUs, such deferral is structured to comply with the requirements of Section 409A. Note that divorce is not a permissible distribution date under Section 409A. Therefore, the settlement of RSUs should not be accelerated in the event of divorce to pay out the NEFS's share of the awards.

10.7 State-Level Issues

The issues that arise at the state court level are too broad to exhaustively address in this chapter. However, there are several, in addition to the distinction between community and non-community property states (discussed above), which are: (1) consideration as a basis of division, (2) the value of tax in the marital estate, and (3) the division of non-transferable options.

Several states, such as Colorado and Indiana,[8] have made determinations as to whether a portion of the stock options to be divided should be transferred on the basis of whether there has been consideration, i.e., services rendered, for such stock options. This is conceptually a nuance for community property states, where it is generally accepted that the stock options are marital property on the date of grant. Certain states simply inquire whether the stock options were granted in consideration of past or future services. Other states create a mathematical formula factoring in such variables, including the grant date, the date of separation, and the date the option can be exercised.[9]

Tax considerations have also been addressed by a number of states in valuing the marital estate. For example, Alaska stipulates that the future tax consequences of exercising stock options should not be considered in valuing the marital estate.[10] On the other hand Indiana[11] permits the inclusion of taxes payable after exercising a stock option in valuing the marital estate.

Although stock options are generally *prima facie* nontransferable, few states have reviewed the actual transferability aspect of stock op-

---

8. Colorado (see *In re Marriage of Huston*, 967 P.2d 181 [Colo. Ct. App. 1998], and *In re Marriage of Miller*, 915 P.2d 1314 [Colo. 1996]) ; and Indiana (see *Hann v. Hann*, 655 N.E.2d 566 [Ind. Ct. App. 1995]).

9. For example, California; see *In re Marriage of Nelson*, 177 Cal. App. 3d 150 (Cal. App. 1st Dist. 1986).

10. *Broadribb v. Broadribb*, 956 P.2d 1222 (Alaska 1998).

11. *Hiser v. Hiser*, 692 N.E.2d 925 (Ind. Ct. App. 1998) (these states also include Michigan; see also *Everett v. Everett*, 489 N.W.2d 111 [1992]).

tions. The Pennsylvania Supreme Court reviewed a case where the employee spouse could not transfer stock options to the NEFS despite a divorce decree requiring a distribution of property.[12] In this case, the court issued a domestic relations order requiring that the employee spouse pay the NEFS his or her share when the options were executed. The Illinois Appeals Court reviewed a similar case and authorized the trial court to retain jurisdiction until the options could be exercised or the options expired[13] and then to divide the property at such time.

While a single common-law rule regarding divorce and stock options cannot be derived from state precedents, it is clear that there are a variety of issues at the state court level that may further obscure the divorce proceedings, and special attention to these state-level issues is required.

10.8 Same-Sex Unions

For same-sex married couples, until very recently, it was not clear whether their marriages would be recognized as valid for U.S. federal tax purposes, making the taxation of equity awards upon divorce of a same-sex married couple unclear. However, on August 29, 2013, the U.S. Department of the Treasury and the IRS ruled that same-sex couples, legally married in jurisdictions that recognize their marriages, will be treated as married for all federal tax purposes. The ruling applies regardless of whether the couple lives in a jurisdiction that recognizes same-sex marriage or a jurisdiction that does not recognize same-sex marriage. Although this ruling did not specifically address how divorces of same-sex married couples would be treated, it stands to reason that the same federal tax rules will apply on divorce to all married couples that are treated as such for U.S. federal tax purposes. Hence, all the information above for federal taxes is equally applicable to same-sex married couples who are legally married in any jurisdiction if they get divorced. However, treatment under state law will continue to vary by state. Finally, although not all states recognize same-sex marriages, it may be possible to obtain a divorce in another state that does recognize same-sex marriages and have property distributed according to the other state's laws.

---

12. *Fisher v. Fisher*, 769 A.2d 1165 (Pa. 2001).

13. *In re Marriage of Moody*, 457 N.E.2d 1023, 1027 (Ill. App. 1991) ; *see also In re Marriage of Frederick*, 218 Ill.App. 3d 533, 578 N.E.2d 612 (1991).

CHAPTER

11

Designing and Implementing an Employee Stock Purchase Plan

Barbara Baksa

CONTENTS

Portions of this chapter were originally written by Tim Sparks, currently the president of Compensia.

This chapter summarizes the principal features of employee stock purchase plans (ESPPs), especially those that are designed to qualify under Section 423 of the Internal Revenue Code (the "Code"), and highlights some of the practical considerations involved in putting an ESPP into place. The purpose of an ESPP is to encourage broad-based employee ownership of employer stock. Through an ESPP that qualifies under Sections 421 and 423 of the Code, an employee subject to U.S. tax law can purchase stock at a discount from fair market value and, if certain holding period requirements are met, receive preferred tax treatment upon sale of the ESPP shares.

For purposes of all of the examples in this chapter, unless stated otherwise, assume that the employee's entry date into the offering period is considered to be the grant date for purposes of Section 423.

11.1   Operation of an ESPP

Section 423 sets the basic operational parameters of an ESPP, which are discussed in greater detail below. In general, under a typical ESPP, employees are given an "option" to purchase employer stock at a favorable price at the end of an "offering period." While Section 423 does not require that the shares be purchased through accumulated payroll deductions, most employers find this approach administratively simpler than having all of the plan participants pay for the stock on the same day.

Before the beginning of each offering period, eligible employees must indicate whether they will participate in the plan. If so, the employee typically completes a subscription agreement or enrollment form indicating the percentage or dollar amount of compensation to be deducted from his or her paycheck throughout the offering period. This form may be on paper or, as is often the case, may be an online form. During the offering period, the company withholds amounts from participants' compensation and credits the amounts to participant record-keeping accounts established for this purpose.

Under most ESPPs, the purchase price is set at a discount from fair market value. While some plans provide that the discount is to be applied to the value of the stock on the purchase date (e.g., 85% of the fair market value on that date), it is more common to provide that this discount is applied to the value of the stock on the first day of the offering period or on the last day, *whichever is lower* (this is generally called a "look-back" provision).

Most plans permit participants to withdraw from the ESPP before the last day of the offering period (the "exercise date"). If a participant does not withdraw from the plan, amounts held for his or her account under the plan are applied automatically to the purchase of shares on the exercise date for the maximum number of shares at the applicable option price. ESPP purchases often take place through a transfer agent of the company or through a brokerage account established for that purpose.

The original subscription agreement setting forth the payroll deduction percentage can continue as long as the plan remains in effect, unless the participant withdraws from the plan, becomes ineligible to participate, or terminates employment. Many plans permit participants to increase or decrease their payroll deduction percentage at any time during the offering period.

11.1.1 Qualified vs. Nonqualified

Many companies choose to implement an ESPP that qualifies for preferential tax treatment under Section 423. This increases the company's administrative burden because the plan must be operated in a manner that complies with the requirements specified in Section 423 and also imposes certain limitations on the design of the plan (e.g., eligible participants, minimum purchase price, and length of the offering period). In addition to monitoring ongoing compliance with Section 423, the company is also responsible for tracking sales and other dispositions of stock acquired under the plan and for compliance with the notification requirements of Section 6039 of the Code.

Where companies want to implement a plan that provides benefits not permissible under Section 423 or where companies do not want to take on the obligations of complying with Section 423 and related tax codes, they may implement a nonqualified ESPP. Under the tax code, non-Section 423 plans are treated as nonqualified stock options, and any discount at purchase is subject to tax withholding for both income and employment tax purposes. Table 11-1 provides a high-level comparison of Section 423 ESPPs to nonqualified plans.

11.2 Section 423's Requirements

To qualify under Section 423 of the Code, an ESPP must meet the following requirements:

- *Employees only.* Only employees of the plan sponsor (or its parent or subsidiary corporations) may participate in the ESPP. Thus, for example, consultants and nonemployee directors may not participate in an ESPP.

- *Shareholder approval.* An ESPP must be approved by the shareholders of the plan's sponsor within 12 months before or after the ESPP is adopted by the board. Once an ESPP has been approved by shareholders, no further shareholder approval is required except for an increase in the number of plan shares (other than an increase

Table 11-1. Comparison of Section 423 ESPPs vs. Nonqualified Plans

	Section 423 ESPPs	Nonqualified plans
U.S. tax compliance	Ensuring compliance with Section 423, tracking dispositions, reporting disposition income on Form W-2, complying with Section 6039.	Withholding taxes at purchase for U.S. employees and reporting income on Form W-2.
Company tax deduction	Upon disqualifying disposition only.	Upon purchase.
Statutory restrictions	Limitations on eligible participants, amount of stock purchased, transferability, price, and term of offering. Must be offered to substantially all employees on an equal basis.	If plan offers a discount or match, timing and form of payment must comply with Section 409A.
Tax compliance for non-U.S. employees	Varies by county, no difference for Section 423 ESPPs vs. nonqualified plans.	
Shareholder approval	Required	Generally required, except for open market plans in certain circumstances.
Accounting treatment	No difference for Section 423 ESPPs vs. nonqualified plans, except for tax accounting.	
Tax accounting	No tax benefit recorded until tax deduction is realized.	Estimated tax benefit recorded as expense is recognized and trued up to actual tax savings.
Securities law	Treatment is generally the same for Section 423 ESPPs vs. nonqualified plans. Purchases under nonqualified plans may be reportable for Section 16 purposes, depending on the terms of the plan.	

pursuant to an evergreen provision—see below) or an amendment to allow employees of certain related corporations (e.g., a subsidiary) to participate.

- *No 5% shareholders.* Any employee who owns 5% or more of the stock of the plan sponsor may not participate in the ESPP.

- *Eligibility.* All eligible employees must be allowed to participate in the ESPP, although certain categories of employees may be excluded:
  - employees employed less than two years;
  - employees whose customary employment is 20 hours or less per week;
  - employees whose customary employment is for not more than five months in a calendar year; and
  - "highly compensated" employees (as defined in Section 414(q) of the Code).

- *Equal rights and privileges.* All ESPP participants must enjoy the same rights and privileges under the plan, except that the amount of stock that may be purchased may be based on compensation differences (e.g., a percentage of compensation).

- *Purchase price.* The purchase price may not be less than the lesser of 85% of the fair market value of the stock on the (1) grant date (typically the employee's entry date into the offering period) or (2) purchase date.

- *Maximum term.* The maximum term of offering periods under an ESPP may not exceed 27 months unless the purchase price is based solely on the fair market value at the time of purchase, in which case the offering period may be as long as five years. There is no maximum term applicable to the ESPP itself, although most ESPPs have a ten-year term.

- *$25,000 limit.* Under all ESPPs of the employer company and its parent and subsidiary corporations, an employee may not purchase more than $25,000 worth of stock for each calendar year in which the offering period is in effect.

- *Nontransferability.* An employee's right to purchase stock under the ESPP may not be transferred except by will or the laws of descent and distribution and may be exercisable during the employee's life only by the employee.

11.3   Designing an ESPP

Within the broad framework of Section 423, there is a good deal of flexibility in plan design.

11.3.1   Number of Shares

There is no limit per se on the number of shares that can be issued under an ESPP. The number of shares reserved under an ESPP should take into account the number of shares available to employees under other stock-based programs, the value of the stock, the duration of the offering, limits on employee contributions, eligibility requirements, and so on. Some employers include an "evergreen" or automatic stock replenishment provision in their ESPP. With such a provision, the number of shares available for issuance under the plan increases automatically, typically each year, based on a specified percentage of the employer's outstanding shares (e.g., 2.5% per year). For tax reasons, the annual increase must be subject to a fixed and determinable limit (e.g., 250,000 shares). An evergreen provision avoids having to continually seek shareholder approval of plan share increases. This can also help the employer avoid additional compensation charges for financial accounting purposes that can apply when the plan runs out of shares during an offering period (see "Grant Date" under "Accounting Considerations" below). While shareholders, particularly institutional shareholders, do not generally view evergreen provisions favorably, approval of such a provision in an ESPP is apparently more palatable to shareholders than an evergreen provision in the employer's stock option plan.

Some employers limit their ESPP share consumption by imposing a cap on the aggregate number of shares that can be issued in any one offering or purchase period. Such a feature allows employers to plan for future share increases and the associated shareholder approval.

11.3.2   Dilution

Other than the number of shares in the plan, the two factors primarily responsible for the dilutive effect of an ESPP are the purchase price of the stock and the duration of the offering period. As a rule, the longer the offering period, the more dilutive the plan, since employees are more likely to purchase their shares at a substantial discount. For example, assume that the fair market value of the employer's stock on the date of grant is $30, and with a 15% discount, the purchase price would be $25.50 (85% of $30). Assume further that at month 24, the fair market value of the stock is $48. By allowing employees to purchase the shares at 85% of the value on the date of grant (i.e., $25.50), the 15% discount would increase, in this example, to a discount of 47% of the value on the date of purchase. The dilutive effect is even more pronounced in plans that include a feature (discussed in greater detail below) under which participants are automatically rolled into a new offering period in the event of a decline in the value of the company's stock.

11.3.3 Offering Periods

ESPPs typically permit participants to purchase shares at the end of an "offering period," which typically runs from 3 to 27 months. Most plans have offering periods of either 6 months or some multiple thereof (e.g., 12 months or 24 months). Plans with offering periods of more than six months typically include interim "purchase periods." For example, if the offering period is 24 months, employees might be allowed to purchase shares at the end of each of the four 6-month purchase periods within the 24-month offering period. In this situation, the purchase price in any one purchase period is usually based on the fair market value on the first day of the offering period or the last day of the particular purchase period, whichever is lower. Plans with offering periods longer than 6 months are more difficult to administer, both because of the interim purchase periods and the fact that in most plans of this kind there are overlapping offering periods (e.g., a new 24-month offering commences every 6 months).

Some ESPPs include an offering period "reset" provision. These plans typically include offering periods that are 12 or 24 months long and begin every 6 months. For example, a 24-month offering period plan might include four 6-month purchase periods (i.e., purchases occur every 6 months during the offering period). Under such provisions, if the company's stock declines in value, at the end of a purchase period the employees are considered to have automatically withdrawn from that offering period and are enrolled in a new offering period. This feature gives the employee the lowest possible purchase price, since the purchase price is reset as of the first day of the new offering period.

For most purposes, these provisions are generally referred to as "reset" provisions. For accounting purposes, however, ASC 718 distinguishes between "reset" and "rollover" provisions. The standards define a "reset" provision as one in which the length of the new offering is the time remaining in the original offering when the price is reset. For example, under a reset provision, where the automatic withdrawal and reenrollment occurs after 6 months into a 24-month offering, the new offering would be only 18 months in length. Under a rollover provision, as defined under ASC 718, the new offering is the full length of the original offering. Where the provision in our example is a rollover, rather than a reset provision, the new offering would be 24 months in length. See section 11.6 for more information on the accounting treatment that applies to ESPPs.

Some plans offer 12- or 24-month offering periods without interim purchases or otherwise restrict the transferability of purchased shares. These plans preclude employees from selling their shares immediately after purchase and are intended to foster greater employee stock ownership.

The timing of the purchase dates can be a crucial detail. Ideally, the purchase dates will not occur at quarter- or year-end, so as to avoid closed trading windows and also ensure that purchases are not occurring during periods of high activity for the plan administration group.

Purchase Timing

When implementing an ESPP, companies should consider carefully the dates on which purchases will occur under the plan. Ideally, purchase dates are timed so that they do not occur on the final date of any fiscal periods, payroll period end dates, or December 31. Avoiding these dates is important to reducing the risks of errors in purchase calculations by limiting distractions for administrative team members tasked with managing the plan and providing sufficient time to perform the audits and reconciliation necessary to prevent errors.

In addition, to encourage participation in the plan, it is advisable to schedule purchases to occur during open window periods. Companies that have ESPPs with purchases that occur during closed trading windows report lower participation in their plans.[1]

11.3.4 Purchase and Contribution Limits

$25,000 Limitation

Section 423 limits purchases under an ESPP to $25,000 worth of stock in any one calendar year, valued as of the date the right to purchase the shares is granted (typically this is the employee's entry date into the offering). Under this rule, if a plan has a 12-month offering period beginning each January 1, and the value of the stock on a particular January 1 is $10 (assume that the offering beginning is considered the grant date), then no employee may purchase more than 2,500 shares ($25,000 divided by $10) in that offering period.

Employees accrue the right to purchase $25,000 worth of stock for each calendar year in which the offering is outstanding. Once employees have accrued the right to purchase stock under an offering, they retain that right until their participation in the offering ends (not merely until the end of the calendar year in which the right accrued). For multi-year offerings, this can result in employees being able to purchase more than $25,000 worth of stock in subsequent years of the offering.

For example, assume a 24-month offering begins on January 1, 20X0, with purchases occurring every 12 months, on December 31, 20X0 and 20X1. In 20X0, an employee enrolled in the offering can purchase up to $25,000 worth of stock. But assume that the employee only purchases $10,000 worth of stock on December 31, 20X0. The $15,000 worth of stock that the employee still has the right to purchase for 20X0 is rolled over to the second year of the offering, enabling the employee to purchase up to $40,000 worth of stock on December 31, 20X1.

---

1. In the Equity Compensation Outlook June 2022 pulse survey on ESPP policies, nearly 60% of respondents with purchases occurring only during open window periods reported that more than 40% of employees participated in their ESPP. Among respondents with purchases occurring during closed trading windows, only 46% were able to achieve this level of participation. The Equity Compensation Outlook is a collaboration between the NASPP and Fidelity Investments.

Note however, that rights to purchase stock that are accrued under one offering cannot be rolled over to another offering. In this example, once the offering ends, the employee loses the right to the amounts accrued under it. If the employee again only purchases $10,000 worth of stock on December 31, 20X1, the $30,000 worth of stock left over under the limit cannot be rolled over to the next offering. When a new 24-month offering begins on January 1, 20X2, the employee will be limited to purchasing just $25,000 worth of stock in the first year of the offering.

Employees accrue the right to purchase stock in each year that the offering is outstanding, even if a purchase does not occur during the year. Thus, even in offerings that are 12 months or less in length, employees may sometimes be able to purchase more than $25,000 worth of stock if the offering spans more than one calendar year. For example, assume a 12-month offering begins on July 1, 20X0, with the first purchase occurring on June 30, 20X1. Employees enrolled in the offering as of July 1, 20X0, accrue the right to purchase $25,000 worth of stock for 20X0 and again for 20X1 and thus will be able to purchase $50,000 worth of stock on June 30, 20X1.

Where an employee has accrued the right to purchase stock for prior years under the offering, purchases are applied against the rights accrued under the limit on a first-in, first-out basis. For example, assume a 12-month offering begins on October 1, 20X0, with purchases occurring every six months, on March 31, 20X1, and September 30, 20X1. An employee that enrolls at the beginning of the offering will be able to purchase $50,000 worth of stock under the offering in 20X1 ($25,000 worth for 20X0 and an additional $25,000 worth for 20X1). Assume the employee purchases $15,000 worth of stock on each purchase date, for an aggregate of $30,000 worth. The purchases are applied first against the amounts accrued under the limit for 20X0. Consequently, the employee has only purchased $5,000 of the $25,000 worth of stock he accrued the right to purchase for 20X1.

The next offering under the plan begins on October 1, 20X1, with purchases occurring on March 31, 20X2, and September 30, 20X2. Upon enrollment in the new offering, the employee has the right to purchase $20,000 worth of stock; the remaining stock unpurchased under the limit at the end of the prior offering. In addition, the employee accrues the right to purchase an additional $25,000 worth of stock once the new calendar year begins. Thus, the employee will be able to purchase $45,000 worth of stock in 20X2 ($20,000 worth rolled over from 20X1 and an additional $25,000 worth of stock for 20X2).

As mentioned above, however, amounts accrued from prior calendar years cannot be rolled over to a new offering. Assume that, in our example, the employee purchased only $10,000 worth of stock in 20X1 (instead of $30,000 worth). The employee had accrued the right to purchase $50,000 worth of stock for the offering, leaving $40,000 worth of stock unpurchased under the limit. When the offering ends after the September 30, 20X1 purchase, the employee loses the right to the amounts accrued under the limit for the prior calendar year. Thus, when the employee is enrolled in the new offering that begins on October 1, 20X1, the amount that the employee can purchase under the limit is set back down to $25,000 worth of stock for the remainder of 20X1. There are no purchases that occur under the new offering in 20X1, so this amount will roll over to 20X2, and the employee will be able to purchase up to $50,000 worth of stock during this year.

Regardless of how many offerings an employee is enrolled in during a calendar year, the employee can only purchase $25,000 worth of stock during the year (excluding any amounts carried forward under the limit from prior years). For example, where a plan has 6-month offerings, employees are not able to purchase $25,000 worth of stock in each offering; any amounts purchased in the earlier offerings during the year reduce the amount of stock employees can purchase in subsequent offerings in the same year.

Let us return to the previous example involving the 12-month offering. Now assume that the employee purchases $50,000 worth of stock during 20X1. At this point, the employee has purchased all the stock that is permitted under the limit for 20X1. When the new offering begins on October 1, 20X1, the employee does not accrue the right to purchase another $25,000 worth of stock. Instead, the employee cannot purchase any stock under that offering for 20X1. Luckily, the plan is designed so that the employee would not be purchasing any stock in 20X1 anyway, and when the new calendar year begins, the employee does still accrue the right to purchase another $25,000 worth of stock. Thus, the employee can purchase up to $25,000 worth of stock during 20X2.

Using Contribution Limits to Administer the $25,000 Limitation

A common misperception is that the $25,000 limit can be administered by limiting contributions to a percentage of $25,000 commensurate with the discount offered under the plan (e.g., where a plan offers a 15% discount, by limiting contributions to $21,250 per year, or 85% of $25,000). Generally, this is not the case because the value of the shares for purposes of the $25,000 limit is based on the fair market value of the stock at the grant date (typically the employee's entry date into the offering), and the purchase price may be based on the fair market value on the grant date or the purchase date. To effectively administer the $25,000 limit by capping employees' yearly contributions, both the $25,000 limit and the purchase price must be based on the same fair market value.

For example, assume that an employee enrolls in an ESPP when the fair market value is $25 per share. The plan offers a look-back and a 15% discount. The employee purchases stock under the offering later that same year, when the fair market value is $20 per share. If the employee is allowed to apply contributions of $21,250 (85% of $25,000) to the purchase, the employee will purchase 1,250 shares ($21,250 divided by 85% of $20 per share purchase date fair market value). This would exceed the 1,000 shares ($25,000 divided by $25 per share grant date fair market value) that the employee is limited to under the $25,000 limitation.

While it is true that where a plan has a look-back and the stock appreciates in value over the offering, both the purchase price and the $25,000 limitation will be based on the grant date fair market value, there is no way to predict that this will occur at the time the employee is making contributions to the plan, making this an unreliable method by which to administer the $25,000 limitation.

$25,000 Limitation in Plans Without a Look-Back

In an ESPP where the purchase price is based solely on the fair market value on the purchase date, application of the $25,000 limit will vary depending on whether the grant date for tax purposes is the employee's entry into the offering or the purchase date. In the case of a plan with a look-back, the grant date for tax purposes must be the employee's entry date into the offering. But where the plan does not provide for a look-back, the plan could define the grant date to be either the employee's entry into the offering or the purchase date, depending on the features of the plan and the company's objectives. (See section 11.3.8, "Maximum Number of Shares," for more information on determining grant date under a Section 423 qualified plan. Note that the grant date for tax purposes must be determined in a consistent manner for all employees participating in the same offering; it is not permissible to use the offering entry date for some employees and the purchase date for others.)

For purposes of valuing shares under the $25,000 limit, Section 423 looks to the fair market value on the grant date. Where the offering entry date is the grant date, the $25,000 limit applies in the same manner to plans without a look-back as those with a look-back. Consequently, the value of the shares purchased for purposes of the $25,000 limit will be based on a different value than the purchase price.

For example, assume that an employee enrolls in an ESPP offering with a 15% discount when the fair market value is $25 per share and purchases stock under the offering later that same year when the fair market value is $30 per share. Assuming the offering entry date is the grant date, the employee will be able to purchase a maximum of 1,000 shares ($25,000 divided by the $25 per share fair market value). If the purchase price is based on the purchase date fair market value, however, those 1,000 shares will have a total price of $25,500 (1,000 shares multiple by 85% of $30 per share) and will have a purchase date value of $30,000 (1,000 shares multiplied by the $30 per share fair market value on the purchase date).

Similarly, if the fair market value on the purchase date is $20 per share, the employee's purchase will still be limited to 1,000 shares ($25,000 divided by the $25 fair market value at grant). In this case, however, the shares will have a total price of $17,000 (1,000 shares multiplied by 85% of $17 per share) and a purchase date value of only $20,000 (1,000 shares multiplied by $20 per share).

Where the plan defines the purchase date as the grant date, the value of the shares will be based on the purchase date fair market value for purposes of the $25,000 limit. In the example above, the value of the shares on the employee's entry date into the offering is irrelevant.

In the case where the fair market value on the purchase date is $30 per share, the employee will be able to purchase a maximum of 833 shares ($25,000 divided by $30 per share). The employee's purchase price will be approximately 85% of $25,000, or $21,241.50 (833 shares multiplied by 85% of $30 per share). In the case where the fair market value is $20 on the purchase date, the employee will be able to purchase 1,250 shares ($25,000 divided by $20 per share). The employee's purchase price will again be 85% of $25,000, or $21,250 (1,250 shares multiplied by 85% of $20).

Thus, where the purchase price is based on the purchase date fair market value, defining the grant date for tax purposes as the purchase date offers the advantage of aligning the $25,000 limitation with the calculation of the purchase price. The $25,000 limitation can thereby be easily administered by limiting contributions to percentage of $25,000 commensurate with the discount offered under the plan (e.g., $21,250 for plans that offer a 15% discount). This approach has the disadvantage, however, of starting the two-year holding period for qualifying dispositions at the time of purchase. In addition, the calculation of ordinary income on a qualifying disposition will be tied to the purchase date; depending on the employee's circumstances and the price path of the stock purchased, this could be an advantage, a disadvantage, or a neutral consideration.

Purchase and Contribution Limits

While not required under Section 423, most ESPPs impose further limits on the amounts that can be contributed to or purchased under the plan, in addition to the $25,000 statutory limitation. These additional limits serve three primary purposes: where the plan is qualified under Section 423, they ensure that the enrollment or offering begin date is considered the grant date; they protect against a shortfall in shares available for purchase under the plan; and where the plan is compensatory under ASC 718, they assist with management of plan expense.

Because the number of shares purchased under the plan is a function of how many employees elect to participate in it, how much they contribute, and the purchase price, it can be difficult to accurately predict how many shares will be purchased under the plan during a given time period. This is particularly challenging when the company's stock price is declining because, as the purchase price under the plan is reduced, participants are able to purchase more shares. But even an increase in stock price can cause an unexpected increase in share usage by encouraging additional employees to enroll in the plan or current participants to increase their contributions. Imposing appropriate limits on the number of shares that can be purchased can preserve the life of the plan by capping the number of shares that will be purchased during a given time period. The most common form of share limit is a maximum on the number of shares an individual can purchase on any given purchase date (see section 11.3.8, "Maximum Number of Shares"). Other alternatives include imposing a maximum on the number of shares that can purchased during an offering (where there are multiple purchases during the offering, this allows the maximum shares to be purchased at the lowest price throughout the offering) or limiting the aggregate number of shares that can be issued on any given purchase date. Individual share limits are more likely to affect higher-compensated employees since they generally contribute more to the plan (and thereby purchase more shares); if triggered, an aggregate limit affects all participants since each individual purchase will be prorated to ensure the limit is not exceeded.

While very effective in terms of preserving the plan's share reserve, share limits can be problematic because, when triggered, a portion of the affected participants' contributions are generally refunded without interest. Because participants are not able to apply their full contributions to the purchase, this reduces their return under the plan. Participants are often distressed to learn that their purchases will be limited; thus, if the limit is triggered routinely, it could affect overall employee satisfaction with and participation in the plan. While it is important that the plan have a share limit, the limit should be high enough that it is triggered only under extreme circumstances (e.g., a severe decline in stock price or an overwhelming increase in participation). If share limits under the plan are triggered routinely, the company should consider imposing contribution limits instead of or in addition to the share limits.

Limiting the amount employees can contribute to the plan both preserves the plan's share reserve and also helps the company manage plan expense (where applicable). These limits typically are in the form of a maximum percentage of compensation that can be contributed (typically 10% to 15%) or a flat dollar amount. Flat dollar amount limits have a greater impact on highly compensated employees; limiting the percentage of compensation that can be contributed affects all participants. Contribution limits are typically enforced through payroll; once the limit is triggered, the participant's contributions to the plan are tolled. This prevents the need to refund amounts to participants after the purchase occurs and also ensures that participants receive a return on all amounts they are able to contribute.

Where contributions to the plan remain constant, overall expense for the plan will also remain constant, regardless of the current value of the stock or the purchase price. While an appreciating stock price will increase the fair value per share of each new offering under the plan, because the purchase price will also increase, thereby decreasing the number of shares purchased by a proportionate amount (assuming contributions remain constant), this increase in fair value will not result in an increase to the plan's aggregate expense. Thus, fluctuations in stock prices will result in greater expense only to the extent that they drive higher levels of participation in the plan, making contribution limits a critical tool for managing and forecasting plan expense under ASC 718.

Changes in Contribution Rates

Most plans permit participants to adjust their level of participation in the plan by either increasing or decreasing their rate of contribution. A generous policy will allow participants to increase or decrease their rate of contribution at any point and will allow multiple adjustments between purchases, but this generosity may create an undue administrative burden on the company. For compensatory plans, this generosity can also increase the cost associated with the plan (in this chapter, see sections 11.6.6, "Increases in Contribution Rates," and 11.6.7, "Decreases in Contribution Rates and Withdrawals").

It is reasonable and appropriate for the company to limit when and how often participants can adjust their contribution rates. It is not necessary to have the same policy for both increases and decreases. A policy could allow participants to decrease the contribution rate at any point (to become effective immediately), limit participants to only one reduction per purchase period, and only allow increases in contribution rates at the start of each purchase period. While significantly easing the administrative burden for the company, this policy is not so restrictive as to interfere with participants' enjoyment of the plan. A policy that is too restrictive might discourage participation in the plan. For example, if participants are prohibited from ever decreasing their contribution rates, they may be reluctant to enroll in the plan or may enroll at a lower rate than they would otherwise. The company should strive to create a policy that is administratively feasible but does not discourage employees from participating.

If participants are allowed to reduce their contribution levels, it also is necessary to establish whether or not participants may cease contributing to the plan without formally withdrawing from the plan. This would allow participants to remain in the plan and purchase shares with the contributions they have made thus far, but not make any further contributions. Some plans permit this course of action only when it is clear that further contributions will not be applied to the purchase of shares due to the statutory $25,000 limitation or another plan limitation.

11.3.5 Compensation

Closely related to the percentage limitation is the plan definition of compensation. Generally, base pay is the simplest, but another definition can be used if base pay does not accurately reflect the makeup of the employees' compensation. However, the definition of compensation cannot operate to discriminate against certain employees. For example, defining compensation as base salary above a certain level (e.g., above $30,000) would violate the equal rights and privileges requirement (discussed above).

If the plan is compensatory under ASC 718, the expense associated with the plan is more readily forecasted when contributions are limited to sources of compensation that are generally predictable in nature, such as base pay. If employees are allowed to contribute from variable pay, such as bonuses, overtime, and commissions, the company will find that its expense for the plan varies from period to period as the number of shares employees purchase increases and decreases in relation to their level of compensation.

11.3.6 Eligibility

Generally, all employees of any corporate entity designated for participation in the ESPP must be eligible to participate. Section 423 permits a plan to exclude employees who have been employed for less than two years, who are employed for 20 hours per week or less or not more than five months per year, or who are considered highly compensated employees. Also, owners of 5% or more of the common stock of a company by statute are not permitted to participate. No other employees may be excluded.

Most companies impose either no service requirements or require only a brief employment period to participate, such as three months. Any service requirement should be considered in light of the company's employee population (e.g., does this population include a significant number of seasonal or part-time employees?), employee turnover, competitive practices, and the eligibility requirements of other company plans. Also, keep in mind that offering periods often commence every three to six months. As a result, new hires may have to wait up to three to six months to participate in an ESPP, in addition to any service requirement.

Under the provision of the Code allowing the exclusion of highly compensated employees, companies can exclude employees that earn a specified amount in excess of the threshold defined in Section 414(q) of the Code. This threshold is adjusted annually for inflation; for 2023, it is $150,000. Companies can set an exclusion threshold that is higher than this amount but cannot exclude employees earning less than this amount. Thus companies could exclude, say, all employees that earn in excess of $200,000 per year but could not exclude, say, employees earning more than $90,000 per year. Where implemented, this limit must be applied equally to all employees of the corporate entities that are eligible to participate in the same offering under the plan. Companies can also exclude Section 16 officers, regardless of their level of compensation.

Under Section 423, only employees are allowed to participate in the plan. Specifically, participants must be employed continuously from the date of grant (typically the date of their enrollment in to the offering) until three months before the date of their purchase. From a practical standpoint, most plans do not provide for participation after termination of employment; typically, upon termination, former employees are immediately withdrawn from the plan and any unused contributions are refunded to them. But, technically, former employees that terminated in the three months leading up to a purchase date can be allowed to participate.

Because the statute requires continuous employment from the date of grant (i.e., enrollment in the offering) until three months before the date of purchase, employees that take a leave of absence could forfeit their right to participate until the first offering that begins after they return from leave. This applies only to leaves that are longer than three months and that do not provide the employee with a guaranteed right of reemployment (through either statute or contract). Thus, statutory leaves (such as maternity leave, military leave, disability leave, and leaves under the Family Leave Act) will not disqualify an employee from participation in a Section 423 ESPP, regardless of the length of the leave. Likewise, a nonstatutory leave under which the company contractually guarantees right of reemployment (such as a company-sponsored sabbatical program) will not disqualify an employee from participation in the ESPP, regardless of the length of the leave. Finally, leaves of less than three months will not disqualify an employee from participation in the ESPP, even where the leave does not provide a guaranteed right of reemployment.

However, employees on leave will be disqualified from participating in the ESPP, where the following three conditions exist:

• The leave is not under a federal, state, or other statutory leave program.

• The leave does not otherwise provide a contractual right of reemployment.

• The leave is longer than three months.

Where these conditions exist, on the first day following the conclusion of the three-month period, the employee is considered terminated for tax purposes. Upon termination, employees can participate in the ESPP for three additional months, after which they should be withdrawn from the plan and receive a refund of any unused contributions. If they are allowed to remain in the plan for more than six months after the start of their leave (the employee is considered terminated after three months and then has another three months in which his or her purchases receive qualified treatment), their purchases should be treated as the exercise of nonstatutory stock options for tax purposes.

Note that, unless prohibited from participating by law as described above, employees cannot be excluded from participating in an ESPP solely because they are on leave. As a practical matter, however, at least in the case of unpaid leaves, where plans require contributions to be made through payroll deductions, employees that are on leave will be unable to contribute to the plan and thus unable to participate, except to the extent that they have unused contributions that were made before the start of their leave.

11.3.7 Participation by Non-U.S. Employees

Often, U.S. employers with employees working outside of the U.S. wish to extend ESPP participation to such employees. Before expanding an ESPP outside the United States, however, employers should become familiar with the applicable laws and regulations of each of the foreign countries where participation will be extended. A discussion of these laws and regulations is beyond the scope of this chapter.

Employers will also need to consider the impact of such participation on qualification of their ESPP under Section 423. Among other things, Section 423 requires (1) that all otherwise eligible employees of any corporation whose employees participate be allowed to participate in the ESPP, and (2) that such participants be allowed to participate on the same terms and conditions. These requirements can be problematic with respect to non-U.S. participants. Local laws sometimes impose requirements that are unique to employees in a particular country, which could violate the equal rights and privileges requirement under Section 423.

Employers can exclude employees in foreign entities (e.g., a foreign subsidiary or parent company) simply by choosing not to designate the entity as one of the corporate entities participating in the plan. While all employees of the U.S. employer (the plan sponsor) must be allowed to participate, it is not necessary to allow employees of foreign entities to participate, provided that the foreign entity is considered to be a separate corporate entity from the U.S. employer.

If a foreign corporate entity (either a subsidiary or parent company) is allowed to participate in the U.S. entity's plan, it is permissible for those employees to participate in a separate offering than the offering U.S. employees participate in. The offering can have the same terms and conditions as the offering to U.S. employees or can have differing terms and conditions. Establishing a separate offering for the non-U.S. entity can enable the company to accommodate requirements under local laws without modifying the terms and conditions under which U.S. employees participate in the plan. Where employees of the foreign entity participate in the same offering as U.S. employees, all employees (both U.S. employees and those of the foreign entity) must be permitted to participate on an equal basis.

Challenges can arise where the non-U.S. employees work out of branch offices or divisions, since the non-U.S. employees will be considered employees of the U.S. employer for purposes of Section 423, and thus must be allowed to participate in the plan and offerings that the U.S. employees participate in.

Employers are permitted to exclude non-U.S. employees if local law prohibits their participation in the plan or if they would have to be allowed to participate in a manner that would cause the plan to violate the requirements of Section 423. Employers can also permit non-U.S. employees to participate in the plan on a less favorable basis than U.S. employees, if so required under local law. The reverse is not true, however; if local law requires additional benefits under the plan to be extended to non-U.S. employees, those benefits must also be extended to U.S. employees if the non-U.S. employees participate in the plan. The only exception is where the non-U.S. employees work for a subsidiary; in that case, as described above, a separate offering could be established for the subsidiary that provides additional benefits that are not allowed under the offering the U.S. employees participate in.

As an alternative to adding non-U.S. employees to the ESPP, many employers implement mirror ESPPs for their non-U.S. employees. These plans, which are not intended to qualify under Section 423, give employers more flexibility in designing the plan to meet the particular requirements of each country and with respect to each employee group. Moreover, it preserves the 423 plan for the benefit of U.S. employees who can benefit from the favorable tax treatment offered under tax-qualified plans. Establishing a separate offering for employees of non-U.S. entities may be a preferable alternative to mirror plans.

Even when not legally required, it is advisable for employees of non-U.S. entities to participate in either a mirror plan or separate offerings from U.S. employees. Because Section 423 requires that all participants in an offering receive equal treatment, administrative errors, such as inadvertently excluding an eligible employee or not allowing an employee to contribute all eligible compensation, can disqualify the entire offering from Section 423. These types of administrative errors are not uncommon in foreign entities, often resulting from miscommunications between the U.S. stock plan administration group and the local payroll group (sometimes compounded by language barriers). Restricting the foreign entity's employees to a separate offering or mirror plan ensures that any administrative errors will not jeopardize the qualified status of the offerings the U.S. employees participate in.

11.3.8 Maximum Number of Shares

In addition to the $25,000 limit discussed above, most plans establish a limit on the number of shares that may be purchased by any one participant in an offering period. For an employee's entry date into an offering to be considered the grant date for tax purposes, the maximum number of shares the employee can purchase must be fixed and determinable at that time. Where no such maximum is established, the grant date for tax purposes only would not occur until the purchase date (the grant for accounting and other purposes would still be the employee's entry date into the offering). The grant date serves four critical purposes under Section 423:

- Establishing the minimum purchase price that must be paid for shares under the plan. As mentioned above, the purchase price cannot be less than the lesser of 85% of the fair market value on the grant date or the purchase date. Because of this minimum price requirement, if the grant date does not occur until the purchase date (i.e., if the plan does not specify an individual purchase limit), the purchase price cannot be based on the lesser of the fair market value at the beginning or the end of the offering; the price would have to be calculated as a percentage of the purchase date fair market value.

- Establishing the value of the shares for purposes of the $25,000 limitation.

- Establishing the start of the statutory holding period necessary to receive preferential tax treatment. Shares acquired under an ESPP must be held for two years from the date of grant (as well as one year from the date of purchase).

- Determining the amount of ordinary income recognized on a qualifying disposition.

Most employers that offer a Section 423 ESPP, and especially those that want to offer a plan where the price is based on the fair market value at the beginning of the offering or the lesser of the fair market value at the beginning or the end of the offering, will want to establish a maximum number of shares that each participant can purchase during an offering period, so that employees' entry dates into each offering are considered their grant dates under Section 423. Neither the $25,000 limitation nor the maximum number of shares that can be issued under the plan is sufficient for this purpose; a separate, per-person, per-offering limit must be specified. This limit can be a specified number of shares or can be determined via a formula, provided that the maximum number of shares can be computed upon each employee's entry into the offering. The limit can be specified in the terms of the plan or can be discretionary, so long as the maximum is established and is no longer subject to adjustment before the beginning of each offering. It is permissible for the maximum to be large enough that no employees are ever expected to be subject to it.

In addition to establishing employees' entry dates into the offering as the grant date, a limit on purchases is recommended to help regulate use of the plan's share reserve.

11.3.9 Price Discount or Contribution Match

Most ESPPs offer an economic incentive for employees to participate in the form of a discount or a match on employee contributions. This economic benefit is one of the key drivers of employee participation; plans that do not offer such an incentive or offer a minimal incentive (e.g., a 5% discount) are likely to experience considerably lower participation rates.

For Section 423 ESPPs, the most common practice is to offer a discount of 15%, the maximum allowed under the tax code. Even for nonqualified plans, although though there is no statutory limit on the amount of discount that can be offered, it is rare that plans offer a discount in excess of 15%.[2] It is also common for nonqualified plans to not offer any discount. Plans that do not offer a discount serve as a convenient way for employees to by company stock without paying brokerage fees on their purchases; they otherwise offer no benefits over simply buying the stock on the open market.

Economically, a match on employee contributions delivers the same benefit as a discounted purchase price. A 15% discount equates to 17.6% match on contributions. For example, say that an employee contributes $1,000 to an ESPP and the company matches the contribution by $176 (17.6% of $1,000). If the stock is purchased at $10 per share, the employee purchases 117 shares (rounded down to the nearest whole share). Alternatively, if instead of matching the employee's contributions, the company discounts the purchase price by 15% to $8.50, the unmatched contributions of $1,000, divided by a price of $8.50, also result in a purchase of 117 shares.

From a perceived value standpoint, however, a match may have a significant advantage over a discount. It is arguably easier to communicate the value of an extra $176 to employees than to explain how a 15% discount equates to the same thing. Unfortunately, it is not clear that a match is permissible under Section 423; the statute simply does not contemplate this benefit being delivered in the form of a contribution match.

---

2.   The 2020 NASPP and Deloitte Consulting Domestic Stock Plan Administration Survey reported that among companies that offered a Section 423 ESPP, 70% offered a 15% discount. Among companies that offered a nonqualified plan (only 24% of the total respondents that offered an ESPP), 32% did not offer a discount, and no respondents offered a discount of greater than 15%. A match (instead of a discount) was offered by 23% of respondents with nonqualified plans (data was not collected on the amount of the match).

11.3.10 Interest

Money contributed to the plan by employees becomes part of the employer's general assets. In the event the employee terminates employment, this money is refunded, typically without interest.

11.3.11 Open-Market Plans

Although most companies that implement ESPPs choose to set aside authorized but unissued or treasury shares to be purchased under the plan, it is also possible for the shares employees acquire under the plan to be purchased from the open market rather than from a pool of reserved shares. Not surprisingly, there are both pros and cons to open-market ESPPs:

- *No discounts.* It is not possible to offer a discounted price in an open-market ESPP. When employees are purchasing treasury or authorized but unissued shares directly from the company, the company can determine the price. But when employees are buying stock from the open market, they have to pay full price for the stock, even if the company is facilitating the purchase. Companies can, however, offer an economic benefit to employees by matching the contributions employees make to the plan. As noted above, this delivers the same economic benefit as a discount (but will result in a cash outflow for the company—see below).

- *No dilution.* One of the most significant advantages of open-market ESPPs is that the shares employees are purchasing are already issued and outstanding, so the plan is not dilutive. (To clarify, an open-market plan does not result in any additional dilution in that it does not result in the issuance of new shares; assuming employees hold the stock acquired under the plan, voting power is still transferred from outside investors to employees. For most companies, however, the votes held by employees are likely insufficient to swing a shareholder election, nor can companies assume that employees will vote with management.)

  The plan does not have any effect on basic or diluted earnings-per-share calculations (because the shares are already issued and outstanding and thus are already included in EPS), and companies do not need to implement a repurchase program to offset the shares issued under the plan.

• *Impact on stock price.* Some companies that offer ESPPs find that their stock price declines slightly after a purchase because their stock's daily trading volume is not sufficient to absorb the employee sales. It is possible that an open-market ESPP would have the opposite effect. The large acquisition of stock needed to fill employee purchase requests might cause the company's stock price to increase slightly (of course, if a majority of employees immediately sell the stock, the increase would be short-lived).

This is a potential challenge to implementing an open-market ESPP, particularly if the plan offers a match that incents participation: the company's stock must have sufficient trading volume to support the purchases. Moreover, companies would not want to give investors or regulators the impression that the plan is a vehicle for manipulating the company's stock price. More frequent purchase intervals (e.g., monthly or bimonthly) could help alleviate this concern by reducing the aggregate number of shares purchased on any given purchase date.

• *Shareholder approval may not be required.* Both the NYSE and Nasdaq exempt open-market purchase plans from the requirement that listed companies obtain shareholder approval for equity compensation plans that they offer. Note, however, that it does not appear that this exemption can be relied on for plans that match employee contributions.

• *Cash flow considerations.* ESPPs in which shares are purchased directly from the company create positive cash flow for the company in the form of the purchase price. These funds are typically available to the company as soon as they are contributed (i.e., the company does not have to wait until the purchase occurs to use the funds) and can be used for any legitimate business purpose. An obvious disadvantage of open-market purchase plans is that these plans do not result in positive cash flow for the company. Moreover, if a match is paid on employee contributions, the plan will result in cash outflow. While ESPPs generally are not implemented for purposes of raising capital (plans that are implemented primarily for capital-raising purposes cannot be registered on Form S-8), some companies value the cash flow generated by the plan.

- *SEC registration.* Because the shares purchased under the plan will be bought from the open market and thus are already registered, it may not be necessary to register the plan with the SEC.

11.3.12 Cashless Funding

In addition to, or instead of, funding purchases in the plan through payroll deductions, purchases can be funded through a "cashless" feature under which some of the purchased shares are sold and the sale proceeds are used to pay the purchase price. This feature operates in much the same way as a sell-to-cover exercise of an employee stock option.

Typically, companies expect employees to contribute a minimum amount to the plan (although this is not required), and additional funds are provided to the employee through a sale of the purchased shares. For example, in a plan that caps contributions at 10%, an employee might agree to contribute 1% of pay and to sell shares to raise proceeds equal to 9% of his or her pay, resulting in a total contribution equal to 10% of his or her pay.

In ESPPs that offer a discount or contribution match, the number of shares purchased will exceed the number of shares that need to be sold to cover the cost of the purchase. Generally, just enough shares are sold to cover the funds necessary for the purchase and any transaction fees resulting from the sale; the remaining net shares are issued to the employee. This funding mechanism is not available for ESPPs that do not offer a discount or contribution match.

11.3.13 Whole or Fractional Shares

ESPPs can permit employees to purchase only whole shares or can allow employees to purchase fractional shares. Where only whole shares are purchased, the number of shares that employees purchase is rounded down to the nearest whole share, resulting in a small amount of unused contributions for each employee after the purchase. These unused contributions can be refunded through payroll or carried forward to the next purchase.

Allowing employees to purchase fractional shares ensures that their contributions are applied in full to the purchase (unless their purchase is subject to a statutory or plan limitation). When a company's stock price is appreciating, this provides a greater economic benefit to employees than simply carrying forward their unused contributions.

At companies that have a high stock price (e.g., hundreds of dollars per share), some employees may be unable to contribute funds sufficient to purchase a whole share. Allowing fractional share purchases can help ensure that all eligible employees are able to participate in the plan.

11.4 U.S. Federal Income Tax Considerations for Section 423 ESPPs

Note: The tax treatment explained in this section applies to U.S. taxpayers only. Section 423 is part of the U.S. federal tax code; as such, it governs taxation only for purposes of U.S. federal income taxes. Section 423 does not govern the tax treatment of ESPPs in any other tax jurisdictions, including at the state and local level in United States (although most states parallel the federal tax treatment) or non-U.S. tax jurisdictions. Taxpayers of other jurisdictions are subject to relevant tax laws in those jurisdictions; most jurisdictions outside the United States do not provide preferential or deferred taxation for Section 423 ESPPs. A discussion of the tax treatment in these other jurisdictions is beyond the scope of this chapter.

In the United States, where a plan meets all the requirements discussed above, an employee who purchases stock under the ESPP will not recognize income for U.S. federal income tax purposes on the purchase; instead, the tax consequences are deferred until the employee sells or otherwise disposes of the stock.

If stock that was purchased under an ESPP is held for more than one year after the date of purchase *and* more than two years after the beginning of the offering period, or if the employee dies while owning the shares, the disposition of the shares is considered a "qualifying disposition." As such, a portion of the overall gain will be taxed as ordinary income upon the sale (or other disposition). The amount of ordinary income equals the lesser of: (1) the actual gain (the amount by which the fair market value of the shares on the date of sale, gift, or death exceeds the purchase price), or (2) the purchase price discount determined using the stock price on the date of grant (typically the beginning of the offering period). For example, if the ESPP purchase price is 85% of the lesser of the beginning or ending fair market value, the "purchase price discount" is 15% of the beginning fair market value. Alternatively, if the price is 90% of the lesser of the beginning or ending stock price, the "purchase price discount" is 10% of the beginning fair market value. And if the purchase price is 85% of the ending fair market value (i.e., if the plan has no "look-back" provision), the "purchase price discount" is still 15% of the beginning fair market value (assuming that the beginning of the offering is considered the grant date). All additional gain upon the sale of stock is treated as long-term capital gain. If the shares are sold and the sale price is less than the purchase price, there is no ordinary income, and the employee has a long-term capital loss for the difference between the sale price and the purchase price.

If the stock is sold, or is otherwise disposed of, including by way of gift, within either of the Section 423 holding periods (a "disqualifying disposition"), the employee recognizes ordinary income at the time of sale or other disposition taxable to the extent that the fair market value of the stock at the date of purchase was greater than the purchase price (i.e., the "spread" at purchase). This amount is considered ordinary income in the year of sale or other disposition even if no gain is realized on the sale or disposition. This would be the case, for example, in the event of a gift or if the shares were sold at a loss. The difference, if any, between the sale proceeds and the fair market value of the stock at the date of purchase is a capital gain or loss, which is long-term if the stock has been held more than one year.

Ordinary income recognized by the employee upon either a qualifying or disqualifying disposition constitutes taxable income that must generally be reported on a Form W-2.

Subject to the limitations of Code Section 162(m) (the $1 million deduction limit), the employer receives a tax deduction only to the extent that a participant recognizes ordinary income on a disqualifying disposition. The employer does not receive a deduction if the participant meets the holding period requirements. To enable the employer to take full advantage of its tax deduction, participants should be required to notify the employer in writing of the date and terms of any disposition of stock purchased under an ESPP.

When participants sell stock acquired under an ESPP, the broker facilitating the transaction is required to issue a Form 1099-B reporting the sale. For stock acquired after 2010, brokers are required to report the tax basis of securities that are sold on the Form 1099-B issued for the sale. Although shares acquired under an ESPP have a stepped-up basis that includes any ordinary income recognized in connection with the disposition of the shares, brokers are required to report only the purchase price of the shares as the tax basis and cannot include this income in the basis reported on Form 1099-B.[3] Any ordinary income recognized in connection with the disposition of the shares reduces the capital gains (or increases the capital losses) employees report for their sales. Employees will have to report an adjustment to their gain on their tax return using Form 8949 to take this income into account when computing their capital gains or losses. While not legally required, companies may find it advisable to provide instructions to employees on how to report this adjustment so as to ensure that employees do not overestimate the tax they owe as a result of their sale.

The appendix to this chapter illustrates the tax treatment of employees under a Section 423 ESPP.

11.4.1 Tax Withholding

The American Jobs Creation Act, enacted in 2004, exempts Section 423 ESPPs from tax withholding and also excludes purchases under these

---

3. For shares acquired from January 1, 2010 until December 31, 2013, brokers could choose to voluntarily include the compensation income recognized in connection with the disposition of the shares in the tax basis reported on Form 1099-B, to the extent that this information was available to them (in many cases, brokers did not have this information for shares acquired under an ESPP). For shares acquired after January 1, 2014, however, this is no longer permissible. Companies should contact the brokers that service their stock plans to determine their reporting procedures for shares acquired through December 31, 2013, to ensure that any educational materials provided to employees appropriately reflect the brokers reporting procedures. Where employees hold shares at brokers that the company does not have a relationship with (and thus where the company has no insight into the brokers' reporting procedures), it may be necessary to provide employees with additional education on this topic.

plans from the definition of wages for FICA/FUTA tax purposes. (Even transactions that occurred before the enactment of the American Jobs Creation Act are exempted from withholding for federal income, Social Security, and Medicare tax purposes, under a moratorium established in 2002 by IRS Notice 2002-47.) Therefore, employers are not required to withhold federal income tax, Social Security, or Medicare on either purchases or dispositions of shares acquired under a qualified ESPP. In addition, because dispositions of shares acquired under a Section 423 ESPP are exempt from FICA/FUTA, any income recognized in connection with the dispositions is not counted toward the maximum wage base for Social Security or FUTA purposes or toward the threshold at which the additional Medicare tax applies. Note, however, that state tax treatment may differ from the federal treatment described here.

11.4.2 Information Returns and Statements

Section 6039 of the Code requires employers to file a return with the IRS for the first transfer of legal title of shares acquired under a Section 423 ESPP where the purchase price is less than the fair market value on the date of grant or where the price is not fixed and determinable as of the date of grant. The return is required only for the first transfer of the shares, not subsequent transfers. Where, upon purchase, shares are immediately deposited into an employee's account at the employer's captive or designated broker, the deposit of the shares is considered the first transfer, triggering the requirement to file the return. Where the shares are issued in certificate form, are held in a book entry account or with the transfer agent in the employee's name, or are deposited into an account at a broker that the employer does not have a contractual arrangement with, the requirement to file a return under Section 6039 is not triggered until the employee subsequently transfers legal title of the shares.

The returns must be filed on Form 3922 by February 28, if filed on paper, or March 31, if filed electronically (electronic filing is required when an employer has more than 250 returns to file). The returns must include the following information:

- The name, address, and employer identification number of the corporation whose stock was transferred under the plan;

- The name, address, and tax identification number of the participant;

- The date the right to purchase the shares was granted (typically the participant's enrollment date in the offering);

- The fair market value of the stock on date of grant;

- The purchase price as if the shares were purchased on the grant date (required only if the price is less than the fair market value on the grant date or if the price is not fixed and determinable on this date);

- The date the shares were purchased;

- The purchase price;

- The fair market value of the stock on the date of purchase;

- The number of shares transferred; and

- The date the shares were transferred.

In addition, the Code requires that the employer provide participants with a copy of the return filed with the IRS (or an appropriate substitute statement) by January 31.

11.5 Federal Income Tax Considerations for Non-Section 423 ESPPs

In some cases, an ESPP may not qualify under Section 423, either by design or as a result of plan operation.

11.5.1 General Rule

In the case of a broad-based ESPP that does not qualify under Section 423, stock purchased will be treated, for tax purposes, as though it had been acquired under a nonstatutory stock option. As a result, a plan participant will recognize ordinary compensation income for federal income tax purposes at the time of purchase measured by the excess, if any, in the fair market value of the shares at the time of purchase over the purchase price. Subject to the deduction limitation under Code Section 162(m), the company will be entitled to a tax deduction in the amount and at the time that the plan participant recognizes compensation income with respect to shares acquired under the plan.

If the participant is also an employee of the company, the compensation income recognized at the time of purchase will be treated as wages and will be subject to tax withholding by the company and reporting (e.g., on Form W-2). Upon a sale of shares by the participant, any difference between the sales price and the purchase price (plus any compensation income recognized with respect to such shares) will be a capital gain or loss and will qualify for long-term capital gain or loss treatment if the shares have been held for more than one year. The company has no reporting or withholding obligations with respect to capital gains and losses.

Section 6039 does not apply to ESPPs that are not qualified under Section 423, so the company is not required to file the IRS returns or provide the participant statements described in section 11.4.2 for non-Section 423 ESPPs.

11.5.2 Code Section 409A (Nonqualified Deferred Compensation Plans)

The American Jobs Creation Act of 2004 added new Section 409A to the Internal Revenue Code. Section 409A applies to nonqualified deferred compensation (NQDC) and provides that compensation deferred under a NDCP is includible in gross income in the year of deferral, unless (1) certain requirements are met or (2) the compensation is subject to a substantial risk of forfeiture. Failure to comply with Section 409A with respect to a deferred amount results in current taxation of the deferred amount, interest, penalties, and an additional 20% tax.

NQDC is broadly defined under Section 409A as any arrangement that provides for the deferral of compensation to a year later than the year in which the service provider (e.g., the employee) acquires a legally binding right to the compensation. Section 423 ESPPs are not subject to Section 409A, nor are options with an exercise price that is set at or above the grant date fair market value. However, options granted with an exercise price less than the grant date fair market value (i.e., "discount options") are subject to Section 409A. As a result, ESPPs with a discount feature that do not qualify under Section 423 must be considered in the context of Section 409A.

As a general matter, Section 409A subjects the holder of discount options to taxation as and to the extent the option vests, unless the option satisfies the requirements of Section 409A. One way to accomplish this is to fix the option exercise date at the time of grant.

Although typical ESPPs involve the grant of discount options, this should not be fatal under Section 409A since ESPP options become exercisable on predetermined dates (i.e., the options "vest" and are exercised at the same time). As a result, it should be possible to design non-Section 423 ESPPs without running afoul of Section 409A.

11.6   Accounting Considerations

Employers are required to account for ESPPs under Accounting Standards Codification Topic 718 (ASC 718), under which ESPPs can be considered compensatory or noncompensatory. Plans that are noncompensatory are implemented for a purpose other than compensation (e.g., to raise capital or distribute stock to employees) and consequently do not result in any income statement expense. Plans that are compensatory will result in compensation expense in much the same manner as traditional stock options and other forms of stock compensation. To qualify as noncompensatory under ASC 718, a plan must meet the following requirements:

1. The plan must not incorporate any "option-like" features.

2. The plan must allow for the participation of substantially all full-time employees meeting limited employment qualifications on an equitable basis. The standard cites customary employment of 20 hours per week or minimum employment of at least six months as examples of limited employment qualifications that are acceptable. Employment qualifications that are designed to exclude a large group of employees could cause the plan to be considered compensatory.

3. The plan cannot provide for a discount from fair market value for the purchase price that exceeds the reasonable costs of raising capital or stock must be offered to all shareholders under the same terms.

If a plan does not qualify as noncompensatory (and most traditional plans cannot, even under the revised requirements), then it is necessary to estimate the "fair value" of the participation rights or "options" that are granted to participants in the plan.

This discussion of the accounting consequences of ESPPs does not distinguish between qualified and nonqualified ESPPs because, with the exception of the tax implications, both types of plans are generally accounted for in the same manner under ASC 718.

11.6.1 "Option-Like" Features Limitation

To be noncompensatory under ASC 718, an ESPP may not contain any "option-like" features, such as a provision permitting a participating employee to cancel participation before a purchase date or a provision establishing the purchase price as an amount based on the lesser of the fair market value of the company's stock on the date of enrollment or the date of purchase (referred to in ASC 718 as a "look-back option").

There are two limited exceptions to this restriction. First, a plan may contain a provision under which employees are permitted a short period of time (not to exceed 31 days) after the purchase price has been fixed in which to enroll in the plan. Second, the plan may contain a provision that permits a participating employee to cancel participation before a purchase date and receive a refund of amounts previously paid where the purchase price is based solely on the fair market value of the company's stock on the purchase date.

11.6.2 Purchase Discount Limitation

Under ASC 718, there are no restrictions on the discount that can be offered under a noncompensatory ESPP, provided that the stock sold under the plan is offered to all shareholders of that same class of stock under the same terms as those that apply under the plan. If this is not the case, then the discount cannot exceed the cost of raising capital in a public offering. A discount from fair market value of 5% or less is considered to be per se reasonable and does not have to be justified. Where the discount from fair market value is more than 5%, however, the company would have to demonstrate that the cost of raising capital is equal to or exceeds the discount for the plan to be considered noncompensatory. This must be demonstrated not only upon implementation of the plan but also on an ongoing basis, making a discount of greater than 5% impractical for most companies that want to offer a noncompensatory plan. Where the greater discount cannot be justified, the entire discount (not just the portion of the discount that exceeds 5%) is treated as compensatory.

11.6.3 Plans with "Look-Back" Features

An ESPP where the purchase price of the stock is based on 85% of the lesser of the fair market value of the company's stock at the beginning of the offering (the date of "grant") or the date of purchase (the date of "exercise") is considered to provide for so-called "look-back" options. Under ASC 718, these plans are considered compensatory in nature and require the determination of a "fair value" estimate at the time of enrollment (or "grant") for the participation rights (or "options") granted to participating employees.

11.6.4 ESPP Fair Value

The fair value of each participation right or "option" is to be estimated at the grant date (typically the enrollment date—see discussion below) by dividing the right into its components and valuing the instrument as a combination position.

Component 1—Discount. The first component represents the inherent discount in the purchase price formula. A participation right or "option" with an exercise price that equals 85% of the value of the underlying stock on the exercise date is considered to always be worth 15% of the stock price upon exercise. (For a stock that pays no dividends, the "option" is the equivalent of 15% of a share of stock.)

Component 2—Look-back. The second component represents the value of the look-back provision. This value reflects 85% of an at-the-money call option with the specific characteristics of the participation right being granted, as estimated using a standard option-pricing model. The look-back, which is essentially an option to purchase stock in the future at a price set on the enrollment date, is viewed as economically equivalent to a call option (which gives the holder the right to buy stock at a specified price). The look-back is represented by an at-the-money option (rather than a discounted option) because the value of the discount has already been included under the first component; it is for this reason as well that only 85% of the call option value is included in the ESPP option fair value.

Component 3—Additional Shares. While the foregoing reflects the accounting treatment for one common type of ESPP, it does not adequately address the accounting treatment for a variety of plans with "look-back" options that contain additional, and often different, features. In December 1997, the Financial Accounting Standards Board issued FASB Technical Bulletin No. 97-1, now contained in ASC Subtopic 718-50. This section provides guidance on how to account for many of the more common types of ESPPs with a "look-back" option and one or more of the following features: multiple purchase periods, price reset mechanisms, and the ability to change the withholding amount or percentage after the enrollment date.

One of the more significant topics addressed by ASC Section 718-50-55 is the differing accounting treatment for ESPPs that establish a maximum on the enrollment date as to the number of shares of stock that can be purchased (identified as a "Type A plan") and those that permit the employee to purchase as many shares as the full amount of the employee's withholdings will permit, regardless of whether the company's stock price is lower on the purchase date than on the enrollment date (identified as a "Type B plan").

The example given previously for estimating the fair value of a participation right or "option" on the enrollment date is for a Type A plan. In the case of a Type B plan, the prior example is modified to take into consideration the fact that, under this type of plan, the number of shares that an employee may purchase is not fixed. Instead, if the purchase price declines during the period, employees are permitted to purchase additional shares. For example, assume an employee enrolls in an ESPP with a 15% discount and a look-back when the market value is $10 per share. Over the course of the offering, the employee contributes $1,000 to the ESPP. If the stock price increases during the offering, the employee can purchase a maximum of 117 shares. But let us say the fair market value declines to $8 on the purchase date. This reduces the purchase price to $6.80, enabling the employee to purchase a maximum of 147 shares (30 more than he or she could have purchased if the fair market value had increased). These additional shares serve to preserve or "lock in" the gain that existed on the employee's enrollment date. In our example, the spread or gain on the employee's enrollment date is $176 ($1.50 multiplied by 117 shares). If, after the fair market value declines to $8, the employee is limited to only purchasing 117 shares, his or her actual gain on the purchase will be only $140 ($1.20 multiplied by 117 shares). Allowing the employee to purchase the additional 30 shares ensures that he or she realizes the same gain that existed on the employee's enrollment date, or $176 ($1.20 multiplied by 147 shares). This is essentially the benefit provided by a put option, which enables the option holder to sell stock at a guaranteed price, thereby ensuring that the holder receives a minimum amount of gain regardless of market fluctuation. Therefore, under ASC 718, the additional shares employees can purchase if the fair market value declines during the offering period is represented by a third component in the valuation: 15% of the fair value of an at-the-money put option. (Only 15% of the fair value of a put option is included because the guarantee relates only to the 15% discount.)

Calculating the Fair Value

As a consequence of the above factors, the fair value estimate for a Type B plan includes three separate components. The first component is to reflect the inherent discount in the purchase price formula. A participation right or "option" with an exercise price that equals 85% of the value of the underlying stock on the exercise date is considered to always be worth 15% of the stock price upon exercise. (For a stock that pays no dividends, the "option" is the equivalent of 15% of a share of stock.) The second component, which is to be estimated using a standard option-pricing model, is to reflect 85% of a call option with the specific characteristics of the participation right being granted. The third component, which is to be estimated using a standard option-pricing model, is to reflect 15% of a put option using the same measurement assumptions that were used to value the call option component. The sum of these three components would be multiplied by the number of shares being issued under the plan and would result in a compensation cost estimate that would be recognized in the company's income statement. The fair value for a Type A plan includes only the sum of the first two components: the discount and the look-back.

Important note: The preceding discussion assumes an ESPP with a 15% discount. If the discount is a different amount, the percentage of the call and put option included in the ESPP option fair value would be adjusted proportionately. For example, for an ESPP with a 10% discount, the fair value would include 10% of the fair market value on the enrollment date (component 1), 90% of the fair value of a call option (component 2), and, if applicable, 10% of the fair value of a put option (component 3).

Example 1

Assume that a six-month offering begins under an ESPP when the fair market value is $10 per share. The purchase price under the offering is 85% of the lower of the fair market value on the enrollment date or the purchase date, and there is no limit on the number of shares that participants can purchase should the price decline during the period. The company anticipates that $850,000 in contributions will be applied to purchase shares under the offering. Participants have essentially been granted an option: the grant date is their enrollment date and the purchase date is the date the option will be exercised (thus, the option has an expected term of six months). The fair value of the option is calculated as in table 11-2.

Table 11-2

Component 1 (discount)	$1.50	(15% of enrollment/grant date fair market value)
Component 2 (look-back)	$1.25	(85% of at-the-money call option)*
Component 3 (additional shares)	$.20	(15% of at-the-money put option)*
ESPP option fair value	$2.95	
Expected shares to be purchased	100,000	($850,000 in contributions divided by $8.50 price)
Aggregate option fair value	$295,000	

* The option fair value was computed using the Black-Scholes module, assuming 50% volatility, a 3% risk-free interest rate, and no dividend yield.

It is not necessary to know the actual purchase price (or the actual number of shares to be purchased) to value the option granted under the ESPP. Instead, the third component of the valuation (the value of the put option) represents the economic benefit the employee would receive should the price decline, allowing him or her to purchase additional shares.

Example 2

Where there are multiple purchases in an offering, each purchase can be valued as a separate option. If an offering was 24 months in length with purchases occurring every 6 months, at the outset of the offering, four options would be valued: a 6-month option, a 12-month option, an 18-month option, and a 24-month option.

For example, assume a 12-month offering begins when the market value is $10 per share, with purchases occurring every 6 months. The purchase price under the offering is 85% of the lower of the fair market value on the enrollment date or the purchase date, and there is no limit on the number of shares that the employee can purchase should the price decline during the period. The company expects that contributions of $850,000 will be applied to each purchase under the offering. The total expense for the offering is computed as in tables 11-3 and 11-4.

Grant Date

ASC 718 requires a grant date valuation; i.e., the fair value of the right to participate in an ESPP is determined on the grant date. Under ASC 718, the grant date occurs when four conditions have been met:

1. The employer and employee have a mutual understanding of the key terms and conditions of the award.
2. The employer is contingently obligated to issue equity instruments or transfer assets to an employee who renders the requisite services.
3. The employee begins to benefit from, or be adversely affected by, subsequent changes in the price of the employer's equity shares.
4. The required approvals for the grant have been obtained.

Table 11-3. Value of 6-Month Option

Component 1 (discount)	$1.50 (15% of enrollment/grant date fair market value)
Component 2 (look-back)	$1.25 (85% of at-the-money call option)*
Component 3 (additional shares)	$.20 (15% of at-the-money put option)*
Six-month option fair value	$2.95
Expected shares to be purchased	100,000 ($850,000 in contributions divided by $8.50 price)
Aggregate option fair value	$295,000

Table 11-4. Value of 12-Month Option

Component 1 (discount)	$1.50 (15% of enrollment/grant date fair market value)
Component 2 (look-back)	$1.80 (85% of at-the-money call option)*
Component 3 (additional shares)	$.30 (15% of at-the-money put option)*
Six-month option fair value	$3.60
Expected shares to be purchased	100,000 ($850,000 in contributions divided by $8.50 price)
Aggregate option fair value	$360,000
Aggregate offering fair value	$655,000 ($295,000 value of 6-month option plus $360,000 value of 12-month option)

In most cases, all of these conditions will be met on the enrollment date, thereby establishing the grant date for valuation purposes. Even where the grant date for tax purposes does not occur until the purchase date (i.e., because the plan does not specify a per-person, per-offering limit), the grant date for accounting purposes will still likely be the enrollment date. In some cases, however, employees may be permitted to enroll in a plan that has not yet been approved by the company's shareholders. When a new plan is implemented (or an existing plan is amended in a manner that requires shareholder approval), Section 423 simply requires that shareholder approval be obtained within one year of when the board adopts the plan (or amendment). This will defer the grant date to the date shareholder approval is obtained (for ASC 718 purposes only; the grant date for tax purposes is still determined based on the terms of the plan, e.g., whether or not the plan includes a per-person, per-offering limit). No expense will be recognized for the plan until shareholder approval is obtained.

Where companies experience a shortage of shares under the plan in the midst of an offering period, one solution to this shortfall is to make a mid-offering allocation of shares to the plan. If participants are permitted to purchase shares that were allocated to the plan (and approved by the company's shareholders) after the enrollment date, the grant date for these newly allocated shares will be the date the shareholders approved the share allocation (no expense will be recognized for the shares until such date). This treatment can be avoided by limiting purchases to only those shares that were already allocated to the plan and approved by shareholders on the enrollment date.

11.6.5 Automatic Reset and Rollover Mechanisms

Many ESPPs that have multiple purchases within a single offering period include a reset or rollover provision that is triggered when the fair market value has declined during the period. These provisions require that if the fair market value of the stock on the purchase date is less than the fair market value at the beginning of the offering, all employees enrolled in that offering are automatically withdrawn from the plan and immediately reenrolled in a new offering period. Under a reset provision, the employees are reenrolled for only the remainder of the current offering (for example, if the reset mechanism is triggered 6 months into a 24-month offering period, the employees are reenrolled for the remaining 18 months only). Under a rollover provision, the employees are reenrolled in new offering period equal to the length of the original period (for example, if the offering was originally 24 months in length, the employees are reenrolled in a new 24-month offering regardless of when the rollover mechanism is triggered).

ASC Section 718-50-55 addresses both reset mechanisms (a "Type D Plan") and rollover mechanisms (a "Type E Plan"), requiring that both be treated as a modification of the original option. To account for the modification, the employer recognizes all of the cost associated with the original offering period but now also recognizes the incremental cost of the new offering period. The incremental cost is equal to the fair value of the new offering less the fair value of the original offering at the time the reset or rollover mechanism was triggered.

Example 3

Assume the same facts as in Example 2, but assume that the fair market value on the first purchase date is $8 per share, triggering a reset provision in the plan. All participants are automatically withdrawn after the first purchase and re-enrolled at $8 per share for the remaining 6 months of the offering. This is viewed as a modification, i.e., a cancellation of the original offering and the start of a new offering. The company must continue to recognize the $655,000 of expense computed for the original offering, but it now must also recognize the incremental expense of the new offering. The incremental expense is computed as in tables 11-5 and 11-6 (assuming 50% volatility, 5% risk-free interest rate, and no dividend yield on the underlying stock).

In computing the fair value of the cancelled 12-month offering, since the 6-month purchase was completed before the reset, only the value of the 12-month purchase period is applied against the value of the new offering. The value of the 12-month offering is recomputed based on current conditions, as in table 11-6.

The aggregate incremental expense for the new offering is $93,750. This is the fair value of the new offering ($293,750) less the current fair value of the cancelled offering ($200,000). This incremental expense is recognized over the remaining six-month term of the new offering, along with any remaining unamortized expense from the original offering.

11.6.6 Increases in Contribution Rates

ASC Section 718-50-55 treats increases in contribution rates that occur during an offering period as modifications of the original option. By allowing employees to increase their contributions and thereby purchase additional shares under the offering, the employer is considered to have modified the terms of the original option. To account for the modification, the employer recognizes all of the cost associated with the original option but now also recognizes the incremental cost of the new option. The incremental cost is equal to the fair value of the new option less the fair value of the original option at the time the increase occurred.

Table 11-5. Fair Value of New 6-Month Offering

Component 1 (discount)	$1.20	(15% of current fair market value)
Component 2 (look-back)	$1.00	(85% of at-the-money call option.)*
Component 3 (additional shares)	$.15	(15% of at-the-money put option)*
Six-month option fair value	$2.35	
Expected shares to be purchased	125,000	($850,000 in contributions divided by $6.80 price)
Aggregate option fair value	$293,750	

* Both options are assumed to have an $8 exercise price, since both are granted on the reset date when the market value is $8 per share. The fair market value of the underlying stock assumed for valuation purposes is also $8 per share, the value on the reset date.

Table 11-6. Fair Value of Cancelled 12-Month Offering

Component 1 (discount)	$1.20	(15% of current fair market value)
Component 2 (look-back)	$.45	(85% of underwater call option)*
Component 3 (additional shares)	$.35	(15% of in-the-money put option)*
Six-month option fair value	$2.00	
Expected shares to be purchased	100,000	($850,000 in contributions divided by $8.50 price)
Aggregate option fair value	$200,000	

* The exercise price of both options is assumed to be $10 per share, the fair market value when the offering originally began. This means that the call option is underwater (since it provides the right to buy stock at $10 when the current fair market value is only $8), and the put option is in the money (since it provides the right to sell stock at $10 when the current fair market value is only $8). The expected term assumed for both options is 6 months, since there are only 6 months remaining under the offering at the time the reset occurs.

Example 4

Assume the same facts as in Example 1, but also assume that midway through the offering, when the fair market value is $12 per share, a number of participants increase their contribution rate such that the company now anticipates $900,000 in contributions will be applied to purchase shares under the offering. This increase is viewed as a modification that will result in incremental expense, computed as in tables 11-7 and 11-8.

Table 11-7. Fair Value of the New Offering

Component 1 (discount)	$1.80	(15% of current fair market value)
Component 2 (look-back)	$2.00	(85% of in-the-money call option)*
Component 3 (additional shares)	$.05	(15% of underwater put option)*
ESPP option fair value	$3.85	
Expected shares to be purchased	105,882	($900,000 in contributions divided by $8.50 price)
Aggregate option fair value	$407,646	

* The exercise price of both options is assumed to be $10 per share, the fair market value when the offering originally began. This means that call option is in the money (since it provides the right to buy stock at $10 when the current fair market value is higher than this amount) and the put option is underwater (since it provides the right to sell stock at $10 when the current fair market value is higher than this amount). The expected term assumed for both options is three months, since there are only three months remaining under the offering at the time the increase in contribution rates occurs.

Table 11-8. Fair Value of Cancelled Offering

Component 1 (discount)	$1.80	(15% of current fair market value)
Component 2 (look-back)	$2.00	(85% of in-the-money call option)
Component 3 (additional shares)	$.05	(15% of underwater put option)
ESPP option fair value	$3.85	
Expected shares to be purchased	100,000	($850,000 in contributions divided by $8.50 price)
Aggregate option fair value	$385,000	

Table 11-9. Fair Value of the Additional Shares

Component 1 (discount)	$1.80	(15% of current fair market value)
Component 2 (look-back)	$2.00	(85% of in-the-money call option)*
Component 3 (additional shares)	$.05	(15% of underwater put option)*
ESPP option fair value	$3.85	
Additional shares to be purchased	5,882	($50,000 added contributions divided by $8.50 price)
Incremental fair value	$22,646	

The incremental expense resulting from the increase in contribution rates is $22,646. This is the fair value of the new offering ($407,646) less the current fair value of the cancelled offering ($385,000). The incremental expense will be recognized over the remaining three months of the offering, along with any unamortized amounts remaining from the original $295,000 of expense computed for the offering. Thus, the total expense for the offering will be $317,646 ($295,000 original expense plus $22,646 incremental expense).

When contribution rates are increased, the fair value of the cancelled and new offerings will always be the same on a per-share basis. Looking at Example 4, you can see that the only factor that changes in the before-and-after valuations is the number of shares involved in the valuation. This is because an increase in the contributions does not change the price the participants will pay for the stock or any of the other factors required for valuation; the increase only changes the number of shares participants can purchase. Therefore, the incremental value of the increase can be determined by simply computing the fair value of the additional shares as of the date the increase occurs, as in table 11-9.

11.6.7 Forfeitures and Decreases in Contribution Rates and Withdrawals

Under ASC 718, the employer is not required to recognize expense for shares that are forfeited under an ESPP. Therefore, if a plan participant's employment terminates (on either a voluntary or involuntary basis) and the participant consequently forfeits the right to participate in the ESPP, the shares that the former employee would have been able to purchase had he or she not terminated are not treated as a cost to the employer. ASC 718 affords employers the following choice in how they account for forfeitures:

- Estimate forfeitures in advance and adjust the expense recognized for the estimated forfeitures, or
- Account for forfeitures as they occur.

If employers choose to estimate forfeitures, the estimate (and expense recognized for the ESPP) should be adjusted as the employer's expectations change. In addition, if actual forfeitures differ from the estimate, the expense recognized for the plan should be adjusted commensurately.

Accounting for forfeitures as they occur does not require any forfeiture estimates but will cause the employer to recognize a greater amount of expense initially. The employer will adjust the expense recognized for the plan as employees terminate, forfeiting their right to participate in the ESPP. Ultimately, the same amount of expense is recognized under both approaches.

The decision as to how to account for forfeitures is an accounting policy election. A change in election is considered a change in accounting policy, requiring a preferability letter from the employer's auditors and retrospective application to the employer's financials. Employers should account for ESPP forfeitures in the same manner that they account for service-based forfeitures of other awards issued to employees.

Employees' decisions to withdraw from the plan or reduce their rates of contribution are not considered forfeitures because these decisions are voluntary. Just as an employer must recognize expense for an employee stock option that expires unexercised, the employer must recognize expense for the ESPP as if the withdrawals and decreases in contribution rates had not occurred. The shares that the employees could have purchased, if they had not withdrawn or decreased their contribution rate, are treated as a cost to the employer.

11.6.8 Attribution of ESPP Expense

Where the offering period and purchase period are the same length, as in example 1 above (involving a 6-month offering with purchases occurring only at the end of the offering), expense is recognized on a straight-line basis over the length of the offering.

Where purchases occur periodically throughout the offering, as in the case of example 2 above (involving a 24-month offering with purchases occurring every 6 months), companies can choose to recognize expense on a straight-line basis over the duration of the offering or can choose to record expense for each purchase period from the start of the offering (sometimes referred to as the "accelerated attribution method").

Where expense for an example 2 ESPP is accrued on a straight-line basis, there are two approaches that can be used: the traditional method and the ratable method. Under the traditional method, expense is accrued evenly over the entire offering period. Under the ratable method, expense for each purchase is recorded evenly over its purchase period.

When the accelerated attribution approach is applied in the case of example 2, expense for the first purchase under the offering is recognized over 6 months, expense for the second purchase is recognized over 12 months, and so on. This effectively front-loads the expense recognition (hence the term "accelerated attribution"), since, in all but the last purchase period, the company is recognizing expense for multiple purchases at the same time. In this example, the company is recognizing expense for a portion of all four purchase periods during the first six months of the offering.

Example 5: Straight-Line Accrual, Traditional Method

Assume that an ESPP has a 24-month offering beginning on January 1. The offering has two purchase periods of 12 months each. The company's fiscal year corresponds with the calendar year. The expense associated with the first purchase period is $800,000 and the expense for the second purchase period is $1,000,000, resulting in a total expense of $1,800,000 for the offering.

Using a straight-line accrual with the expense allocated evenly throughout the two-year offering period, the company simply allocates an equal portion of the total expense for the offering to each fiscal period in the offering. As a result, the company records $900,000 of expense per year for the offering ($225,000 per quarter).

Example 6: Straight-Line Accrual, Ratable Method

Assume the same facts as in example 5. Using a straight-line ratable accrual, the expense for each purchase is recorded evenly over its respective purchase period. As a result, the company records $800,000 of expense ($200,000 per quarter) in the first year of the offering and $1,000,000 of expense ($250,000 per quarter) in the second year of the offering.

7: Accelerated Attribution

he accelerated attribution approach, expense for each purchase is recorded over a period measured from the start of the offering ե. the purchase date.

In the first year of the offering, the company records the expense for the first purchase period in full and records half of the expense for the second purchase period. This results in expense of $1,300,000 in the first year of the offering ($800,000 for the first offering and $500,000, half of $1,000,000, for the second offering). This equates to $325,000 per quarter. In the second year of the offering, the company records the remaining $500,000 of expense for the second purchase period ($125,000 per quarter).

Table 11-10 compares the expense recorded under each of the three attribution methods used in examples 5 through 7 above. The total expense under each expense attribution approach is the same; the only difference between the three approaches is the timing of expense recognition.

Table 11-10. Comparing ESPP Attribution Methods

Attribution method	Year 1 expense	Year 2 expense	Total expense
Straight-line, expense accrued evenly			
Purchase periods 1 and 2	$900,000	$900,000	$1,800,000
Straight-line, ratable accrual			
Purchase period 1	$800,000		$800,000
Purchase period 2		$1,000,000	$1,000,000
Total	$800,000	$1,000,000	$1,800,000
Accelerated			
Purchase period 1	$800,000		$800,000
Purchase period 2	$500,000	$500,000	$1,000,000
Total	$1,300,000	$500,000	$1,800,000

Upon implementing an ESPP, a company must make a policy decision as to which attribution method it will apply. This decision should not be treated lightly; companies wishing to change attribution methods will have to demonstrate that the new method is better suited to the ESPP and may even be required to file a preferability letter from the company's auditors with their financial statements for the period in which the change is made. Generally, it is expected that most companies will use the same attribution method for the ESPP that they use for other service-based awards under their stock compensation program.

11.7 Additional Considerations

11.7.1 Shareholder Approval

Section 423 of the Code requires that an ESPP be approved by company shareholders within 12 months of its adoption by the board of directors. No further shareholder approval is required unless the company amends the plan to increase the number of shares available for issuance or changes the designation of corporations whose employees may participate in the plan (unless the plan provides that such designations may be made from time to time).

11.7.2 Federal Securities Law

For public companies, shares issued under an ESPP are typically registered with the Securities and Exchange Commission (SEC) on Form S-8. Registration of shares by means of Form S-8 is relatively straightforward. Form S-8 consists of two parts, a prospectus and an information statement. The prospectus is intended to be distributed to participants but is not filed with the SEC. The information statement, which must be filed with the SEC, largely consists of documents, such as annual financial reports, that have been prepared by the company for other purposes and are incorporated in the S-8 by reference.

As a result of the 1996 changes to Rule 16b-3 of the Securities and Exchange Act of 1934, ESPP transactions (other than sales of shares purchased under any ESPP) are exempt from Section 16(b) of the Exchange Act (i.e., the short-swing profit rules). Transactions under any ESPP are exempt from the reporting requirements of Section 16(a) as well.

APPENDIX
Illustration of Section 423 ESPP Tax Treatment

The following examples illustrate the federal income tax consequences when a participant sells stock purchased under a Section 423 ESPP. They assume that the grant date is the enrollment date and a purchase price of 85% of the lower of (1) market value on the enrollment date or (2) market value on the purchase date.

Example 1—Qualifying Disposition: The participant sells stock one or more years after the purchase date *and* two or more years after the enrollment date (i.e., a qualifying disposition). The tax consequences at a variety of sale prices are shown below:

Assumptions:

Enrollment date market value	$5.00	$5.00	$ 5.00	$5.00	$5.00	$5.00
Purchase date market value	10.00	10.00	10.00	4.00	4.00	4.00
Purchase price	4.25	4.25	4.25	3.40	3.40	3.40
Sale price	12.00	8.00	2.50	10.00	3.75	3.00
Actual gain (loss)	$7.75	$3.75	$(1.75)	$6.60	$ .35	$ (.40)

Tax Consequences:

Ordinary income (the lesser of 15% discount at enrollment date or sale price minus purchase price)	$ .75	$ .75	$ —	$ .75	$ .35	$ —
Long-term capital gain (or loss) (sale price, less ordinary income, less purchase price)	$7.00	$3.00	$(1.75)	$5.85	$ —	$ (.40)

Example 2—Disqualifying Disposition: The participant sells stock within one year after the purchase date or within two years after the enrollment date (i.e., a disqualifying disposition). The tax consequences at a variety of sale prices are shown below:

Assumptions:

Enrollment date market value	$5.00	$ 5.00	$ 5.00	$5.00	$5.00	$ 5.00
Purchase date market value	10.00	10.00	10.00	4.00	4.00	4.00
Purchase price	4.25	4.25	4.25	3.40	3.40	3.40
Sale price	12.00	8.00	2.50	10.00	3.75	3.00
Actual gain (loss)	$7.75	$ 3.75	$(1.75)	$6.60	$ .35	$ (.40)

Tax Consequences:

Ordinary income (market value on date of purchase minus purchase price)	$5.75	$ 5.75	$ 5.75	$ .60	$ .60	$ .60
Capital gain (or loss)* (sale price, minus ordinary income, minus purchase price)	$2.00	$(2.00)	$(7.50)	$6.00	$ (.25)	$(1.00)

*If shares are held for more than one year, the capital gain or loss is long-term.

The Role of the Transfer Agent

Joshua McGinn

CONTENTS

An integral part of the stock option process is the issuance and delivery of the shares, which will involve a transfer agent who is responsible to register share issuance and transfer the shares. In addition to these basic functions, transfer agents also perform many other services, such as dividend payments, administering direct stock purchase plans, proxy tabulation for annual stockholder meetings, escheating property deemed abandoned, and merger exchanges, with some transfer agents offering fully integrated stock plan administration services. With most transfer agents operating on proprietary systems, which may result in differing practices, it is highly recommended to contact your representative to review the stock option interface and discuss the process flow, applicable formats, templates, notices, and acceptable mediums to be used.

12.1 Equity Issuance Instructions

For the most part, the main contact an equity professional will have with his or her transfer agent is with communicating the exercise of a stock option or the vesting of a restricted stock award or restricted stock unit and directing the agent to deliver shares. The common practice is to provide an equity issuance letter, which should detail the amount, origin, effective date, and delivery information for the shares. This equity issuance notification should clearly identify the reserve(s) to be debited and provide additional direction if treasury shares should also be debited. Should any shares be used to satisfy tax withholding, instructions should also be provided as to the disposition of such shares (i.e., cancel and retire or post to treasury). Again, one should discuss the format with his or her transfer agent representative and inquire whether the transfer agent has a recommended template to use. An optimal letter will be structured in such a way that a copy of the letter can be also transmitted to the broker, eliminating the need for a separate communication (see the appendix to this chapter). Alternatively, some agents offer web-based online DWAC portals, which offer an efficient and convenient method of conveying share deliveries.

12.2 Control Numbers

A common best practice is to use a sequential control numbering sequence on each option issuance to assist in identifying the transactions. Control numbers will eliminate duplicated transactions and allow the transfer agent to notify the equity professional of any missing instructions. Additionally, transfer agents usually request brokers to reference the respective control number with the electronic delivery requests because it helps verify each transaction (such as delivering the correct director's stock payment when you may have other director deliveries to the same brokerage house but from different offices). Furthermore, a control number will allow the transfer agent to notify the equity professional of any late delivery requests and allow for easier research when conducting reconciliations for any discrepancies.

12.3 Transaction Date

The transaction date for the transfer agent to record an equity issuance is important because it affects the number of shares issued and outstanding, which is relied upon for many calculations and securities filings. One must carefully consider whether to direct the transfer agent to use the exercise date or the settlement date for the date of issuance, especially for companies that pay dividends. Shares exercised and sold on an ex-dividend date ("ex-date") (defined as one business day before a dividend record date under regular T+2 settlement)[1] yet issued and delivered on the record date will actually be paid the dividend payment although the shares were sold without the dividend right. For example, XYZ Corp.'s common stock pays a dividend, and the next record date is February 8, 2023. Under T+2 settlement, the ex-dividend date is February 7, 2023. Ali buys 10 shares on February 6 and will receive the next dividend payment on those shares. Ali buys 10 more shares on February 7 (the ex-date) and so will not receive the dividend payment on those shares (but will receive the dividend after that if Ali still owns those shares as of the next quarterly ex-dividend date).

Equity professionals should also be cautious of delayed share deliveries being made after the dividend record date, in which case the dividend will not be paid to the broker's depository nominee in the normal course of business but rather would need to be processed and paid as an off-cycle payment. As DWAC deliveries to brokers through Depository Trust Company cannot be reflected as of any other date than the actual DWAC delivery date, this can pose both share and cash dividend reconciling challenges.

12.4 Cost Basis Tracking and Reporting

Effective January 1, 2011, issuers, agents, brokers, trustees, and custodians are required to obtain, maintain, and transfer the cost basis

---

1.   The settlement date is expected to be reduced to T+1 in March 2024 (subject to change)

of shares to one another as required under the Emergency Economic Stabilization Act of 2008. As such, the equity professional will need to provide the acquisition date(s) and purchase price(s) to the entity (i.e., the transfer agent or the broker in cases of DWAC deliveries) receiving the shares upon the exercise of options, purchase of ESPP shares, issuance/vestings of restricted stock awards, and so on that occur after January 1, 2011 ("covered" securities). The receiving entity will be responsible for maintaining this cost basis information until the time of transfer or the sale of these covered shares. At the time of transfer of shares from one entity to another, the originating entity is required to deliver a "transfer statement" to the receiving entity within 15 days. If the cost basis information is not received, the receiving entity is obligated to contact the originating entity once and request this information. Should this information be unattainable, the receiving entity may classify the shares as "non-covered." Upon a sale of covered shares, the agent/broker will be responsible to classify the sale as a short-term or long-term transaction and to also calculate the capital gain/loss for each share lot. This information will be reported on Form 1099-B to the holder for each differing share lot and will also be directly furnished to the Internal Revenue Service (IRS). Special care should be taken with selling incentive stock option (ISO) shares and Section 423 ESPP shares under a possible disqualifying disposition because as of January 1, 2014, any ordinary income component is no longer allowed to be added to the cost basis by the agent/broker. Only the actual price paid will be reported as the cost basis, and the employee will need to report any adjustment to his or her gain or loss on Form 8949 when completing his or her individual tax return. As these adjustments can easily be forgotten by the employee or not recognized by a tax preparer at the time the tax return is being prepared, it would be a best practice for the equity professional to include this information in any FAQ document and/or provide alerts or reminder messages with any year-end communications such as Form 3921 and Form 3922. Because the cost basis tracking and reporting regulations are complex, it is advisable for the equity professional to contact his or her transfer agent and broker representative(s) for more information and to discuss the format and requirements for conveying the appropriate cost basis information.

12.5   Reserves

It is common for transfer agents to maintain separate records of individual equity reserves associated with option plans, warrants, private placements, at-the-market (ATM) offerings, and other purposes. It is a good practice to request a listing of the reserves (or view them online) to verify that the correct names and balances are being maintained. It is important that the transfer agent receive appropriate documentation and subsequently record the applicable change to the equity reserves as a result of any stockholder-approved equity plan increase, automatic evergreen increase, and/or possible adjustments caused by a capitalization change, such as a forward or reverse stock split. No one wishes to receive notice that the CEO's option exercise cannot be delivered because there are not adequate shares left in the reserve. One should also update any reserve name changes due to plan amendments and instruct the transfer agent to cancel any residual shares held in expired reserves from old equity plans and unused actions (such as past stock exchanges or secondary offerings). One should also review the reserve balances to ensure that forfeitures and fungible share adjustments are properly being accounted for. It is strongly recommended to establish a monthly or a quarterly reserve reconciliation process with the transfer agent to ensure that all transactions have been properly accounted for and that the reserve has the correct number of shares.

12.6   Authorization Authority

For control purposes, transfer agents usually look for a certificate listing company employees who are authorized to provide option issuance instructions, together with their titles and sample signatures. This certificate can be designed to limit the authority of specific individuals to specific equity plans. If the company requires that dual authorization must be provided with any share issuance request, the certificate should state this as well. An additional certificate may be required if third-party option administrators are allowed to requisition shares directly from the transfer agent. It is important to notify the transfer agent should any individual's authority need to be revoked due to an employment status change. The transfer agent should deactivate any systems access and remove the former employee's authority from the certificate on file. It is a best practice to adopt a process to provide a current certificate to the transfer agent on an annual basis. An issuer may consider providing authorization to its captive broker (usually with an online medium), but the issuer should fully vet the system to ensure that email alerts on DWAC requests are provided to issuer contacts for audit/checks and balances needs as well as to determine whether there are added costs to the issuer for providing the use of such a medium to a third party.

12.7   DWAC Versus DRS

Currently, the most prevalent way to deliver shares from the transfer agent to a brokerage account is through the means of DWAC (deposit/withdrawal at custodian), which is an electronic service offered to broker participants at Depository Trust Company (a central depository that holds book-entry shares for the majority of brokers, banks, and custodians). The broker initiates an electronic request through Depository Trust Company for the issuer's shares, which is presented to the transfer agent, who is linked to the issuer's CUSIP identifier. The DWAC request includes the issue, the originating broker by participant number, the number of shares requested, and a memo field that typically references the transaction or control number. Once the request has been presented to the transfer agent, it is reviewed and either approved, rejected, or set aside with no action taken. If approved, the transfer agent codes the DWAC request for acceptance and increases the Depository Trust Company's FAST book-entry position on the stockholder ledgers while Depository Trust Company credits the broker's participant account for these shares. Although DWACs are not instantaneous, they are fairly immediate depending on the cycle times and systems architecture among the broker, transfer agent, and depository.

It is common for transfer agents to charge the broker or Depository Trust Company directly for processing DWAC transactions in an effort to reduce the costs to the issuer. Some brokers charge these fees back to the issuer or to the optionee(s).

To avoid DWAC fees, it has been suggested to some issuers to deliver a large block of treasury shares to their captive broker from which to draw option exercises. One needs to be aware that this practice results in the treasury stock being registered in a brokerage account and intermingled with outstanding shares, making it difficult to rely on the transfer agent's stock ledgers for ascertaining an accurate number of shares issued and outstanding for dividend payments, proxy voting rights, EPS calculations, and securities filings. As various states prohibit companies holding treasury stock, a request to an issuer to deliver a block of shares from an option reserve could trigger legal issues with issuing shares which have not been fully paid.

An alternative means of delivering stock electronically is through the Direct Registration System (DRS). Brokers have the ability to retrieve book-entry shares from the transfer agent's records as long as they have specific account information, such as (1) the account registration, (2) the account number, (3) the account's Taxpayer Identification Number, and (4) the number of shares. Although primarily used as a means to electronically retrieve shares from an individual person's account at the transfer agent, this service could be used to pull in option shares exercised and credited directly to the optionee(s) or to an account in the broker's name. The broker uses the same equipment as used for a DWAC, but because the DRS request is less manually intensive from the transfer agent's perspective, no DWAC fees are incurred. The limitations with DRS is that it is not immediate but is an overnight process and that individual DRS transactions are limited in value to $3 million, $7.5 million, or $25 million each, depending on the broker's surety level.

12.8   Restricted Stock Awards

For restricted stock awards that are to be issued in the name of the employees and contain voting and dividend rights, most agents record these shares in book form in a protected, separate file. (Similar arrangements can be followed for issuers who allow early exercises of options where the shares have been exercised and issued but not fully vested to the employee, subject to forfeiture or repurchase where the issuer still maintains control over the shares.) It is no longer advisable to issue physical stock certificates with restrictive legends due to the possibility of employees erroneously reporting certificates lost and having them replaced at the transfer agent. Furthermore, relying on book-entry recording avoids time delays and potential "loss in transit" risks associated with physical deliveries of restricted stock certificates.

When setting up the restricted stock file with the transfer agent, the equity professional should provide direction to code the restricted stock file to prohibit sales and share transfers but still allow address changes; possible coding for the direct deposit of dividends; and other general maintenance requests, such as certifying Taxpayer Identification Numbers. The equity professional will need to determine whether the restricted stock information should be made visible to the employee through the transfer agent's Internet and telephone services or shielded from view. Additionally, it needs to be determined whether transaction advices are to be generated and distributed by the transfer agent when any book-entry restricted stock activity occurs or whether they are to be suppressed.

For dividend-paying companies, the issuer further needs to verify that the dividends paid on the restricted stock awards are to be treated as compensation income and reported to the employee by the issuer on Form W-2, and that the transfer agent suppresses any reporting of 1099-DIV income. Although it is highly uncommon, some issuers may decide to treat the dividends paid on restricted stock as 1099-DIV income and have the transfer agent report the payments to the employee and to the IRS.

If it is verified that the dividends on restricted stock are to be treated as compensation, the equity professional should consider whether the full dividend rate is to be paid to the restricted stock participants or whether the dividend rate should be adjusted to reflect withholding (e.g., an adjusted dividend rate of 75% if a withholding rate of 25% is used). Should the adjusted dividend rate be used, the equity professionals will need to work closely with their treasury department to accrue the full dividend but reallocate the difference to their payroll department to be recorded and applied to the employees' paychecks and be filed and paid as tax withholding. The usual practice is to allow for the full dividend to be paid to the employee by the transfer agent and then for the issuer to deduct additional tax from the employee's paychecks.

Further attention is needed if there happen to be any Section 83(b) elections made on the restricted stock awards. As dividends paid on such elections are to be treated and reported as 1099-DIV income, special consideration will need to be made by the transfer agent to account for and administer these accounts appropriately.

12.9 Data Privacy

Extreme care needs to be exercised when transmitting option information and data files to the transfer agent. For standard option exercises using DWAC deliveries, no employee information needs to be transmitted to the transfer agent; only the brokerage house needs to be identified because the shares are being deposited directly to its depository account. There are cases when the transfer agent will need personal employee information, such as when restricted stock awards are to be issued or vested or when an optionee wishes to exercise and hold in his or her own name because he or she does not use a brokerage account. The equity professional should discuss the process for encrypting and protecting files or using a secure Internet portal to deposit records securely into a transfer agent's document repository. Although the recipient's Social Security number will need to be provided with the initial load of a restricted stock issuance, a secondary unique number should also be provided, such as an employee number or, once established and provided by the transfer agent, the transfer agent's account number for the individual. This secondary unique number can then be used as the primary account identifier.

12.10 Form W-9/Form W-8BEN

Social Security numbers or Taxpayer Identification Numbers may be necessary to convey to the transfer agent when loading restricted stock awards or issuing shares into individual's names with exercise-and-hold transactions without a broker. Although the equity professional can furnish these numbers to the transfer agent, in most circumstances the transfer agent will need to obtain its own copy of an executed Form W-9 to comply with U.S. Treasury regulations and eliminate IRS-mandated backup withholding. Transfer agents can solicit this information directly from the individuals, or the equity professional can provide an original or copy of an executed Form W-9. Unfortunately, a copy of a Form W-4 will not satisfy the transfer agent's regulatory compliance requirements. Foreign individuals without Social Security numbers or Taxpayer Identification Numbers may need to execute a Form W-8BEN, which certifies a foreign individual's foreign status and allows the transfer agent to withhold nonresident alien tax at the applicable country treaty rate (10%–20%) instead of the default back-up withholding rate of 24%. Current Treasury regulations require an original copy to be submitted (not a photocopy/facsimile) and that it have a street address (not a P.O. Box address). Furnishing copies of Form W-9s should be done using encryption or a secure Internet portal.

12.11 Online Access

An effective tool provided by most transfer agents is online access to shareholder records. In addition to being able to view specific shareowner activity, these portals provide the ability to retrieve capitalization information and review option issuance activity. A user ID is assigned to an issuer contact; the user ID can be authorized for various levels of access and functionality, including the ability to make address changes and apply special coding to applicable accounts for tracking purposes. These portals also provide various activity reports and lists, such as insider transactions, missing option exercises, and identifying accounts eligible for escheatment.

With the industry undergoing frequent changes, it highly recommended to meet with or call your transfer agent representative regularly to discuss regulatory changes, current offerings, process improvement, new services, industry happenings, and other issues. Some transfer agents publish periodic newsletters addressing important matters, so please ask your representative to be added to their distribution list. Additionally, many transfer agents conduct formal service reviews to ascertain how well they are performing and whether there are opportunities for improvement and additional needs they may be able to serve. So take the opportunity to engage in dialogue with your transfer agent to establish a good rapport and build a relationship on awareness and understanding.

APPENDIX
Sample Equity Issuance Letter

VERIGOOD INC.
123 Main Street
Anywhere, ST 99999

Via Facsimile – (###) ###-#### or
e-mail xxxxxxx@xxxxxxxx.com

Date: xx/xx/2022

Control No. #####

T/A or Option Contact
Transfer Agent
123 First Street
Anywhere, ST 99999

CUSIP: #########

Dear Contact,

You are hereby authorized to issue and deliver the shares of Common stock as indicated below via DWAC.

Date of Exercise: Date ##, 2022

Name of Option Plan:	Number of shares:
Reserve 3 – 2014 Stock Option Plan	12,500
Reserve 4 – 2014 Employee Stock Purchase Plan	
Reserve 5 – 2014 Global Stock Purchase Plan	
Reserve 6 – 2014 Stock Incentive Plan	5,100
Reserve 7 – 2017 Stock Option Plan	
Reserve 8 – 2017 Global Equity Stock Option Plan	8,572
Reserve 10 – 2017 Employee Stock Purchase Plan	
Reserve 11– 2017 Stock Incentive Plan for Non-Employee Directors	
Reserve 12– 2017 Equity Incentive Plan	27,200
Reserve 13 – Assumed 2019 Target Option Plan	
Reserve 14 – 2019 Stock Incentive Plan	
Reserve 14 – 2019 Stock Incentive Plan	1,000
Total Shares to DWAC:	54,372

Broker Name: *Securities Broker*
Broker DTC#:   *0123*
Contact and Phone: *John Smith 555-555-1234*

Sincerely,

Senior Stock Analyst
VeriGood, Inc.
Ph: 555-555-5678

Cc: Broker contact

CHAPTER

13

Annual Meetings

Joshua McGinn

CONTENTS

A company's annual meeting of shareholders is a highly visible and important event at which the company communicates to all of its investors and receives feedback from its investors with responses in the form of favorable or unfavorable voting. The procedural aspects of the shareholder meeting are governed by federal laws (Section 14 of the Securities Exchange Act of 1934, the Sarbanes-Oxley Act of 2002, and the Dodd-Frank Wall Street Reform and Consumer Protection Act of 2010), state laws (Delaware General Corporation Law Sections 211–233, California Corporations Code Sections 600–605, and New York Business Corporation Law Section 602), stock exchange rules (e.g., New York Stock Exchange Listed Company Manual Section 302), and the company's corporate charter and bylaws. As such, the meeting process usually involves in-house counsel and/or outside counsel. As each company has its own needs, preferences, and objectives, the following information is only a general guideline to the annual meeting process; the reader should confer internally and with counsel for planning the annual meeting.

A helpful tool to assist in planning your annual meeting is a "time and responsibility checklist," a document that identifies the responsible party for each task and the respective deadlines. Your counsel or transfer agent can usually provide one to you. It will assist with identifying responsible parties and individuals at the legal department, HR department, compensation department, investor relations department, financial printer, transfer agent, and facilities coordinator. In addition, the schedule will assist you in backing into the various dates/deadlines for filing and mailing the proxy materials, record date, and the broker search date. The checklist will provide a basis for discussion and a framework to verify issues with many variables, such as the form to be used to convey the financials (i.e., a Form 10-K, a Form 10-K wrap, or a more elaborate annual report), whether a Notice of Internet Availability is to be used, what proposals should be added, and a number of other alternatives.

Typically, the equity professional is responsible for providing information in the "Notes to Consolidated Financial Statements" in the Form 10-K, such as confirming the number of shares outstanding as of the fiscal year-end and details on stock-based compensation, such as the number of shares granted, the number of shares exercised and issued, the amount of expense the company reported, and the number of shares remaining under each option plan reserve. There are additional requirements pertaining to directors and officers under Regulation S-K, which may be filed in the Proxy Statement if filed within 120 days of the company's fiscal year-end. The disclosures usually filed in the Proxy Statement are the Summary Compensation Table for the "named executive officers"; tables for grants of plan-based awards, outstanding equity awards, and option exercises and stock vested; potential payments upon termination or change in control; a director and executive stock ownership table; a beneficial ownership table of investors owning 5% or more; and the number of shares outstanding and entitled to vote as of the record date. Again, because the timing and disclosure practices may differ among companies and even possibly between differing years for the same company, one should confer with counsel.

13.1   Key Dates

To return to a more general overview of the annual meeting process, important key dates to review and establish when planning for the shareholder meeting are as follows:

13.1.1   Broker Search

This is a notice from your transfer agent or proxy solicitor to "the street" (banks, brokers, and intermediaries) informing them of your upcoming shareholder meeting, providing the record date, the meeting date, and the type of mailing (a full set of printed proxy materials or mailing a "Notice of Internet Availability") for them to estimate the number of sets of needed materials and to prepare the mailing to their clients. The broker search must be conducted 20 *business* days *before* your record date and please be cautious of any observed industry holidays during that time.

13.1.2   Registering Your Meeting Dates with the Depository Trust Company

As the majority of shares are held by institutional investors in brokerage or bank custody accounts, these shares are actually held in book-entry and registered to the Depository Trust Company's (DTC) nominee name of "Cede & Co." As the official stock ledger will show Cede & Co. being the registered holder on the record date, issuers need to request that DTC assign voting rights to the various banks and brokers who actually hold the shares within DTC as of the record date. DTC accomplishes this by producing an omnibus proxy, which is an official voting document assigning voting rights to the respective brokerage houses and banks holding shares and should be retained with the official records of the meeting. Without the omnibus proxy, votes submitted by the brokers could not be received and tabulated if the shares remained in the name of Cede & Co. The first step to register your meeting with DTC is to complete a letter (see appendix A to this chapter) and send it via email to proxyannouncements@dtcc.com with a courtesy copy to your tabulation agent. You will then need to log into the DTC's website and enter these dates, establish your payment method, and request a Security Position Report (SPR) to be transmitted to your tabulation agent as an authorized third party. Please note that as releasing records to unauthorized parties is a security risk, the DTC system has set up a number of security measures, and it is recommended to begin the registration process early, especially if the issuer may be new, such as the case with a recent initial public offering (IPO),as additional steps will need to be taken in order to set up the company profile and authorized officers from the company. After the record date, the DTC omnibus proxy, which is the actual legal voting assignment, complete with a color stamp, will be available for download. Please arrange to print this document, provide it to your proxy tabulation agent and, if applicable, your proxy solicitor, and retain it to have on hand at the annual meeting.

13.1.3   Record Date

The record date is the date set pursuant to a company's bylaws that establishes which holders of the company's stock are entitled to vote at the shareholders meeting. The record date for most states cannot fall more than 60 days before the meeting date, and it is advised to keep to the 60-day time period because it provides more time to prepare the proxy documents before the filing and mailing date. This additional time will come in helpful, especially if a Notice of Internet Availability is used, as the Notice of Internet Availability must be *completely* mailed 40 days *before* the meeting date. The equity professional will most likely be the one responsible for confirming with the transfer agent the number of shares outstanding and eligible to vote as of the record date, reconciling for last-minute exercises and late Deposit/ Withdrawal At Custodian (DWAC) deliveries. The equity professional should also determine whether the company is holding any treasury shares or unexercised shares in a corporate account with a broker and then coordinate the delivery of these shares to the transfer agent on or before the record date so they can be recognized as company treasury stock and voting rights suppressed.

13.1.4 Preliminary Filing Date (If Applicable)

If your agenda items contain additional proposals other than the regular items, such as adoption of a new stock plan or a shareholder proposal, you may need to file a preliminary copy of your proxy statement with the Securities and Exchange Commission (SEC) for review. This review process may take 10 business days, so you will need to build in enough advance time in your schedule so as to provide action and responses before having to finalize and mail the documents.

13.1.5 Mail Date

A proper mail date should be scheduled after the record date to provide ample time for the final drafting of the proxy materials, the printing and delivery of the materials, and the preparation of the investor files. It should also incorporate an appropriate amount of time should any agenda item be considered sensitive and require additional time to solicit. Also, if using a Notice of Internet Availability, the mail date has to be scheduled for no later than 40 days before the meeting date. The mailing date will also have an impact on when the initial broker voting may be cast because if the brokers mail the materials 25 days before the meeting, they may issue a "15-day vote," or if the materials are mailed within 15 days, they may issue a "10-day vote." Please be aware that 'broker intermediaries' who conduct these mailings on behalf of the brokers/banks may need additional processing time to receive files from the brokers/banks.

13.1.6 Filing Date

On the filing date, the proxy statement and proxy card should be filed with the SEC on Schedule DEF 14A via EDGAR. Seven copies of the company's annual report should be sent to the SEC on the mail date. If your company is listed on the New York Stock Exchange (NYSE), then three definitive copies of all proxy materials (including the proxy card) must be sent with the NYSE no later than the date on which such materials are sent to any security holder.

If you did not file certain required disclosures under Regulation S-K of the Securities Act of 1933 (for example, the named executive officers' compensation) in your 10-K and are not able to file these disclosures in the proxy statement within 120 days from the fiscal year-end, you will then need to file an amendment to the Form 10-K to include the required disclosures within the 120 days from the fiscal year-end.

13.1.7 Hosted Website

An SEC-compliant website hosting the meeting documents is to be made effective on the Filing/Mail date. This website needs to be indexed, searchable, downloadable, printable, and "cookie-free" with no tracking. It is usually linked to the shareholder voting site, and your tabulation agent should have a module available and will request copies of the meeting documents in advance of the mailing date in order to create this website. It is recommended that you review the website in a test mode before the website goes live.

13.1.8 Meeting Date

According to NYSE regulations (which most brokers/banks adhere to), the meeting date cannot fall less than 10 days from the mail date and, for most companies, more than 60 days from your record date (based on the state of incorporation's rules).The company's bylaws may also dictate certain parameters of the annual meeting date, and it is a best corporate governance practice to set the annual meeting date when your board of directors and senior executive officers are available to attend.

13.2   Documents for the Annual Meeting

- *Script.* The primary purpose of the annual meeting is to satisfy state business laws to elect directors and allow shareholders to vote upon other matters to be brought before them. It is recommended that a script be written to first address the business purpose of the meeting. Presentations, remarks, and a question-and-answer period should be placed after the polls close and the results of the voting have been announced. Special addenda should be added so that the chair of the meeting will have a script to follow to address any unruly behavior or unexpected events that may require a need to close the meeting early.

- *Affidavit of Mailing.* The mail house responsible for mailing the proxy materials should issue an Affidavit of Mailing identifying and attesting that the proxy materials were mailed on a specified mail date.

- *Record Date List.* A certified list of shareholders as of the record date should be produced. Pursuant to the company's bylaws and state law, it should be made available for inspection by shareholders 10 days before the meeting date at the meeting location or at the offices of the company. This list should also be retained with the official records of the meeting.

- *DTC Omnibus Proxy.* As mentioned above, the company should have a copy of the DTC Omnibus Proxy because this is the legal voting assignment for the tabulation agent to receive and accept voting from the bank and brokerage houses.

- *Oath of Inspector.* Delaware and most other states request that an independent inspector be appointed to examine proxies and ballots faithfully and with strict impartiality and to accurately report the voting results (see appendix B to this chapter).This independence requirement usually is satisfied with a representative of the tabula-tion agent being appointed as the inspector of election because the agent has been overseeing the voting up to the meeting. This form is usually stamped by a notary public.

- *Proxy Committee Ballot.* As returned proxy votes actually appoint a "proxy" representative to vote their shares in-person at the meeting as directed by the holder, it is important that a Proxy Committee Ballot be prepared presenting all voting received by proxy to be executed by the appointed proxy or proxies (see appendix C to this chapter). This document should be filed with the records of the meeting.

• *Shareholder Ballot.* A shareholder ballot should be prepared and made available during the shareholder meeting for those shareholders who want to vote in-person at the meeting. The inspector of election will verify the identity, validity, and authority of the shareholder ballot and ascertain whether any supporting documentation is required, such as a legal proxy. A legal proxy is a voting assignment from the broker to the shareholder in order to vote in-person since the shares are actually recorded in the broker's name.

• *Certificate of Tabulation/Report of Inspector.* As the role of the inspector of election is to verify and report the official voting results, this is concluded with a report of the inspector certifying the number of shares represented at the meeting for quorum purposes and the results of the voting on the individual proposals (see appendix D to this chapter).Special attention should be given to the non-routine proposals and reporting of the respective number of "broker no-votes."

• *Form 8-K.* The results of the report of inspector need to be filed with the SEC on Form 8-K within four days from the meeting date.

13.3 Other Important Considerations to Be Aware Of

For an annual meeting, one cannot solicit voting without first or simultaneously presenting the financial condition of the company. This is usually accomplished with the annual report or Form 10-K being distributed before or with the proxy statement.

13.3.1 Directors

Depending on the company's bylaws, there may be annual elections for the entire slate of directors or, if a staggered board exists, for a class of certain directors. Additionally, the bylaws will determine the votes required to approve the nominees by either a majority or plurality voting standard for the election of directors. Under the majority vote standard, each nominee must be elected by a majority of the votes cast by the shares present, in-person, or represented by proxy and entitled to vote. Under plurality vote, the nominees receiving the most votes cast by the shares present in-person or represented by proxy and entitled to vote will be elected. Under plurality voting, a withhold vote does not count as a vote against the nominee because it is interpreted more as an abstention from giving authority to vote for the nominee's election. With a set number of director seats for election and a slate of nominees for that same number of seats, nominees can be elected with a single vote being cast in favor of their election with plurality voting.

13.3.2   Auditors

Although the proposal to ratify the board's decision to (re)appoint the auditors is not a required proposal to be brought before the shareholders, most companies do present this to a shareholder vote because it is considered good corporate governance practice and to help obtain a quorum (usually 50% plus one share of all shares entitled to vote) in order to properly hold the meeting. The auditor proposal is considered a "routine" matter under NYSE guidelines, and brokers are able to cast votes on behalf of any non-responding investors in favor of this proposal. In contrast, director nomination and executive compensation proposals are deemed "non-routine," and any non-voted shares cannot be voted and must be classified as a "broker no-vote."

13.3.3   Executive Compensation

Also known as "Say on Pay," is a non-binding vote to approve the company's compensation to the executive officers. This is usually an annual vote unless the shareholders have approved an alternative review period of every two or three years. Companies with IPOs closing after December 8, 2011, and classified as "emerging growth companies" are able to forego the Say-on-Pay proposal for five years unless they exceed $1 billion in gross revenues.

13.3.4   Shareholder Proposals

Shareholders are able to submit certain items for vote by meeting the requirements set forth in the company's bylaws and Rule 14a-8 under the Securities Exchange Act of 1934. Proposals presented by shareholders vary from corporate governance issues to social and environmental issues. Popular shareholder proposals over the past several years have included adoption of a majority vote standard for election of directors; separation of the offices of CEO and chairman of the board; and most recently proxy access.

13.3.5 Mail Type

Historically, past typical mailings of proxy materials have been conducted with mailing a "full set" of proxy materials consisting of a financial report (annual report or Form 10-K), a proxy statement, a proxy card, and a return envelope. An increasing more popular and cost effective method being used more often now is mailing a "Notice of Internet Availability," which is a single-page notice informing the shareholder of the meeting details, voting items, a URL address where they may view the financial document and proxy statement, and further instructions on how to vote their shares. Mailing a Notice of Internet Availability requires that the notices be completely mailed 40 days before the meeting date. It is important to know that a commencement or partial mailing on the 40th day does not comply with the rules. Another type of distribution method is to use electronic distribution of a notice of the annual meeting and proxy materials. This method usually requires receiving consent from shareholders and for them to provide their email addresses. This method is very helpful for employee plans such as a 401(k), whereas if the company uses email as the usual method of communicating to their employees, e-proxy emails can be sent to them without explicit consent. Please check with the plan trustee to find whether the trustee will allow either a Notice of Internet Availability or e-distribution because there may be ERISA concerns disallowing such media to be used.

13.3.6 Meeting Location

The company will need to consider what the best meeting location should be. Weighing costs of external meeting sites with security, liability, and resources (space, catering, audio-visual, parking, etc.) versus hosting the meeting on-site is a discussion that should be held early in the steps with meeting planning.

13.3.7   Virtual Shareholder Meetings

Online, virtual shareholder meetings have become more popular over the past five years, and they were widely adopted in 2020 due to shelter-in-place restrictions as a result of the COVID-19 pandemic. Under the Delaware Business Code (and the laws of most other states), to conduct a virtual shareholder meeting, you must (1) allow voting up to when the official polls close (rather than midnight before the meeting) and (2) allow shareholders to converse with executive management during the meeting. Basically the only requirement (based on SEC guidance and Delaware statutes) is that the annual meeting process must accommodate online voting until the chair officially closes the poll, and shareholders must have the ability to ask questions and engage in dialogue with management. The mailing, tabulation, and proxy solicitation process remain unchanged, but there is the added requirement for shareholders to access an online interface during the annual meeting. Hence, a company should check with its transfer agent contact to see what its offering provides.

13.3.8   Proxy Solicitation

With the investor environment in flux with economic and activist influences, the company should formulate a strategy for its proxy solicitation effort. The basic practice is to mail the proxy materials and wait for investors to vote on their own. Depending on the time between mail and meeting, the mail medium, the investor profile, and the matters to be voted upon, an issuer may not receive a lot of voting or may receive an unexpected "against" vote. It is advisable to determine the amount of institutional, retail, and insider/employee populations and to help conduct vote projections. The company may wish to engage a proxy solicitation firm to help identify perceived sensitive issues and practices observed by institutional and proxy advisory firms. They will identify large investors and will determine how they have voted on similar proposals in the past to obtain a vote projection. They will also assist with monitoring and actively obtaining votes to attain passage.

13.3.9   Proxy Advisory Firms

There are firms that review companies' proxy materials and issue voting recommendations to institutional investors. The analysis provided includes a review of corporate governance and compensation practices as well as a comparison of executive compensation and stock price performance among the issuer's peers and other issuers of similar profile. The report is usually issued approximately two weeks before the meeting date, so any unexpected, adverse recommendation may be challenging to overcome or alter with so little advance notice before the meeting.

13.4 Conclusion

As mentioned in the opening paragraphs, the annual meeting and proxy process is a large and complicated project that requires coordination among many entities. There are many alternatives available to the company, so it is advisable to confer with counsel; to check with a number of resources to receive updates, advice, and recommendations; and to engage assistance from compensation consultants, law firms, the financial printer, the transfer agent, proxy solicitation firms, and peers early in the process to end up with a plan that works best for your company.

APPENDIX A
DTC Omnibus Proxy Request

[Company Letterhead]

[Date]

The Depository Trust Company

via email to: proxy announcements@dtcc.com

                 [proxy tabulator]

Please be advised that [Company Name] has set the following dates relative to its meeting.

Record date: _____

Meeting date: _____

Meeting type: _____

Classes of stock eligible to vote include:

Class   CUSIP#

_____   _____

If you have any questions, please contact me via the phone number or email address included below.

Sincerely,

[Officer's Name]

[Title]

[Tel number, fax number, email address]

APPENDIX B

Oath of Inspector of Election

I, [Name], having been appointed to act as Inspector of Election at the Annual Meeting of Stockholders of [Company Name], a [Delaware] corporation, to be held on [Day], [Month] [Date], [Year], and at any adjournments or postponements thereof, do solemnly swear that I will fairly, impartially and to the very best of my abilities execute the duties of Inspector of Election at such meeting, and I will faithfully and with strict impartiality, examine the proxies and ballots and canvass the votes cast at such meeting and will truthfully and accurately report the results thereof.

By: _____
[Name]

[Notary Seal]

APPENDIX C
Proxy Committee Ballot

[COMPANY NAME]

Annual Meeting of Stockholders

[Date]

Pursuant to the authority vested in us by virtue of proxies granted by the holders of shares of Common Stock of [Company Name] (the "Company"), we hereby cast the votes to which those shares are entitled to as follows:

Proposal 1 Election of the following [Class I] Directors.

Nominee:	Votes For	Votes Withheld
[Nominee 1]	[shares]	[shares]
[Nominee 2]	[shares]	[shares]
[Nominee 3]	[shares]	[shares]

Proposal 2 [Description]

	Shares Voted
For	[shares]
Against	[shares]
Abstain	[shares]

Dated: [Date]

By: _____

[Appointed Proxy]

By: _____

[Appointed Proxy]

APPENDIX D
Certificate of Inspector of Election

The undersigned, having been designated to act as Inspector of Election at the Annual Meeting of Stockholders of [Company Name], DOES HEREBY CERTIFY AS FOLLOWS:

FIRST: The Annual Meeting of Stockholders (the "Annual Meeting") of [Company Name], a [Delaware] corporation (the "Company") was convened at [Time] [Time Zone), on [Month] [Day], [Year], at [Location of Meeting].

SECOND: On the record date for determining the Company's stockholders entitled to notice of and to vote at the Annual Meeting, [Record Date], there were issued and outstanding [Number] shares of Common Stock of the Company.

THIRD: There were present at the Annual Meeting in person or by proxy, stockholders of the Company who were the holders of [Number][Quorum Percentage] shares of Common Stock of the Company entitled to vote thereat constituting a quorum.

FOURTH: The proposals presented received the following votes:

Proposal 1 Election of the following [Class I] Directors.

Nominee:	Votes For	Votes Withheld	Percent of Voted	Broker Non-Votes
Nominee 1	[shares]	[shares]	[%]	[shares]
Nominee 2	[shares]	[shares]	[%]	[shares]
Nominee 3	[shares]	[shares]	[%]	[shares]

The three nominees have been elected as [Class I] Directors for the terms set forth in the company's proxy statement.

Proposal 2 [Description]

	Shares Voted	Percent of Voting
For	[shares]	[%]
Against	[shares]	[%]
Abstain	[shares]	[%]
Broker Non-Vote	[shares]	-0-

The [Description of proposal] was approved.

Dated: [Date]

By: _____

[Name]

Inspector of Election

14

State Mobility Issues for Equity Compensation

Marlene Zobayan

CONTENTS

D oing business often requires that employees travel, whether to establish new offices, meet potential customers and vendors, attend trainings, or even relocate for personal reasons. Some movement is temporary, other moves are permanent, but all can have tax consequences. This chapter addresses the issues regarding such movement between U.S. states. It also briefly addresses the state tax situation for an employee who moves or travels into or out of the United States.[1]

A *mobile employee* is an employee who works in more than one tax jurisdiction between the grant of an equity award and the date when the equity award is taxable under local law. There are different types of mobile employees, as outlined in more detail below. A tax jurisdiction can be a country, state, city, or region. Each jurisdiction that the mobile employee has worked in may tax some or all of the income associated with each equity award.

State rules regarding the taxation of equity awards vary. For example, unlike federal law and the laws of most other states, Pennsylvania state law does not confer tax benefits for ISOs and ESPPs.[2] Other states, such as Rhode Island, have their own versions of qualified plans.[3] When employees work or reside in more than one state while their equity awards are outstanding, each state may have the right to tax the employees on the income from the equity award. An employee may pay tax in more than one state and may be subject to tax in a state where they no longer live or work or have never lived or worked. This chapter focuses on the employer payroll compliance aspects, not the employees' ultimate reporting obligation. Note that payroll compliance may also vary if there is no corporate nexus in that particular state.

14.1 Types of Mobility

Mobility for tax purposes takes different forms:

• *Assignee/Secondee*—an employee who lives in one state but is sent to live and work in another state for a period of time, creating a taxable presence in the other state. The intent with these arrange-

---

1. For the purposes of this chapter, the District of Columbia will be included in the term *state*.

2. For example, see 61 PA Code § 101.6(f), which does not distinguish between incentive, qualified, restricted, or nonqualified stock options for determinations of timing income receipt.

3. See generally RI Gen L § 44-3-44 (2021).

ments is that the employee will return home after the period of assignment. Assignees are likely to stay on their home payroll.

- *Transfer*—an employee who moves from one state to another, with the duration of the move being indefinite. A transfer will likely change payroll to the new location.

- *Traveler*—an employee who goes to work in a new location for a short period of time, usually not establishing residency in the new state. Travelers will remain on their home payroll.

- *Commuter*—an employee who lives in one state but commutes to work in another. The payroll system should already have the live-in and work-in states configured appropriately.

- *Telecommuter*—an employee who lives and works in one state but works remotely for an employer located in another state. The payroll system should already have the live-in and work-in states configured appropriately.

It is possible for an employee to have more than one type of mobility. For example, a traveler may decide to more to the new state and become a transfer. Remote workers may also fall into one of the above mobility types. Remote workers are discussed in section 14.10.

The definitions above are colloquial, and each company or organization may use these terms differently.

Each type of mobile employee presents unique challenges; these are discussed in section 14.5.

14.2 Taxation of Residents and Nonresidents

A common mistake is to think that residency in a state is established based only on the number of days spent in that state. Several factors may lead to tax residency in a state, including:

- the number of days spent in the state,

- the intention regarding the stay, and

- the availability of permanent housing and/or family ties.

> *Example 1.* Bob moves from Massachusetts to Virginia on September 1 with the intention of making Virginia his home indefinitely. He will be deemed to be

a Virginia resident from September 1 even though he will not spend 183 days in Virginia during the year.[4]

Each state's rules vary as to the circumstances in which an individual is considered to be a resident, as do each state's rules on breaking residency. For example, the California Franchise Tax Board considers an individual who leaves California to take up employment elsewhere as a California resident if they return to California for more than 45 days within a taxable year.[5]

Most states tax residents on worldwide income, i.e., the resident individual's entire income, regardless of where it is earned. The resident state may (or may not) give tax credits or exemptions for taxes paid to another state on income earned in such other state.

Most states tax nonresidents on sourced income—that is, income the nonresident individual earns in that state—but not income earned elsewhere. Note, however, this is not true of all states. For example, the District of Columbia taxes residents only.

> *Example 2.* Anne is a resident of California and has a total income of $100,000. However, she has earned $30,000 in Utah and the remaining $70,000 in California. Utah taxes Anne on $30,000. California taxes Anne on the full $100,000 but allows her a credit for Utah taxes paid on the $30,000 of income earned in Utah.[6]

14.3 Sourcing of Income: General Principles

When a person is (or has been) working or living in more than one state, the taxation can become complicated. Every tax jurisdiction that the individual has lived or worked in may want to tax their income. Each state has different laws regarding what income to tax, which means looking to state law to determine the *source* of the income. The underly-

---

4. See Va. Code Ann. § 58.1-302, which defines a resident as any person who either maintains a place of abode in Virginia for over 183 days in a taxable year or is domiciled (i.e., has their permanent place of residence to which they intend to return) in Virginia.

5. See FTB Publication 1031, *Guidelines for Determining Residency Status* (2021) (available at https://www.ftb.ca.gov/forms/Search/Home/FormRequest).

6. See CA RTC § 18001, which describes the credit (and its exceptions) for taxes paid to another state by California residents.

ing principle of mobility taxation is the principle of sourcing income. There is no single methodology for sourcing income to different states (and countries). The general view is that income should be sourced where it is earned. Most states apply this concept on a physical presence basis, so the location where the employee is physically working will determine where the income is sourced. Therefore, if an employee works for one day in Colorado, under the general principle, income for that day is deemed to be Colorado-sourced.[7] This concept works well for regular salary amounts paid on a regular pay cycle. However, multi-year income such as equity compensation makes sourcing more complicated. The employee may earn the income over a long time period, often spanning several years, and recognize the income and be subject to tax at a later point in time, such as upon exercise of an NSO or the release of an RSU. Under the general sourcing principle, the income is earned over the period in which services are performed. If the equity award is not specific about this, the period starts from the grant date. See the discussion under "Sourcing for Equity Compensation" below.

There are certain notable exceptions to the general principle. Jurisdictions that take different perspectives on sourcing include (but are not limited to):

- *"Convenience of the employer" states.* Arkansas, Delaware, Pennsylvania, Nebraska, New Jersey, and New York apply the "convenience of the employer" test to sourcing. Income is sourced where the employer/employment is based unless the employer requests that the employee work elsewhere. For example, the wages paid to a telecommuter who works remotely from home in Tennessee for a New York employer will be sourced entirely to New York under New York's convenience of the employer rules.[8]

- *Location at grant.* Some tax jurisdictions, notably Singapore, take the position that the location of employment at the time of grant is the source of the income even if the individual then moves elsewhere shortly thereafter. Conversely, equity awards granted before establishing residency in Singapore that were not granted in respect

---

7. See Co. Rev. Stat. § 39-22-109 (2)(A)(II), which describes the circumstances for sourcing a nonresident's income to Colorado.

8. See, e.g., *In re Huckaby v. N.Y.S. Div. Tax Appeals*, 4 NY3d 427 (2005)·

of the Singapore assignment or services are not subject to taxation in Singapore. The author knows of no U.S. states that take the same position with the exception of a court ruling in North Carolina that effectively ruled the same way.[9]

For completeness, we should also note that several types of individuals are excluded from the sourcing principles applicable to employees. Special rules apply to sports teams, public figures, and entertainers. Self-employed individuals may have the income sourced to the location of the business for which they are performing services. Many states also have special rules for military personnel and interstate transit workers.

14.4 Sourcing for Equity Compensation

The question then becomes how to source multi-year income such as equity compensation when the award is held by a mobile employee. Different tax jurisdictions take different approaches. Some common approaches are

* based on workdays from grant to vest,
* based on workdays from grant to exercise,
* sourced as wages under the convenience of employer principles, and
* based on employment/location at grant.

Historically, many tax jurisdictions would source equity compensation based on workdays spent in the state from grant to exercise. In 2004, the Organization for Economic Cooperation and Development (OECD) published the report *Cross-border Income Tax Issues Arising from Employee Stock Option Plans*.[10] This report suggests that tax jurisdictions consider the period between grant and vest of the option as

---

9. See N.C. Individual Income Tax Admin. Hearing Docket No. 2004-200 (available at https://files.nc.gov/ncdor/documents/administrative-tax-hearings/2004-200s. pdf), which describes the North Carolina Secretary of Revenue's determination regarding the apportionment of nonqualified stock options.

10. The report is available at http://www.oecd.org/ctp/treaties/33700277.pdf.

the earnings period. Many tax jurisdictions, including the U.S. at the federal level, implemented this suggestion.[11] Similarly, certain states such as New York, Minnesota, and Georgia followed suit.

> *Example 3. Grant to vest sourcing:* While he is employed and working in Georgia, Charles is granted an NSO that cliff-vests on the fourth anniversary of grant. After three years, Charles relocates to take a new position with the same employer in Oregon. He remains employed in Oregon on the fifth anniversary of grant when he exercises the stock option. The portion of the stock option income sourced to Georgia is based on the three years spent in Georgia over the four-year vesting period, or 75%.[12]

Before the publication of the OECD report, many jurisdictions would treat the period from grant to the exercise of a stock option as the earnings period. Some jurisdictions, such as Massachusetts,[13] continue to do so. Similarly, Connecticut considers the period from the first date in the year of grant to the last day in the year of exercise.[14]

> *Example 4. Grant to exercise sourcing:* While she is employed and working in Massachusetts, Diane is granted an NSO that cliff-vests on the fourth anniversary of grant. After three years, Diane relocates to take a new position with her employer in Wisconsin. She remains employed in Wisconsin when she exercises the stock option on the fifth anniversary of grant. The portion of the stock option income sourced to Massachusetts is based on the three years spent in Massachusetts over five-year period from grant to exercise or 60%.

Some states take a completely different approach altogether. In North Carolina Ruling 2004-200, the decision was reached that stock

---

11. See 26 CFR 1.861-4 (b)(2)(ii)(F) ("In the case of stock options, the facts and circumstances generally will be such that the applicable period to which the compensation is attributable is the period between the grant of an option and the date on which all employment-related conditions for its exercise have been satisfied (the vesting of the option).").

12. See Ga. R&R § 560-7-4-0.05 (3)b, which describes the rules and provides examples for equity apportionment in Georgia.

13. See 830 CMR 62.5A.1(3)(c)(2) ("The amount of such [income derived from non-qualified stock options] that is taxable to Massachusetts is determined…for the period between the option grant date and the option exercise date").

14. See Conn. Reg. § 12-711(b)-18(a).

options are sourced to the location of employment at grant, regardless of whether the individual remains in North Carolina at exercise. As mentioned above, Singapore takes a similar approach.

Many states, however, do not have a specified sourcing methodology for equity compensation. In this case, the taxpayer should determine a reasonable position and apply it consistently. The author's preference is to follow the federal sourcing rules in the absence of any other guidance.

14.5 Special Issues Related to Each Type of Mobile Employee

Each type of mobile employee presents its own compliance challenges. An in-depth review is outside the scope of this chapter. However, we will briefly discuss the challenges associated with each type of mobile employee:

- *Assignees/Secondees.* When employees are assigned or seconded from one state to another, the main issue will be identifying the state in which the employee is resident. As the move is intended to be temporary, the employee may not break residency in the former state but may (or may not) establish residency in the new state.

- *Transfers.* With a transfer that is an indefinite move, the employee will likely break residency in the old state and establish residency in the new state.

- *Travelers.* Travelers typically do not break residency in their home states. Depending on the states they travel to and the type of activities they perform there, travelers may or may not be subject to tax in the work (travel) states. Some states have de minimis thresholds for nonresident travelers to be subject to tax. The de minimis threshold may be measured in days or income. New York, for example, requires employer payroll compliance for an employee who has worked in New York for more than 14 days in the tax year; however, compensation paid in one year relating to a prior year is excepted from this rule.[15] Oklahoma applies a threshold for

---

15. See *Withholding on Wages Paid to Certain Nonresidents Who Work 14 Days or Fewer in New York State*, N.Y.S. Dept. of Tax. and Fin., Technical Memorandum

nonresidents working in Oklahoma of $300 of income for each calendar quarter.[16]

Given the difficulties employers face in trying to navigate and comply with the laws of every state where their workers perform services, Congress has tried to pass federal legislation to standardize the taxation of nonresident business travelers for all states. The Mobile Workforce State Tax Simplification Act (or its predecessors) has been introduced in every congressional session since 2009. The Act would impose a 30-day de minimis period, allowing nonresident employees to work in a state without being taxed there, subject to some exceptions such as sports teams, performers, etc., as noted above. The latest version of the bill was introduced in January 2021.[17]

- *Commuters.* Commuters typically live in one state but work in another, e.g., living in Connecticut but working in New York. Often the employer will have payroll compliance responsibilities for both the live-in and work-in states, and the employee may be required to file taxes in both. However, if the states have a reciprocal agreement,[18] then payroll reporting may not be required for the work state. In the case of commuters, most payroll systems can identify the reporting requirements as long as the correct live-in and work-in addresses are populated. It is important for equity compensation administrators to understand how payroll is treating the employee and apply taxation accordingly and consistently.

- *Telecommuters.* Telecommuters work from one (or more) state(s) for an employer based in another state. In general, telecommuters are taxed based on their physical location when performing

---

TSB-M 12(5)I (July 5, 2012) (available at https://www.tax.ny.gov/pdf/memos/income/m12_5i.pdf).

16. See Ok. Stat. § 68-2385.1(e)(4), which excludes remuneration paid for services performed in Oklahoma by a nonresident if that income is not greater than $300 in a calendar quarter.

17. See H.R. 429, the Mobile Workforce State Income Tax Simplification Act of 2021. See https://www.congress.gov/bill/117th-congress/house-bill/429 for the current legislative history of H.R. 429.

18. See section 14.7 of this chapter.

the work. However, see the description of the "convenience of employer" rules under "Sourcing of Income—General Principles" above.

For a discussion of remote workers, see section 14.10.

14.6   Retirement, Termination, and Death

Often an employee will terminate from the employer or retire and move to another state before the transaction date, which triggers taxable income associated with the equity award. The individual is now resident in a state where they have not worked for the employer. As a resident of that state, the individual is likely taxable on worldwide income. In general, any post-termination/retirement period should not be used to source the income. This period is not part of the earnings period because there are no workdays for the employer.

Whether the employer is responsible for withholding state tax and/or reporting income to the resident state depends on the state and possibly on whether the employer is registered for payroll or has corporate nexus in that state.

The income reporting and tax withholding requirements for equity compensation upon the death of the participant are complicated. State mobility may complicate the compliance further. The author is not aware of any specific statutes by U.S. states regarding the sourcing of income in the case of equity compensation being paid out to an estate or beneficiaries. However, in the absence of any guidance, the general tax principles discussed above should apply.

14.7   Avoiding Double Taxation

Given the differences in sourcing methodology, there are several scenarios in which an individual can be subject to tax on the same income in more than one state. Yet there are several ways in which double taxation may be mitigated.

First, some states have reciprocity agreements in which state A agrees not to tax the residents of state B for work performed in state A. These are common between neighboring states in the Northeast. The employee may be required to complete a form stating that they are resident in a reciprocal state before the employer can stop payroll reporting for the work state.

Second, most states allow residents to claim a tax credit for taxes paid to another state for income that is doubly taxed. However, in most cases the amount of income on which a tax credit is allowed is limited to the income sourced to the nonresident state, as determined by the resident state rules. In addition, the tax credit is limited to the resident state tax rate or the actual taxes paid to the other state, whichever is lower (example 5).

> *Example 5.* Edward moves from Nebraska to New Jersey. While living and working in Nebraska, he was granted an RSU that vests and is released after he establishes residency in New Jersey. New Jersey does not have a special rate for supplemental income. His New Jersey tax rate is 7%. New Jersey allows a tax credit for taxes withheld for Nebraska (table 14-1).[19]

Table 14-1. Tax Credit Illustration (Example 5)

	New Jersey (resident)	Nebraska (nonresident)	Total
Income sourced	$7,000	$5,000	$12,000
Income reportable	$12,000	$5,000	$17,000
Tax rate	7%	5%	
Tax withheld	$590 ($840 less credit of $250)	$250	$840

Note that not all states allow the employer to reduce withholding for a tax credit to another state; in these situations, the credit would have to be claimed on the individual's state tax return, resulting in a cash flow inconvenience until the tax return is filed.

Third, some states may exclude income of resident individuals that is sourced to and taxed by another state. For example, Colorado excludes from withholding the amount of residents' income that is sourced to and subject to tax in other states.[20]

---

19. See New Jersey Tax Topic Bulletin GIT-3W (available at https://www.state.nj.us/treasury/taxation/pdf/pubs/tgi-ee/git3w.pdf).

20. See DR 1098, Colorado Income Tax Withholding Tables for Employers (available at https://tax.colorado.gov/sites/tax/files/documents/DR1098_2021.pdf).

Several payroll systems may not be able to process a transaction where the sum of the state taxable incomes is more than the amount of the federal taxable income. As shown in example 5, the sum of the income reportable to both states is $17,000, whereas the total income is only $12,000. Some payroll systems may treat the federal taxable amount as $17,000. For situations like this, readers should seek professional advice on the best route to follow given the states concerned.

14.8   State Disability, Unemployment Insurance, and Other Payroll Taxes

Employers in all states must contribute to Federal Unemployment Tax (FUTA) and the state equivalents (SUTA). Some states also have a corresponding employee deduction for unemployment, disability, paid family leave, or a similar insurance benefit. These payroll taxes are not necessarily allocated the same way as income taxes.

To allow continuity of coverage, all states have agreed to one set of tests to determine where the wages are reportable for SUTA purposes. The state for which SUTA is paid is determined by the first test that produces a definite result. The tests are applied in the order shown below:

1. *Localization.* Services are localized in a state if all the work is performed within one state and constitutes "employment" under the law. Work performed outside the state that is incidental to the work performed in state is ignored.

2. *Base of operations.* When services are normally performed in two or more states, then the test of localization is not applicable, as services cannot be said to be localized in any one state. The next test, base of operations, considers where the employee's base of operations is located; it may be the employee's business office, or an office maintained in the employee's home. In the absence of other and more controlling factors, the base of operations may be the place where the employee receives mail, keeps supplies and equipment, or maintains business records.

3. *Operations and control.* If the base of operations test does not result in a definitive state, the next test is where the employee's work is directed and controlled from, provided the employee undertakes some services in that state.

4. *Employee's residence.* When coverage cannot be determined by the other tests, an employee's service in its entirety is covered in the state in which they live, provided that some of their service is performed in that state.

The state for SUTA purposes may not match the state for income tax purposes. The reader should determine whether the payroll system can manage this difference.

14.9   Local Taxes

According to the Tax Foundation, as of 2019 there were almost 5,000 municipalities and school districts in the U.S. that impose an income tax.[21] Some apply tax on current residents only, such as New York City, and others collect taxes from nonresidents as well as residents, such as Yonkers.[22] Many localities, however, do not have any guidelines on mobile employee taxation. In such cases, the company should take a position and apply it consistently. Some payroll systems require local taxes to be collected on the amount of the relevant state taxable income.

14.10 Remote Workers

The term "remote worker" is generally used to describe an employee who does not work from the employer's office. Instead, the remote worker may work from their existing residence, a new residence, or a temporary location. These may be in the same state as the employer's office or in another state.

In general, if the remote worker continues in the same state (and locality, if relevant) as the employer's office, there is no tax impact. If the remote work is done from another state and the move is permanent (or at least long-term), the remote worker will likely break residency in the original state and establish residency in the new state. This remote worker will likely be treated as a transfer or a telecommuter. If the move

---

21.   See Jared Walcaz, *Local Income Taxes in 2019* (July 30, 2019) (available at https://taxfoundation.org/local-income-taxes-2019).

22.   See *Employer's Guide to Unemployment Insurance, Wage Reporting, and Withholding Tax*, NYS-50, 26–27 (rev. Jan. 2014) (available at https://www.tax.ny.gov/pdf/publications/withholding/nys50.pdf).

is temporary, then the remote worker may be treated as a traveler during the time spent in the other state.

See section 14.2 for a description of each type of mobility and section 14.5 for a discussion of the associated issues. The employer's payroll compliance obligations may depend on whether the employer has corporate nexus in a particular state.

14.11 State Issues for International Mobility

State issues may also arise when employees move or travel to or from the U.S.

For moves into the U.S., some of the equity compensation paid may be excluded from federal income tax through the application of a double tax treaty. However, many states do not follow income tax treaties; therefore, any equity compensation received after moving to the U.S. may be subject to state tax on the full income associated with equity compensation, even when federal taxes may only apply to a portion of the income.

Similarly, a non-U.S. business traveler visiting a particular state may be exempt from federal taxes under the terms of a treaty but may be subject to state taxes for income earned during the business trip.

> *Example 6.* Francois is a French citizen and resident who travels for work to Connecticut for one week every month. Francois qualifies for an exemption from U.S. federal income taxes under the terms of the France-U.S. double tax treaty. Similarly, he is exempt from U.S. social taxes under the terms of the France-U.S. totalization agreement. However, Francois will be subject to Connecticut income tax on the income relating to workdays in Connecticut.

When employees move out of the U.S., their equity compensation may need to be sourced for state and federal purposes. The sourcing may not be the same for federal and state purposes, as noted in "Sourcing for Equity Compensation" above.

Individuals who are U.S. citizens or green card holders may be subject to U.S. federal tax on worldwide income but may break state residency and be subject to state tax on state-sourced income only.

14.12 Practical Considerations

When implementing or evaluating state mobility compliance policy or procedures, there are many considerations each company should think through, including:

* Where are the company's largest exposures, and how can the process effectively address these?

* How can you gather mobility information? Which system is the system of record?

* What are the payroll system's capabilities and limitations? Some payroll systems require that the total of all state taxable income must be equal to the federal taxable income. Some payroll systems cannot accommodate multistate taxation.

* Where the rules are not clear, what positions will the company take?

* How will the new process be communicated to and coordinated among the company's stock plan administration, human resources, payroll, legal, and finance functions?

* Will the company implement policies to help employees with liability in more than one state, such as tax return preparation assistance or tax equalization?

The author would like to thank Mindy Mayo of KPMG LLP; Carol Rutlen, Crystal Gronau, and Nicky Chiuchiarelli of Rutlen Associates LLC; and members of the tax panel of the CEPI Curriculum Committee, namely Haleh Carrillo, Andrea Kagan, and Carl Toppin, for their review and guidance.

A Layperson's Glossary of Employee Stock Plan Terminology

As with any specialized field, the world of employee stock plans has its own vernacular. Stock options and related plans are governed, as well as influenced, by a wide array of laws, regulations, rules, and standards, including tax laws and concepts, securities laws, and accounting principles. Following is a glossary of many of the more commonly used words and phrases in this field. All references to the "Code" in this glossary refer to the Internal Revenue Code of 1986, as amended (which itself is defined below). Any other abbreviations used in the definitions are also defined.

10% Owner

In general: Beneficial owner of more than 10% of a class of equity securities of an issuer that is registered under Section 12 of the Exchange Act.

For ISOs: An employee who, at the time of grant, owns stock possessing more than 10% of the total combined voting power of all classes of stock of the employer corporation or of its parent or subsidiary corporation. Under Section 422(b)(6) of the Code, such an employee is not eligible to receive an ISO unless, as provided in Section 422(c)(5) of the Code, at the time such option is granted the option price is at least 110% of the fair market value of the company's stock subject to the option and such option by its terms is not exercisable after the expiration of five years from the date such option is granted.

Acceleration

With respect to unvested shares, speeding up the vesting schedule (that is, decreasing the period over which vesting restrictions lapse).

Accredited Investor

A term defined in Rule 501 of Regulation D to classify investors who are financially sophisticated to protect their own interests and have a reduced need for the protection provided by certain public filings

Administrator

See "Plan Administrator."

Affiliate

Under Rule 144, a person who directly or indirectly controls, is controlled by, or is under common control with the issuer. As a rule, executive officers and directors are deemed to be affiliates. Affiliates are subject to certain limitations as to volume and timing with respect to sale of unregistered (restricted) stock of the issuer.

Alternative Minimum Tax (AMT)

In general: "Alternative" method of computing federal income tax that recaptures certain preferences and adjustments that are otherwise excluded from gross income.

For ISOs: The difference, if any, between the option price and the fair market value of the stock of the corporation on the date of exercise of an ISO is an AMT adjustment, and therefore—although it is otherwise excluded from gross income in the year of exercise—it will be added back when computing alternative minimum taxable income (AMTI). If an ISO produces AMT, it may result in a tax credit against ordinary income tax in future years.

AMEX (American Stock Exchange)

The second largest organized stock exchange, on which corporate securities are traded. Because the listing requirements of this exchange are considered to be less stringent than those of the New York Stock Exchange, the exchange generally trades the securities of small-to-medium-sized corporations.

Annual Meeting

A meeting of a corporation's directors, officers, and shareholders/stockholders, held for the purpose of communicating the operating and financial results of the business for the prior fiscal year, the corporation's prospects for the future, and major decisions of management, and for deciding matters requiring the approval of the corporation's shareholders/stockholders. Generally, the election of the corporation's board of directors occurs at the annual meeting. Shareholders/stockholders who are not able to physically attend the annual meeting may vote on the election of directors and other matters brought before the meeting by submitting a proxy before the meeting authorizing a third party to vote their shares of stock.

Anti-dilution Adjustment

A change to the terms, conditions, and/or price of a security to prevent a diminution in value as the result of a change in the capital structure of a corporation. Typically, an employee stock option plan will provide for an appropriate adjustment in the number and kind of securities subject to the plan and to all outstanding employee stock options in the event of a change in the capitalization of the corporation.

APB 25

Accounting Principles Board (APB) Opinion No. 25, issued in 1972, set out the accounting standards for both compensatory and noncompensatory options before FAS 123(R) (now codified as ASC Topic 718 for grants to employees and ASC Subtopic 505-50 for grants to nonemployees), which supersedes it.

ASC Subtopic 505-50

Accounting Standards Codification (ASC) Subtopic 505-50, "Equity-Based Payments to Non-Employees," governs the accounting treatment in the U.S. of equity awards to nonemployees. Before FASB's 2009 codification of GAAP, it was part of FAS 123(R). See "FAS 123(R)."

ASC Topic 718

Accounting Standards Codification (ASC) Topic 718, "Stock Compensation," governs the accounting treatment in the U.S. of equity awards to employees. Before FASB's 2009 codification of GAAP, it was part of FAS 123(R). See "FAS 123(R)."

Authorized but Unissued

The difference between the number of securities of a given class authorized for issuance under a corporation's charter documents and the number of securities of that class that are issued and outstanding.

Available for Grant

The incremental difference between the number of shares of stock authorized for issuance under a stock option plan and the number of shares already subject to option. Cancelled shares that are added back to the plan and any increase in the number of shares available for issuance pursuant to the plan are included in the calculation of shares "available for grant."

Backdating

The practice (whether or not fraudulent) of setting an option exercise price that is less than fair market value on the grant date. The term "backdating" has been used to describe practices as varied as intentional discounting (i.e., intentionally stating that the option was granted on a date different than the actual grant date), misdating (unintentionally stating the incorrect grant date price), "spring-loading" (granting options before good news breaks), "bullet-dodging" (granting options after bad news breaks), "forward-dating" (approving options with a grant date set after approval), and 30-day pricing (approving options with grant price to be set at the average or best price in a 30-day window). Backdating may raise accounting, SEC disclosure, and tax issues (particularly under Section 409A of the Code).

Basis

See "Tax Basis."

Beneficial Owner

Under the Exchange Act generally: a person who, directly or indirectly, through any contract, arrangement, understanding, relationship, or otherwise, has or shares voting power (which includes the power to vote or to direct the voting of) a security and/or investment power (which includes the power to dispose of or to direct the disposition of) such security.

For Section 16: a person who, directly or indirectly, through any contract, arrangement, understanding, relationship, or other means has or shares a direct or indirect pecuniary interest in equity securities. Securities are "beneficially owned" for these purposes if the holder is entitled to the economic benefits resulting from a transaction in them, whether or not the holder is the record, or registered, owner of the securities.

Black-Scholes Option Pricing Model

A mathematical formula used for valuing employee stock options that considers such factors as the volatility of returns on the underlying securities, the risk-free interest rate, the expected dividend rate, the relationship of the option price to the price of the underlying securities, and the expected option life. Developed in 1973 by three economists, the model was originally created to value options traded on European commodity exchanges.

Blue Sky Laws

State securities laws governing the purchase and sale of securities. The phrase "blue sky" originates from a federal case that described such laws as aimed against "speculative schemes which hold no more basis than so many feet of blue sky."

Board of Directors

A group of individuals elected by a corporation's shareholders to set the policies and oversee the affairs (but not the day-to-day management) of the corporation.

Broker/Brokerage Firm

An individual or a company that acts as an intermediary between a buyer and seller of securities. A broker receives compensation, in the form of a commission, for assisting in or effecting the purchase or sale of securities. A broker is "registered" with the NASD and the exchange on which the securities are traded. Brokers are also regulated under federal and state securities laws.

California Commissioner's Rules

Regulations implementing the California Securities Act of 1968.

Cancellation

In the context of an employee stock option plan, a transaction (usually triggered by a specific event, such as an optionee's termination of employment) in which an outstanding employee stock option is rescinded and the unexercised shares of stock subject to such option are returned to the pool of shares reserved for issuance under the plan.

Capital Asset

Property that meets the definition in Section 1221 of the Code, as follows: property held by a taxpayer, other than (1) stock in trade, inventory or property held primarily for sale to customers in the ordinary course of business, (2) real property or depreciable property used in a trade or business, (3) a copyright, a literary, musical, or artistic composition or similar property of a taxpayer who created such property, (4) accounts or notes receivable acquired in the ordinary course of a trade or business, or (5) publications of the United States government received at a discount. In general, securities (including stock purchased upon exercise of an option) are a capital asset.

Capital Gain

The increase in value, or profit, realized from the sale or exchange of a capital asset; that is, the excess of the proceeds received from the transaction over the basis of the asset. Capital gains can be short-term (where the capital asset was held for one year or less) or long-term (where the capital asset was held for more than one year). Generally, long-term capital gains are taxed at rates more favorable than those applicable to ordinary income.

Capitalization

The total value of all securities that have been issued by a corporation. A corporation's capitalization may include both equity securities and debt securities.

Capital Loss

The decrease in value realized from the sale or exchange of a capital asset; that is, the excess of the basis of the asset over the proceeds received from the transaction.

Cashless Exercise

Form of stock option exercise in which the option price for the number of shares of stock being purchased is paid with consideration other than cash. Common cashless exercise methods include stock swap, net exercise, delivery of a promissory note, and (broker-assisted) same-day-sale transaction. Frequently used to refer to an arrangement between a corporation and a third party, such as a securities brokerage firm or a financial institution, whereby the third party will provide funds, on a temporary basis, to an employee to exercise an employee stock option, immediately upon which some or all of the shares of stock acquired upon exercise of the employee stock option will be sold to repay the funds advanced to initiate the transaction.

Change in Capitalization

An adjustment to the capital structure of a corporation—for example, due to a stock dividend, stock split, or reverse stock split—that results in either an increase in the number of outstanding securities, with a corresponding reduction in the value of each security, or a decrease in the number of outstanding securities, with a corresponding increase in the value of each security.

Change in Control

A transaction that alters the ownership of a corporation, including a merger, consolidation, stock sale, or asset sale. With respect to options, events that constitute a change in control are generally defined in the plan.

Cliff Vesting

Form of vesting in which shares fully vest on a single date rather than ratably over a period of months or years. For example, a typical cliff vesting schedule might provide that 100% of the total shares vest on the fourth anniversary of the grant date.

Closed Trading Window

The period, as determined by a corporation, during which the securities of the corporation may not be sold by certain designated individuals, typically the corporation's insiders. Generally, the period runs from some predetermined time following the release of the corporation's quarterly or annual financial results until 24 to 48 hours following the release of the subsequent period's financial results. Also, a period during which the ability of participants or beneficiaries in a corporation's pension plan to direct or diversify assets credited to their accounts, to obtain loans from the plan, or to obtain distributions from the plan is temporarily suspended, limited, or restricted.

Code

The Internal Revenue Code of 1986, with such modifications, revisions, and additions as are made from time to time.

Collateral

Property given as security for a loan (e.g., a promissory note).

Common Stock

Basic unit of corporate ownership interest that typically confers on the holder of the security the right to vote, select directors, receive dividends, and share in the residual assets upon the dissolution or winding up of the business. Unlike preferred stock, common stock has no preference to dividends or to any distribution of assets by the corporation.

Compensation Committee

Committee of the board of directors that evaluates and approves executive compensation (including equity compensation plans).

Compensation Expense (for Equity)

For financial reporting purposes, the "cost" recognized by a corporation on its financial statements with respect to the issuance of its securities in connection with a stock-based compensation plan or arrangement. Under ASC Topic 718 (formerly FAS No. 123(R)), the amount of compensation expense associated with an employee stock option represents the "fair value" of the employee stock option calculated as of the date of grant of the option using a mathematical option pricing model (such as the Black-Scholes Option Pricing Model).

Compensation Income (for Equity)

Gross income recognized and taxed as ordinary income by a service provider in connection with the transfer of equity from the service recipient (e.g., exercise of an NSO, disqualifying disposition of an ISO, or purchase or receipt of restricted stock).

Confirmation of Exercise

A written statement issued by a corporation to an optionee setting forth specific information about a stock option exercise transaction. In the case of an exercise of an ISO, this statement is sometimes used to provide the information required by Section 6039 of the Code to be provided to an employee.

Constructive Receipt

For tax purposes, income has been constructively received (and is subject to taxation) at the first time that the taxpayer has an unrestricted right to receive such property, regardless of whether or not he chooses to do so. Note that Section 409A of the Code essentially treats any "nonqualified deferred compensation" that does not satisfy specific requirements as constructively received as of the date the taxpayer had a legally binding right to the payment.

Corporate Tax Deduction (for Equity)

The amount realized on exercise of an option (or other compensatory transfer of equity) that is deductible on the corporate income tax return as a trade or business expense under Section 162 of the Code (subject to the application of Section 162(m)). Generally, the amount of deductible compensation expense is equal to the amount of compensation income recognized by the employee for federal income tax purposes.

Corporation

A legal entity that is separate from, and independent of, the persons who formed and/or own the business. A corporation possesses the attributes of (1) limited liability (that is, its shareholders/stockholders are not personally liable for the debts of the corporation), (2) centralized management (that is, responsibility for managing the business and affairs of the corporation resides with designated directors and officers rather than with the owners, the shareholders/stockholders), (3) continuity of life (that is, the corporation has a perpetual existence that is not affected by the death or departure of its shareholders/stockholders), and (4) free transferability of interest (that is, the shareholders/stockholders have the ability, subject to any contractual limitations, to freely transfer or otherwise dispose of their shares of stock without affecting the corporation's status).

Derivative Security

A security that takes, or "derives," its value from another instrument. For purposes of Section 16 of the Exchange Act, a derivative security includes any option, warrant, convertible security, stock appreciation right or similar right with an exercise or conversion privilege at a price related to an equity security, or similar securities with a value derived from the value of an equity security.

Director

An individual elected by the shareholders/stockholders of a corporation to serve on the corporation's board of directors who performs the functions of a director set forth in the corporation's charter documents and bylaws.

Discount Stock Option

A stock option granted with an option price that is less than the fair market value of the corporation's stock on the date of grant. By virtue of the requirement under Section 422(b)(4) of the Code that an ISO must have an option price that is not less than the fair market value of the corporation's stock on the date of grant, a discount stock option will necessarily be a nonqualified stock option. Under ASC Topic 718 and ASC Subtopic 505-50 (formerly FAS 123(R)), discounting that is disclosed properly at the time of grant is less of an issue than it was under APB 25. However, undisclosed discounting may raise serious SEC disclosure issues. Discounting in general may cause tax issues under Section 409A of the Code.

Discretionary Transactions

Transactions in a 401(k), profit sharing, pension, or similar retirement plan that involve the movement of funds between investment alternatives or a distribution. Where the discretionary transaction involves movement of into or out of a company stock investment or involves the distribution of funds invested in company stock, the transaction is reportable for Section 16(a) purposes and may be subject to the short-swing profit recovery provisions of Section 16(b).

Disposition

Sale, gift, or other transfer of property (such as shares of stock) by a person.

Disqualifying Disposition

Disposition of shares of stock acquired upon the exercise of an ISO or Section 423 ESPP option before meeting the statutory holding period set out in Section 421 of the Code of period of one year from exercise and two years from grant. In the year of the disqualifying disposition, the employee recognizes compensation income equal to the difference, if any, between the option price and the fair market value of the stock of the corporation on the date of exercise (or, if unvested at the time of exercise, at the time of vesting). Any post-exercise appreciation recognized by the employee as a result of the disposition is taxable as capital gain. Under Section 422(c)(2) of the Code, the amount included as ordinary income on a disqualifying disposition will be the lesser of the actual gain at sale or the spread on exercise (or vesting).

Early Exercise

The exercise of an option before the time that the shares issued pursuant to such option have vested under the option's vesting schedule.

EDGAR (Electronic Data Gathering, Analysis, and Retrieval System)

The automated computer system developed and implemented by the SEC for the filing of registration statements, periodic reports, and other filings mandated under the federal securities laws by issuers registered under Section 12 of the Exchange Act.

Employee

An individual who performs services for an employer, subject to the direction and control of the employer as to the type of work and manner of performance. Employee status is distinct from that of an independent contractor. For income tax purposes, W-2 withholding of income taxes on wages applies only to employees.

Employee Stock Option

See "Option" or "Stock Option."

Employee Stock Option Agreement

See "Option Agreement."

Employee Stock Option Plan

See "Option Plan."

Employer

Person who directs and controls the performance of services by an employee.

Employment (or "Payroll") Taxes

Generally, a term used to describe taxes imposed under FICA and FUTA. These taxes are assessed against employers and, in the case of FICA taxes, employees with respect to the wages paid to such employees.

Equity

Term that refers to an ownership interest in a corporation. Equity also represents the amount of capital invested by the shareholders/stockholders plus the retained earnings of the business. The term is also used to denote the capital stock of a corporation.

Equity Compensation

Use of equity (rather than or in addition to cash) to compensate a service provider. The most common forms of equity compensation include restricted stock, stock options, and "phantom" stock.

Equity Security

A stock or similar security, or a security that is convertible, with or without consideration, into such a security, which security in either case provides an equity interest in the corporation.

ESPP (Employee Stock Purchase Plan)

Type of stock option plan that provides for ongoing stock purchases by employees pursuant to a subscription agreement. May be a tax-qualified statutory option plan under Section 423 of the Code, or may result in nonstatutory option treatment under Section 83. Tax-qualified plans generally include a discount from market price, determined as of either the first day or the last day of the applicable exercise period. See "Section 423 Plan."

Evergreen Provision

A replenishment feature in a stock plan that automatically increases at regular intervals the number of shares reserved under the plan.

Exchange Act

See "Securities Exchange Act of 1934."

Ex-dividend Date (Ex-date)

The date (one day before the record date under T+2 settlement) on and after which the next dividend is not owed to an investor purchasing a dividend-paying stock.

Exempt Transactions (Section 16)

For Section 16 purposes, this term typically refers to transactions that are exempt from the short-swing profit recovery provisions of Section 16(b). Most exempt transactions are still reportable under Section 16(a), although in some cases, this term refers to transactions that are exempt from both the short-swing profit recovery provisions of Section 16(b) and the reporting requirements of Section 16(a).

Exercise

Purchase of stock pursuant to an option.

Exercise Date

The date on which an employee stock option is exercised.

Exercise Notice

Form completed and submitted by an optionee to the issuer that provides notice of the optionee's intention to exercise an option. Generally, an exercise notice requires the optionee to identify the option being exercised, indicate the number of shares of stock being purchased, provide payment of the aggregate option price for the shares of stock being purchased in a form permitted under the option agreement, make certain representations to the corporation concerning the optionee's investment intent, and agree to certain restrictions imposed on the shares of stock.

Exercise Price

The consideration in money or property that, pursuant to the terms of an employee stock option agreement, is the price at which the shares of stock subject to an employee stock option may be purchased. The exercise price is typically expressed on a per-share basis. Also referred to "option price" or "strike price."

Expiration Date

The last date on which an employee stock option may be exercised by an optionee. This date is typically set forth in the option agreement for the employee stock option and usually ranges from five to ten years following the date of grant of the employee stock option. Also refers to the date on which an employee stock option plan expires.

Fair Market Value

For tax purposes, the value of a share of stock on any given date. The concept of "fair market value" is a tricky one, made even more so by the enactment of Section 409A. For both NSO and ISO purposes, the IRS has traditionally deferred to the public market or, in the case of a private company, to the good-faith valuation of the issuer's board of directors. However, the regulations under Section 409A require that to support the position that a grant has been made at fair market value, privately held companies must either follow one of three specific safe harbor valuation methods or demonstrate that the valuation method actually used was reasonable. Depending on the stage of a company's life cycle, the safe harbor could include using an independent appraiser, providing an in-house written valuation that satisfies certain specified criteria, working with a non-lapse restriction based on a formula price, or using the price for which shares were purchased in a recent arm's-length sale. The IRS will respect a valuation based on a safe harbor unless the issuer's reliance is "grossly unreasonable." A company that chooses not to use a safe harbor method must be prepared to show that its valuation made reference to the valuation factors set out in Section 409A, and there is no assurance that the IRS will agree that the method is reasonable for these purposes. In a public company, of course, fair market value is determined with reference to the price posted on the applicable stock market (generally this is closing price, but it depends on how the plan was drawn up).

Fair Value

For accounting purposes, the value of an option determined in accordance with ASC Topic 718 and ASC Subtopic 505-50 (formerly FAS 123(R)), using a pricing model such as Black-Scholes or a lattice model. An amendment of ASC 718 issued in 2021, ASU 2021-07, offers a practical expedient that private companies can use to determine the fair market value of their stock when valuing awards that receive equity treatment under ASC 718. This practical expedient cannot be relied on for liability awards, nor can it be used to determine the fair market value of company stock for non-accounting purposes.

FAS 123

Statement of Financial Accounting Standards No. 123, "Accounting for Stock-Based Compensation." FAS 123 requires companies to place a "fair value" on employee stock options not otherwise covered by APB 25 as of the date of grant and to either reflect such value as a charge to earnings during the service period or disclose the amount that would have been charged in a footnote to the company's financial statements.

FAS 123(R)

Statement of Financial Accounting Standards No. 123 (revised 2004), "Share-Based Payment." The Financial Accounting Standards Board's revision of its FAS 123 accounting standard. Mandates that compensation expense for options and awards granted to employees is determined at grant and is generally not adjusted for subsequent events (with the exception of forfeitures), provided that the option or award can only be settled in stock. Under FASB's 2009 codification of GAAP, FAS 123(R) has now been codified as ASC Topic 718 for grants to employees and ASC Subtopic 505-50 for grants to nonemployees. See "ASC Subtopic 505-50" and "ASC Topic 718."

FASB (Financial Accounting Standards Board)

A private sector organization recognized by the Securities and Exchange Commission as the source for generally accepted accounting principles for corporations that offer and sell securities in the United States.

FICA (Federal Insurance Contributions Act)

A series of employment taxes imposed on employees and employers with respect to employee wages, including Social Security and Medicare taxes.

FINRA (Financial Industry Regulatory Authority)

A self-regulatory organization subject to the Exchange Act, comprising brokers and dealers. Created in 2007 to incorporate oversight of U.S. securities markets into one organization. Among the organizations incorporated was the National Association of Securities Dealers (NASD), which comprised brokers and dealers in the over-the-counter (OTC) securities market.

Fiscal Year

The annual accounting period for a corporation. A fiscal year is a period of 12 consecutive months. It frequently coincides with the calendar year, but can conclude at the end of a different month. For example, a fiscal year can run from October 1 to September 30.

Form 3

The initial ownership report for directors, officers, beneficial owners of more than 10% of a class of an issuer's registered equity securities, and any other person subject to Section 16 of the Exchange Act. A Form 3 requires information on the number of non-derivative securities and derivative securities beneficially owned at the time the reporting person becomes subject to Section 16 and, except in the case of an issuer's first registration of a class of equity securities pursuant to Section 12 of the Exchange Act, must be filed with the SEC within 10 calendar days of that date. A Form 3 must be filed with the SEC even if the reporting person does not own any securities of the issuer at the time the filing is required.

Form 4

Change in beneficial ownership report for directors, officers, beneficial owners of more than 10% of a class of an issuer's registered equity securities, and any other person subject to Section 16 of the Exchange Act. A Form 4 requires information on any change in beneficial ownership of non-derivative securities and derivative securities by a reporting person that is not eligible for deferred reporting. With limited exceptions, a Form 4 must be filed with the SEC within two business days after the date of execution of the transaction that results in a reportable change in beneficial ownership.

Form 5

Annual change in beneficial ownership report for directors, officers, beneficial owners of more than 10% of a class of an issuer's registered equity securities, and any other person subject to Section 16 of the Exchange Act. A Form 5 requires information on holdings and changes in beneficial ownership by a reporting person of non-derivative securities and derivative securities that are exempt from current reporting. A Form 5 must be filed with the SEC within 45 calendar days after the end of the issuer's fiscal year.

Form 1099

Information report that must be provided to the service provider by the service recipient with respect to any non-wage compensation income earned or received during the taxable year covered by the report.

Form 10-K

An annual disclosure report for issuers subject to the reporting requirements of Section 13(a) or 15(d) of the Exchange Act. The report contains information about the business and management of the issuer, legal proceedings involving the issuer, management compensation, and the issuer's latest audited financial statements.

Form 10-Q

A quarterly report for issuers subject to the reporting requirements of Section 13(a) or 15(d) to the Exchange Act. The report contains information about the business and management of the issuer, and other specified information.

Form S-8

Form of registration statement under the 1933 Act that may be used by issuers subject to the reporting requirements of Section 13(a) or 15(d) of the Exchange Act to register securities issuable to participants in an employee benefit plan, such as an employee stock option plan.

FUTA (Federal Unemployment Tax Act)

An employment tax imposed on employers with respect to employee wages.

GAAP (Generally Accepted Accounting Principles)

Substantive rules for the practice of accounting as established by the body of opinions and decisions issued by the FASB.

Golden Parachute

Under Section 280G of the Code, the value of certain compensation-related benefits (including options) receive by an employee contingent upon a change in control.

Grace Period

Period of time provided under an option agreement for the exercise of an employee stock option following termination of the optionee's employment. Typically, this period of time ranges from 30 days until the expiration of the original option term, may vary depending upon the reason for the termination of employment, and is limited to the exercise of shares of stock that were vested as of the date of termination.

Grant Date

The date upon which an employee stock option is formally approved by the company's board of directors. The grant gives rise to certain contractual rights and obligations on the part of the optionee and the corporation.

Holding Period

For tax purposes: The length of time stock must be held before transfer for any gain to be eligible for capital gain treatment. For statutory option purposes, the period is one year from exercise and two years from grant (set out in Section 421 of the Code); for general capital gains purposes, the period is one year from the date of transfer of capital property (Sections 1221–1223 of the Code). The tax holding period begins on the date the property is first transferred (regardless of whether purchased with a note or subject to contractual restrictions).

For Rule 144 purposes: The length of time unregistered stock must be held before transfer. If purchase is with a note, the securities holding period begins only when the note is paid off or fully collateralized with property other than the underlying stock.

IASB (International Accounting Standards Board)

Voluntary global accounting standards-setting organization whose member nations include the U.S., Australia, Canada, France, Germany, Japan, New Zealand, and the U.K. IASB standards are intended to establish GAAP on an international basis.

Income Tax Regulations

Rules promulgated by the Internal Revenue Service implementing and interpreting the statutory provisions of the Code, which have the force of law. Congressional authority for the issuance of regulations is set forth in Section 7805 of the Code.

Independent Contractor

A service provider who is not an employee.

Indexed Stock Option

A stock option with an option price that is periodically adjusted in relation to a market, industry or peer group performance (such as the Standard & Poor's 500). Economically, for the stock option to have value to the optionee, the corporation's stock must outperform the designated performance indicator. While it is possible that the stated option price can be decreased if the designated performance indicator declines over the option term, many employee stock option plans do not permit the option price to drop below the fair market value of the corporation's stock on the date of grant. Since the option price for this type of employee stock option changes over time, for financial reporting purposes it is considered a "variable" award that results in periodic compensation expense until the option price is finally fixed.

Insider

A general term referring to persons who, by virtue of their positions within a corporation, have access to confidential information about the corporation. Frequently used to denote the directors, officers, beneficial owners of more than 10% of a class of an issuer's registered equity securities, and persons otherwise subject to Section 16 of the Exchange Act.

Insider Trading

A person's wrongful use or wrongful communication, whether directly or indirectly, of confidential information to purchase or sell securities.

Institutional Investor

An organization, rather than an individual, that invests on behalf of the organization's members. There are generally six types of institutional investors: pension funds, endowment funds, insurance companies, commercial banks, mutual funds, and hedge funds. Institutional investors must generally file a Form 13F with the SEC to report their quarterly holdings; they must also file a Form 13G if they own more than 5% of a company's stock.

Internal Revenue Code (the "Code")

The Internal Revenue Code of 1986, as amended; the key federal statute providing for the taxation of individuals, corporations, and other persons.

In-the-Money

Term used to describe an employee stock option where the current fair market value of the shares of stock subject to the option is greater than the exercise price.

IPO (Initial Public Offering)

A corporation's first offering of securities to the general public under a registration statement prepared and filed with the Securities and Exchange Commission in accordance with the 1933 Act. The offering must also be made in compliance with the requirements of the securities laws of the various states where the securities will be offered for sale and sold.

IRS (Internal Revenue Service)

An agency of the federal government, under the supervision of the Department of the Treasury, that is responsible for administering the federal tax laws, including the Code.

ISO Amount Limitation

A dollar limitation to the amount of stock that can receive preferential tax treatment under an ISO grant. As set forth in Section 422(d) of the Code, to the extent that the aggregate fair market value of the shares of stock with respect to which ISOs are exercisable for the first time by an employee during any calendar year (under all plans of the employee's employer corporation and its parent and subsidiary corporations) exceeds $100,000, such stock options shall be treated as nonqualified stock options to the extent of the amounts in excess of $100,000. For purposes of applying this rule, options are to be taken into account in the order in which they were granted. In addition, for purposes of applying this rule, the fair market value of any shares of stock is to be determined as of the time the ISO with respect to such shares of stock was granted.

ISO (Incentive Stock Option)

An employee stock option that meets the requirements of Section 422(b) of the Code and, therefore, qualifies for the preferential tax treatment under Section 421 of the Code. Generally, an ISO does not give rise to federal income tax consequences for the employee either at the time of grant or at exercise. Instead, the employee is subject to taxation at the time of disposition of the shares of stock acquired upon the exercise of the ISO.

Issuer

A corporation that issues securities.

Lattice Models

Models for determining the fair value of employee stock options that use a decision-tree approach of possible future outcomes. A value is arrived at based on the weighted probability of all possible future outcomes. There are many different kinds of lattice models including binomial models and trinomial models, among many others.

Leave of Absence

A temporary, approved absence from employment. For purposes of applying the ISO rules, a leave of absence is not considered an interruption of the employment relationship if the leave is shorter than 91 days or the employee's right to reemployment is guaranteed by statute or contract.

Legend

Statement printed on a stock certificate to indicate that the securities represented by the certificate are subject to limitations or restrictions on transfer. Generally, used to denote that the securities were issued in a private placement and, therefore, are "restricted securities" and "legended stock" for purposes of the federal securities laws. May also reflect a contractual restriction that has been placed on the securities by the issuer as a condition to their original issuance.

"Lock-Up" Restrictions

Transfer restrictions imposed by the underwriters of a public offering of securities on the directors, officers, principal shareholders, and, possibly, others associated with the issuer in order to maintain an orderly trading market in the issuer's securities.

Matchable Transactions

Two transactions that can be matched against each other to trigger recovery of short-swing profits under Section 16(b). Both transactions must be nonexempt (i.e., not exempt from the requirements of Section 16(b)), the transactions must be opposite-way (i.e., an acquisition and a dispositions), and the transactions must occur within a period of less than six months. The earlier of the two transactions must occur while the individual executing them is subject to Section 16. It does not matter whether the acquisition or the disposition occurs first.

Measurement Date

For accounting purposes, the first date on which both the number and the price of shares subject to an option are known. The measurement date for a fixed award is the date of grant, while the measurement date for a variable award is the date of vesting (or expiration).

Modification

For purposes of a statutory option, a beneficial change to the terms of an option (including by way of example, the number of shares, an extension of the term, pricing, or the method of financing). Under Section 424 of the Code, the underlying option will be disqualified from statutory option treatment unless it is treated as a new option as of the date of the modification.

Nasdaq

A computerized network showing quotations and transaction information with respect to securities traded in the over-the-counter market which meet the size and trading volume requirements to be quoted on the system. Nasdaq tends to reflect prices for the more active OTC-traded securities.

National Association of Securities Dealers, Inc. (NASD)

A self-regulatory organization subject to the Exchange Act, comprised of brokers and dealers in the over-the-counter (OTC) securities market. The NASD was established in the late 1930s to regulate the over-the-counter securities market.

Net Exercise

An exercise technique that permits the optionee to buy shares with no cash down by agreeing to allow the issuer to withhold (at exercise) that number of shares with a value equal to either the full exercise price or the exercise price plus an amount sufficient to cover taxes. The optionee receives only the balance of the shares and pays ordinary income tax on the full exercise price, which is equivalent to the difference between the amount paid for the withheld shares (zero) and their fair market value at exercise.

New York Stock Exchange (NYSE)

The oldest organized stock exchange.

No-Action Letter

Interpretive letter issued by the SEC to a specific requestor, indicating the SEC staff's advice regarding the application of specific securities forms or rules; available to the public.

Nonapproved Plan

A stock option plan that has not been approved by the shareholders.

Nonexempt Transactions (Section 16)

For Section 16 purposes, this term refers to transactions that are subject to the short-swing profit recovery provisions of Section 16(b).

Nonrecourse Loan

Term used to describe a loan or other obligation that does not provide for personal liability against the debtor. In the event of a default on the obligation, the creditor is limited to recovery on the collateral provided for in the loan.

Nonreportable Transaction (Section 16)

A transaction that is not required to be reported on either a Form 4 or a Form 5. Note that the effect of a nonreportable transaction on an insider's holdings should be reflected on the next Form 4 or 5 filed for the insider on which the holding in question appears.

Nontransferability Restriction

Term used to describe a restriction imposed on a security that precludes its transfer or conveyance to a third party.

NQSO, NSO (Nonstatutory [or Nonqualified] Stock Option)

A stock option that does not satisfy the requirements of a statutory stock option under the Code. The spread (if any) on exercise of an NSO is includable in ordinary income and subject to tax under Section 83 of the Code.

Offering Period

With respect to an ESPP, the period starting with the grant or offering date and ending with the exercise date.

Officer

A corporate official responsible for managing the day-to-day operations of a corporation. For purposes of Section 16 of the Exchange Act, an issuer's president, principal financial officer, principal accounting officer (or if there is no such accounting officer, the controller), any vice-president of the issuer in charge of a principal business unit, division or function, any other officer who performs a policy-making function or any other person who performs similar policy-making functions for the issuer.

One Million Dollar Cap

Under Section 162(m) of the Code, the maximum amount of certain kinds of compensation paid to "covered employees" that may be deducted by a publicly traded corporation.

Opposite-Way Transactions

Two transactions that have an opposite effect on a Section 16 insider's holdings; i.e., one transaction increases the insider's holdings and the other decreases his or her holdings. A purchase and a sale are an example of opposite-way transactions.

Option Date

See "Grant Date."

Optionee

The recipient of a stock option. In the case of an ISO, the optionee must be an employee of the granting corporation or a parent corporation or subsidiary corporation of the granting corporation at both the time of grant of the stock option and the time of exercise of the stock option (or have been an employee within three months of the date of exercise). In the case of an NSO, the optionee may be either an employee of the granting corporation or, if provided in the employee stock option plan, a nonemployee (such as a nonemployee director or a consultant or other independent contractor providing services to the granting corporation or a parent corporation or subsidiary corporation of the granting corporation).

Option Price

See "Exercise Price."

Option/Stock Option

A contractual right granted to an individual to purchase a specified number of shares of stock of the granting corporation at a specified price for a specified period of time. As set forth in the regulations to Section 83 of the Code, the term "option" includes the right or privilege of an individual to purchase stock from a corporation by virtue of an offer of the corporation continuing for a stated period of time, whether or not irrevocable, to sell such stock at a pre-determined price, such individual being under no obligation to purchase. Such a right or privilege, when granted, must be evidenced in writing. The individual who has such right or privilege is referred to as the "optionee."

Option/Stock Option Agreement

A written contract setting forth the terms and conditions of an employee stock option grant. While no particular form of words is necessary, the written agreement should express, among other things, an offer to sell at the option price and the period of time during which the offer shall remain open. Typically, the written agreement also contains the complete name of the individual receiving the stock option, the effective date of the stock option, the type of stock option granted, such as ISO or NSO, the number of shares of stock covered by the option, the option price, and the vesting schedule for the shares of stock covered by the option.

Option/Stock Option Plan

A formal program adopted by a corporation, often in writing, that provides for the grant of employee stock options to one or more individuals upon the terms and conditions set forth in the plan document and the issuance of shares of stock of the corporation upon the exercise of such stock options.

Option Term

The period of time granted to an individual to exercise an employee stock option. Generally, the term of an employee stock option ranges from five to 10 years.

Out-of-the-Money or Underwater

When the option price is greater than the current fair market value of the shares of stock subject to the stock option.

Outstanding Option

An employee stock option which has been formally granted by a corporation and not cancelled, exercised, or expired. The shares of stock underlying an employee stock option have their own status, which is affected by exercise and expiration of the stock option as well as cancellation.

Overhang

Used as a measure of dilution, this is the percentage of company stock represented by all potentially grantable shares under the plan. It is calculated by adding the total number of shares represented by outstanding, unexercised stock options to the number of additional shares available for grant and then dividing that sum by the total number of shares of common stock outstanding.

Over-the-Counter (OTC) Market

The public trading market for securities which are not traded on either the AMEX or the NYSE. It is composed of brokerage firms making a market and executing transactions in non-listed securities. The over-the-counter market operates primarily through telephone transmissions rather than through the auction-style market found at the exchanges.

Parent Corporation

A corporation that owns a controlling interest in the securities of another corporation. For purposes of the ISO rules, any corporation (other than the employer corporation) in an unbroken chain of corporations ending with the employer corporation if, at the time of grant of the employee stock option, each of the corporations other than the employer corporation owns stock possessing 50% or more of the total combined voting power of all classes of stock in one of the other corporations in such chain.

Par Value

A dollar amount assigned to shares of stock by the corporation's charter documents. It may be used to compute the dollar accounting value of common shares on a corporation's balance sheet. Many corporations issue no-par stock. Par value has no relation to fair market value.

Performance-Based Stock Option

An employee stock option granted with terms that provide that the stock option will be exercisable as to the shares of stock subject to the stock option only upon the attainment of one or more performance-based objectives (that is, objectives other than merely continued service with the corporation). For financial reporting purposes, a performance-based stock option is considered a "variable" award that results in a periodic compensation expense for the corporation until the stock option vests or is settled.

Plan Administrator

In general: An individual or committee of individuals authorized under an employee stock option plan to administer and carry out the objectives, purposes, terms, and conditions of an employee stock option plan. The plan administrator usually selects the individuals to whom stock option grants are to be made, determines the number of shares of stock to be covered by a particular grant, sets the option price at which the grant is made, approves the form or forms of written agreement to accompany each grant, and determines all other terms and conditions of the grant (consistent with the employee stock option plan). Typically, the plan administrator will have the power to establish, amend, and rescind rules and policies deemed necessary or appropriate for the proper administration of the employee stock option plan, to make all necessary determinations under the plan, to construe and interpret the provisions of the plan, and to amend or terminate the plan and, under certain circumstances, outstanding stock option grants. Often a corporation's board of directors will act as the administrator of the employee stock option plan or will delegate responsibility for administering the plan to a subcommittee of the board of directors.

For purposes of Section 16 of the Exchange Act: The plan administrator of an employee stock option plan of an issuer with a class of equity securities that has been registered under Section 12 of the Exchange Act will often be composed of individuals who qualify as "nonemployee" directors for purposes of Rule 16b-3.

Plan Expiration Date

The date after which shares of stock may no longer be granted, awarded, or issued pursuant to the terms and conditions of a stock plan.

PLR

See "Private Letter Ruling (PLR)."

Post-Termination Exercise Period

Period of time provided under an option agreement for the exercise of an employee stock option following termination of the optionee's employment. Typically, this period of time ranges from 30 days until the expiration of the original option term, may vary depending upon the reason for the termination of employment, and is limited to the exercise of shares of stock that were vested as of the date of termination.

Preferred Stock

Equity securities of a corporation that carry certain rights, preferences, and privileges superior to the common stock. Preferred stock generally receives an investment return at a specific rate whenever dividends are declared, and it has priority to the earnings and assets in the event of a sale or liquidation of the corporation before distributions may be made to the common shareholders.

Premium-Priced Stock Option

An employee stock option with an option price that is greater than the fair market value of the corporation's stock on the date of grant.

Private Letter Ruling (PLR)

A ruling issued by the IRS to a specific taxpayer, indicating the IRS interpretation of the tax law with respect to a stated set of facts. PLRs include private letter rulings and technical advice memoranda, and are available to the public, although they may not be cited as precedent and do not bind the IRS other than as to the taxpayer requesting the ruling Other forms of nonprecedential IRS rulings include field service memoranda and IRS Chief Counsel Advisory memoranda.

Privately (or "Closely") Held Company

A corporation the securities of which are not publicly traded.

Promissory Note

A written promise to pay a specified amount of money at a specified time in the future; may be unsecured or secured with collateral acceptable to the holder of the note. If recourse is not limited specifically to the underlying collateral, holder will be entitled to recourse against all of the assets of the maker.

Prospectus

A written document used as a selling piece in an offering of securities that contains certain specified information about the issuer, its business and financial condition, and the terms and conditions of, and risks associated with, the offering. A prospectus is a condensed version of the registration statement filed with the SEC in connection with the offering of securities.

Proxy

A grant of authority to vote the securities of another person. Also refers to the person authorized to vote the securities on behalf of another and/or the written document granting the authority.

Proxy Notice

A written notice to a shareholder/stockholder providing notification of the date, time, and place of a corporation's annual meeting of shareholders/stockholders and describing the matters to be submitted for the approval of the shareholders/stockholders at such meeting.

Proxy Solicitation

A request to be empowered to vote the securities of another person. Typically, a corporation will solicit the authority to vote the securities of its shareholders/stockholders at the corporation's annual meeting of shareholders/stockholders.

Proxy Statement

Solicitation materials relating to an issuer's annual meeting of shareholders, which must be delivered in advance of the meeting. Generally, these materials describe the agenda items for the meeting and contain certain specific information about the directors and principal shareholders/stockholders of the corporation, the compensation of management, and detailed information on proposals to be submitted to the shareholders/stockholders for approval.

Public Company

A company whose stock is publicly traded on a recognized stock exchange; subject to the registration, disclosure, and related rules enforced by the SEC.

Public Offering

An offering of securities to the general public under a registration statement prepared and filed with the SEC in accordance with the 1933 Act and any applicable blue sky laws.

Pyramid Exercise

A transaction in which an optionee exercises a minimum number of shares of stock underlying an employee stock option for cash and then immediately tenders such shares of stock back to the corporation at their appreciated value to exercise additional shares of stock under the stock option. Through a series of successive stock swaps in this manner, the optionee is able to fully exercise the shares of stock subject to the employee stock option. In this manner, the employee stock option can be fully exercised with a minimum cash investment. This results in the optionee receiving shares of stock with an aggregate value equal to the total amount of appreciation in value inherent in the stock option at the time that the transaction is initiated.

Qualifying Disposition

For purposes of stock purchased pursuant to a statutory stock option, a disposition made after satisfying the statutory holding period set out in Section 421 of the Code of two years from grant and one year from exercise.

Readily Ascertainable Fair Market Value

Under Section 83 of the Code, an option must have a "readily ascertainable fair market value" in order to be taxed at the time of grant. In order to have a readily ascertainable fair market value, the income tax regulations require that the stock option either be actively traded on an established securities market or, if not actively traded on an established securities market, the fair market value of the stock option be measurable with reasonable accuracy. The income tax regulations further provide a series of conditions that must be satisfied in order for an employee stock option to meet the "reasonably accurate measurement" test, including, among other things, free transferability of the stock option and the absence of restrictions that could significantly affect the value of the stock option or the underlying shares of stock. Since employee stock options are virtually always nontransferable and subject to vesting restrictions, such stock options seldom would have a readily ascertainable fair market value at the time of grant. As a result, the compensatory element of the acquisition of the employee stock option will not be subject to taxation under Section 83 of the Code until the stock option is exercised.

Realization

Tax concept that describes when gain (whether or not reduced to cash) is treated as compensation. Generally, a gain is considered "realized" when it has been received by a person for such person's use, benefit or disposal. For example, the exercise of an employee stock option to purchase shares of stock that have appreciated in value will be considered a realization of gain since the optionee has taken the final steps to obtain the benefits of economic gain that had previously accrued to the optionee. Realized gain is not necessary taxed at the time of the realization: see "recognition."

Recapitalization

An internal reorganization of the capital structure of the corporation. Typically, a reorganization involves a change to the type or number of securities outstanding. Sometimes the transaction will involve an amendment to the corporation's charter documents.

Recognition

Tax concept that describes when realized gain becomes taxable. Most realized gains are taxable at the time reported; however, tax recognition of some realized gains may be deferred under the Code. For example, Section 1036 of the Code is a nonrecognition provision that provides that any gain realized from an exchange of shares of stock of a corporation for other shares of stock of the same corporation (such as in a stock swap exercise of an employee stock option) is not to be recognized at the time of the exchange. Instead, typically an adjustment to the basis of the property involved is made to preserve any unrecognized gain or loss, which may eventually be subject to taxation at a later time.

Record Date

A date set by the corporation for purposes of determining stock ownership for purposes of voting, dividends, and adjustments resulting from a change in capitalization (for example, a stock split, a stock dividend or a reverse stock split).

Recourse

Term used to describe a loan or other obligation that provides for personal liability against the debtor. In the event of a default on the obligation, the creditor can seek to foreclose on the personal assets of the debtor.

Registered Owner

A shareholder who holds shares directly, i.e., whose name is recorded in a security issuer's register as the security's owner (also called the "record holder"). A registered owner is entitled to receive a proxy and cast votes directly with the issuer.

Registration

The formal process for the issuance of securities under federal and/or state securities laws that permit the public sale of securities.

Regrant

The reissuance or replacement of a previously granted employee stock option, often with terms and conditions that differ from those in the original stock option.

Regulation D

Exemption promulgated by the SEC under the 1933 Act for the private placement of securities that permits limited offerings of securities made in compliance with the conditions of the regulation and exempts such offerings from the registration requirements of the 1933 Act.

Regulation G

Provision promulgated by the Board of Governors of the Federal Reserve System to regulate the extension of credit by persons other than banks or brokers and dealers in connection with the purchase or carrying of marginable securities. Generally, this provision would apply to the extension of credit by certain corporations in connection with the purchase of shares of stock under an employee stock option plan.

Regulation T

Provision promulgated by the Board of Governors of the Federal Reserve System to regulate the extension of credit by brokers and dealers in connection with the purchase or carrying of securities.

Reload Option

A stock option granted to an individual who has exercised an option (typically by a stock swap) that restores the original number of shares under option; the terms of the option (e.g., the price) need not be the same as those of the swapped option.

Replacement Grant

A new employee stock option grant that is intended to replace a previously granted stock option, often with terms and conditions that differ in some respect from those contained in the original stock option. Frequently, when an employee stock option is repriced, the transaction will take the form of a cancellation of the original employee stock option and the grant of a new "replacement" stock option.

Reportable Transaction (Section 16)

A transaction that must be reported on a Form 4 or a Form 5.

Reporting Person

A general term referring to directors, officers, beneficial owners of more than 10% of a class of an issuer's registered equity securities, and any other person otherwise subject to Section 16 of the Exchange Act.

Repricing

The adjustment of the option price of an outstanding employee stock option to reflect a decline in the value of the corporation's stock subject to the stock option. Typically, a stock option "repricing" takes the form of either an amendment of an outstanding stock option to reduce the exercise price or a cancellation of an outstanding employee stock option in exchange for the grant of a new stock option that has an option price equal to or greater than the current fair market value of the corporation's stock. The repricing of employee stock options is subject to extensive regulation and may trigger, among other things, significant income tax, securities law, and accounting consequences.

Repurchase

The reacquisition of shares of stock from an individual by a corporation. Depending on the nature of a corporation's repurchase rights, the corporation may pay the original cost of the shares of stock to the individual or the fair market value of the shares of stock at the time of repurchase.

Repurchase Option/Right

Contractual right reserved by the issuer to repurchase shares from employees (or service providers) at the time of their termination of employment (or service contract) or on another specified event. In general, the issuer will always reserve the right to repurchase unvested shares at their original purchase price. In privately held companies, the issuer may also reserve the right to purchase vested shares at their then-fair market value. Note that many forms of repurchase rights will expire under their terms at the time of an IPO.

Restricted Securities

For securities law purposes, shares of stock issued in a transaction that was not registered under the 1933 Act in reliance on an exemption. Resale of such shares is generally subject to Rule 144 (or subsequent registration). Sometimes called "restricted stock," not to be confused with the term as defined below.

Restricted Stock

A stock grant that is nontransferable until vesting.

Revenue Procedure

A notice published by the IRS giving administrative guidance on the application of tax laws; intended to be relied upon by taxpayers.

Revenue Ruling

A ruling published by the IRS that states the IRS audit position on the application of the tax law to specific facts; establishes precedent that may be relied upon.

Reverse Stock Split

Generally, a change in the capitalization of a corporation that decreases the number of securities outstanding and adjusts the value of the securities upward.

Right of First Refusal

Contractual restriction imposed on shares of stock that entitles a corporation to match any third party offer to purchase the shares of stock subject to the restriction on the same terms and conditions as the third party offer.

Rule 144

Rule promulgated by the SEC as a "safe harbor" for the resale of "restricted securities" (that is, securities that were acquired other than in a public offering) and "control securities" (that is, securities owned by affiliates of the corporation).

Rule 16b-3

Rule promulgated by the SEC that provides that transactions between an issuer that has registered a class of equity securities under Section 12 of the Exchange Act (including an employee benefit plan sponsored by the issuer) and a director or officer of the issuer that involve equity securities of the issuer will be exempt from the operation of the "short-swing profits" recovery rule of Section 16(b) of the Exchange Act if the transaction satisfies the applicable conditions set forth in the rule.

Run Rate

Used as a measure of dilution, this is the number of options granted annually (less option cancellations) as a percentage of total shares issued and outstanding.

Sale

A transaction involving the disposition of property, such as shares of stock, in exchange for the receipt of consideration for such property.

Same-Day Sale (or "Broker Same-Day Sale")

A form of cashless exercise of an employee stock option in which an individual sets the sale price with a broker on the exercise date (in the case of options) or the purchase date (in the case of a purchase under a Section 423 plan), has the shares delivered directly to the broker, and, on delivery of the shares, receives payment for the shares sold.

Same-Way Transactions

Two transactions that have the same effect on a Section 16 insider's holdings; i.e., both transactions increase the insider's holdings or both decrease his or her holdings. A purchase and the grant of a stock option are an example of same-way transactions.

SAR/SSAR

See "Stock Appreciation Right (SAR)."

Section 12 Registration

Registration of a class of an issuer's equity securities under Section 12 of the Exchange Act. Registration under Section 12 is required if securities of the class are listed on a national securities exchange or are held by 2,000 or more individuals or 500 or more non-accredited investors and the issuer has total assets exceeding $10 million, as of the last day of the issuer's most recent fiscal year.

Section 16(a) of the Exchange Act

Provision of the Exchange Act that requires the directors and officers of an issuer that has registered a class of its equity securities under Section 12, as well as the beneficial owners of more than 10% of any class of the issuer's registered equity securities, to file periodic reports with the Securities and Exchange Commission disclosing their holdings and changes in beneficial ownership of the issuer's equity securities.

Section 16(b) of the Exchange Act

Provision of the Exchange Act that requires the directors and officers of an issuer that has registered a class of its equity securities under Section 12, as well as the beneficial owners of more than 10% of any class of the issuer's registered equity securities, to return over to the issuer any profits realized from the purchase and sale, or sale and purchase, of the issuer's equity securities within a period of less than six months.

Section 83 of the Code

Provision of the Code that governs the taxation of property (including stock) received in connection with the performance of services. Section 83 provides that the difference between the fair market value of such transferred property and the amount (if any) paid for such property must be recognized on the first date that the property is freely transferable or not subject to a substantial risk of forfeiture (i.e., vested). Section 83 governs the federal income tax consequences of the grant and exercise of a nonqualified stock option.

Section 83(b) Election

Under Section 83(b), a taxpayer may elect to treat the spread (if any) on transfer of property as vested for purposes of federal income tax (and the capital gains holding periods) on the date of transfer, even if such property is otherwise unvested for non-tax purposes. If the spread on transfer is minimal, ordinary income tax attributable to the spread may be significantly reduced from what it would otherwise be at the time of vesting. The election is a technical device and requires the taxpayer to file a written statement with the IRS no later than 30 days after the date of transfer of property.

Section 162(m) of the Code

Provision of the Code that limits the ability of publicly traded corporations to deduct as an ordinary and necessary business expense certain employee remuneration in excess of $1 million paid to specified "covered employees" of the corporation.

Section 423 Plan

An employee stock purchase plan (ESPP) that qualifies under Section 423 of the Code.

Section 6039 of the Code

Provision of the Code that requires corporations to provide, by January 31 of the following year, certain specified information to employees who have exercised an ISO or transferred stock under a Section 423 plan.

Securities Act of 1933 (1933 Act)

A federal statute governing the offer and sale of securities in interstate commerce; prescribes registration, disclosure, and anti-fraud rules.

Securities and Exchange Commission (SEC)

An agency of the federal government created under the Exchange Act that administers the federal laws regulating the offer and sale of securities within the United States.

Securities Exchange Act of 1934 (Exchange Act)

A federal statute that requires stock exchanges to register with (or qualify for an exemption from registration) as a prerequisite to doing business; includes reporting, proxy solicitation, tender offer, and insider trading rules.

Security

General term, used to describe instruments, such as shares of stock, bonds, and debentures, as well as other instruments that have one or more characteristics of a security. The traditional definition of a security is an instrument that involves an investment where the return is primarily or exclusively dependent on the efforts of a person or persons other than the investor.

Share

An individual unit of a class of equity securities that represents the basic ownership interest of a corporation.

Shareholder/Stockholder

A person who owns one or more of the outstanding shares of stock of a corporation. These shares of stock may be either shares of common stock or shares of preferred stock. "Shareholder" and "stockholder" are synonymous; however, the corporate laws of different states assign the term to corporations incorporated in their jurisdictions. For example, Delaware corporations have stockholders; California corporations have shareholders.

Shareholder Approval

Authorization by shareholders of a corporate transaction or event. Generally, shareholder/stockholder approval is sought in connection with the adoption of an employee stock option plan and, in certain instances, with the amendment of such plans.

Share (or Stock) Certificate

A document that evidences ownership of a specific number of securities of a corporation. The certificate typically contains an alpha-numeric identifier, the name of the issuing corporation, the number of securities represented by the certificate, and the name and address of the shareholder/stockholder.

Share Reserve

The number of shares of stock that have been authorized and reserved by a corporation's board of directors for issuance pursuant to an employee stock option plan.

Shares Outstanding

The equity securities of a corporation that have been issued to, and are currently held by, the shareholders/stockholders of the corporation. In the context of an employee stock plan, the shares of stock of a corporation that have been sold and issued to, and are currently held by, the participants in the plan.

Short-Swing Profits Recovery Rule

Under Section 16(b) of the Exchange Act, a rule requiring directors and officers of an issuer that has registered a class of its equity securities under Section 12, as well as the beneficial owners of more than 10% of any class of the issuer's registered equity securities, to disgorge to the issuer any profits realized from the purchase and sale, or sale and purchase, of the issuer's equity securities within a period of less than six months.

Social Security Tax

An employment tax for retirement income imposed on employees and employers under the Federal Insurance Contributions Act with respect to the wages paid to employees.

Spread

For shares purchased under an option, the difference, if any, between the option price and the fair market value of the shares on the date of exercise (or, if exercise is for unvested shares, on the date of vesting).

Statutory Holding Period

Holding period established by Sections 422 and 423 of the Code for ISOs and ESPP options: one year from exercise and two years from grant.

Statutory Stock Option

An employee option accorded favorable tax treatment under Sections 421–424 of the Code; that is, an ISO or Section 423 ESPP option.

Stock

The basic form of equity issued by a corporation (other than a limited liability company). A corporation may issue different classes and series of stock, including common and preferred stock, as well as voting and nonvoting stock.

Stock Appreciation Right (SAR)/Stock-Settled Stock Appreciation Right (SSAR)

A contractual right granted to an individual that gives the recipient the right to receive a cash amount equal to the appreciation on a specified number of shares of stock over a specified period of time. An SSAR pays out the appreciation in the form of stock rather than cash.

Stockbroker

An individual that acts as an intermediary between a buyer and seller of securities. A stockbroker receives compensation, in the form of a commission, for assisting in or effecting the purchase or sale of securities. A stockbroker is "registered" with the National Association of Securities Dealers and the exchange on which the securities are traded. Brokers are also regulated under federal and state securities laws.

Stock Certificate

A document that evidences ownership of a specific number of securities of a corporation. The certificate typically contains an alpha-numeric identifier, the name of the issuing corporation, the number of securities represented by the certificate, and the name and address of the shareholder/stockholder.

Stock-for-Stock Exercise

See "Stock Swap Exercise."

Stockholder

See "shareholder."

Stock Option Committee

Committee of the board of directors of a corporation responsible for decisions pertaining to employee stock option grants under the corporation's employee stock option plan.

Stock Option Plan

See "Option Plan"

Stock Option Repricing

See "Repricing."

Stock Split

A change in the capitalization of an issuer that increases or decreases the number of securities outstanding, and adjusts the value of the securities accordingly, without a corresponding change in the assets or capital of the issuer. Generally, used to denote a change in capitalization that increases the number of securities outstanding and adjusts the value of the securities downward.

Stock Swap Exercise

A transaction in which already-owned shares of stock are exchanged in lieu of cash to pay the option price for the exercise of a stock option.

Street Name Issuance

The registration of a security in the name of a securities brokerage firm as a nominee for the beneficial owner of the securities. Securities are often held in "street name" to expedite transfers of the securities when the securities are sold, since no delivery of the certificate or signature of transfer by the beneficial owner is required.

Strike Price

See "Exercise Price."

Subsidiary

A corporation that is majority owned or wholly owned by another corporation. For purposes of the ISO rules, any corporation (other than the employer corporation) in an unbroken chain of corporations beginning with the employer corporation if, at the time of grant of a stock option, each of the corporations other than the last corporation in the unbroken chain owns stock possessing 50% or more of the total combined voting power of all classes of stock in one of the other corporations in such chain.

Substantial Risk of Forfeiture

Tax concept under Section 83 of the Code that describes a situation in which an individual's rights to the full enjoyment of property is conditional upon the future performance of substantial services.

Swapped Shares

The number of shares of stock tendered to the corporation in a stock swap exercise. The swapped shares are assigned a value, typically the fair market value of the corporation's stock on the date of exercise. To complete the transaction, the optionee must deliver to the corporation a certificate or certificates covering enough previously issued and presently owned shares of stock to pay the aggregate option price for the share of stock being acquired through the stock option exercise.

Tandem Stock Option

An employee stock option that also provides the optionee with a related right, such as a stock appreciation right, covering an equivalent number of securities. Generally, the exercise of one right affects the holder's ability to exercise the other right. For example, to the extent that an optionee exercises the employee stock option portion of a tandem employee stock option/stock appreciation right, the related stock appreciation right is cancelled, and vice versa.

Tax Basis

A tax concept representing the actual and constructive "cost" of property to a taxpayer; for purposes of stock purchased under an option, the tax basis is equal to the amount paid on exercise plus any amount included in ordinary income prior to disposition.

Tax Deferral

The ability to postpone the payment of taxes from the date of a specific transaction until a later date. For example, assuming that a stock option designated as an ISO satisfies the conditions of Section 422(b) of the Code, upon exercise of such ISO the employee is permitted to defer the recognition of taxable income in connection with the acquisition of the shares of stock received upon exercise of the stock option until the disposition of such shares of stock.

Tax Offset Bonus

A cash bonus payable to an employee upon the exercise of a nonqualified stock option to cover, or "offset," the withholding taxes due as a result of the exercise. Generally, the amount of the bonus will be based upon a percentage of the total amount of compensation income recognized by the optionee plus additional amounts needed to "gross up" the bonus to fully offset the tax effect of the transaction on an after-tax basis.

For financial reporting purposes, the use of a tax offset bonus to reimburse an employee for the withholding taxes due on the exercise of a nonqualified stock option will result in "variable" accounting treatment for the transaction. That is, the corporation will record a compensation expense for financial reporting purposes equal to the amount of the cash bonus plus the entire difference between the option price and the fair market value of the corporation's stock on the date of exercise.

Tax Regulations

Rules promulgated by the Internal Revenue Service implementing and interpreting the statutory provisions of the Code. Congressional authority for the issuance of regulations is set forth in Section 7805 of the Code. While such rules are not law, they represent the Internal Revenue Service's interpretation of the proper application of the law and are presumed to be valid.

Tax Withholding

The retention of certain amounts from an employee's wages or compensation by a corporation to satisfy income tax and/or employment tax obligations.

Tax Withholding with Shares

An exercise feature that allows the optionee to request that the corporation withhold some of the shares of stock being acquired upon the exercise of the stock option in order to satisfy the optionee's withholding tax liability arising in connection with the transaction. The traded shares are assigned a value, usually the fair market value of the corporation's stock on the date of exercise. This value is divided into the total taxes due to determine the number of shares of stock required to be withheld. The number of shares of stock exercised is then reduced by the number of shares of stock to be withheld and only the net balance is issued to the optionee.

Term

The stated period of time within which an option may be exercised (before it expires). Generally, the term of an employee stock option will be a period of up to 10 years. Also may refer to the duration of an employee stock option plan, during which time the plan administrator may grant stock options to eligible participants in the plan.

Termination Date (Option)

The date on which an option terminates, which may be either at the end of a stated term or at the time of the optionee's termination of employment (or service contract) with the company.

Termination of Plan

The termination of a stock option plan resulting from either the affirmative decision of the plan administrators to wind up the plan, the exhaustion of the plan share reserve or the expiration of the stated plan term.

Time-Accelerated Restricted Stock Award Plan (TARSAP)

A form of restricted stock purchase award that provides for a fixed, service-based vesting schedule with certain vesting accelerators tied to the achievement of specified performance criteria. If properly structured, for financial reporting purposes, the amount of compensation expense associated with the award is measured at the date of grant. This type of arrangement enables a corporation to grant an award that, from a practical standpoint, operates as a performance-based award but which receives "fixed" accounting treatment rather than the "variable" accounting treatment that is typically associated with performance-based arrangements.

Time-Accelerated Stock Option

A form of employee stock option that provides for a fixed, service-based vesting schedule with certain vesting accelerators tied to the achievement of specified performance criteria. If properly structured, for financial reporting purposes, the amount of compensation expense associated with the stock option is measured at the date of grant. This type of arrangement enables a corporation to grant an employee stock option that, from a practical standpoint, operates as a performance-based award but which receives "fixed" accounting treatment rather than the "variable" accounting treatment that is typically associated with performance-based arrangements.

Trade Share Value

The value assigned to an exercised share that is traded back to the corporation to satisfy a withholding tax liability arising in connection with a stock option exercise. Commonly the trade share value is equal to the fair market value of the corporation's stock on the date of exercise.

Transfer

Conveyance of property, such as shares of stock, from one individual to another individual, followed by recording the ownership of the property on the records of the issuer.

Transferable Stock Option (TSO)

An NSO that permits the optionee, under the terms and conditions set forth in the option agreement, to transfer the option to one or more third parties. Because of the limitation on transferability set forth in Section 422(b)(5) of the Code, an ISO cannot be a transferable stock option. Most corporations that permit transferable stock options limit the group of permissible transferees to immediate family members of the optionee or to entities (such as trusts or partnerships) for the benefit of immediate family members. A number of federal income and gift tax issues must be considered in connection with the implementation and use of transferable stock options.

Transfer Agent

An institution selected by an issuer to issue and transfer share certificates representing the ownership of the outstanding securities of the issuer. An agent of the corporation responsible for registering shareholder/stockholder names on the corporation's records. The transfer agent maintains a current list of shareholders/stockholders for purposes of distributing dividends, reports, and other corporate communications.

Transfer Date

The date upon which securities are considered to have been transferred from one person to another.

Treasury Shares (Treasury Stock)

Shares of the capital stock of a corporation that were previously issued by the corporation and have been reacquired and are being held in "treasury" rather than retired. Substantively, treasury shares are equivalent to authorized but unissued shares. However, the corporation may reissue treasury shares without having to satisfy the minimum consideration requirements of state corporate law. Several states do not recognize the concept of treasury shares.

Underwater or "Out of the Money"

Terms used to describe an employee stock option where the option price is greater than the current fair market value of the shares of stock subject to the stock option.

Unvested Shares

Shares of stock that an individual has not yet earned and, therefore, may not transfer to a third party. Entitlement to the shares of stock is subject to the satisfaction of one or more contingencies (generally service-based) that are attached to the receipt of the shares of stock.

Vesting

With respect to shares of stock, the process through which shares are earned over a period of employment (or provision of services); for purposes of Section 83 of the Code, shares become vested on the first date they are transferable or not subject to a substantial risk of forfeiture. Conditions for vesting are generally stated in either the option grant (for stock options) or the restricted stock purchase agreement (for stock purchase).

Vesting Period

In general, the time period over which shares become vested, as set out in the option grant or purchase agreement.

Vesting Schedule

The specific schedule that dictates vesting. For an option, the vesting schedule may be the same as the exercise schedule (i.e., the option may only be exercised as to shares that are already vested) or may be different (i.e., the option may be exercised "early" as to shares that are not already vested). If early exercise is permitted, the shares themselves will be subject to vesting (see "repurchase option").

Wages

Under Section 3401 of the Code, remuneration (in any form) paid to an employee in connection with services rendered to the employer.

"Window" Period

A period of time during which, under a corporation's trading policy, it is permissible for a director, officer or employee to trade in the corporation's securities if the individual is in compliance with the terms of the policy (that is, the individual is not in actual possession of material, non-public information concerning the corporation). Typically, these periods run from ten days to two months following the release of quarterly or annual financial information by the corporation.

Withholding

The retention of certain amounts from an employee's wages or compensation by a corporation to satisfy the income tax and/or employment tax obligations of the employee that arise in connection with the exercise of a nonqualified stock option.

About the Authors

Michael J. Album is a partner in New York office of Proskauer Rose LLP, where he is part of the firm's Employee Benefits & Executive Compensation Group. He represents companies and compensation committees; private equity firms and hedge funds; and CEOs, senior executives (in numerous business sectors), and portfolio managers on a full range of executive compensation matters. Michael has written and spoken extensively in the area of executive compensation. He has written a lead article for an annual issue of the *Dow Jones Private Equity Analyst–Global Compensation Study* ("Human Capital Considerations for Maturing Private Equity Firms"), and he has contributed chapters on MBO compensation issues to publications, including *Private Equity Mathematics* and *Human Capital in Private Equity*. His other articles have appeared in *The Business Lawyer, New York Law Journal, Employment Relations Today, Venture Capital Review,* and other legal publications, and he has been a featured speaker on executive compensation developments at ALI-ABA, Dow Jones Private Equity, and other webinars and seminars. He also has been featured in interviews in *Private Equity Manager* on topics relating to private equity compensation and portfolio company matters.

Barbara Baksa is the executive director of the National Association of Stock Plan Professionals (NASPP). She is a frequent speaker on equity compensation-related topics and has spoken at NCEO, NASPP, and other industry events. In addition to her speaking engagements, she has authored several white papers and contributed chapters to four books on stock compensation and is the author of the book *Accounting for Equity Compensation,* also published by the NCEO. Barbara also serves as the editor of the *NASPP Advisor.* She holds the Certified Equity Professional (CEP) designation, serves on the Certified Equity Professional Institute's advisory board, and is an executive fellow of the Institute for the Study of Employee Ownership and Profit Sharing at Rutgers University School of Management and Labor Relations.

Colin Diamond is a partner in White & Case's New York office and is chair of the firm's Public Company Advisory Group. He represents investment banks and issuers in a range of registered and unregistered U.S. capital markets transactions, and has particular experience advising on IPOs. He was the lead securities lawyer on the $19.3 billion IPO by Visa and has advised on over 30 IPOs. Mr. Diamond also counsels public companies on all aspects of their Exchange Act reporting and stock exchange obligations, as well as best practices with respect to corporate governance matters and the securities law aspects of equity incentive plans and compensation-related disclosures. Mr. Diamond also has extensive experience addressing the capital raising and trading challenges faced by companies emerging from Chapter 11.

William Dunn is a retired partner in PricewaterhouseCooper's Human Resource practice, where he led the U.S. firm's executive compensation practice. Mr. Dunn and his colleagues consulted with clients on a variety of strategic and technical compensation issues, including the use of stock-based compensation plans, compensation issues associated with business reorganizations, deferred compensation planning, and the multinational effects of deferred and equity-based compensation. He has more than 25 years' experience in assisting clients in executive compensation matters and has worked as the liaison between the firm's clients, the IRS National Office, the Treasury Department, Congress, and other global regulatory authorities in matters relating to rulings, tax legislation, and regulatory guidance. Mr. Dunn has a master's degree in taxation from the American University, Washington, D.C., and a bachelor's degree from the University of Maryland. He is a Certified Public Accountant, is a member of the American Institute of Certified Public Accountants and serves on the advisory boards of many executive compensation support organizations. Mr. Dunn has published articles in many technical publications and is often quoted in tax matters, appearing in both print and broadcast tax features. Finally, Mr. Dunn has instructed at Georgetown and American University and has appeared on a variety of technical and industry video programs.

Steven D. Einhorn was a partner in the New York office of Brown Rudnick LLP, where he was a member of the firm's Tax Practice Group. He focused his practice on a broad range of executive compensation and employee benefits matters, including compliance with ERISA, tax, corporate, and securities laws and regulations affecting employee benefit plans, programs, and arrangements. He passed away in 2021.

Jennifer George is a partner at PwC. For more than 18 years, Jennifer has focused her practice on assisting U.S. multinational companies with the regulatory and tax issues related to offerings of equity incentives and other benefits to employees and consultants outside the United States. Most of the companies Jennifer works with are U.S. multinational companies. Her experience ranges from assisting small private companies to Fortune 500 companies. Her work on the implementation of employee incentive plans involves tax laws (both employee and company perspectives), securities laws, exchange control regulations, labor laws, and related issues. Jennifer assists companies not only with complying with current foreign rules and regulations but also with strategizing for upcoming changes and reacting quickly to these changes. She also advises companies on how to efficiently manage global programs and make smart choices regarding grant types to minimize legal filing requirements to the extent possible. And she has extensive experience with the foreign tax and legal issues for equity awards in M&A transactions and other corporate transactions. Before joining PwC, Jennifer was a partner at two different global law firms. Jennifer is an attorney and practiced as a C.P.A. before law school.

Sorrell Johnson is the head of equity plan administration for Advanced Micro Devices (AMD). She began working in the equity compensation industry in 1997 and has worked as an equity plan professional on both the consulting and issuer side, authoring several white papers on a variety of equity compensation-related topics. Sorrell earned her Certified Equity Professional (CEP) designation in 2003, currently serves on the Certified Equity Professional Institute's curriculum committee, and was honored three times with the CEP Volunteer Excellence Award. She has taught for NASPP University, contributed to a NASPP podcast, and served as the vice president of the Silicon Valley NASPP chapter. She was also featured in an article in the Wall Street Journal regarding public company tender offers. She is a frequent speaker at various industry events, including NASPP chapter meetings, NASPP's national conference, and Global Equity Organization (GEO) meetings.

Thomas LaWer is a principal at Compensia, a compensation consulting firm, in its Silicon Valley (California) office. Tom advises compensation committees, boards of directors, and senior management regarding executive and board pay, reward strategies, equity compensation programs, and corporate governance issues related to compensation programs. Before joining Compensia, Tom was a partner in the law firm of Greenberg Traurig and one of the leaders of its national executive compensation group. Tom received his JD from the University of Chicago Law School and received a BS in Economics from the Wharton School of Business of the University of Pennsylvania. Before law school, Tom was a Certified Public Accountant at KPMG in New York City.

Joshua McGinn is the senior vice president for the Western Region at AST and has more than 35 years of industry experience. In his current role, Josh manages shareholder services for corporate issuers with IPOs, M&A transactions, and activist situations. Before joining AST in April 2012, Josh was with Computershare and its predecessor EquiServe, and with Bank of Boston. There, he was involved with planning, developing, and administering a wide range of services, including forward and reverse stock splits, acquisitions involving both stock and cash exchanges, corporate spinoffs, implementing and administering direct stock purchase plans, and assisting clients with DRS and full dematerialization programs. While working at Bank of Boston, he helped develop the company's first book-entry ESPP program. Josh also has a solid background with annual meetings, proxy mailings, solicitations, and proxy contests. He started Bank of Boston's proxy solicitation department in the late 1980s and contributed to that organization's e-proxy, e-distribution, and proxy householding services. He was also instrumental with rolling out AST's virtual shareholder meeting plat-form during the COVID-19 pandemic in 2020. Josh received both his bachelor's and MBA degrees from Boston University, has earned his Series 7 license, and has attained the Certified Equity Professional (CEP) designation. He is a director of the San Francisco chapter of the National Association of Stock Plan Professionals (NASPP) and a director of the San Francisco chapter of the National Investor Rela-tions Institute (NIRI) as well as a past contributor to the Society of Governance Professionals.

Eric Orsic is co-head of the Capital Markets and Public Companies Practice Group at the international law firm of McDermott Will & Emery LLP, resident in its Chicago office. He has extensive experience with insider trading and reporting under Section 16 of the Securities Exchange Act, executive compensation and other proxy disclosures, corporate governance, and resales of restricted securities under Rule 144. He has also worked with public and private companies in the de-sign and structuring of executive compensation programs, including stock and stock-based compensation plans.

Henrik P. Patel is global head of employment, compensation and benefits at the global law firm White & Case LLP. Henrik advises many U.S. and non-U.S. clients (including public and private companies, boards of directors, and executives) on executive compensation and employee benefits aspects of various corporate transactions, includ-ing mergers, acquisitions, divestitures, spin-offs, succession planning, debt and equity financings, initial public offerings, private equity and leveraged buyout transactions, and banking transactions. He has ex-tensive experience with financial services institutions, private equity, and hedge fund clients. Henrik was named to the "40 Under 40" list of outstanding M&A lawyers by *The M&A Advisor* and has been named a recognized individual by *Legal 500* in Employee Benefits & Executive Compensation.

Joseph Phelps is an attorney and former senior associate in the Seattle office of K&L Gates LLP, where he was part of the firm's Corporate/ M&A practice group.

Carlisle F. Toppin is a senior associate at Cleary Gottlieb Steen & Hamilton LLP. His practice focuses on executive compensation and employee benefit matters, principally in connection with mergers and acquisitions, spin-offs, initial public offerings, and other business transactions. He also regularly advises public and private companies on the design, implementation, and disclosure of equity and cash incentive compensation programs; nonqualified deferred compensation arrangements; negotiating employment and separation agreements; and traditional employee benefit plan matters. Carlisle currently serves on the Certified Equity Professional Institute's curriculum committee.

Marlene Zobayan is a partner at Rutlen Associates LLC. She has over 20 years of international tax and benefits experience, including global equity plans, mobile employee taxation, global compensation, and benefits. Her clients range from startups to Fortune 10 companies. She provides a range of services including remote work policy, mobile employee policy, global equity plan design, mobility compliance, compliance reviews, assistance with local approvals and filings, communications, employer tax compliance advice, and designing administrative processes; she is known for her expertise with mobile employee issues. Marlene is a regular speaker and author on global stock plan and reward issues. Marlene is a member of the U.K. Association of Tax Technicians, a U.S. Enrolled Agent, a Certified Equity Professional, and a Fellow of Global Equity. A former chair of the Advisory Board of the Certified Equity Professional Institute (CEPI) of Santa Clara University, Marlene is currently a member of the CEPI's Curriculum Committee.

Jacobin Zorin is the chief privacy officer at Cepheid, supporting it and the other five operating companies of Danaher Corporation's Diagnostic Platform with worldwide data privacy issues such as HIPAA and GDPR. She previously was the director of the privacy office and stock administration and served as the assistant corporate secretary of Cepheid before its acquisition by Danaher. At that time, she managed day-to-day stock activity and data privacy, as well as corporate and securities issues, Section 16 filings, and insider trading policy compliance. She has more than 20 years of experience in global equity compensation and corporate legal affairs, is a Certified Equity Professional, and has written and updates the IPO-related chapters in Selected Issues in Equity Compensation. She is also a Certified Information Privacy Professional/US, Certified Information Privacy Professional/Europe, Certified Information Privacy Manager, and Fellow of Information Privacy, and is a frequent speaker at industry events. She continues to volunteer with the Certified Equity Professional Institute (CEPI) and previously served as a member of the CEPI's curriculum committee.

About the NCEO

The National Center for Employee Ownership (NCEO) is a nonprofit organization that has supported the employee ownership community since 1981. Our mission is to help employee ownership thrive. We have more than 3,000 members because we help people make smart decisions about employee ownership, with everything from reliable information on technical issues to helping companies reach the full potential of employee ownership.

We generate original research, facilitate the exchange of best practices at our live and online events, feature the best and most current writing by experts in our publications, and help employee ownership companies buisld ownership cultures where employees think and act like owners.

Although most of our activities and most of our membership base center around broad-based plans such as employee stock ownership plans (ESOPs) rather than equity compensation, we are the main publisher in the field, with dozens of titles, and a number of our books, such as this one, are on equity compensation.

To learn more about us or order our publications, visit us at www. nceo.org or telephone us at 510-208-1300. To go directly to a list of our equity compensation titles and bypass our ESOP and other non-equity publications, go to **www.nceo.org/r/equitybooks** in your web browser.

CEPI Exam Resources

Studying for the CEPI exams? See **www.nceo.org/CEP** for our CEP Exam Prep Course plus CEPI required texts in paperback and PDF format.

Made in the USA
Las Vegas, NV
09 March 2023

68819998R00282